Jewish Philosophical Polemics Against Christianity in the Middle Ages

Jewish Philosophical Polemics Against Christianity in the Middle Ages

by
DANIEL J. LASKER

Ktav Publishing House Inc.
Anti Defamation League of B'nai B'rith
New York
1977

Library of Congress Cataloging in Publication Data

Lasker, Daniel J. 1949–

Jewish philosophical polemics against Christianity in the Middle Ages.

Bibliography: p.
Includes index.
1. Christianity—Controversial literature—History.
2. Judaism—Relations—Christianity. 3. Christianity and other religions—Judaism. I. Title.
BM590.L37 296.3 76-50657
ISBN 0-87068-498-1

MANUFACTURED IN THE UNITED STATES OF AMERICA

To my Dear Wife Debbie

רבות בנות עשו חיל ואת עלית על כלנה

Acknowledgments

The present work is substantially identical with my doctoral dissertation (Brandeis University, February, 1976). It was written under the direction of my teacher, Prof. Alexander Altmann, whose inspiration and advice have been invaluable to me. I am grateful to him for introducing me into the field of medieval Jewish philosophy and greatly influencing the course of my studies.

I would like to thank also a number of colleagues whose counsel has been greatly appreciated. Profs. Frank Talmage and Lawrence Schiffman read most of the manuscript and offered quite helpful suggestions in both content and form. In addition, I am grateful to Profs. Russell Blackwood and Jay Williams for their assistance.

A number of foundations have assisted this project financially. They were the Memorial Foundation for Jewish Culture, the National Foundation for Jewish Culture, and the Huber Foundation. Their support has been greatly appreciated.

The bulk of the research that made this book possible was conducted at the Library of the Jewish Theological Seminary of America. I would like to thank the Librarian, Prof. Menahem Schmelzer, for putting the Library's facilities at my disposal and for permitting me to quote from its extensive manuscript collection. I would like also to acknowledge the invaluable help of the Library's Research Assistant, Susan Winter Young.

The facilities of a number of other libraries were useful in my research. I appreciate the courtesy extended by the Burke Library, Hamilton-Kirkland Colleges, the Union Theological Seminary Library, New York Public Library, and Columbia University Library. In addition, I would like to thank the Librarians of the Bodleian, Parma, and Paris National Libraries for the use of microfilm copies of manuscripts. Quotations from S. Pines' translation of Maimonides' *Guide of the Perplexed* are by permission of the University of Chicago Press.

Finally, I would like to acknowledge the help and assistance of members of my family. My parents, Rabbi and Mrs. Arnold A. Lasker, and my in-laws, Mr. and Mrs. Joseph Dworkin, added immeasurably to the progress of my research.

This book is lovingly dedicated to my wife, Debbie. She has been not only a source of encouragement, but also a valuable helper in the course of the research and writing of this work. Her suggestions were always well considered and quite useful. "Many daughters have done valiantly, but you have excelled them all."

Daniel J. Lasker
Columbus, Ohio

February 10, 1977
22 Shevat, 5737

Table of Contents

CHAPTER ONE

Introduction

General Principles

The historical relationship between Judaism and Christianity has not been peaceful, and it has left us with a polemical literature which is a very rich source for scholarly investigation. Through the ages, Christian thinkers had made Judaism the object of attack, hoping thereby to convince Jews to abandon their ancestral faith. From the earliest days of the new religion, when Christianity was just emerging from Judaism, Christians sought to demonstrate to Jews that Jesus was the expected messiah and that the doctrines he taught were true. At first, the debate was three-sided, with Jews, Christians, and pagans all taking part.[1] As Europe became Christianized, the Jews remained as the only nonconverted minority.[2] They therefore became the object of intensified pressure. Since Christianity had its origin in the Jewish religion and saw itself as the true heir to biblical Israel, the presence of Jews in its midst was often a source of discomfort.

The Christian attempt to missionize the Jews took many forms. Jews were often forced to listen to conversionary sermons and to participate in public disputations concerning the merits of their faith. At times, Jews were offered financial inducements to change their religion. In extreme cases, Christians made converts by means of forced baptisms. As the Christians tried to win over the hearts and minds of the Jews, they developed a wealth of arguments to aid their cause. Many of these contentions were collected in works given such titles as *Adversus Judaeos* or *Contra Judaeos,* though these polemical treatises were not the only literature produced by the Christian attack upon Judaism.[3]

Many Jews did not remain passive in the face of the Christian challenge to their religion. Even in the early periods of Christianity, when Judaism was not unduly pressured by the new faith, arguments were formulated to combat the Christian claims. Talmudic and midrashic literature offers evidence that Jews were aware of the story of Jesus as related in the Gospels and basic Christian doctrines, against which they argued.[4] In a later period,

Jewish thinkers in Muslim countries polemicized against Christianity, even though neither Judaism nor Christianity was dominant, and the Jews were not under compulsion to convert to Christianity.[5] It was in Western Europe, however, that the defense of Judaism, with its concomitant attack on Christianity, reached its fullest development.

The first European Jewish anti-Christian arguments did not appear in specifically polemical works. Though many Jewish compositions, notably biblical commentaries, included refutations of Christian doctrines,[6] it was not until the twelfth century that there appeared treatises totally dedicated to defending the Jewish position and contending against the Christian one. As the Christian pressure intensified in that century, Jews felt a need to compose books that would help them meet the challenge of the dominant religion.[7] This type of polemical work, which is usually designated in Hebrew as a *vikuaḥ*[8] or a *sefer niẓẓaḥon,*[9] became a quite common feature of medieval Jewish literature. In every succeeding medieval century in practically every Western European country, Jewish thinkers wrote either original polemical works or accounts of the public disputations in which they took part. The Jewish arguments against Christianity were taken from a wide range of disciplines reflecting the specific interests of the various authors. When read in conjunction with other Jewish treatises which contain anti-Christian material, these polemics offer an extensive, comprehensive critique of Christianity and provide an insight into medieval Jewish-Christian relations.[10]

Since Jewish polemical literature represents a wide variety of approaches originating from differing geographical areas during the course of a long period of time, it provides a fertile source of study. Many fields of scholarship, including biblical exegesis, Jewish history, and Jewish-Christian social relations, can gain by an analysis of this material. Unfortunately, little work has been done in this area. The few studies that have concerned themselves with polemics have not selected any large topic and examined it through the whole range of the extant sources. Though there are some valuable works on certain polemical treatises, or on narrowly delineated minor topics, e.g., the polemical discussion of a particular biblical passage, no comprehensive investigation of the Jewish anti-Christian literature has as yet been attempted.[11]

Since no systematic examinations of polemical literature exist, one cannot adequately answer some of the most basic questions of medieval Jewish-Christian intellectual relations. For instance, no one doubts that many Jews were familiar with Christian doctrines. Nevertheless, how familiar they were with these doctrines and what the sources of their knowledge were remain obscure. The aim of the present study is to begin to answer some of these fundamental questions by means of an analysis of one specific aspect of Jewish polemical literature. That aspect is the Jewish philosophical polemic against Christianity in the Middle Ages. It is assumed that the presentation of a systematic overview of one characteristic and vitally important area of the Jewish-Christian debate will provide information that will cast light on the whole field. In addition, it is hoped that such a study will provide guidelines for further investigation of the other aspects of the Jewish-Christian polemical literature.[12]

Philosophical Arguments

In combating the doctines of Christianity, Jewish polemicists employed a variety of types of argumentation to strengthen their own beliefs. These arguments may be divided into three distinct categories: (1) exegetical arguments *(min ha-ketuvim)*, (2) historical arguments *(min ha-meẓi'ut)*, and (3) rational arguments *(min ha-sekhel)*.

These kinds of argumentation were also used by Christian polemicists. "Christian apologetics is of three kinds: that which appeals to prophecy, that which appeals to reason, and that which appeals to history—not to imply that these three kinds are always kept distinct in practice."[13] Each of these categories can be further subdivided, as we shall see.

Exegetical Arguments

The primary texts included in medieval exegetical arguments were (1) the Hebrew Bible, (2) the New Testament, and (3) the Talmud. Each of the texts were subjected to different types of exegesis and interpretation.

1. Even though both Christians and Jews were united in their acceptance of the authority and divine nature of the Hebrew Bible (to the Christians, the Old Testament), they were divided by their diverse interpretations of it. Since this text did enjoy the acceptance of both sides, it served as the chief literary source in the Jewish-Christian dispute. Both sides quoted from the Hebrew Bible either in support of their own beliefs or in the attempt to refute the contentions of their opponents. Thinkers of both religions admitted the overriding necessity of correct interpretation of Scripture while, at the same time, differing greatly on the nature of correct interpretation.

Some questions did arise concerning textual problems. Whereas the Masoretic text was held to be authoritative for Jews, the Western Church accepted Jerome's translation, the Vulgate, as canonical. Thus, a Jew and a Christian reading the same verse, one in Hebrew, the other in Latin, might come to two different conclusions, each of which might be justified by the differing versions.[14] Certain verses quoted by the Christians as being found in the "Old Testament" are not in the Hebrew text.[15] As a result of these discrepancies of text and translation, each side accused the other of falsification.[16]

To dispel some of these textual ambiguities and to prove the authenticity of the Masoretic text, Profiat Duran devoted one chapter of his *Kelimat Ha-Goyim* "to explaining the corruptions of Jerome the corrupter, who translated the Holy Books from Hebrew to Latin, and to adducing proof that those Holy Books which we have are the exact truth to which one may not ever add and from which one may not ever detract (cf. Deut. 13:1)."[17] Duran stated that most of these textual corruptions were not the result of deliberate deception but were rather the result of Jerome's having employed a Jewish ignoramus *(Yehudi 'am ha-'areẓ)* to help him.[18] Basing himself on Judah Halevi, Duran argued that the authenticity of the Hebrew text is verified by its uniformity in all copies of the Bible throughout the scattered Jewish communities of the world.[19]

Even when Jews and Christians agreed on the text, they disagreed on its exegesis. One important point of divergence centered on the question whether the text was to be understood literally or figuratively, the Jews usually opting for the former, the Christians for the latter.[20] Another important issue concerned the question whether or not the prophecies of the Hebrew Bible were indeed fulfilled by the advent of Jesus.[21] Disagreements arose also as to the exact meaning of specific terms, e.g., *'almah* in Isaiah 7:14,[22] or whole passages, e.g., the identity of the "suffering servant" in Isaiah 53.[23]

One could cite any number of verses from the Hebrew Bible which were employed by the Jewish and Christian debaters in their polemical works. Exegetical arguments from the Hebrew Bible were included in almost every controversial work in reference to almost every point of debate. Overall, this type of contention was the most prevalent one in Jewish-Christian polemics.

2. Since the New Testament was rejected by the Jews as not authoritative, the Christian polemicists rarely tried to argue from it. Arguments from New Testament verses would have had little effect on Jews, who did not impute validity to the text. The Jews, for their part, referred to the New Testament as *aven gillayon* (falsehood of blank paper) or *'avon gillayon* (sinfulness of blank paper), making a play on the Greek

evangelion.[24] Nevertheless, they felt free to use the New Testament in their arguments against the Christians.

In their use of the New Testament for controversial purposes, the Jewish polemicists followed two general methods. The first was to denigrate New Testament stories. The second was to demonstrate that latter-day Christianity, with which they were familiar, was unfaithful to its own sacred writings and hence had no validity even for the Christian, let alone the Jew.

Jewish denigration of the New Testament is recorded as early as the second century.[25] While there are various hints of such treatment in different sections of the Talmud,[26] the classic example of Jewish defamation of the New Testament is the parody *Toledot Yeshu.*[27] In this work, the miracles attributed to Jesus are said to have been performed by means of magic, and Jesus is regarded not as the son of God but as the illegitimate offspring of Mary and a Roman soldier.[28] Other Jewish criticisms referred to the contradictions among the Gospels.[29] Similarly, some polemicists repeated Jewish assertions recorded in the New Testament, e.g., that Jesus was not the messiah because he could not save even himself (Mark 15:29-32),[30] and that the disappearance of Jesus' body was the result of chicanery, not a miracle (Matthew 28:11-15).[31] A few Jews also noted that a number of verses from the Hebrew Bible were incorrectly quoted in the New Testament (cf. Deuteronomy 6:4 with Mark 12:30, Luke 10:27).[32] How could Jesus be the messiah, and his followers the true Israel, the Jewish polemicists asked, if Jesus and his disciples were ignorant of verses that even the youngest child would know?[33]

The Jewish polemicists also employed the New Testament to point out the contradictions between this textual source of Christianity and Christian doctrines which arose later and became established in the Church. Whereas in the discussion of the Hebrew Bible the Christians accused the Jews of taking the text too literally, here it was the Jews who said that certain passages must be understood figuratively. When Christians read Matthew 26:26-28 ("This is my body . . . This is my blood"), they understood it to mean that the Eucharist really became the body and blood of Jesus. The Jewish polemicists, for their part, maintained that these verses were obviously a parable and were not meant literally.[34] Profiat Duran's *Kelimat Ha-Goyim* was specifically intended for this type of ad hominem argument *(kefi ma'amar ha-'omer),* namely, that of attacking the Christian doctrines from their own sources. Duran attempted to demonstrate contradictions between the New Testament and the Christian doctrines of Jesus' divinity, the Trinity, incarnation, original sin, abrogation of the Law, transubstantiation, baptism, papal authority, and virgin birth with its attendant devotion to Mary.[35]

3. Just as the Christians did not use the New Testament as a source of weaponry in polemics but responded when called upon to defend it, so, too, did the Jews have to defend the Talmud, though they could not employ it in their own arguments, since the Christians did not accept it as authoritative. The Christians made reference to the Talmud for two reasons. First, they attacked the Talmud as being anti-Christian and blasphemous. Second, the Christians employed the Talmud as a source of exegetical arguments, asserting that it provided proof that Jesus was the messiah.

There are a number of statements in the Talmud directed against Jewish intimacy with idolaters. For instance, the Tractate *'Avodah Zarah* is replete with prohibitions of Jewish contact with idol-worshipers. Many of these laws refer to such non-Jews in derogatory terms.[36] On the basis of these texts, Christians accused the Jews of harboring ill will toward them and of cursing them in the synagogues. The Christians also complained about various statements in rabbinic literature concerning Jesus which they felt were blasphemous.[37] The Jews, who could not deny the authority of these talmudic statements, employed a reply originated by Yeḥiel of Paris in the Disputation of 1240. He argued that the idolaters referred to by the Talmud were not Christians and that the Jesus of the Talmud was not Jesus of Nazareth.[38]

The Christians also contended that the Talmud and related midrashic material give evidence that the messiah had already come and that other Christian doctrines were true.[39] The first to use these arguments appears to have been Alan of Lille (ca. 1114–ca. 1203);[40] other notable polemicists to employ such arguments were Paul Christiani (Disputation of Barcelona, 1163),[41] Raymund Martini (thirteenth century),[42] Abner of Burgos (Alfonso of Valladolid, 1270–1348),[43] and Geronimo de Santa Fe (Joshua Lorki, Disputation of Tortosa, 1413–14).[44]

The Jewish reply to the argument that the Talmud proves the truth of Christianity was fourfold: (1) The Midrash, which was the source of the statements cited by the Christians, was not as binding upon the Jewish believer as the Halakhah, the legal norms which every Jew must obey. (2) All talmudic statements about the messiah put his birth after the death of Jesus. (3) The rabbis who were the authors of rabbinic literature were believing Jews and not Christians. (4) Midrashim were allegorical and not to be understood literally.[45] When the Jews argued this last point, they employed a method of exegesis dissimilar to the one they used in interpretation of the Hebrew Bible. Likewise, Christians who maintained that the Bible was to be understood figuratively insisted that the Talmud should be interpreted literally.

In addition to their citations from the Hebrew Bible, the New Testament, and the Talmud, Jewish and Christian polemicists occasionally quoted and analyzed critically passages written by the acknowledged authorities of the other religion. This practice, which served a number of polemical purposes, is found in the works of only the most knowledgeable of the polemicists, e.g., Profiat Duran[46] and Judah Aryeh de Modena[47] among the Jews, and Abner of Burgos among the Christians.[48] Of course, each side was quite selective in its citations, taking only the texts which suited its purposes.

From the above brief account, it is evident that the usefulness of exegetical arguments was definitely limited. Neither side had clear-cut rules of exegesis that applied impartially. One verse or citation was interpreted literally if that helped the general argument; another one was read figuratively if such an exegesis was called for to support a theological position. There were also no criteria for determining which side had, indeed, the correct interpretation. For the most part, then, Jewish and Christian polemicists were simply talking past each other, even though they were ostensibly discussing the same text.

There were, nevertheless, some positive results of exegetical argumentation. Since each side held the canonical texts discussed to be divine and uncorrupted, emendations or disavowals of passages were not possible.[49] Each side, then, was forced to read its sacred works very closely and to formulate clear and convincing interpretations. Just as Rabbanite-Karaite debates stirred thinkers of both factions to read the Bible more carefully, so too Jewish-Christian debates encouraged greater textual study.

Historical Arguments

Not content to argue merely from sacred writings, the polemicists employed another category of argument—one which could be termed historical. These were contentions derived not from divine texts but from the real world, a reality also considered ordained by God. Both sides agreed that the condition of the world was divinely ordered; they disagreed as to how one should interpret the raw data that reality provides.

The most frequent Christian historical argument directed at Judaism was to the effect that the depressed state of the Jewish people testified to their rejection by God. The Christians asserted that the Jewish people were being punished by God because they were collectively guilty of the crucifixion of Jesus and because they continued to reject him and his religion. This claim appeared in many anti-Jewish writings and was reflected in Jewish apologetics. Solomon ibn Verga, for instance, quoted a Christian as stating in reference to the Jews: "Reality proves it; why do they sit in exile pressured, oppressed, drawn out, and plucked up? It is only revenge for the blood of Jesus."[50] According to the Christians, the Temple was destroyed and the Jews remained in exile because of their stubbornness and perversity.[51]

While the polemicists were propounding this argument from social conditions, the Christian authorities were careful to make sure that the status of the Jews remained at a low level. Constant persecutions, pogroms, forced baptisms, and expulsions all contributed to the reality which seemed to reaffirm the Christian contention. The Christians appeared to have forgotten that when they were subject to persecutions and martyrdom, they had argued that their willingness to suffer for their religion proved its value and truth.[52]

The Jews agreed that their sufferings were a punishment for their sins but not for the sin of rejecting Christianity. Indeed, argued some Jewish thinkers, Jewish conversions to Christianity, such as they existed, were one of the reasons for Jewish suffering. Other Jewish sins also contributed to the length of the exile, the polemicists averred. Redemption, however, would eventually come.[53]

Other authors responded to this argument by pointing out the relative weakness of Christianity vis-à-vis Islam. If worldly success were the true criterion of a religion's worth, they contended, would not Christianity have to be the dominant religion everywhere in order to substantiate this claim? The Jews specifically referred to Muslim control of Christian holy places in the Land of Israel as further proof that Christians should not cite their worldly superiority to the Jews as evidence that their religion was divine.[54]

Further Christian historical argument was to the effect that Jews acted immorally. Evidence for this charge was adduced from the fact that Jews exacted interest on loans to Christians. Though the Jews engaged in many other occupations besides moneylending, and the Christians themselves lent at usurious rates, the anti-Jewish polemicists remonstrated with the Jews concerning this practice. The Christians based this argument on Psalms 15:5, which seemed to indicate an absolute denunciation of lending at interest. The Jews responded with their own exegetical argument derived from Deuteronomy 23:21, which permitted Jews to exact interest from Gentiles.[55]

Jewish polemicists also accused the Christians of immorality. Some medieval debaters maintained that contemporary Christians were guilty of lack of hospitality, thievery, and sexual immorality. Their priests and nuns officially practiced celibacy, but this did not prevent them from frequently succumbing to their passions. Indeed, added some Jews, by listening to confession the priests knew which women were most likely to be responsive to their advances. If Christianity were a true religion, these Jews argued, its practitioners, and especially its leaders, would not act immorally.[56]

On occasion, historical arguments were backed up by reference to Scripture. Thus, Genesis 49:10, "The scepter shall not depart from Judah," was cited to reinforce the Christian argument that, since there existed no Jewish government headed by a member of the tribe of Judah, Shiloh (the messiah, according to Christian exegesis) must have already come.[57] On the Jewish side, the lack of world peace, combined with such prophecies as Isaiah 11:1-9, "The wolf shall dwell with the lamb," was sufficient to disprove any claims that the world was enjoying the messianic era.[58]

The Jewish and Christian use of historical arguments points out the basic weakness of such contentions. Thinkers of each religion interpreted what they perceived in the world as being in accordance with their preconceived doctrines. God was considered the author of history; theologians were needed to explain history's significance. Historical arguments were not very strong, then, for the differing religions could account for the same reality in varying ways.

Rational Arguments

The third major category of polemical arguments were those derived from reason *(min ha-sekhel)*. In addition to contentions arguing from textual exegesis and historical facts, polemicists of both religions turned to speculative reason to reinforce their claims. The debaters asserted that rational arguments were neither based on a text nor founded in reality; rather, they were the result of ratiocination alone. Nevertheless, not all rational contentions were of the same type. Some can be designated as "common-sense" arguments, others as "philosphical" arguments.

How does one distinguish between rational arguments based on common sense and those which are philosophical? The following examples should help to demonstrate the difference between the two. Jewish polemicists offered two main rational arguments against incarnation: (1) If God had become man, He would have become impure by being born of a woman (impurity having come from physical contact with her), and He would have been subject to suffering. Since God cannot be impure or suffer, He cannot become incarnate.[59] (2) God is the incorporeal, immutable Prime

Mover of the world; therefore He cannot be said to have changed into a material human being.[60] Similarly, some Jews presented varying arguments against transubstantiation: (1) Host worship is idolatrous. (2) According to the principles of logic, physics, and metaphysics, one body cannot be in more than one place at the same time. Hence a literal understanding of the presence of Christ in the Eucharist is precluded.[61]

When Jews claimed that incarnation was unbefitting God or that host worship was idolatrous, they were making a value judgment which the Christians did not share. To the Christians, incarnation was most befitting the Deity, since it showed God's love for mankind.[62] Similarly, to the Christians, host adoration was not idolatrous because it did not amount to worshiping bread, but God, who made Himself present in the bread.[63] Jews and Christians started from differing premises; a discussion on the level of those premises was indeed pointless, since the two sides were inevitably talking at cross-purposes. These arguments were not rooted in a shared philosophical tradition; they were derived from common sense value judgments made by theologians of both religions, "common sense" being not so common.

On the other hand, the premises of the philosophical arguments were valid to both Jewish and Christian polemicists. Philosophers of the two religions agreed that God was incorporeal and immutable and that one body could not be in more than one place at the same time. Despite the agreement on these fundamental speculative principles, Jewish and Christian thinkers arrived at different conclusions. The Jews believed that these principles ruled out the acceptance of the Christian doctrines of incarnation and transubstantiation; the Christians argued that the very same principles were not incompatible with their faith. One may say that when polemical discussion moved on this level, i.e., when it revolved on the question as to whether or not mutually agreed upon philosophical doctrines refuted theological claims, one can speak of philosophical arguments. While the Jews and Christians might have remained in disagreement, they proceeded, at least, from the same philosophical premises.

Philosophical arguments, as the term will be used in this study, are those which take up the results of philosophical reasoning in logic, physics, or metaphysics, and apply them to theological concepts. Disputants who were in basic agreement in matters philosophical might reach radically different conclusions when applying philosophy to theology. As will become apparent in the course of this study, Jewish and Christian philosophers who might both be Aristotelians would disagree sharply as to the value of Aristotelian philosophy in determining the truth of religion in general and specific doctrines in particular. The Jewish philosophical polemicists asserted that philosophy was sufficient to demonstrate the inconsistency and contradictory nature of Christian beliefs. Christian philosophers responded that this was not the case; reason and the Christian religion were not incompatible.[64] Philosophers of both religions, however, were generally in agreement concerning the philosophical principles upon which the Jewish critique of Christianity was based.

Procedure to Be Followed

Medieval Jewish polemical literature is replete with philosophical arguments against Christianity. Though not every polemicist was also a student of philosophy, most had some knowledge, however superficial, of certain principles of logical reasoning. The Jews employed these principles in their anti-Christian works quite often. In addition, Jewish philosophers who were not specifically polemicists also directed philosophical arguments against Christianity on occasion. From the wealth of these arguments emerges a specifically philosophical polemic against Christianity. It is this polemic that will serve as the focus of the present work.

In order to analyze the Jewish philosophical polemic against Christianity in the Middle Ages, it is necessary first to isolate, collect, and enumerate all the Jewish philosophical arguments. Since it is not possible in the confines of the present study to list refutations of every Christian belief, only four doctrines will be discussed, i.e., Trinity, incarnation, transubstantiation, and virgin birth. Not only are these extremely important Christian beliefs but also they are the tenets most often subjected to Jewish philosophical criticism. An enumeration of the arguments against these specific doctrines should be sufficient to draw a general outline of the Jewish philosophical polemic.

The primary aim, then, of this study is to provide a catalogue of the medieval philosophical arguments as a first step toward a fuller evaluation of the philosophical polemic against Christianity. In addition, reference will be made to the philosophical framework in which the arguments appear, the probable sources of the Jewish contentions, and the Christian counter-arguments. It is hoped that from such an investigation a coherent picture of the use of philosophy in the Jewish-Christian debate will emerge.

The format of the present work is as follows. First, the sources of the philosophical polemic will be presented. Second, the general method of the Jewish philosophical polemicists will be analyzed. Third, the philosophical arguments against Trinity, incarnation, transubstantiation, and virgin birth will be discussed. The conclusions that arise from this study will be drawn in the final portion of the work.

CHAPTER TWO

The Sources

The Various Methods of the Polemicists

The arguments which are the components of the Jewish philosophical critique of Christianity in the Middle Ages are found in a variety of sources. The one genre of literature in which most of these contentions are located is the polemic *(vikuaḥ / sefer niẓẓaḥon).* The Jewish polemical works exhibit great diversity both in method of argumentation and in style. These differences were noted by Joseph ben Shem Tov (ca. 1400–ca. 1460), who opened his commentary on Profiat Duran's *Iggeret Al Tehi Ke-'Avotekha* with a description of six types of polemical treatises.[1] Though his categorization is perhaps too simplified, it might be a good framework into which to place the various Jewish polemical works which form the basic source material for the present study.

Exegesis of the Hebrew Bible

The first, and by far the largest, category contains works which dealt primarily with the exegesis of the Hebrew Bible. Their purpose was to demonstrate that the Christian interpretation of the Scriptures was misguided. Under this category Joseph ben Shem Tov listed the following works:

1. *Sefer Milḥamot Ha-Shem* by Jacob ben Reuben, the Rabbanite (twelfth century). This treatise, written in 1170, was one of the earliest works, if not the earliest, devoted entirely to Jewish polemics. It consists of twelve chapters, the first offering a refutation of Christian doctrines, the eleventh a critical review of New Testament passages, and the twelfth a series of proofs that the messiah had as yet not come. The intermediate nine chapters contain a discussion of the correct exegesis of the Torah, Psalms, Jeremiah, Isaiah, Ezekiel, the Twelve Prophets, Daniel, Job, and Proverbs. This treatise served as the basis for many other polemical works. Jacob ben Reuben was apparently a Neoplatonist, but he quoted a variety of Jewish

philosophers, including Saadia Gaon, Isaac Israeli, and Abraham bar Ḥiyya.[2]

2. *Sefer 'Ezer Ha-'Emunah* by Moses Ha-Kohen of Tordesillas (fourteenth century). The author, writing in 1375, divided his work into nineteen sections, dealing with verses from the Torah, Psalms, Isaiah, Jeremiah, Ezekiel, the Twelve Prophets, Proverbs, Job, Daniel, Song of Songs, and Lamentations, with a section devoted to talmudic *haggadot*. This treatise contains material which was employed by Moses Ha-Kohen in a number of public disputations in Avila.[3]

To these works cited by Joseph ben Shem Tov may be added the following treatises:

3. *Sefer Ha-Berit* by Joseph Kimḥi (ca. 1105–ca. 1170).[4] This work is from the same period as *Milḥamot Ha-Shem* (no. 1). Besides its discussion of biblical verses, the treatise is notable for its critique of Christian life and morality.

4. *Sefer Niẓẓaḥon Yashan,* an anonymous Franco-German work of the twelfth to thirteenth century. In addition to the discussion of biblical verses, there is a great deal of material critical of the Christian religion and the New Testament. The author(s) also answered Christian charges relating to the Jewish people. The tone of the book is very acerbic.

5. *Sefer Yosef Ha-Meqanneh* by Joseph ben Nathan Official (thirteenth century).[5] This work is similar to the preceding one (no. 4) in both structure and method of argumentation. The first part, divided into 137 chapters, deals with the Hebrew Bible, specifically the Torah, the Former Prophets, Jeremiah, Ezekiel, Isaiah, the Twelve Prophets, Psalms, Proverbs, Song of Songs, Ecclesiastes, Lamentations, Job, and Daniel. The second part, criticism of the New Testament, contains 43 chapters.

6. *Teshuvot Radaq La-Noẓrim* by David Kimḥi (1160–1235).[6] Kimḥi did not write this as a separate treatise; rather, it is a compilation of excerpts from his commentary on Psalms which are specifically directed against the Christian interpretation.

7. *Milḥemet Miẓvah* by Meir ben Simeon of Narbonne (thirteenth century).[7] This unedited work is a major compilation of Jewish arguments against Christianity. The main feature of this treatise is the author's record of a public disputation on the question of Jewish moneylending in which he participated in Narbonne, 1245.

8. *'Edut Ha-Shem Ne'emanah* by Solomon ben Moses ben Yekutiel (thirteenth century). Besides the discussion of biblical verses, this polemic is notable for its guidelines to Jewish polemicists and its explanations for the length of the Jewish exile.

9. *Even Bohan* by Shem Tov ben Isaac Ibn Shapruṭ (fourteenth century).[8] Basing himself on *Milḥamot Ha-Shem* (no. 1), Ibn Shapruṭ, writing in 1385–1405, repeated Jacob ben Reuben's answers and then added his own replies. In addition to the sections dealing with scriptural verses, the author discussed talmudic *haggadot,* the book of Matthew (of which he provided a translation), a refutation of Christian dogmas (based on Profiat Duran's works, nos. 39, 41), discussions of the messiah and resurrection, and refutations of Abner of Burgos's critique of *Milḥamot Ha-Shem.*

10. *Sefer Niẓẓaḥon* by Yom–Tov Lipmann Mühlhausen (fourteenth to fifteenth century).[9] The author, writing in approximately 1399, followed the order of the Bible as he explained difficult passages, thereby refuting both Christians and Karaites. An account of a disputation with a Jewish apostate, Pesaḥ/Peter, is appended.

11. *Aḥiṭov Ve-Ẓalmon* by Mattityahu ben Moshe Ha-Yiẓhari[?] (fifteenth century).[10] This Spanish work is in the poetic form of a *maqama,* detailing a debate among converts to Judaism, Christianity, and Islam. The author dealt with a number of theological questions along with his treatment of scriptural exegesis.

12. *Magen Va-Romaḥ* by Ḥayyim ibn Musa (1380–1464).[11] This treatise, written in 1456, was meant as a refutation of the works of Nicholas de Lyra.[12] The main issue of discussion is the interpretation of messianic verses promising future happiness to the Jews.

13. *Teshuvot Ha-Noẓrim* by Benjamin ben Moses of Rome (fifteenth century).[13] This Italian work concerns itself mainly with biblical verses.

14. *Magen Avraham* by Abraham Farissol (ca. 1451–1525).[14] A prominent geographer, Farissol, writing in approximately 1500, combined scriptural exegesis with refutations of various Christian doctrines. This native of Avignon recorded some of the arguments he employed in a public disputation in Ferrara, the place where he composed most of his literary works.

15. *Ḥerev Pifiyot* by Yair ben Shabbetai of Correggio (sixteenth century). This is another Italian composition. Besides his discussions of biblical verses and various theological questions, the most notable feature is the author's list of one hundred signs of the messianic period which had not as yet been realized.

16. *Zikheron Sefer Niẓẓaḥon* by Meshullam ben Uri (sixteenth century).[15] This poetic work is based on the arguments of *Sefer Niẓẓaḥon Yashan* (no. 4) and Mühlhausen's *Sefer Niẓẓaḥon* (no. 10).

17. *Ḥizzuq Emunah* by Isaac ben Abraham of Troki (ca. 1533-ca. 1594). This is one of the most celebrated of Jewish polemics though the author was a Karaite. Written in Poland, the work is divided into discussions of Hebrew

scriptural passages and New Testament verses. The influence of this work can be seen by the number of Christian refutations of it.[16]

18. *Kevod Elohim[?],* an anonymous work of the sixteenth century.[17] This polemic, which is very dependent upon a large number of earlier writings, exists in a large number of recensions. The exact name of the work, as well as the author, the date, and the place of composition, all remain in doubt, with several manuscripts having incorrect titles. There is little original material in this work.

19. *Kur Maẓref Ha-'Emunot U-Mar'eh Ha-'Emet* by Isaac Lupis (seventeenth century). This work is also based on *Milḥamot Ha-Shem* (no. 1), though it discusses talmudic passages. The results of the five centuries between the latter work and itself are also apparent in the development of the arguments. It was written in Aleppo, Syria, in 1695.

Exegesis of Rabbinic Literature

The second type of polemic enumerated by Joseph ibn Shem Tov is similar to the first in that the main focus is exegesis. The texts which were considered for interpretation are in this case rabbinic, not biblical. Cited in this category were the following:

20. *Vikuaḥ Ramban* (The disputation at Barcelona, 1263).[18] This work is Naḥmanides' (1194–1270) account of his disputation with Fra Paul Christiani concerning whether the Talmud indicated that the messiah had already come. The disputation is notable in that Nahmanidies argued that *midrashim* were not binding upon the Jews. This contention was repeated by most Jewish polemicists who discussed *haggadot.*

2a. One chapter of *'Ezer Ha-'Emunah* (no. 2).

In addition to these works, one can add the following polemics that deal mainly with rabbinic literature.

21. *Vikuaḥ Rabbi Yeḥiel Mi-Paris* (The disputation at Paris, 1240).[19] This account of the disputation between Rabbi Yeḥiel (d. ca. 1265) and other French Jewish leaders, and the apostate Nicholas Donin tells of the trial of the Talmud which resulted in its burning. Rabbi Yeḥiel's arguments were not sufficient to convince the Christians that the Talmud should not be burnt.

22. *Vikuaḥ Tortosa* (The disputation at Tortosa, 1413–1414).[20] This debate, between Spain's Jewish leaders and Joshua Lorki (Geronimo of Santa Fe), revolved mainly around talmudic passages concerning the coming of the messiah.

23. *Milḥemet Miẓvah* by Solomon ben Simon Duran (ca. 1400–1467).

This treatise, written in 1437, against Joshua Lorki, differentiated between law, which must be obeyed, and Midrash, the belief in which is optional.

24. *Yeshu'ot Meshiḥo* by Don Isaac Abravanel (1437–1508). Part of Abravanel's trilogy on the messiah, this work is an explanation of talmudic passages that seem to indicate that the messiah had already come and that he was divine, not human.

Added to the above polemics dealing with the Talmud and Midrash might be a number of chapters in the works cited in the first category of polemics.

Attacks on Christianity

According to Joseph ben Shem Tov, the third method employed by the polemicists went beyond a simple defense of Judaism. Such a tactic might imply that whereas Judaism was not false, neither was Christianity necessarily wrong. Thus, polemicists now moved on to an attack of Christianity, showing the superiority of Judaism. In this category, Joseph ben Shem Tov referred to the following:

25. *Nusaḥ Ha-Ketav* by Joshua Lorki (d. ca. 1419).[21] Written before the author's conversion to Christianity and subsequent conversionary attempts, this letter to Paul of Santa Maria, another Jewish apostate, tries to set some guidelines for the investigation of religions. The falseness of Christianity was seen in that it would be unfair for those who had never heard of Christianity to be deprived thereby of reward.

Joseph ben Shem Tov also made mention of a number of later scholars, probably referring to some of the chapters in the later polemical treatises mentioned above. It is possible that he had some of the following works in mind also. These compositions concern themselves more with Christian doctrine than with scriptural exegesis.

26. *Sefer Nestor Ha-Komer,* an anonymous work of an unknown date.[22] This treatise is attributed to a priest named Nestor who converted to Judaism. If a sixth-century date is correct for this work, it is the first specifically anti-Christian Jewish polemic. It is possible that *Nestor* was originally written in Arabic.

27. *Ta'anot* of Moses ben Solomon of Salerno (thirteenth century).[23] The author, who was a Neoplatonic follower of Maimonides, also wrote another anti-Christian polemic entitled *Ma'amar Ha–'Emunah,* which has not been preserved. The first section of *Ta'anot* is devoted to a critique of the doctrines of Trinity and incarnation based on principles stated in Maimonides' *Guide.* The second section treats various biblical verses.

28. *Vikuah Radaq.*[24] This polemic, attributed incorrectly to David Kimḥi, attacks both orthodox Catholic and heterodox Catharist doctrines. It appears to have been written in thirteenth-century Italy.

29. *Livyat Ḥen* by Levi ben Abraham of Villefranche (1245–1315).[25] This author, in the chapter of his work devoted specifically to a refutation of Christianity, dealt with such doctrines as the Trinity, incarnation, original sin, and others.

30. *'Ezer Ha-Dat* by Moses Ha-Kohen of Tordesillas.[26] This work, written originally in Spanish by the same author as of *'Ezer Ha-'Emunah,* devotes itself mainly to theological questions, especially the unity of God.

31. *Keshet U-Magen* by Simon ben Ẓemaḥ Duran (1361–1444). There is little original in this treatise, which is a chapter from Duran's *Magen Avot.* This chapter, II:4, was censored from the printed edition because of Duran's defense of the perfection of the Torah as compared to the doctrines of Christianity. An anti-Muslim polemic forms half of this work.

32. *Sefer Ha-'Iqqarim,* III:25, by Joseph Albo (d. ca. 1444). This chapter is devoted to a general refutation of Christian criticism of the Torah. Albo's method was to show that Christian doctrines were deficient, especially compared to Jewish beliefs.

33. *Sefer Hoda'at Ba'al Din* by Don David Nasi (fifteenth century).[27] The author, writing in 1430, compared the principles of the Jewish religion, as outlined by Maimonides, with those of Christianity. Even the New Testament attested to the truth of the Jewish principles, but the Christian doctrines had no support.

34. *Vikuaḥ* of Elijah Ḥayyim ben Benjamin of Genazzano against Fra Francisco di Aquapendente (sixteenth century).[28] The subjects of this disputation are original sin, abrogation of the Torah, and the lowly state of the Jewish people.

35. *Vikuaḥ* of Azriel Petaḥia ben Moshe Alatino against Alphonso Caraciolla (seventeenth century).[29] In this account of the disputation that occurred in April 1617 in Ferrara, the author explained why Jews did not accept Christianity.

36. *Magen Va-Ḥerev* by Judah Aryeh de Modena (1571–1648). This work treats Christian doctrines on a variety of levels, both exegetical and philosophical. De Modena did not finish this work, which discusses original sin, Trinity, incarnation, virgin birth, and the conditions of the messianic age.

37. *Pilpul 'Al Zeman Zemanim Zemanehem* by Jonah Ha-Kohen Rappa (eighteenth century).[30] The author used a parody of the Passover Haggadah as a framework for criticizing Christian doctrines.

38. *Makkot Li-Khesil Me'ah* by Aaron Ḥayyim Voltera[?] (eighteenth

century).[31] In this poem of one hundred verses, plus a commentary apparently by the author, various Christian doctrines are mentioned and refuted.

Comparisons of Christian Doctrines with the New Testament

Those who followed the fourth method of debate directed their attention to the principles of Christianity as compared to the teachings of the New Testament. Not only were these doctrines false in themselves, argued the polemicists, but also they were contradicted by the New Testament. Therefore, there was no basis upon which the Christians could believe their doctrines. While some early polemicists adopted this method sparingly, Joseph ben Shem Tov stated that it was perfected in:

39. *Sefer Kelimat Ha-Goyim* by Profiat Duran (ca. 1345-ca. 1414).[32] This author, whose *Iggeret* is the subject of Joseph ben Shem Tov's commentary, analyzed the various Christian doctrines and showed how they departed from New Testament teachings. As noted, he also discussed mistakes in Jerome's translation of the Hebrew Bible and misquotations of the Bible in the New Testament.

Attacks on the Articles of Christianity

The fifth type of polemic is that which attacks the "articles" *(artiqolos)* of Christianity by showing their contradictory nature. This method was intended to demonstrate that major Christian beliefs were false in that they were self-contradictory. Joseph ben Shem Tov cited the following as an example:

40. *Biṭṭul 'Iqqare Ha-Noẓrim* by Ḥasdai Crescas (1340-1410).[33] Joseph ben Shem Tov himself translated this treatise into Hebrew from the original Spanish and commented upon it. The Christian doctrines treated are those of original sin, salvation, Trinity, incarnation, virgin birth, transubstantiation, baptism, the messiah, abrogation of the laws, and demons. Though Crescas was an opponent of Aristotelianism, he used Aristotelian principles extensively in his critique of Christian doctrines.

Comparisons of Christianity with the Principles of Philosophy

The sixth category of polemics includes those works which purported to show that Christian doctrines were inconsistent with philosophy, namely, the findings of logic/mathematics, physics, and metaphysics. One who accepts Christianity must, perforce, reject both sense perception, first principles, and commonly accepted notions. Joseph ben Shem Tov put into this category of polemics the work upon which he was writing his commentary.

41. *Iggeret Al Tehi Ke-'Avotekha* by Profiat Duran.[34] This is a satirical letter written to David Bonet Bonjorn, who, after accepting baptism unwillingly, became convinced of the truth of Christianity. This work, known in Latin as *Alteca Boteca,* was misunderstood by the Christians, who thought that the constant refrain, "Be not like your fathers," was to be taken literally, not satirically. Duran, who also composed a commentary to Maimonides' *Guide,* depended upon Aristotelian philosophy for his critique of Christianity. Though Duran's *Iggeret* was the only polemical work which specifically used the method of showing the inconsistency between reason and Christian doctrines almost throughout (though other methods were employed), many succeeding treatises were influenced by Duran's arguments. A number of authors already mentioned employed this technique along with others.

The above list of polemical works is by no means complete. The treatises just enumerated represent the major Jewish medieval polemics. Other compositions will be quoted in the course of this study. In addition, the categorization is also not perfect. Many polemicists employed a wide variety of argumentation, trying thereby to give as full and well-rounded a rebuttal of Christianity as possible. Joseph ben Shem Tov's classification system is helpful, since it offers an indication of the great variety in Jewish polemical works.

The Literary Style of the Polemics

Not only did the various polemicists use a number of different methodologies, but also they employed a variety of forms in which to place their polemics. The most common forms were the dialogue or disputation, the expository treatise, following either the biblical or a topical arrangement, the poem, the letter, and the parody.

Dialogues. The dialogue genre of polemics attempted either to recreate a real disputation, e.g., nos. 20, 21, 22, 34, 35, or to give the impression of a disputation, or at least a conversation that actually occurred, e.g., nos. 1, 2, 3, 9. Authors using the dialogue form related the Christian arguments as having actually been articulated by a Christian antagonist. Sometimes the

Christian was portrayed as actively debating, as in the disputations, while at other times he just offered his interpretations and then was left speechless by the Jewish reply.

Expository treatises. The expository treatises took two approaches. In the first, discussion followed the general order of the books in the Hebrew Bible (and sometimes the New Testament). The Christian interpretation was represented, and then the Jewish author refuted it. When the New Testament was the subject of the polemic, the author offered Jewish objections to the various passages. Examples of this genre of polemic are nos. 4, 5, 6, 10, 17, 19.

In the second approach, the author presented the discussion topically. Specific doctrines of either Judaism or Christianity were analyzed and debated until the author believed he had shown that the Jewish position was correct and that the Christian one was in error. This was probably the most common style, used in nos. 12, 14, 15, 23, 24, 26, 27, and a number of others.

Poems. Representatives of the poem form are *Zikheron Sefer Niẓẓaḥon* (no. 16), *Makkot Li-Khesil Me'ah* (no.38), and *Aḥiṭov Ve-Ẓalmon* (no.11), which also took the form of a disputation. The authors of these works attempted to add the literary beauty of the poem to their arguments.

Letters. The most famous examples of the letter genre are Profiat Duran's *Iggeret* (no.41) and Lorki's *Nusaḥ Ha-Ketav* (no.25).[35] These letters were usually the outgrowth of a particular situation in which the author was trying to convince his correspondent of the truth of Judaism. At the same time, the letter could be used as a general polemic in the larger Jewish-Christian debate.

Parody. Authors using the parody form relied on humor to convey their arguments. Examples are Rappa's *Pilpul* (no. 37) and the anonymous *Toledot Yeshu,* which is a parody of the Gospels but not a polemic per se.

Other Sources of Jewish Philosophical Arguments

As stated above, references to Christianity and refutations of Christian doctrine can be found in any number of works whose major purpose is not polemical. The following are some of the categories of compositions in which such material is present.

Biblical commentaries. Since one of the major issues under contention in the Jewish-Christian debate was the correct interpretation of the Bible, it was only natural that Jewish biblical commentators would include anti-

Christian interpretations in their works. Care should be taken, though, not to assume that every Jewish interpretation that disagreed with the Christian exegesis was written with the latter in mind. Commentaries especially noted for anti-Christian material, either explicit or implicit, are those of Rashi,[36] Abraham Ibn Ezra,[37] and David Kimḥi.[38]

Mysticism. Anti-Christian material in Jewish mystical works is not always explicit. Indeed, many Christians were convinced that the Kabbalah confirmed Christian doctrines, especially the Trinity.[39] A careful examination, however, can uncover various refutations of Christianity in mystical works.[40]

Poetry and liturgy. Since the Jews were living in an atmosphere of repression, it was only natural that when they turned to poetry and to prayer, they would try to find solace for their plight. This attempt expressed itself a number of times in anti-Christian remarks, sentiments, and arguments being included in poems and in the liturgy. Not all the references are readily apparent; a careful reading of uncensored texts is necessary for finding this material.[41]

Chronicles. The most outstanding example of a polemic in the form of history is the *Toledot Yeshu* already referred to above. Chronicles of Jewish history also contained anti-Christian and polemical material. Examples of this are Abraham Ibn Daud's *Sefer Ha-Qabbalah*[42] and Solomon Ibn Verga's *Shevet Yehudah.*[43]

Legal Works. Since dealings with Christians were an everyday occurrence for Jews in Christian lands, the Jewish law had to adjust to this situation. What sort of relations Jews should or should not maintain with the Christians became an important topic for the halakhists.[44] Examples of how specific anti-Christian polemics came into the legal material can be seen in Maimonides' *Mishneh Torah*[45] and the Responsa of Rabbi Solomon ben Adret (Rashba).[46]

Philosophical treatises. Most Jewish philosophical works were composed in order to demonstrate the compatibility of philosophy and Judaism. It is natural that in this context Jewish thinkers might attempt to show that the doctrines of other religions were rejected by reason. Indeed, Christianity was often the target of criticism, implicit or explicit, in Jewish philosophical works. After the polemical treatises themselves, these compositions form the second main source of the medieval Jewish philosophical critique of Christianity. In the course of this study, reference will be made to a number of works of Jewish philosophy, including those of Dāwūd al-Muqammiẓ,[47] Saadia Gaon,[48] Baḥya ibn Pakuda,[49] Judah Halevi, Maimonides,[50] Ḥasdai Crescas,[51] Abraham Bibago,[52] and Elijah del Medigo.[53]

The Christian Sources

Comment must be made on the Christian sources of this study. The different types of polemics that were common among the Jews, differing as they were in both content and form, were also employed by the Christians. They, too, had specific works devoted to polemics, which were presented as either dialogues, straight exposition, poetry or letters.[54] One genre of polemic which was quite rare among the Jews, whether for polemical or other purposes, and was used by the Christians for polemics, was the play.[55] Anti-Jewish polemical material is often found in other literary forms as well, e.g., philosophy or biblical commentaries.

It is easier to find the anti-Jewish material in Christian works than it is to locate anti-Christian material in the Jewish counterparts. This is so because the Christians wrote with no fear of censorship or concern for avoiding antagonism of the Jews. Another factor is also important. For Christianity, Judaism presents a theological problem, while for Judaism, as a religion, Christianity is relatively unimportant. Therefore, it is much more likely that an internal Christian composition, be it philosophical, exegetical, legal, or other, would make references to Judaism. A similar Jewish work, though, might have little or no reason to discuss Christianity.[56]

In this study, Christian sources will be cited in order to shed light on the Jewish philosophical critique. Some works will be quoted because they help place the Jewish arguments inside a larger context. Other sources will show the background of the controversy, while further quotations will be adduced in order to present the Christian refutations of some of the Jewish arguments. Though it is thought that the Christian works so considered are representative of the whole range of medieval Christian literature, by no means is there a claim that all or even the majority of relevant passages have been consulted. The present study does not offer an exhaustive investigation of Christian polemical literature. Rather, selections of this material will be employed to elucidate the Jewish arguments.

CHAPTER THREE

The Use of Reason in Religious Debates

Before proceeding to the Jewish polemic against specific Christian doctrines, it is necessary to outline the theoretical basis upon which such criticism was made. The Jewish polemicists' assertion that the central Christian dogmas were illogical and self-contradictory presupposed a firm philosophical foundation for its justification. Similarly the use of philosophical arguments implied a definite view of the relation between religion and reason. How the Jewish polemicists perceived this relationship will be discussed here.

According to the Jewish philosophical polemicists, one of the main differences between Judaism and Christianity lay in the former's conformity to reason and the latter's irrationality. To support this contention, the polemicists developed methods of distinguishing between their own doctrines, which they claimed to be rational, and Christian beliefs, which, they argued, contradicted the findings of reason. An examination of their approach will elucidate the theoretical basis of the various Jewish philosophical critiques of Christianity.[1]

Explanations of Christian Belief in Irrational Doctrines

Jewish theologians sought, in the first place, to render an account to themselves of the phenomenon of Christian belief in rationally unacceptable doctrines. They tried to gain some psychological insight into this kind of belief by pondering the force of training and habit.

This insight appears to have been offered first by Judah Halevi (1085–1141) in the opening passages of his *Kuzari,* a philosophical defense of Judaism. He began this work with succinct statements of the doctrines of the philosophers, Christians, Muslims, and Jews, fictionally presented to the King of the Khazars. In rejecting, in turn, philosophy, Christianity, and Islam, the King did not, in fact, address himself to any specific doctrines. For instance, philosophy was rejected because it did not provide an answer to the King's personal quest.[2] Similarly, he did not accept Islam because one of its claims to truth was based on the beauty of the Quran, which was written in a language the King did not understand.[3] In his reply to the Christian scholar, the King said:

> I see here no *logical* conclusion; nay, *logic rejects* most of what you say. If both appearance and experience are so palpable that they take hold of the heart, compelling belief in a thing of which one is not convinced, they render the matter more feasible by a semblance of logic. This is how natural philosphers deal with strange phenomena which come upon them unawares, and which they would not believe if they only heard of them without seeing them. . . As for me, I cannot accept these things, because they come upon me suddenly, not having grown up in them. My duty is to investigate further.[4]

The objection of the King was based on the assumption that logic rejected the Christian doctrines of incarnation, virgin birth, and Trinity. On occasion, one might accept a belief which reason apparently contradicted, if sufficient empirical evidence existed to substantiate such a doctrine. In the case of Christianity, however, such evidence did not exist. Why, then, did the Christians themselves maintain such tenets? Halevi answered through the mouth of the King that they have "grown up in them"; the doctrines have not "come upon them suddenly." He apparently claimed, then, that only those who are born and raised as Christians could believe in Christian doctrines even though reason rejected them.[5]

The ideas fictionally espoused by Judah Halevi through the King of the Khazars were, in reality, advocated by Moses ben Naḥman (Naḥmanides) before another King, James I of Aragon. In the Barcelona Disputation, 1263, Naḥmanides, according to his own testimony, said:

> And you, our lord and king, are a Christian born of a Christian [man and of a Christian woman] and all your days you have listened to priests [and Minorites and Preaching Friars talking of the nativity of Jesus] and they have filled your brain and the marrow of your bones with this doctrine, and you have believed it out of habit. Of a certainty the doctrine which you believe and

> which is a dogma of your faith cannot be accepted by *reason*. Nature does not admit of it. The prophets have never said anything that would support it. Also the miracle itself cannot be made intelligible by the doctrine in question as I shall make clear with ample proofs at the proper time and place. That the Creator of heaven and earth [and all that is in them] should withdraw into [and pass through] the womb of a certain Jewess and should grow there for seven months and be born a small child and after this grow up to be handed over to his enemies who condemn him to death and kill him, after which, you say, he came to life and returned to his former abode—neither the *mind* of Jew nor of any man will sustain this. Hence vain and fruitless is your arguing with us, for here lies the root of our disagreement.[6]

Naḥmanides affirmed, then, these two major points: Christianity was illogical, and only one brought up as a Christian could believe in its doctrines.

Ḥayyim ibn Musa also recognized the importance of upbringing in determining attitudes and beliefs. He concluded his treatise, *Magen Va-Romaḥ*, with the account of a minor disputation held before a noble. After rejecting basic Christian doctrines, the Jewish polemicist stated:

> All the books in the world could not by any means force this into the mind of a rationalist, especially one who has grown up believing in the Torah, which is far removed from these beliefs . . . for his [the Jew's] whole belief agrees with reason.[7]

A Jewish upbringing caused one to reject Christianity; conversely, it may be inferred, only a Christian upbringing allowed one to accept Christian doctrines.

Isaac of Troki (ca. 1533–ca.1594) continued to argue in the same vein. How is it that the Christian sages, with all their wisdom in secular sciences, can accept beliefs which are foreign to reason and are not proven from the words of the prophets?[8] Troki answered that Christian beliefs were ultimately derived from pagan doctrines originally held by the Gentiles before they became Christians.

> It became known to me without doubt that these strange beliefs and these corruptions remained as an inheritance from their predecessors. The lies to which their ancestors had become accustomed from their youth deceived them and became for them as natural things that did not appear strange because habit is second nature.[9]

In other words, irrational Christian beliefs were seen as holdovers from an earlier period when the Gentiles were pagans. Again, upbringing was seen to be more influential than reason.

What was it about Christianity that the Jews found so irrational? Why did the Jewish polemicists assert that only a born Christian could believe in this religion? Most important, what distinguished the doctrines of Christianity, which the Jews considered as irrational and, therefore, rejected, from those of Judaism, which the Jews claimed to be rational and worthy of acceptance? What criteria were to be employed when considering the respective rationality of differing religious claims? Indeed, could reason play any role in questions of religion?

Maimonides' Guidelines

Maimonides was concerned with some of these very same questions. He dealt with them in the *Guide* under the topic of distinguishing that which is rationally possible, though naturally impossible, from that which is totally impossible since reason does not admit it as a possibility. His treatment of this problem served as a guide to the anti-Christian polemicists as they discussed the use of reason in religious debates.

According to Maimonides, "the impossible has a stable nature, one whose stability is constant."[10] This means that God is not omnipotent in the sense that He can do anything and everything. There are certain things which even God cannot accomplish.

> Thus, for example, the coming together of contraries at the same instant and at the same place and the transmutation of substances, I mean the transformation of a substance into an accident and of an accident into a substance, or the existence of a corporeal substance without there being an accident in it—all of these things belong to the class of the impossible according to all men of speculation. Likewise that God should bring into existence someone like Himself, or should annihilate Himself, or should become a body, or should change—all of these things belong to the class of the impossible; and the power to do any of these things cannot be attributed to God.[11]

On the other hand, there were certain beliefs which were held by some to be possible, and by others, impossible. The Mu'tazilites taught that God could create an accident that existed without a substratum; Jews taught "the bringing into being of a corporeal thing out of no matter whatever" (i.e., *creatio ex nihilo*). Philosophers, namely, strict Aristotelians, denied even the possibility of these doctrines.[12] How, then, can one decide which things are possible and which are impossible?

Maimonides dealt with the very same problem when he treated the doctrines of Kalam. One of the theories espoused by the Mutakallimun was the following:

> They are of the opinion that everything that may be imagined is an admissible notion for the intellect. For instance, it is admissible from the point of view of the intellect that it should come about that the sphere of the earth should turn into a heaven endowed with circular motion and that the heaven should turn into the sphere of the earth. Or to take another example, it is admissible that the sphere of fire should move toward the center of the earth and that the sphere of the earth should move toward the encompassing heaven. For as they say, according to intellectual admissibility, one place is not more appropriate for one particular body than another place. They also say that with regard to all things that are existent and perceptible that supposing anything among them should be bigger than it is or smaller or different from what it is in shape or place—should a human individual, for instance, have the size of a big mountain having many summits overtopping the air, or should there exist an elephant having the size of a flea, or a flea having the size of an elephant—all such differences would be admissible from the point of view of the intellect. The whole world is involved in this method of admissibility as they practice it. For whatever thing of this kind they assume, they are able to say: it is admissible that it should be so, and it is possible that it should be otherwise; and it is not more appropriate that one particular thing should be so than that it should be otherwise.[13]

According to this doctrine, there are no philosophically determined immutable rules of nature; everything runs merely according to custom. Things in the world are not as they are because divine wisdom ordains them; they are the product of divine will.[14] Therefore, the world could be almost totally different from what it is now.

Despite the belief that anything imaginable is possible, even the Mutakallimun held certain things to be impossible.

> At the same time they are unanimous in holding that the coming-together of two contraries in the same substratum and at the same instant is impossible, cannot be true, and cannot be admitted by the intellect. They further assert that it is impossible and cannot be admitted by the intellect that a substance should exist without there being any accident in it; or, as some of them say, it is also impossible and cannot be admitted by the intellect that an accident should exist without being in a substratum. Similarly they say that it cannot be true that a substance should be transformed into an accident or an accident into a substance or that a body should compenetrate another body; they

> acknowledge that these are impossibilities from the point of view of the intellect. Now it is a true assertion that none of the things that they consider as impossible can be mentally represented to oneself in any way whatever, whereas the things they call possible can be.[15]

Some notions, then, are impossible, since the intellect does not allow them in that they cannot even be imagined; reason is not really the determining factor. Yet according to Maimonides and the philosophers, reason, not imagination, should be the final arbiter of what is possible.[16]

But are there not notions which the philosophers, employing reason, rejected as impossible, and Maimonides himself, also employing reason, accepted as possible? How could Maimonides state that certain things held possible by Kalam were, in fact, impossible, while maintaining that other things denied by the philosophers were possible? To answer these questions Maimonides posited a tentative principle of distinguishing the possible from the impossible.

> Consider, thou who art engaged in speculation, and perceive that a method of profound speculation has arisen. For with regard to particular mental representations, one individual claims that they are intellectual representations, whereas another affirms that they are imaginative representations. We wish consequently to find something that would enable us to distinguish the things cognized intellectually from those imagined. For if the philosopher says, as he does: That which exists is my witness and by means of it we discern the necessary, the possible, and the impossible; the adherent of the Law says to him: The dispute between us is with regard to this point. For we claim that that which exists was made in virtue of will and was not a necessary consequence. Now if it was made in this fashion, it is admissible that it should be made in a different way, *unless intellectual representation decides,* as you think it decides, *that something different from what exists at present is not admissible.*[17]

The intellect can refute certain notions as impossible. Anything not specifically rejected by reason is possible.

There existed, then, three schools of thought concerning the differences between the possible and the impossible. (1) The followers of the Kalam held that anything imaginable is possible. Anything not allowed by the imagination is impossible. Imagination is the absolute arbiter of the possible. (2) The philosophers believed that only doctrines proven by reason, as based on what actually exists, are possible. Anything not proven by reason is impossible. Reason is the absolute arbiter of the possible. (3) The religious

Jew (Maimonides) believed that the intellect is the arbiter, but not the absolute arbiter, between the possible and the impossible. There are, however, certain beliefs that, although they are not supported by reason, are not rejected by it. These notions, though they may be contrary to nature, are possible if reason does not refute them. Still, not everything imaginable is possible.

In concrete terms: The Kalam beliefs mentioned earlier, e.g., that there be a man the size of a mountain or an elephant the size of a flea or the earth and fire in different places, are ruled out by reason. They are not only impossible in nature, but they are also excluded by the definitions of "man," "elephant," "earth," and "fire." Thus, such existents are impossible.[18] On the other hand, *creatio ex nihilo* has not been disproven by reason.[19] There is nothing intrinsically illogical or contradictory about the notion of creation, despite the philosophical questions it raises and despite its presumed natural impossibility. Creation is not in the category of notions like the existence of a "square whose diagonal is equal to one of its sides or a corporeal angle encompassed by four plane right angles."[20] These are notions ruled out by logic, i.e., by definition; only he who is ignorant of the definition of the terms could believe in the possibility of such ideas. The Mutakallimun, then, believed in the possibility of some logical impossibilitites; the Jews believed in some natural impossibilities, but not in logical impossibilities. Philosophers did not believe in either natural or logical impossibilities.

> It has then become clear that, according to every opinion and school, there are impossible things whose existence cannot be admitted. Power to bring them about cannot be ascribed to the Deity. The fact that He does not change them signifies neither inability nor deficiency of power on His part. Accordingly, they are necessarily as they are and are not due to the act of an agent. It has then become clear that the point with regard to which there is disagreement concerns the things that could be supposed to belong to either of the two classes—whether they belong to the class of the possible or to the class of the impossible. Learn this.[21]

How, then, does one distinguish between logical and natural possibilities? Maimonides, who at one point said "would that I knew,"[22] gave some indication of an answer in his theory of the purpose of the world. He raised the question as to whether one can determine the reason the world is as it is. In responding to this issue, Maimonides distinguished between the Aristotelian view of the world's eternity and his own view that the world was created. If Aristotle was correct, then one cannot even ask what is the purpose of the world, since only that which is brought into being can be said to have a reason for its existence; an eternal substance is not the result of will, and therefore can exhibit no ultimate end. A created being, however, usually does show that there is a purpose for its existence. What, then, is the reason for the world? Maimonides answered that any attempt at solving this problem ultimately leads one to say "God has wished it so, or: His wisdom has required this to be so."[23]

Could the world have been different? Maimonides answered in the affirmative. Since the world is the product of divine will, God could have made that which exists, its causes, and its effects much different from what they are now. Everything depends on the divine will, or, "if you prefer you can also say: on the divine wisdom."[24]

Since it is the case that divine will, or wisdom, is the arbiter of what exists, and, therefore, of what is possible, why is the Kalam theory of admissibility not to be accepted? Maimonides stated that, indeed, it "is not something one hastens to reject in its entirety with nonchalance."[25] One must be very careful when distinguishing what is possible from what is impossible. Philosophers, using only reason, would consider certain things impossible because they were not in conformity with nature. The Mutakallimun would accept almost anything imaginable as possible, relying on God's omnipotent will to uphold its possibility. Maimonides steered a middle course. God can will into existence that which appears to be a natural impossibility; He cannot, however, cause a logical contradiction to exist. If reason rejects something as logically inconsistent, it cannot exist despite God's will and power. If reason allows something as possible, though it does not support it as necessary, it is, in fact, possible. Maimonides admitted that the details of this theory, i.e., how one draws the exact distinctions, must still be worked out.[26]

Before turning to the polemical use of Maimonides' theory of possibility, there is one more consideration to be discussed in connection with this thinker. When Maimonides raised the issues analyzed above, he did so in reference to the Mutakallimun and the Mu'tazilites in particular. Did he possibly have the Christians in mind also? The answer is probably yes.

In *Guide* III:15 Maimonides listed the following impossibilities: that God should bring into existence someone like Himself, or should annihilate Himself, or should become a body, or should change. Do these notions not correspond, however crudely, to the Christian doctrine that Jesus was the created incarnation of God and that in him God was crucified, as it were?

That Maimonides was arguing here against Christianity is supported by a number of considerations. First of all, Maimonides was well aware of Christian doctrines, as is evident from his denial of Trinity (*Guide* I:50),[27] divine impregnation (II:6),[28] and the messiahship of Jesus *(Hilkhot Melakhim* 11:4[29] and *Iggeret Teman*[30]*)*. Second, Joseph Kaspi (1279–1340) interpreted the above passage as being anti-Christian in its denial of incarnation and divine change.[31] Further, Simon Duran identified Christian beliefs with those of the Mu'tazilites.[32] It is, therefore, possible that Maimonides also had the Christians in mind when writing these passages about the Kalam.[33]

Even though the refutation of Christianity was not a major concern of Maimonides, he was aware of,. and he opposed, Christian doctrines. Whether or not he had Christianity in mind when distinguishing between logical and natural impossibilities, the distinction he drew became one of great importance in the history of Jewish-Christian polemics, as we shall see.

The Polemical Approach of the Jewish Averroists

How did the distinction drawn by Maimonides apply to Jewish-Christian polemics? The answer to this question is furnished by an analysis of the position of Averroistic Jewish polemicists. Averroes, in his *Faṣl al-Maqāl,*[34] argued that religious truths and philosophical verities were distinct, with no relation between them. One could not use the canons of philosophy to prove religion, since religious truths were not supported by rational speculation. Nevertheless, Jewish polemicists argued that Judaism was a true religion while Christianity was a false one. They did employ reason to validate this claim, which seemed to negate the Averroistic position. In what sense, then, could an Averroistic Jewish polemicist use philosophical arguments against Christianity? On what grounds could he contend that Judaism was more rational than Christianity? Indeed, did a Jewish debater have any rational means at his disposal on which to base the claim of the superiority of Judaism over Christianity?

These questions take on even greater importance when seen in their historical perspective. The late fourteenth and the fifteenth centuries were marked by great pressure on the Jews, particularly those in Spain, to convert to Christianity.[35] Given an Averroistic viewpoint, namely, that reason cannot be invoked in support of religious doctrines, could rational arguments be proposed to keep Jews from converting? In an atmosphere in which all religions were seen to have somewhat equal validity, reason per se not favoring any of them, why should a Jew defy the temptation of conversion and thereby face continued discomfort?

It is when they were confronted by these questions that the Averroistic Jewish polemicists turned to Maimonides' distinction between possible and impossible things. They developed his theory into the following assertions: Jewish doctrines, though they appear to be naturally impossible, are not logically impossible. Christian doctrines are both logically and naturally impossible, and they are, therefore, not at all admissible. Even though reason cannot be used to prove religious doctrines, it can be employed to distinguish between possible and impossible religious beliefs.

When claiming that Judaism was rational, one meant only that its doctrines were not found by reason to be logically self-contradictory and, hence, impossible. There was no claim here that Judaism was the result of rational speculation. Similarly, a polemicist who averred that Christianity was irrational asserted that reason judged its beliefs to be incompatible with philosophical logic. Philosophy cannot be used to "prove" a religion; it may be employed, though, to "disprove" one.

A prime example of how this problem was treated in the Averroistic milieu is presented in Joseph Albo's *'Iqqarim* (fifteenth century). He laid down a distinction between the possible and the impossible in his discussion of the question whether faith or reason leads man to happiness *(haẓlaḥah)*. Albo emphatically stated that faith brings such a reward. Philosophers never had miracles performed for them; only prophets were so worthy. After enumerating a large number of changes in nature (miracles) wrought for men of faith, Albo stated that if during their lives believers had such a close relationship with God that they were able to bring about miracles, certainly after their deaths they would continue to cleave to God and attain the highest happiness.

> This is why we find that miracles are performed for men of faith, and not for men of speculative knowledge, so as to show that faith stands higher than speculation and the things of nature. Therefore one may through it attain true union with God during life and after death, which is higher than nature.[36]

Even though belief, and not philosophy, leads to happiness, it is not possible that all beliefs lead to this end. Surely, false beliefs do not have the ability to produce such results.

> The question therefore arises, how can we tell whether a thing is true and demands implicit belief or is not true and should not be believed. If we say that the question must be determined by reason, it will follow that ratiocination stands higher than faith, which contradicts what was laid down before. This is a difficult matter which we must endeavor to solve.[37]

Albo solved this question in the manner suggested by Maimonides, namely, by positing two kinds of impossibilities. The first category of impossible notions are those which are "essentially impossible" *(nimna'ot qayyamot be-'aẓmam),* over which God has no power. For example, God cannot make the part equal to the whole, or the diagonal of a square equal to a side, or the affirmative and negative be applied at the same time to the same thing in the same relation.[38] Such notions could never be admitted as even possible, let alone commanded by faith.

> Such things therefore should not be believed. Thus it can never be accredited by tradition that God can create another being like Him in all respects. For the one would necessarily be the cause and the other the effect, and they would no longer be similar in all respects.[39]

The other category of the impossible are those beliefs which are "merely impossible according to the laws of nature" *(ha-nimna'ot eẓel ha-ṭeva' bilvad).* Such beliefs, e.g., in resurrection of the dead, or in the possibility that a human being can survive forty days and nights without food or drink, are not impossible for God to actualize. If the intellect can conceive of the existence of a notion, then that notion is possible.

> We may lay it down as a rule, therefore, that anything which the mind can conceive, though it be impossible by the laws of nature, may be believed to have existed in the past, to be existing now, or to come to exist in the future. This is particularly true if experience testifies to the existence of the thing, though the mind denies its existence because it does not know the cause.[40]

The polemical nature of this distinction becomes apparent in the anti-Christian section of Albo's treatise (III:25). After stating some typical Christian arguments against Judaism, Albo offered the following guidelines to the question of faith and reason.

> Anything that is the subject of belief must be conceivable by the mind, though it may be impossible so far as nature is concerned. . . . But a thing which the mind cannot conceive, for example that a thing should be and not be at the same time, or that a body should be in two places at the same time, or that one and the same number should be both odd and even, and so on, cannot be the subject of belief, and God cannot be conceived as being able to do it, as God cannot be conceived being able to create another like Him in every respect. . . . For since the mind cannot conceive it, God cannot do it, as it is inherently impossible. Therefore, it cannot be the subject of belief, for belief in impossible

> things does not give perfection to the soul, else reason would have been given to man to no purpose, and man would have no superiority to the animals, since the mind does not affect belief.[41]

Albo went on to argue that Christianity taught some doctrines which were, indeed, inconceivable to the intellect and, therefore, impossible.

In the light of Albo's lengthy discussion on this question, two propositions advanced by Ḥasdai Crescas, Albo's teacher, in his work *Biṭṭul 'Iqqare Ha-Noẓrim* become clearer. Before stating his anti-Christian contentions, Crescas formulated two principles which he felt should be acceptable to both sides.

> (1) Faith cannot force the intellect to believe something that is self-contradictory. (2) The divine power cannot be imagined to be able to contradict first principles, nor derivatives which are explained by absolute proofs, because these are derived from the first principles.[42]

What Crescas was saying was that not all beliefs are possible, and that reason decided between the possible and the impossible. Faith cannot force us to believe in something self-contradictory because God Himself has no power over the logically impossible. Crescas then proceeded to show that Christianity taught doctrines which were self-contradictory and impossible.

Continuing in this vein, Joseph ben Shem Tov stressed the difference between religious truths derived from prophecy, which were above the intellect, and untrue beliefs whose impossibility was established by reason. Prophecy might have taught doctrines (e.g., creation) which were unsubstantiated by philosophy without necessarily implying a logical contradiction. On the other hand, true prophecy could not impart a belief which was incompatible with first principles, e.g., that the part equaled the whole.[43]

Elijah Del Medigo (ca. 1460–ca. 1497), one of the most important Jewish Averroists, developed the discussion one step further. True, reason could not be used in supporting the validity of religious doctrines. What, then, would the Jew do if his own religion taught something which contradicted either his sense of perception or reason? If a Jew rejected such a doctrine on the basis of reason, then in his determination of religious doctrines, he would be employing reason, and not just faith or revelation. And if he used reason to reject some beliefs, should he not reject all religious doctrines not supported by reason, even Jewish ones?

Del Medigo's answer is three fold. First, the Jewish religion could not command belief in a self-contradictory notion. If the Jews were enjoined to accept such a belief, they would have to reject it, since God Himself has given man the rational ability to distinguish true from false. Second, any possible irrational beliefs that the Jew might be commanded to hold, e.g., incarnation, could not be necessary for the maintenance of the Jewish religion. Thus, if Judaism demanded belief in incarnation, a Jew should disown such a view, since it could not be a very important doctrine. The third answer to whether Jews could accept an irrational belief if so commanded by Judaism consisted of the assertion that this was not a problem for Jews. Since even the masses would not accept irrational beliefs, certainly God would not command them. Del Medigo argued that Christian doctrines, such as the Trinity and transubstantiation, were so foreign to the intellect that no one could possibly accept them. But if someone chose to believe in them, Del Medigo said, he would not discuss the issue with him, since this was not his concern.[44] Del Medigo's argumentation here is rather tenuous and not very convincing.

One more problem presented itself to Del Medigo. If one insisted that only religious doctrines which reason did not reject were acceptable, was one not thereby diminishing God's power? Did not the Jews agree that God was omnipotent *(yakhol 'al kol davar)*?[45] We have already seen a possible answer: God does not have the power to do something which is logically self-contradictory. Del Medigo added that the reason for this apparent lack of power was that God would have absolutely no desire to do such a thing, nor would He want to change Himself or one of His attributes. Del Medigo refused to argue with someone who held a contrary view.[46]

In his short account of the disputation with Fra Francisco di Aquapendente, Elijah Ḥayyim of Genazzano stressed the above distinctions in two different sections of the work.

> God forbid that we believe in a doctrine not in great accord with the intellect. Anything which the intellect refutes cannot be called Torah since Torah will not come to nullify the intellect.[47]

> We Hebrews do not say that one should believe only in those doctrines which the intellect affirms by demonstration. We do say, however, that one cannot believe that which the intellect refutes and rejects altogether so that their existence is seen to be impossible.[48]

Judah Aryeh de Modena followed Maimonides and Joseph Albo in distinguishing between possible and impossible religious beliefs. One may believe in what appears to be a natural impossibility but not in a logical impossiblity.[49] Proceeding further, he contended that reason was often necessary not only to reject certain notions as impossible, but also to give some basis for belief. Thus, if one asked a Christian for proof of the Trinity, he would say that this is a doctrine derived from faith. But if one then suggested that the Christian believes in one God with four Persons, he would ask for proof. If one responded that this belief may be derived from a faith which is similar to the Christian's in that it was not amenable to proof, nevertheless the Christian would not accept it. Obviously, then, argued de Modena, "Faith must be intermediate between proof and reason *[sevara']*, namely, it cannot be proven absolutely, for if it were so proven, it would not be faith. Yet faith must have some aspect of reason, lest it be complete foolishness."[50] A true religion did not have to be proven by philosophy; however, philosophy must not contradict a religion if one is to judge the latter as true.

This position did not disappear with the end of the Middle Ages. Moses Mendelssohn (1729–86) echoed it almost word for word. Thus, in his letter to Karl Wilhelm Ferdinand, hereditary Prince of Brunswick, Mendelssohn explained why he could not accept Christianity.

> And I must confess that the doctrines I have just listed [Trinity, incarnation, passion, gratification of first person of Deity by suffering of second person] strike me as an outright contradiction of the fundamental principles of reason. I simply cannot harmonize them with anything that reason and cogitation have taught me about the nature and attributes of the Deity.[51]

Echoing Del Medigo, Mendelssohn answered the question of what he would do were irrational beliefs demanded of him by Judaism.

> Of course, if I were to find such doctrines in the Old Testament, I would have to reject the Old Testament, too. . . . In the Old Testament, however, I find nothing that resembles these doctrines nor anything that I consider incompatible with reason. Therefore, I feel I am wholly justified in having faith in the historical authenticity that we unanimously ascribe to these writings. Consequently, I make the following fundamental distinction between the books of the Old and New Testaments: the former are in harmony with my philosophical views, or at least do not contradict them, while the latter demand a faith I cannot profess.[52]

For Mendelssohn, as for the medieval Averroists, it was inconceivable that religion would force someone to believe an irrational doctrine. This was what Christianity attempted to do. It was, therefore, to be rejected.[53]

We might summarize the position of the Averroistic Jewish polemicists as follows. The truths of philosophy were accepted because reason required it. The doctrines of Judaism were believed because revelation taught them and reason did not reject them. Christian beliefs, on the other hand, were not at all believable because reason disproved them. Theoretically, Christian doctrines would be as probable as Jewish ones if they were consistent with reason. This, however, was not the case.

How did the Christians respond to the accusation that they held illogical beliefs? Those of the dialectical school of thought, most notably Thomas Aquinas (1225–74), flatly denied any incompatibility between reason and Christian doctrines. The dialecticians concentrated on demonstrating this fact. In terms which echoed the statements of the Jewish Averroists, Thomas said:

> Now, although the truth of the Christian faith which we have discussed surpasses the capacity of reason, nevertheless that truth that the human reason is naturally endowed to know cannot be opposed to the truth of the Christian faith. For that with which the human reason is naturally endowed is clearly most true; so much so, that it is impossible for us to think of such truths as false. Nor is it permissible to believe as false that which we hold by faith, since this is confirmed in a way that is so clearly divine. Since, therefore, only the false is opposed to the true, as is clearly evident from an examination of their definitions, it is impossible that the truth of faith should be opposed to those principles that the human reason knows naturally.[54]

If someone were to adduce rational arguments against Christianity, it would be apparent that these arguments were "conclusions incorrectly derived from the first and self-evident principles imbedded in nature. Such conclusions do not have the force of demonstration; they are arguments that are either probable or sophistical. And so, there exists the possibility to answer them."[55]

Criteria for Determining Logical Impossibility

Members of both religions, then, asserted that reason did not contradict their doctrines. While Jews maintained that certain Christian beliefs were logically impossible, the Christians claimed that they were only apparently impossible. A true investigation of philosophical principles, they averred, demonstrated that logic and Christianity were not incompatible. What basis, then, was there to the Jewish polemical assertion that philosophy contradicted Christianity? What guidelines were drawn to distinguish between the naturally impossible and the logically impossible? Could there be consistent criteria by which one determined what was, in fact, possible?

We have already seen a possible answer given by Elijah Del Medigo: God has no power to make the logically contradictory possible, nor has He any desire to exercise such power. Similarly, we may say that God has no ability to change Himself or one of His special attributes[56] nor has He any desire to do so. His use of power is confined to the things external to Him. Del Medigo concluded that because of its complexity, the matter should not be discussed further.[57]

In this statement, Del Medigo did not substantially enlarge upon Maimonides' conclusions about the logically impossible. He merely reiterated that there were certain contradictory things which even God could not bring into existence. Not only did God have no such power, but also He would not even have the will to exercise it. God's will, or "if you prefer you can also say: divine wisdom,"[58] had established immutable laws of reason which God Himself could not transgress. The problem, however, remained: how could one distinguish between the logically possible and the logically impossible?[59]

Other Jewish polemicists offered another criterion for distinguishing possible and impossible doctrines. A possible doctrine was one that was not only logically consistent, but also implied no defect *(ḥisaron)* in the divine nature. One might maintain a belief if it was seen to be consistent with God's perfection and greatness. If, however, the doctrine in question implied some defect in God, it was not a possible belief.[60]

How could one determine, though, what doctrines taught such a defect in God? On what basis could one decide if a particular belief befitted the divine nature? In attempting to answer this question, one must turn to the polemicists themselves and see how they defined what cannot properly be ascribed to God.

Joseph Kimḥi gave some indication of what constituted a doctrine which taught a defect in the divine nature. In his arguments against incarnation, Kimḥi asserted that it was inconceivable that God would become defiled by entering into a woman's womb or would allow Himself to be a helpless child. A belief of this kind, Kimḥi argued, did not befit divine perfection.

> Thus I do not hold this belief which you profess, for my reason does not allow me to diminish the greatness of God, be He exalted, for He has not lessened His glory, be He exalted, nor has He reduced His splendor, be He extolled. If I do not hold this faith which you profess, I am not blameworthy.[61]

In his commentary on *Guide* III:15, Joseph Kaspi also gave an indication of what doctrines cannot properly be maintained. As noted above, Kaspi interpreted Maimonides to be speaking about Christianity when the latter stated that incarnation and divine change were impossible. The question arose why the Jews accepted creation and resurrection of the dead if they denied incarnation and divine change. Were not both equally unreasonable? Kaspi replied:

> This is no argument since we reply to them: Those notions concerning which we admit that God has power [e.g., creation] do not involve a defect. God forbid that in God's essence there be the power and possibility of evil, defect, or lack of dignity.[62]

For Kaspi, then, incarnation was logically impossible because it implied divine imperfection. Creation and resurrection, both of which demonstrated God's power and greatness, could be maintained even if they appeared to be impossible doctrines. One enhanced the concept of God by believing that He could create *ex nihilo* or resurrect the dead; one diminished the concept of God by maintaining that He became human.

This criterion was also applied by Shem Tov ibn Shapruṭ, who portrayed a Christian as arguing in the following manner: It was true that reason and logical proof should not be used in religious matters; if, however, a Jew did employ reason to reject Christian doctrines, why did he himself maintain belief in creation and revelation at Sinai, which were also apparently logically impossible? Ibn Shapruṭ answered that "there is a great difference between those things which are an insult to and a defect in God's essence," and those concepts about which there is a lack of knowledge (e.g., creation). Ibn Shapruṭ asserted that Christianity taught doctrines which implied divine deficiency and were, therefore, to be rejected. Judaism, on the other hand, taught rationally acceptable beliefs even if they were not perfectly understood.[63]

Abraham Bibago (fifteenth century) stated that he made a similar claim in front of King Don Juan II of Aragon. In the presence of this king, a Christian scholar asked Bibago if he were a Jewish philosopher. The latter responded that he was an observant Jew who had also studied philosophy, though he was not a philosopher. The Christian then asked why the Jew rejected incarnation, claiming that it is an inconceivable doctrine and therefore impossible, while at the same time he accepted creation, which Aristotle had disproved. The Jew should be consistent and reject everything of which reason disapproves, or he should accept all religious beliefs including incarnation. Bibago responded:

> The answer to your question has two aspects. First, the proofs of Aristotle are not proofs but only arguments, as we the students of Maimonides establish.[64] When we reject them and believe in creation, we are not believing in something impossible, for this doctrine is intellectually possible. Second, if we were to believe the first impossibility [incarnation], we would be ascribing a defect to the divine nature, but [a belief in] the second impossibility [creation] ascribes a perfection to the divine nature. If we were to say that God, may He be blessed, was acted upon, became incarnate, was murdered and died, this is an imperfection in divinity, and we would be positing that something which is not God, because it is only possible of existence and is in need of something else and is acted upon by something else, is indeed God.[65]

Bibago further explained that creation was possible, implying as it did God's divine perfection, as evidenced by his ability to do something which appears impossible.[66]

This brief survey indicates that the polemicists who asserted that Christian doctrines diminish God's greatness pointed out incarnation as their prime example. The belief that God became man and underwent the tribulations of the human condition was seen as unbefitting the Deity. Christians, on the other hand, responded that the opposite was the case. God's willingness to become incarnate in order to save mankind was a sign of His great love. One did not diminish God's glory by believing in incarnation but rather enhanced it.[67]

Given this polarity in initial premises between Jews and Christians, could the idea of that which befits God be employed as a criterion of judging logical impossibility? The answer is apparently in the negative. In fact, when the Jewish polemicists drew the distinction between what was fitting and what was not, they seemed to posit this distinction not as a real criterion for judging possibility, but only as a reply to the accusation that they were not consistent. As Bibago stated, the question of propriety was not the only basis for accepting creation. The other reason one allowed *creatio ex nihilo* consisted in the intellect's not judging it to be absolutely impossible (and it was taught by revelation). The implication was that there was sufficient logical justification for rejecting Christian doctrines.

Conclusions

It is this last point, i.e., the logical justification for the rejection of Christianity, that was most often stressed by the Jewish philosophical polemicists. It was not solely a matter of God's will, which was difficult to determine, or of ascribing a defect to divinity, the interpretation of which depended on varying world views. The Jewish polemicists asserted that it was logical reasoning which prohibited one from accepting Christianity as true. Christian doctrines were those which Maimonides would classify as logical impossibilities. Reason could not conceive that they might be true, since even God is not able to bring logical impossibilities into existence. Jewish doctrines were natural impossibilities; they could be true if God so willed it. Jewish Averroists, then, did not employ reason to support religious claims. Reason was to be used solely to refute the possibility of a religious doctrine.

Having established these principles, Jewish philosophical polemicists turned to exposing the logical impossibility of Christian doctrines. In order to be convincing, they had to demonstrate that the beliefs they were criticizing fell into the category of logical impossibilities, which were invariably false, and not into the classification of natural impossibilities, which could be true. In proceeding to this task, the Jewish polemicists employed philosophical principles which were acceptable to the Christians also. It was the Jewish contention that the Christian theologians taught doctrines which were not only logically self-contradictory in themselves, but also inconsistent with other Christian beliefs. The Jewish methods of argumentation will be shown in the coming chapters.

CHAPTER FOUR

Trinity

The Christian doctrine which the medieval Jewish polemicists subjected to the most comprehensive and varied philosophical criticisms was that of the Trinity. Though this belief is not fully developed in the New Testament, it was adopted by the Church Fathers, who taught it as authoritative and who gave it its philosophical foundations.[1] Though not all Christians with whom the Jews were familiar agreed on all the details of the trinitarian doctrine,[2] most followed the formulation of the Quicumque (Athanasian) Creed.

> We venerate one God in the Trinity, and the Trinity in oneness; neither confounding the persons, nor dividing the substance; for there is one person of the Father, another of the Son, (and) another of the Holy Spirit; but the divine nature of the Father and of the Son and of the Holy Spirit is one, their glory is equal, their majesty is coeternal. Of such a nature as the Father is, so is the Son, so (also) is the Holy Spirit; the Father is uncreated, the Son is uncreated, (and) the Holy Spirit is uncreated; the Father is immense, the Son is immense, (and) the Holy Spirit is immense; the Father is eternal, the Son is eternal, (and) the Holy Spirit is eternal: and nevertheless there are not three eternals, but one eternal; just as there are not three uncreated beings, nor three infinite beings, but one uncreated, and one infinite; similarly the Father is omnipotent, the Son is omnipotent, (and) the Holy Spirit is omnipotent: and yet there are not three omnipotents, but one omnipotent; thus the Father is God, the Son is God, (and) the Holy Spirit is God; and nevertheless there are not three gods, but there is one God; so the Father is Lord, the Son is Lord, (and) the Holy Spirit is Lord; and yet there are not three lords, but there is one Lord; because just as we are compelled by Christian truth to confess singly each one person as God and [and also] Lord, so we are forbidden by the Catholic religion to say there are three gods or lords. The Father was not made nor created nor begotten by anyone. The Son is from the Father alone, not made nor created, but begotten. The Holy Spirit is from the Father and the Son, not made nor created nor begotten, but proceeding. There is therefore one Father, not three

> Fathers; one Son, not three Sons; one Holy Spirit, not three Holy Spirits; and in this Trinity there is nothing first or later, nothing greater or less, but all three persons are coeternal and coequal with one another, so that in every respect, as has already been said above, both unity in Trinity, and Trinity in unity must be venerated. Therefore let him who wishes to be saved, think thus concerning the Trinity.[3]

A number of concepts are presented in this formulation of faith. First, there is only one God, who is one substance or divine nature. Second, this one God has three Persons: the Father, the Son, and the Holy Spirit. Each Person is God; still, there is only one God. Third, the Father was not begotten, the Son was generated from the Father, and the Spirit proceeded from the Father and Son. Fourth, all three Persons are coequal and coeternal. Despite the seeming causative relation between the Persons, they are not distinguished from each other in terms of priority or importance.[4]

Now the Jewish polemicists agreed that there was only one God and only one divine nature. They also believed that whatever might be said about God did not imply priority or greater importance to any specific aspect of divinity over another. They disagreed, though, with the division of God into three Persons and with the assumption that the three Persons were apparently causally connected. The Jews rejected this Christian concept of a triune God as being incompatible with the principles of God's unity, which even the Christians claimed they maintained. This divergence in theology was one of the crucial differences between Judaism and Christianity. It was natural, then, that the debate over the Trinity was a central feature of almost every Jewish anti-Christian polemical work. A study of the philosophical aspects of this debate will show quite well the Jewish use of philosophy to criticize the Christian religion.

As we have seen, the Jewish polemicists considered most Christian doctrines to be not only false but also illogical and nonsensical. The Trinity was no exception. Some Jews contended that this notion was so incompatible with human reason that one could not even verbally express it. Any attempted explanation would, of necessity, be mere words, since logical impossibilities could never be conceptualized adequately. Thus Maimonides cited the Christians who employed the trinitarian formula, "God is one, but also three, and the three are one," as an example of people who say one thing but must believe something quite different. The Christian statement was self-contradictory because the doctrine it meant to express was itself unintelligible.[5]

Maimonides was not alone in considering the Trinity a belief which could not be explained because of its illogical nature. Yūsuf al-Baṣīr, for instance, contended that the Christians, when referring to the doctrine of the Trinity, contradicted themselves in expression as well as in concept.[6] Profiat Duran wrote that the Trinity was a belief which "the mouth is not able to say, and the ear is too heavy to hear,"[7] in addition to being something which is said but is not intelligible.[8] Levi ben Abraham of Villefranche said: "According to their belief, God's unity does not lend itself to conceptualization, but this [the Trinity] is one of the doctrines which is logically impossible."[9] Quoting Maimonides,[10] Simon Duran stated that this belief was "uttered by the mouth without being represented in the soul," i.e., any verbal explanation could never be based on an adequate logical conceptualization.[11] This opinion was echoed also by Joseph Albo,[12] Judah Aryeh de Modena,[13] and Isaac Lupis.[14] The author of *Ḥerev Pifiyot* (Samson ben Joshua Moses Morpugo?) had the Jewish disputant say to his Christian adversary: "This is something which I do not understand, nor are you able to explain it to me."[15]

The Christians were aware of the difficulties which their trinitarian doctrine raised. Augustine commenced his *De Trinitate* with the statement that the purpose of his work was "to guard against the sophistries of those who disdain to begin with faith and are deceived by a crude and perverse love of reason."[16] Thomas Aquinas acknowledged that human reason experienced great difficulties with the concept of Trinity.[17] Whereas a person could acquire knowledge of the essence of God from his own reason, the Trinity was known only from faith. One could not hope to prove the Trinity to nonbelievers; one could only show that it was not an impossible doctrine.[18]

What was it that was so intrinsically difficult about the Trinity that caused its opponents to say it was inexplicable, and even its proponents to admit that it could be known only through faith, not reason? How did the Jews proceed to demonstrate that God was totally one and simple, not a Trinity of Father, Son, and Holy Spirit? What was it about the Trinity that the Jews considered inherently contradictory, and thus inexpressible? How did the Jewish polemicists and theologians use specifically philosophical arguments to refute this doctrine? It is to these questions that we now turn.

There was no one Jewish philosophical critique of the Trinity. Though many of the same arguments were repeated time and time again, the frameworks in which they appeared differed greatly. The varied philosophical contentions usually reflected the schools of thought of the different polemicists. Some writers stressed exegetical arguments,[19] referring only briefly to philosophical issues. Others disregarded the Scriptures in order to focus on the claimed rational inconsistency of the trinitarian doctrine. Some arguments were to the point; others seem to have been misdirected.

In the following analysis of the Jewish philosophical critique of the Trinity, attention will be paid to each type of argument employed, its philosophical background and context, and its relation to the Christian sources. The arguments have been classified into four major categories: (1) Trinity implies matter. (2) The divine attributes are not Persons. (3) Generation disproves unity. (4) Syllogistic logic refutes the Trinity. An additional section will be devoted to (5) images of the Trinity.

Trinity Implies Matter

One of the most common Jewish arguments against the Trinity was based on the Aristotelian dictum that "all things that are many in number have matter."[20] Using the argument in its simplest form, many Jews contended that since God was devoid of matter, He could not be many in number. Thus, He could not be a Trinity of three distinct Persons. This type of refutation is found in the works of Saadia,[21] David Kimḥi,[22] Levi ben Abraham of Villefranche,[23] Simon Duran,[24] and in *Kevod Elohim.*[25]

A more intricate form of the argument was offered by Jacob ben Reuben. Quoting his Christian antagonist, who said that God was "personas distintas realmente, tres in persona et una in sustancia," he responded:

> There are two alternatives in regard to your statement: (1) The Creator is [composed of] matter and form and, therefore, not one, or (2) He is one without matter and form. Now if there are three Persons and each one is separate and distinct *[guf bifene 'aẓmo],* then already they have some distinction between them. They each must have a beginning and end, and their existence has dimension and magnitude; thus, each one is limited. The philosophers have already testified that every limited thing is distinct; every distinct thing is composed; every composed thing is created; every created thing needs an external creator and cannot itself be God.[26] Therefore, there can be only one Creator, one who is without matter and form, without dimension or magnitude, without any disjunction or composition or new creation; rather He is first without beginning, and last without end, eternal without cause, and He can be no other thing.[27]

Jacob ben Reuben's refutation was copied almost verbatim by Shem Tov ibn Shapruṭ,[28] Isaac Lupis,[29] and the author of *Kevod Elohim*[30] for use in their own works.

Though many Jewish polemicists employed this argument, some realized that they might be accused of a possible contradiction. Aristotle taught, and Jewish Aristotelians accepted, that the separate intellects, which caused the spheres to revolve, were both incorporeal and numerically distinct.[31] Apparently, the Jewish philosophical polemicists were not consistent in their application of the principle "all things which are many in number have matter." How, then, could they justify their rejection of the Christian doctrine? Possible answers were provided by Moses ben Solomon of Salerno and Joseph ben Shem Tov.

Moses ben Solomon dealt with this problem in the following manner. First, he quoted Maimonides' formulation of the aforementioned principle, which concluded: "No multiplicity at all can be cognized by the intellect in the separate things, which are neither a body nor a force in a body, except when they are causes and effects."[32] Next, Moses ben Solomon argued that a Trinity would be possible only if the Father were a cause and the Son were an effect, but if the Son were an effect, then, as an effect, he could not be the Son of God.[33] He then recounted a discussion on this point held with Nicolo of Giovenazzo (b. 1197). The Christian argued that Aristotle had not said that incorporeal things were devoid of multiplicity, but rather their multiplicity could not be cognized. Moses ben Solomon dismissed this argument by saying that if incorporeal things were many in number, the intellect would be able to cognize this multiplicity. He argued further that the reason why Aristotle did not use the expression "incorporeal things are devoid of multiplicity" was because he realized that the separate intellects had multiplicity in respect to their being causes and effects, but otherwise they exhibited no multiplicity.[34] Another reason for the sage's use of the term "cognition of multiplicity" was the fact that men could comprehend the separate intellects only by means of their own intellect.[35]

Another Christian asked the following question: "Did not Aristotle state that the number of intellects is such, and such is the number of spheres?"[36] Moses ben Solomon again responded that the multiplicity of the intellects was a function of their being causes and effects. Furthermore, one was able to distinguish their number only by means of motion, for the intellects moved the spheres. It is from the strength of their motion that one knew the number of the intellects and the fact that they were causes and effects. If the Persons of God were many in number, they would have to be causes and effects.[37]

Joseph ben Shem Tov responded to the charge of inconsistency in the following manner:

> When you think in your intellect of an incorporeal intelligible, or even a material intelligible which we render an intelligible, you will not find in your mind any multiplicity in this intelligible, nor can you conceive it to be more than one. An example: when you consider in your intellect the form of the letter aleph abstracted from matter and accidents (for this is intellectual representation as is explained in *On the Soul),*[38] you will not have in your intellect two alephs. One is the other. But in your imagination you will find multiplicity if you distinguish between them in respect of accidents. For this one is large, and that one is small. This one is black, and that one is white. Likewise, you will find multiplicity outside the intellect in their material, accidents, and other qualities. In the intellect, however, there remains only one concept of the aleph. This has already been proven in *On the Soul,* chapter 2.[39] This is why Aristotle says in *Metaphysics* that multiplicity comes only from the aspect of matter. Incorporeal things can have multiplicity only in essence, e.g., the essence of the intelligible aleph is different from the intelligible bet. The essence of the mover of the sphere of the zodiacal signs is distinct from the mover of Saturn's sphere. But it is utterly impossible that their essence be one intelligible which is multiple individually. Therefore, the Philosopher explains in *Metaphysics*[40] that the heavens and their movers are many in species, i.e., essence, unlike Reuben and Simon, who are many individually though they have a common intelligible essence.[41]

As Joseph ben Shem Tov saw it, the Christians' mistake was in trying to say that the three Persons were distinct but neither separate essences (thus three Gods) nor material individuals (thus making God corporeal). The trinitarians could not posit individualized nonmaterial essences because an incorporeal essence could only be one. In this way, Joseph ben Shem Tov refuted the Trinity as inconsistent with Aristotle's principle and still defended the Jewish belief in numerically distinct separate intellects.[42]

These statements by Moses ben Solomon and Joseph ben Shem Tov represent the two medieval solutions to the problem of multiplicity of immaterial movers. Numerical distinctions were possible either because the intellects were related by cause and effect or because they were diverse in species, i.e., each mover was its own species.[43] The earliest Christian Apologists offered this latter interpretation of the Trinity, namely, each Person was its own species, and therefore numerable.[44] For later Christian thinkers, who held God to be one essence, with all three Persons of that one essence and none of them the cause of another, neither diversity in species nor a relationship of cause and effect could be suggested as interpretations of the Trinity. How, then, could the immaterial Persons be numbered?

Thomas Aquinas dealt with this problem in a somewhat different context. Asking how the Persons could be numbered when number implied that God was a whole that had parts, something which was manifestly impossible, Thomas answered by distinguishing between two types of number. There were both simple, or absolute, number, e.g., two, three, four, and also applied number, e.g., two men, two horses. Since absolute number existed only in the intellect, there was no reason why it could not be employed when discussing God. On the other hand, one might not ascribe applied number to God. Thus, whereas in creatures one was part of two, as one man was part of two men, this could not be said of God, since the Father was as much as the whole Trinity. The immaterial Persons, then, could be numbered but only by absolute number.[45]

The Divine Attributes Are Not Persons

The largest portion of the Jewish philosophical polemic against the Trinity was devoted to a polemical discussion of the divine attributes. The Jewish polemicists rightly perceived that the Christian polemicists attempted to explain the concept of Persons, which the Jews found unacceptable, by reference to various theories of attributes, which many Jewish thinkers accepted. The Christians drew a parallel between the two doctrines, hoping thereby to convince the Jews of the possibility of a divine Trinity.[46] The Jewish polemicists argued that the parallel was specious and irrelevant. Though there was no one Jewish theory of attributes, certain common features are apparent in the distinctions Jews drew between divine attributes and the Trinity.

The Jewish polemical treatment of the divine attributes can be divided into the following sections: (1) Kalamic refutations, and (2) Aristotelian refutations of both (a) the Persons as attributes, and (b) a connection between the Trinity and God as intellect, intellectually cognizing subject, and intellectually cognized object *(sekhel, maskil, muskal)*.

Jewish Kalamic Refutations of the Trinity

The first major Jewish philosophical movement in the Middle Ages was the Kalam, and the first Jewish philosophical arguments against Christianity were derived from this method of rational speculation.[47] The

Mutakallimun, expecially the Mu'tazilites, stressed two major themes in their philosophy, i.e., the unity of God and His justice.[48] It was in the context of their treatment of God's oneness that the Mutakallimun discussed doctrines which they thought were incompatible with God's absolute unity. One of those doctrines was the Christian Trinity.[49]

The Jewish Mutakallimun were in general agreement with the Muslim thinkers on the question of God's unity. They, too, attempted to prove that God was one, both in terms of number and in terms of simplicity. Following the Kalamic pattern, these Jewish thinkers usually began with a proof for God's existence (by demonstrating that the world was created, and thus needed a creator) and proceeded to show that God was one. They then refuted the Dualists, who held that there were two supreme beings,[50] and the Christians, who believed that the one God was a Trinity of three Persons (hypostases).[51]

The Kalamic Jewish critique of the Trinity was the product mainly of three important thinkers: (1) Dāwūd ibn Marwān al-Muqammiẓ (late ninth century), (2) Saadia ben Joseph Gaon (892–942), and (3) Abū Yūsuf Ya'qūb al-Qirqisānī (tenth century). In addition, (4) other Jewish Mutakallimun will be considered briefly. Though the various Jewish Kalamic refutations of the Trinity were quite similar, the differences were significant enough to warrant a full treatment of each polemicist.

Dāwūd ibn Marwān al-Muqammiẓ. The Kalamic pattern of argument is seen clearly in the works of the first Jewish Mutakallim of note, Dāwūd al-Muqammiẓ.[52] After proving God's existence and providing four demonstrations of God's numerical oneness, al-Muqammiẓ then raised the question as to the sense in which God was to be considered one. This problem, namely, what was meant by the term "one," had already been treated by Aristotle, who distinguished between things which were one by accident and those which were one by nature. Things which were one in virtue of their own nature could be one by continuity, e.g., a number of objects combined to form a single collection. Likewise, they might exhibit unity of substratum, e.g., water and oil have a common underlying element; unity of genus, e.g., a horse and a man are both animals; or unity of species, e.g., Socrates and Plato are one because they belong to the species man.[53]

In his own discussion of the senses of unity, al-Muqammiẓ did not follow Aristotle exactly.[54] He did, however, enumerate "one in species" as a possible explanation of God's unity. This meant that Godhood was one species composed of individuals who were members of the species. He saw this definition of God's unity as the meaning of the Christian doctrine which taught that God was "one substance with three Persons *[jawhar wāḥid 3 aqānīm].*" The common substance was the species Godhood; the three Persons were individuals participating in this species. These Persons were three and distinct from eternity; still, they did not constitute three Gods. There was only one God.[55]

In citing the trinitarian formula that God was "one substance, three Persons," al-Muqammiẓ was on firm ground. The concept that God was one substance *(jawhar/substantia/ousia)* with three Persons *(aqānīm/personae/prosopa)* went back to Tertullian.[56] The use of this formulation in the Christian-Arabic world can be seen, for instance, in the works of Yaḥya ben 'Adī (tenth century), who stated that God was "one substance possessing three properties *[ḥawāẓẓ]*, which the Christians call Persons *[aqānīm].*"[57] Thus, al-Muqammiẓ's citing of this standard Christian formula is not remarkable.

What is somewhat surprising, however, is al-Muqammiẓ's assertion that Christians understood God's oneness in terms of unity of species. This was the doctrine of the Cappadocians (Basil of Caesaria, Gregory of Nazianzus, and Gregory of Nyssa),[58] but it was rejected by Augustine.[59] It appears that, despite the latter's authority, some Christians continued to cite unity of species as an explanation of the Trinity.[60] Al-Muqammiẓ's direct source was Nonnus, though, as Vajda pointed out, the former appears to have misunderstood his teacher deliberately.[61] On the other hand, the influence of the Cappadocians is unmistakable, since al-Muqammiẓ quoted three images of the Trinity that derived from the theologians of this school.[62]

Having stated that the Christians believed God to be one in species, al-Muqammiẓ proceeded to show that God's unity could not be so conceived. The argument ran as follows: If the three Persons participated in one substance, then they were either identical with that substance or not identical with it. If one assumed that the Persons were identical with the substance, as did the Jacobites,[63] then one asked: (1) Is this identity exclusive so that there is nothing other than the substance, or (2) are these three Persons, while being identical with the substance, something other than the substance? If the first case holds, and the Persons are exactly identical with the substance, then there is no distinction between the Persons.[64] Thus, if one took this position that the substance was absolutely identical with the Persons, then he must concede either that the substance was not really one, or that there was no distinction between the Persons.[65]

Al-Muqammiẓ continued: on the other hand, let us suppose that one adopts the view that the three Persons are one substance, plus something else. The question can be asked, what is that "something else"? If one answers that the "something else" is the properties *(ḥawāẓẓ)* of the Persons which distinguish them, then a further question arises, are they substances or accidents? If the properties are substances, then within God would exist noneternal substances.[66] If the properties are accidents, then God would be composed of substance and accident, and, thereby, not be eternal.[67] What if the properties are neither substances nor accidents? A lacuna in the text deprives us of al-Muqammiẓ's answer.[68] We may assume that al-Muqammiẓ provided a reason why this alternative was impossible, thereby demonstrating that the Christian formula "one substance, three Persons," was logically contradictory.

The above treatment of the Trinity appeared in a discussion of what was meant by God's unity. When al-Muqammiẓ turned to the subject of God's attributes, he again raised the question of the Trinity. The appropriateness of the context is seen when we look at the background of the Kalamic theory of attributes. As Wolfson has shown, Muslims adopted the theory of attributes mainly in order to refute the Christian Trinity.[69] It made sense, then, that a discussion of attributes took the Trinity into account.

In the section treating the question of God's attributes, Treatise Nine of his *Twenty Treatises,* al-Muqammiẓ defined the Trinity as follows: "God lives with life, which is the Holy Spirit, and knows with knowledge, which is the Word which they call the Son. This is pure polytheism."[70] This formulation reflected Eastern Christian teaching. The identification of the Son with God's knowledge and the Spirit with God's life was made by such thinkers as Yaḥya ben 'Adī, who stated: "The Father has a life, which is the Holy Spirit, and a Word, which is the Son."[71] Eliyya of Nisibis[72] and Paul Rahib[73] taught similar doctrines.

Al-Muqammiẓ attributed this Christian doctrine to a misunderstanding of the semantic meaning of God's attributes. The Christians took God's "wisdom" and "life" to have the same meaning as man's wisdom and life. They were then led to ascribing ontological status to the attributes, believing that the attributes of wisdom and life had real, distinct existence, separate from God's essence.[74] This was the position held by the Muslim Attributists (Ṣifātiyya), who stopped short, though, of a trinitarian belief.[75] Al-Muqammiẓ, for his part, rejected the positions of both the Christians and the Muslim Attributists. It was true that God lived, he argued, but not by virtue of life; He knew, but not by virtue of knowledge. His life and His knowledge were by virtue of Himself, not by virtue of anything outside Himself.[76]

The Christians rejected this theory of attributes, claiming that it was logically impossible for God to live not by virtue of life, or to know not by virtue of knowledge, because we witness that life and knowledge are always by virtue of life and knowledge. Al-Muqammiẓ replied that if this be the case, then God should also die and be bereft of knowledge, since we witness that all who lived or knew eventually died or lost their knowledge. Now some may say that indeed their God did live and die, did know and also was ignorant.[77] Those, however, who did not use this retort stated that contrary to what occurred in our world, God could live by virtue of life and still never die; He could know by virtue of knowledge and still never be ignorant. Al-Muqammiẓ answered that using the same method we could say that, contrary to what occurs in our world, God lives not by virtue of life and knows not by virtue of knowledge. According to al-Muqammiẓ, the Christian had no answer to this argument.[78]

In his polemic against the Trinity, al-Muqammiẓ sought to demonstrate the two aspects of the problem of God's unity. First, he asserted that the only way to understand God's unity was in terms of total simplicity. No other meaning of unity could be allowed when referring to God. Second, since God's unity was absolute, any attributes ascribed to Him had to be understood as having different meanings from those ascribed to humans.[79] Thus, there could not be two real distinct attributes in God which corresponded to the Christian concept of Son and Holy Spirit. The Christian doctrine of the Trinity could not be maintained.

Saadia ben Joseph Gaon. Saadia Gaon also discussed God's unity immediately after proving His existence as Creator of the world. Following the standard Kalamic pattern, Saadia refuted the opinions of the Dualists and the Christians in this context. First, Saadia proceeded with a general introduction stating the fact of God's unity and essential attributes. Second, he demonstrated God's numerical unity against Dualist claims. Third, he set the stage for his refutation of the Trinity by explaining God's attributes in an anti-Attributist fashion. Fourth, he argued against the Trinity and incarnation. Fifth, and finally, Saadia discussed anthropomorphism in the Bible.[80]

Saadia's interest was in the trinitarian doctrine held by the Christian "elite," not that of the "common people," namely the Tritheists, who believed in three Gods.[81] How have the elite been led to adopt the concept of a Trinity? "They arrived at these three attributes [Persons] and adhered to them by asserting that only a thing that is living and knowing can create and, because they believed that life and knowledge of that thing which is the Creator are two things other than His essence, these became for them three."[82] It is not clear from this formulation whether Saadia understood that Christian doctrine held that the Son was knowledge and the Holy Spirit was life, as stated by al-Muqammiẓ, or vice versa.[83]

Saadia proceeded to attack the trinitarian doctrine with two arguments. The first stated that a Trinity, with its assumption of real attributes, implied that God was corporeal. Though the Christians denied a belief that God was a physical body, they had to hold such a view in order to assert that each person of the Trinity was distinct from each other one. As we have seen, this was based on Aristotle's statement that "all things that are many in number have matter."[84]

What, then, was the status of the attributes which Saadia ascribed to God—living, knowing, powerful? These are not three separate existents. The three terms express piecemeal what the mind intuits at one stroke, namely, that the Creator must live, know, and be powerful.[85] In the case of man, life and knowledge were attributes distinct from man's essence, because, as we perceive, a man could live and then not have life or know and then be devoid of knowledge. Since it is out of the question that God be dead, ignorant, or powerless, He had the attributes of life, knowledge, and power as part of His essence.[86]

The distinction which Saadia drew between God's attributes and man's attributes seems to have an ontological basis. Saadia apparently believed that man's attributes had existence independent of him while God's attributes had no such external subsistence. Still, some semantic aspects were involved.[87] This can be seen in al-Muqammiẓ's discussion of attributes cited above. The question was raised as to whether attributes ascribed to God mean the same as when they are ascribed to man. Al-Muqammiẓ answered: "God forbid." God was considered living and knowing, not because He at one time lacked these properties and then acquired them, nor because He had them now and will, at some time, lose them. God had these attributes eternally. A man, on the other hand, lived after not having lived and will eventually die. He had knowledge after having been ignorant and may again be ignorant. God is not like this. He is always living and knowing. Therefore, the attributes life and knowledge, as indeed other terms predicated of God, such as power, hearing, and sight, were used in a totally different manner when referring to God than when referring to man.[88] Saadia seems to be employing this type of semantic distinction in his argument against the ontological status of God's attributes.[89]

Saadia's second argument against the Christians centered on the number of Persons in the Trinity. If the claim were made that the three Persons corresponded to God's essence, life, and knowledge, why were there not more Persons corresponding to God's power, hearing, and seeing? If these latter attributes were held to be implied by God's life (and, thus, unnecessary as separate attributes or Persons), was not God's life implied by His knowledge? Only a living being could have knowledge. The Christians, then, should follow this argument to its logical conclusion and adopt any number of Persons, not just three. That they were not consistent proved that "they merely make up this artificial thesis in order to uphold what they have been told [by their teachers]."[90]

Saadia concluded this section dealing with the Trinity by refuting some standard Christian proof-texts from the Hebrew Bible. He stated that a correct understanding of each verse would not undermine a belief in God's absolute unity.[91]

Abū Yūsuf Ya'qūb al-Qirqisānī. Ya'qūb Qirqisānī, who was a Karaite, was quite familiar with Christianity, and he made numerous references to its history and doctrines in his major work, *Kitāb al-Anwār wal-Marāqib (Book of Lights and Watchtowers).*[92] Unlike al-Muqammiẓ and Saadia, Qirqisānī did not make his refutation of the Trinity part of a larger discourse on God's unity.[93] The apparent reason for this divergence is that *al-Anwār* is a compendium of Karaite law, and not a systematic philosophical work. Qirqisānī's concern was to present the truth of his opinions and the falseness of other, non-Karaite doctrines. His critique of Christianity, then, came in the treatise devoted to the refutation of many divergent views.[94] Qirqisānī's arguments against the Trinity were the most numerous and comprehensive ones among Jewish Mutakallimun.

Qirqisānī commenced his work with an enumeration of the doctrines and practices of various sects. As one part of this exposition, he presented the view of the Christians, distinguishing between Jesus himself and Christians contemporary to Qirqisānī, who followed the teachings of Paul.[95] Qirqisānī branded the religion of the latter as "outright heresy" and described their belief in God as follows:

> The Creator is one substance in three hypostases; that He is one in three and three in one, for, according to them, He is living and knowing; but life and knowledge are two qualities of the substance, therefore the substance is one hypostasis and the two qualities are two hypostases, together three hypostases. They assert that Jesus is the Messiah who was predicted by the prophets and whose advent was promised by them; that he is one of the three hypostases, and that the three hypostases are Son, Father, and (Holy) Spirit; the Son is Jesus who is divine and human, for the Creator who is the substance personified Himself in him. This is all that they say, though they differ among themselves in particulars.[96]

In his refutation of this Christian doctrine, Qirqisānī attacked not only the idea of three Persons, but also the statement that God is a substance.[97]

Qirqisānī presented the Christians as arguing in the following manner: God is self-existent, and everything which is self-existent is a substance. This is a principle of the logicians, who declare that the definition of substance is that which is self-existent and does not require for its existence anything else.[98] Since the definition and the object defined are co-exclusive,[99] in the sense that every substance is self-existent and everything that is self-existent is a substance, it follows that God as self-existent is a substance.[100]

On the other hand, answered Qirqisānī, if we were to follow the logicians, why not also employ another of their definitions of substance, namely, that which is subject to contrary qualities in its essence?[101] Similarly, every subject of accidents (the nine categories excluding substance) is a substance.[102] Since the Christians said that God was a substance, because He was self-existent, they should also have said that He was subject to accidents.[103] It would be better, argued Qirqisānī, to say that God was self-existent but not a substance. In this way, one was not caught in contradictions.[104]

Actually, added Qirqisānī, though the Christians ostensibly denied that God was subject to accidents, they nevertheless, by holding the trinitarian doctrine, attributed the nine categories (other than substance) to Him. Thus, when they said that He was three Persons, they attributed to Him number and, thus, the category of quantity. By believing that God lived with life and knew with knowledge, the Christians attributed quality to Him; by saying that He was Father and Son, they entered Him into the category of relation. These were the three basic categories of accidents that Christians attributed to God.[105] As for the other six categories, these were attached to the Son, who was one of the Persons. They thought Jesus was the Son who was born in time (category of time). They said he existed in a particular place (place). They said he dressed and rode (state/position), and sat, rose, and worked (position), and ate, drank, fought, received, and gave (action). Eventually, he was killed and crucified (affection).[106] It was obvious, then, that the Christians attributed to God all the categories of accidents.[107] To avoid this consequence, it was better to deny both that God was a substance and that there were three Persons.

Qirqisānī now turned to a further demonstration that the concept of three Persons in God was impossible. He asked what proof the Christians had that God's knowledge was the Son and His life was the Spirit. Their answer was that every agent must live with a life other than himself and know with a knowledge which was other than himself. Since God was an agent, He must live with a life and know with knowledge. If this were so, then His knowledge and His life were two hypostases (Persons), and the essence was the third hypostasis. Since knowledge is generated from the knower, as a son is generated from his father, God's knowledge was the Person of the Son. Likewise, since life is only through the spirit, God's life was his (Holy) Spirit. There were, then, of necessity, three Persons. The Father was the substance, the Son was knowledge, and the Holy Spirit was life.[108]

Using the same methodology employed to refute God's being a substance, namely, extending the analogy to its logical conclusion, Qirqisānī questioned the validity of the Christian proof for the three Persons. If one attributed life and knowledge to God because every observed agent had life and knowledge, why did the Christians deny that God had limbs and organs just as every observed agent had? Since the Christians said that God did not have limbs and organs, why did they not just say that God was an agent who lived and knew by virtue of His essence, and not by virtue of life and knowledge? Qirqisānī pointed out that the Christian analogies did not work; one could just as easily insist that a dimensionless body exists, contrary to what we perceive concerning bodies. In addition, they should have said that God was sensate and movable, because all observed agents are sensate and movable.[109]

The next argument against the Trinity came from the impossibility that the Persons could be both distinct in number and identical in essence *(fī-l-maʿnā).* If the Christians said that the Father was not the Son and not the Spirit, how could they reject the thesis that the Trinity was not one in essence? If they said that the three could be one in essence, would they agree that two things, one eternal, one created, could be actually one in essence.[110] If they said yes, then the eternal thing would be created, the created thing would be eternal, and the eternal thing would have to have created itself. If they said no, these two things could not be two in number, one in essence; then, similarly, the Father, Son, and Spirit could not be one in essence and three in number.[111]

Qirqisānī added yet another argument against the Trinity. One asked the Christians, was God's life eternal? If they said yes, then it could be asked further whether God's life was living and reasoning, and his reason, living and reasoning.[112] If they again said yes, then one asked whether each member of the Trinity was itself a Trinity (since the Father had a Son and Spirit for his wisdom and life). Should they deny that the Spirit had life and reason, and the Reason had life and reason, then one asked whether the Reason was an agent or creator (as was the Father, thus necessitating its having life and reason). How one should complete this line of questioning has not been preserved because of a lacuna in the text.[113] Presumably, Qirqisānī established that either each Person must be a Trinity (which the Christians denied) or God Himself could not be a Trinity.[114]

After a digression intended to prove that God's word *(logos)* was created and not eternal,[115] Qirqisānī proceeded with two more anti-trinitarian arguments. Again, he asked whether the Christians had a proof for the Trinity, since any doctrine which cannot be proved should not be believed. Their proof was from both reason and Scriptures. This, Qirqisānī maintained, was contrary to what the Christians claimed concerning the previous generations which did not believe in the Trinity.[116] Even though these latter could demonstrate creation and God's existence and unity with intellectual proofs, they did not believe in a Trinity. Surely, they realized that God knew and lived, just as they knew that bodies with composition and accidents must have had a creator. Nevertheless, their intellects did not come to the same conclusions as the Christians claimed. Similarly, if one asserted that Scriptures proved the Trinity, how could the prophets have said things about a triune God when they themselves were ignorant of this doctrine? Qirqisānī maintained, then, that there were no proofs, either rational or scriptural, for the Trinity.[117]

The last of Qirqisānī's arguments ran as follows. If the Christians admitted that, before the life of Jesus, people were ignorant of the three Persons because of the weakness of their intellectual abilities, then was it not possible that there may really be more attributes, say five or ten, which will at some future time be revealed to a generation with greater intellectual ability?[118] God could create a new people with such a greater capacity which could understand more Persons. Moreover, if God created humanity, from Adam through Moses, including many prophets, why could He not have created in them sufficient ability to understand the nature of God, i.e., according to the Christians, the Trinity? That God did not do so was evidence that the Trinity did not exist.[119]

Qirqisānī's philosophical critique of the Trinity was comprehensive and to the point. His major contention was that Christians claimed they used the canons of logic as a basis for their beliefs, yet nonetheless they actually rejected the ultimate conclusions of their own premises. They wished to hold that God was a substance, who, as an agent, lived through life and knew through knowledge. But, argued Qirqisānī, a substance bears accidents, and all agents are sensate and have bodily limbs. God could not bear accidents or have bodily limbs. The Christians, inasmuch as they refused to accept the consequences of their own teachings, contradicted themselves.

Other Jewish Mutakallimun. Yūsuf al-Başīr (eleventh century, Karaite) continued in the Kalamic pattern.[120] He established God's existence and oneness, accepting the three attributes of power, knowledge, and life as being essential to God, not as distinct, separate entities. Once this was demonstrated, al-Baṣīr proceeded to offer an abbreviated refutation of a number of sects whose views would deprive God of absolute unity. These groups included Dualists (Manichaeans, Dayṣanites, and Zoroastrians), Christians, Attributists (Ṣifātiyya), and believers that God's attributes were neither identical with nor different from Him (Kullābiyya). He stated that a detailed refutation was superfluous, since the truth of his already stated position implied the falseness of any other doctrine.[121]

The definition of the Trinity proffered by al-Baṣīr is similar to the ones we have already seen—God's Word was the Person of the Son, His life was the Person of the Holy Spirit.[122] There was one sole substance, one sole God, three Persons *(aqānīm).*[123] Al-Baṣīr added one more element to this doctrinal formulation. Though each Person was distinct and nonidentical with the other two, still each one was not different from the others.[124] This formulation may have one of two meanings. First, it may simply be a restatement of Gregory of Nazianzus' doctrine that though each Person was not the others, they were not to be considered different (in essence).[125] On the other hand, al-Baṣīr's statement may reflect a belief in modes *(aḥwāl),* interpreting the attributes as neither identical with God nor other than God.[126] This theory, devised by Abū al-Hudhayl (d. 841 or 850) and Abū Hāshim (d. 933), was intended to mediate between the varying current theories of attributes. The modalists taught that the divine attributes were neither existent nor nonexistent, neither identical with God nor other than God.[127] That such a view concerning the Persons was held by some Christians was attested by Shahrastānī, who reported it as a Nestorian belief. True Nestorians, however, did not hold such a doctrine.[128]

Al-Baṣīr did not use the arguments against the Trinity which al-Muqammiẓ, Saadia, and Qirqisānī employed. Rather, he attacked the trinitarian doctrine on the basis of arithmetic logic. The number three (as in three Persons) meant a composition of three distinct entities; furthermore, it was impossible for God to be composed of parts.[129] It followed, then, that God could not possess attributes which were distinct, nor could He exhibit any alternation. Hence, the Christian doctrine of the Trinity, which stated that God was one substance with three attributes, involved a logical contradiction.[130]

Judah Hadassi (twelfth century, Karaite) did not present an orderly account and refutation of Christian doctrines. Instead, he offered an abbreviated description of certain Christian beliefs accompanied by short refutations of them. For instance, he stated that the Christians conceived of

God as "Father, Son, and Holy Spirit"; that "the Father contains the principle of Godhood, the Son is God's Word which became incarnate after the manner of men, and the Holy Spirit is His wisdom and the prophecy of His prophets; these three are considered equal and they are one."[131] Hadassi did not contest this formulation, being content solely to ridicule the idea of incarnation.[132]

In another passage, Hadassi equated Christian doctrine with the tenets of the Ṣifātiyya, the Attributists.[133] He rejected the latter's belief that God had real, distinct attributes by stating that a multiplicity of real attributes implied that God was created, was not homogenous (i.e., not perfectly simple), and was, thus, changeable. Obviously, Hadassi held that God was none of these, since He was uncreated, totally simple, and nonchanging.[134] Since this was Hadassi's argument against Attributists, whom he equated with Christians, we may conclude that the same refutation would apply to the latter's trinitarian doctrine.

Hadassi recorded in another passage that the Christians believed Jesus to be God, thereby making a Trinity of three Persons, the Father, the Son, and the "Spirit of Impurity," while they still maintained that God was one. Hadassi did not offer another refutation.[135]

Not every Jewish Mutakallim who referred to the Trinity mentioned the problem of attributes, nor did everyone who discussed attributes put them in an anti-Christian polemical framework. Baḥya ibn Pakuda, for instance, listed a number of arguments for God's numerical unity, concluding that he thereby refuted the doctrine of the Christians concerning the Trinity.[136] In his refutation of the same doctrine, Joseph Kimḥi repeated part of Baḥya's argumentation against more than one God.[137] Since, however, these arguments were actually directed against a plurality of Gods, not a Trinity in one God, they were not really to the point. On the other hand, Aaron ben Elijah used the standard Kalamic proofs for essential divine attributes, claiming that they implied no multiplicity in God, without referring, however, to the Christians in this context.[138]

The importance of the Jewish Kalamic arguments against the Trinity lay in the fact that they pointed out clearly the difference between the varying concepts of God's unity. Christian theologians, as well as Muslim Attributists, taught that God was numerically one, yet that real, distinct, existent attributes could be predicated of Him. One of these attributes, according to the Christians, but not according to the Attributists, became incarnate as the messiah. Jewish Mutakallimun and anti-Attributist Muslim thinkers denied the separate existence of such attributes, believing that they would compromise God's absolute unity. As Jewish philosophers turned to

Aristotelianism, Kalamic refutations of the Trinity continued to be employed.

Aristotelian Refutations

THE PERSONS AS ATTRIBUTES.

We have seen that the Jewish Mutakallimun had attempted to refute the doctrine of the Trinity by rejecting any resemblance between God's essential attributes and the Persons of the Trinity. They claimed that the essential attributes had no real, distinct individual existence, whereas, according to the Christians, the Persons did have such existence. If, indeed, the divine attributes were to be distinct, argued the Jewish Mutakallimun, God's absolute unity, simplicity, and incorporeality would be compromised.

The identification of God's attributes and the Persons was not confined to the East, nor were Kalamic-type refutations restricted to Mutakallimun. As stated, the Eastern Christians held that God had three essential attributes corresponding to the Father, the Son, and the Holy Spirit. These three attributes were usually considered to be self-existence (essence), life, and wisdom.[139] In the West, the first to introduce such a teaching was John Scotus Erigena (ca. 810–ca. 877), who said the Father was *essentia,* the Son, *sapientia,* and the Holy Spirit, *vita.*[140] Erigena's teachings, though, were condemned,[141] as were those of Peter Abelard (1079–1142), the next Christian of note to suggest such a trinitarian interpretation. Abelard identified the Father with power *(potentia),* the Son with wisdom *(sapientia),* and the Holy Spirit with goodness *(benignitas).*[142] Abelard's opponents interpreted this to mean that "the Father is complete power, the Son a certain power, the Holy Spirit no power." The Council of Sens (1140) condemned Abelard's teaching thus understood.[143]

One would assume that after the condemnation of Erigena and the specific disavowal of Abelard's trinitarian doctrine, the identification of each Person with a divine attribute would not continue to be taught. This, however, was not the case. Abelard's students kept his interpretation of the Trinity alive until it became an acceptable, if not very common, explanation of the Christian doctrine.[144] William of Conches (d. 1145), who was also condemned, held the Persons to be *potentia, sapientia,* and *voluntas.*[145] Hermann taught the same thing.[146] Hugh of Saint Victor (1096–1141) combined a number of interpretations to conclude that the Father was power, the Son wisdom, and the Spirit goodness *(bonitas sive benignitas),* or love *(amor),* or will *(voluntas).*[147] Peter Lombard (ca. 1100–1160) taught the three attributes as power, wisdom, and goodness, [148] as did Thomas Aquinas, who ascribed the source of this doctrine to Augustine.[149] In all of these latter cases, care was taken to emphasize that though each attribute was identified with one Person, one should not believe that only one Person had that attribute. Thus, all the Persons had wisdom, since God had wisdom. The Son alone, however, was appropriately designated by the name wisdom.[150] The Eastern formula: "God lives with life, knows with knowledge," was rejected by the Western Church.[151] In general, the Eastern emphasis on the Persons as divine attributes was lacking in Western Christianity.

Western Jewish polemicists, however, often made reference to the Christian notion of Persons as attributes. This may be the case because this doctrine, or one very similar, was propagated among the Jews. Peter Alfonsi (1062–ca. 1140), a Jewish convert to Christianity, wrote in his anti-Jewish *Dialogus* that the Father was *substantia,* the Son, *sapientia,* and the Spirit, *voluntas.*[152] In an anonymous thirteenth-century anti-Jewish polemical poem written in French in the form of a dialogue between a Christian and a Jew, the author had the Jewish debater admit that God had power *(poissance),* wisdom *(sapience),* and goodness *(bontez).* The Christian then identified these three attributes with the Father, the Son, and the Holy Spirit.[153] A similar doctrine was taught by the Christian polemicists Peter of Blois (ca. 1135–1212)[154] and Nicholas De Lyra (ca. 1270–1349).[155] Borrowing from kabbalistic doctrine, Abner of Burgos ((1270–1348) referred to the Trinity as wisdom *(ḥokhmah),* understanding *(tevunah),* and knowledge *(da'at).*[156] Apparently, Christian polemicists attempted to convince Jews of the possibility of a divine Trinity by reference to a theory of attributes which was acceptable to Jewish thinkers. It is clear from Jewish polemical literature that the Jews were aware of this. Even those polemicists who did not mention three specific attributes showed familiarity with the Christian teaching when they compared their own theory of attributes with the trinitarian belief.

There were two basic schools of thought concerning attributes among Jewish Aristotelians. Maimonides and his students held that there were no positive attributes which could be predicated upon God. The most that could be ascribed to Him were negative attributes and attributes of action.[157] The Jewish followers of Averroes (1126–98), however, believed that God might be described by positive essential attributes, as long as they were understood ambiguously, *secundum prius et posterius.*[158] Now, for a Maimonidean, there was not even an apparent problem in reconciling his theory of attributes with a denial of the Trinity. If one held that there were absolutely no positive attributes, and the Christians interpreted the three Persons as positive, distinct attributes, then the refutation of attributes was sufficient to rebut the Christian doctrine.[159] An Averroist, on the other hand, who accepted some positive attributes, found himself in the same situation as the Jewish Mutakallim who believed in essential attributes. The question was raised as to why Jews would allow positive attributes, which they claimed did not compromise God's simplicity and unity, though at the same time they rejected the Christian interpretation of attributes as Persons.[160]

Averroes himself dealt with this same question, though it appears that he was only slightly conversant with Christian doctrine. In his *Tahāfut at-Tahāfut (The Incoherence of the Incoherence),* he stated that plurality in an incorporeal being could exist only in definition.

> This is the doctrine of the Christians concerning the three hypostases in the divine Nature. They do not believe that they are attributes additional to the essence, but according to them they are only a plurality in the definition—they are a potential, not an actual, plurality. Therefore they say that the three are one, i.e. one in act and three in potency.[161]

Averroes also distinguished between Ash'arites, who believed in attributes additional to the essence, and Christians, who held God's attributes to be essential.[162]

Averroes' explanation of the Trinity was not the usual interpretation of the Persons, and this was noted by Moses Narboni (d. 1362). After quoting the above two references to Christianity in *Tahāfut at-Tahāfut,* Narboni said: "It appears to me that for the Christians these three attributes are *in actu,* while the substance remains one, not *in potentia* as Averroes says."[163] Narboni's own refutation of the Trinity will be discussed below.[164]

In another work, Averroes was closer to the recognized Christian doctrine. He referred to those who believed in divine attributes, stating that they must either hold that God was self-existent and the attributes existed through Him, or that the attributes were self-existent and there were many Gods.

> This [latter doctrine] is the doctrine of the Christians, who thought that there were three Persons, namely, existence, life, and knowledge. God has already referred to this saying: "Certainly they disbelieve who say: God is the third of three" (Quran, Sura 5:77).[165]

This second reference of Averroes to the Christian Trinity was also quoted in Jewish literature. Simon Duran said approvingly: "Averroes, in his discussion of attributes, said that if one should say that every attribute is self-existent, then there are many Gods. This is the doctrine of the Christians, who posit the three Persons as existence, life, and knowledge."[166] Duran proceeded to state that contemporary Christians considered the Persons to be power, wisdom, and will. We see here very clearly that a Western Jew equated the Western Christian doctrine of attributes with the traditional Eastern Christian trinitarian theory. What Duran did not realize was that the difference between the doctrine reported by Averroes and the one with which he was familiar was more geographical than temporal.

The Western philosophical critique of the Trinity as divine attributes was quite extensive and continued through many centuries. Most polemicists distinguished between their own acceptable theory of attributes and the Christian Trinity. Others were content to show inconsistencies between a belief in divine unity and the identification of attributes as Persons. In our discussion of the Jewish arguments, we will deal chronologically by centuries.

Twelfth century. The first European Jewish polemicist to refer to the problem of God's attributes was Jacob ben Reuben in his *Milḥamot Ha-Shem.* He made mention of no specific trinitarian theory but only to a Christian claim that the Jewish belief in attributes implied multiplicity in God. Jacob ben Reuben used in his answer Saadia's arguments for the unity of essential attributes. He quoted Saadia explicitly but added nothing new of consequence.[167]

Thirteenth century. It is only in the thirteenth century that the designation of God as *potentia, sapientia, voluntas* first appeared in Jewish polemical works. Such a doctrine was cited by Meir ben Simeon of Narbonne, Moses ben Solomon of Salerno, and Naḥmanides.

Meir ben Simeon referred on a number of occasions to the Christian identification of the Father as power, the Son as wisdom, and the Spirit as will. He argued against this doctrine as follows: Does the Son, he asked, have the power which is called the Father? If the Christians answer in the negative, then the Son is deficient of power. If they say that he has the power called Father, then the Father was born as was the Son, and they both must have been born.[168] Further, Meir ben Simeon stated:

> Every Jew and every true intelligent person in the world admits that the Creator is wise, powerful, and willing without doubt. Still, we do not go so far as to say that He has three bodies. He is the true one, and there is nothing like His unity, which is without body. His power, wisdom, and will are all one in true unity with neither beginning nor end.[169]

Before referring to the specific attributes power, wisdom, will, Moses ben Solomon discussed in general terms the relation between divine attributes and Persons. He argued that if there were three Persons and they were one, then there must be something which united them and something else which distinguished them into three. If the substance were the unifying factor, there would be four things—three attributes and one substance. It was not a Trinity but a Quaternity. A Christian responded to this line of reasoning by averring that the Person was one part of the essence and there were three Persons. Moses ben Solomon retorted that if the Person were solely part of the substance, then one Person would be no different from any other, since there was only one substance.[170]

In addition, he argued, if God were one substance and three attributes, it would follow that the First Cause was not truly one but composed of many things, namely, substance and attributes. Further, if the attributes were part of the essence, God would be divisible. If, on the other hand, the substance and attributes were not one thing, one attribute would be totally different from the other attributes and there would be no Trinity.[171] If God were three Persons, He would be composed and not the necessary of existence.[172]

Turning to the specific attributes, Moses ben Solomon recorded the following discussion with the Christians: He asked them whether God's power was different from His wisdom and His wisdom different from His will, since it was known that human wisdom and will were different. "But how are they in the case of God?'[173]

When some Christians answered that they were one, the Jewish polemicist argued that the Trinity was thus negated. Others responded that the attributes were distinguishable one from another. If that were the case, Moses ben Solomon continued, the attributes would be separate, and God, as it were, would be subject to diversity in His essence. This was impossible. Since even the Christian bishop *(hegmon)* agreed that it was a positive commandment to believe in God's absolute, uncomposed unity, His power, wisdom, and will must be identical with the essence.[174]

In his account of the Disputation of Barcelona, 1263, Naḥmanides recorded that the Christian disputants gathered in the Barcelona Synagogue on the Sabbath following the conclusion of the disputation. At this time, Raimund de Penaforte announced that the Trinity was wisdom, will, and power. In addition, he claimed that Naḥmanides had previously admitted this in Gerona (Naḥmanides' home city) to Fra Paul Christiani (the convert who was the instigator of the disputation).[175]

Naḥmanidies answered:

> At this I got to my feet and spoke as follows: I ask both Jews and Gentiles to give me their attention on this matter. When Fra Paul asked me in Gerona if I believed in the Trinity, I replied: "What is the Trinity? Do you mean three material bodies, of the sort that men have, constitute the Godhead?" He said: "No." Then I asked: "Do you mean that the Trinity consists of three subtle substances, such as souls, or that it is three angels?" He said: "No." "Or do you mean," I inquired, "that the Trinity is one substance which is a compound of three substances, such as are those bodies which are compounded of the four elements?" He said: "No." "If that is the case" said I "then what is the Trinity?" He answered: "Wisdom, and will and power." To which I replied that I acknowledge the Deity to be wise and not foolish, to will without sense perception, and to be powerful and not weak, but that the expression Trinity was a complete mistake. For wisdom in the Creator was not an accident, but He and His wisdom were one and He and His will were one and He and His power were one—and, if this was so, the wisdom and the will and the power were one whole. And even if these were accidents in God, the thing which is the Godhead was not three but one, bearing three accidents.[176]

Naḥmanides proceeded to say that the Christians actually taught a fivefold Deity, since, first, there must be a subject of these three attributes, and second, one should enumerate life along with wisdom, power, and will.[177]

The Christians were aware of the argument as to why there were not more than three Persons. Abelard himself questioned why, if the Persons were really attributes, there were not more Persons corresponding to God's other attributes. He answered that despite God's innumerable qualities, only the three Persons, Father, Son, and Holy Spirit, could be determined.[178] Thomas Aquinas cited a similar problem. He stated that one might object that there could be no other procession in God in addition to the one which resulted in the generation of the Son. If there were another procession, i.e., of the Spirit, one might be led to admit that further processions could exist to infinitude. Thomas concluded that the procession of the Spirit was not only possible, but also necessary.[179] No other procession, however, was possible. Thomas argued further that if, it seemed, both knowledge and will each corresponded to separate processions of the Son and Spirit, then there should be another procession corresponding to power. Similarly, God had other attributes which seemed to require further processions. Nevertheless, Thomas claimed that this was not the case.[180] On the other hand, in the argument advanced by the Jewish polemicists, the assumption of one procession already led to the possibility of an unlimited number of Persons.[181]

Reference may be made here to one more thirteenth-century Jewish thinker, Moses ben Joseph Ha-Levi (Ha-Lavi), who followed Averroes closely in his treatment of divine attributes. He accepted the three essential attributes of wisdom, will, and power. At the same time he realized the problems raised by such a position. "Since some men thought that these attributes are numerically distinct they said that there is a Trinity with essential unity."[182] Ha-Levi evidently rejected such a consequence of his theory.

As we have seen, the thirteenth-century Jewish polemicists were aware of the Christian identification of the Persons as divine attributes, and they offered arguments against this doctrine. Generally, their contentions derived from neither a Maimonidean nor an Averroistic interpretation of attributes. It is only in the fourteenth century that Jewish philosophical polemicists became acutely aware of the possible contradiction between their theories of attributes and their denials of the Trinity. These polemicists' arguments were, however, very similar to those of their earlier predecessors.

Fourteenth century. In his refutation of an identification of the Persons with divine attributes, Moses Ha-Kohen of Tordesillas combined a philosophical with an exegetical argument. Noting that some Christians said that God was will, power, and wisdom, and that these were in the Creator in a manner unlike what they were in the creatures, Moses Ha-Kohen argued that the Christians were short-changing God. Quoting I Chronicles 29:11–12, "Thine, O Lord, is the greatness, and the power, and the glory, and the victory and the majesty . . . both riches and power come from thee," he said that one should give God many more than three Persons.[183]

The most comprehensive Western philosophical critique of the theory of the Trinity as divine attributes was presented by Ḥasdai Crescas in his *Tratado (Biṭṭul 'Iqqare Ha-Noẓrim).* Before turning to Crescas' refutation, it is instructive to review his own theory of attributes as presented in *Or Ha-Shem,* his major philosophical work. While there is no general agreement as to the meaning of all the details of this doctrine, we can see, at the very least, Crescas approved of positive essential attributes which were neither the essence itself nor something additional to the essence. Quoting the image of *Sefer Yeẓirah* of a flame united with a burning coal *(shalhevet ha-qeshurah be-gaḥelet)* as an illustration of God's irruptible unity, Crescas went on to say:

> Just as essence cannot be conceived without existence nor existence without essence, so the attribute cannot be conceived without its subject nor the subject without its attributes; and all the attributes are comprehended in absolute goodness, which is the sum total of all perfections.[184]

As part of his proof that God's attributes were essential, though not the essence itself or part of the essence, Crescas said:

> Since we comprehend the meaning [of the attributes] it follows that knowledge is neither power nor will, and, therefore, they are three separate things. But since God's essence is one in all aspects, if the attributes were His essence or part of His essence, it would be like the doctrine of those who say that He is one but He is three and the three are one.[185]

How was Crescas' theory different from that of the Christians? The latter believed that the three Persons were each the essence or part of the essence, while Crescas maintained that the attributes were essential, but were not the essence itself. Nevertheless, according to him, the attributes were conceptually distinct.[186]

The thin line between conceptually distinct essential attributes and the Christian Persons became a source of misunderstanding for Crescas' readers. Joseph ben Shem Tov, the translator and commentator of Crescas' *Tratado,* made the following comment after the chapter dealing with the Trinity.

> It was necessary for me to point out [the difference between Crescas and the Christians] because I have noticed that some scholars had raised the same difficulties with respect to our author's theory of divine attributes. This is the reason why they did not understand the truth of his opinion nor the difference between the theories [Crescas' and the Christians']. Now, what misled them is the word attribute *[to'ar],* which is not a correct translation of *persona.* Others have translated it by *parẓof*[187] meaning that the Father appears in His essence, and also the Son and Spirit. In truth, they *[to'ar* and *persona]* do not mean the same thing, and this misled those who accuse the holders of the attribute theory. Further, since they [the Christians] claim that the *personas* are power, wisdom, will, and the attributists say that God has power, wisdom, will, it was thought that both [theories] mean the same thing. This is not so.[188]

What were the difficulties which Crescas raised against the Christians, and which his critics raised, in turn, against him? First, let us see how he understood the Trinity. According to Crescas, there were three principal propositions underlying the Christian doctrine. (1) "The Christian says that there exist in God, may He be blessed, three distinct attributes, in their language, *persona.*" (2) "The Christian says that God, may He be blessed, has an attribute called Son, born of the Father." (3) "The Christian believes that God, may He be blessed, has an attribute proceeding from the Father and Son called Spirit."[189] He stated further:

> The Christian belief posits that the divine essence includes three attributes, *personas* in their language, but one essence. [The Persons are] Father, Son, and

> Holy Spirit, or power, wisdom, will. The Father generates the Son and from the love of both the Holy Spirit is emanated. The Father is the power, the Son is the wisdom, and the Spirit is the will, and the essence of all three is one God. They are distinct as attributes, but each one of them is God.[190]

Crescas offered first two refutations not based on a theory of attributes,[191] then proceeded to enumerate five arguments which were so constructed. Each refutation started with a proposition common to Judaism and Christianity and proceeded to show how the Trinity contradicted this mutually agreeable proposition.

1. The first argument was based on the belief that God's essence had eternal life, power, wisdom, will, and many other perfections. This was clearly believed by members of both religions.[192] Crescas then argued that if power, wisdom, and will were hypostasized as Persons, God's life and other perfections should also be so considered. There should be more than three attributes. Otherwise, God would not be alive, contrary to the previously stated proposition.[193] This, we have seen, was a common argument.

2. Crescas' second argument was based on the common assumption that God's simplicity was infinite, and that one infinite was not larger than another one.[194] This was also in accord with standard Christian doctrine.[195] But, argued Crescas, one can imagine an infinite simplicity greater than that taught by the Christian doctrine of Trinity, namely, a simplicity without attributes. Now, since the essence was other than the attributes, which was determined by the fact that the essence was one and the attributes were many, it followed that God had in Him actually four things, namely, an essence and three attributes, not even just three things (as the Christians thought they claimed). This, of course, contradicted the proposition that God was infinitely simple.[196]

3. The next common proposition was that God was not composed of parts. This was obvious to both Jews and Christians, because if God were composed of parts, there would have to be a cause of the composition. God was causeless, and therefore not composed of parts.[197] Yet, argued Crescas, according to the Christians the essence and the attributes were different, as was already stated. It was further clear that an attribute generated or emanated but that the essence did not generate or emanate.[198] Hence, essence and attributes were different. Therefore, according to the Christians, God was composed of different things, essence and attributes, subject and object. This contradicted the assumption that God was not composed.[199]

As we have seen, Crescas was not the only Jewish polemicist to argue that God's simplicity and lack of composition precluded the possibility of a

Trinity. Moses ben Solomon of Salerno,[200] Moses Ha-Kohen,[201] Yom-Tov Lipmann Mühlhausen,[202] Joseph ben Shem Tov,[203] Abraham Farissol,[204] Isaac of Troki,[205] and the author of *Kevod Elohim*[206] all offered similar arguments. As Crescas stated, the Christians agreed that God was simple and not composed. The real issue here was whether or not the Trinity impinged on these principles. The Jews saw the Christian doctrine as teaching that God was composed of three separate things; the Christians understood themselves to be saying that God was totally one, but He had in him relations which resulted in there being three Persons. No composition or preclusion of simplicity was implied by such a doctrine.[207] The Jewish polemicists, however, argued that this was a contradictory belief.

4. The Christian concept of the Trinity also contradicted the mutually accepted proposition that there was no alternation *(ḥilluf)* in God.[208] According to Crescas, the Trinity implied such alternation, and, indeed, infinite alternation. Whereas the essence had no multiplicity, the attributes did. Also, the Father generated, but the Son did not. The Father and Son emanated (the Spirit), but neither the Spirit nor any one attribute by itself can emanate; in addition, they cannot emanate infinitely.[209] There is, then, infinite alternation in God.

Thomas mentioned a similar objection.

> Opposed predicates, furthermore, show a plurality in that of which they are predicated. But opposites are predicated of God the Father and of God the Son. The Father is God unbegotten and generating, but the Son is God begotten. Therefore, it does not seem possible that the Father and Son are one God.[210]

The Christian answer was that these distinctions were not in God's essence, but were only distinctions of relation, which did not imply a plurality in God.[211]

5. The last of Crescas' arguments was based on the proposition that there was nothing in God which was not God. This was taught by the Christians in the decree of the Council of Rheims, which stated that only God—the Father, Son, and Spirit—was eternal, and no other things, e.g., relations, properties, singularities, or onenesses, which were not God, were eternally present in God.[212] But, argued Crescas,

> If God is one essence and three attributes, no one [attribute] by itself is God. This can be explained as follows: If [each attribute] were God, each one would have to be one essence and three attributes, each of which must be one essence

and three attributes, and, thus, *ad infinitum*. Therefore, not every [attribute] is God.[213]

Thomas mentioned a similar objection. The Father produced another divine Person because of his infinite goodness. But the Holy Spirit also had infinite goodness. Therefore, Thomas said, one would think that the Holy Spirit should also produce another Person, who would produce another infinitely. The Christian answer to this objection was that the Holy Spirit would produce another Person if his goodness were numerically distinct from the Father's goodness. Since they shared in the same goodness, differing only in relation, other Persons did not proceed.[214]

These, then, are Crescas' arguments against the Trinity, which concentrated on the question of Persons as attributes. They were all predicated on the notion that the Christians claimed real existence for the Persons, and contended that each was different from the others and each had different properties. The positing of such Persons in God, Crescas argued, was irreconcilable with His unity and simplicity. The doctrine of Persons meant alternation and composition in God's essence.

What, then, of Crescas' own theory of attributes? Were his critics correct that the same arguments might be used against his own doctrine? At first sight, it appears that his critics were correct. Was not a God without attributes—even if they were held to be essential—simpler than a God who had them? If God had both essence and essential attributes, was He not a composite being? If God's will and power were distinct, as Crescas claimed, did this not imply alternation? Should we conclude, therefore, that Crescas did contradict himself?

In trying to answer these questions, we should remember that Crescas' *Tratado* was a polemical work. He was more interested in refuting Christian doctrine than propounding his own. The question of attributes was not the only part of the *Tratado* which apparently contradicted his *Or Ha-Shem.*[215] Crescas may simply have wanted to offer arguments against Christianity, regardless of his own theories, assuming that Crescas' true beliefs were outlined in *Or Ha-Shem.*[216]

On the other hand, Crescas explicitly stated in his *Or Ha-Shem* that his doctrine of attributes was dissimilar to that of the Christians. Perhaps the difference is made clear by another comment of Joseph ben Shem Tov.

> You should know that the upholder of essential attributes is not of this kind [i.e., is not a trinitarian]. . . . This is clear, for they say that the Father generates the Son, but he who ascribes to God, may He be blessed, power and

wisdom does not think, God forbid, that power produces wisdom nor that power is God nor that wisdom is God. Likewise, one who ascribes to God existence or other attributes, as does the rabbi [Crescas] of blessed memory, does not posit them as the essence but only as essential. Therefore, this doctrine is not liable to any of the difficulties necessitated by the Christian belief, nor does he believe that they [the attributes] are both three and one.[217]

Joseph ben Shem Tov was undoubtedly correct in saying that Crescas' theory of attributes differed from the Christian doctrine. His critics were also right in pointing out that anti-Christian arguments did not necessarily have to be restricted to Christian beliefs. In the last analysis, however, it is clear that Crescas' rejection of the Trinity and other Christian doctrines was based on more than a disagreement about attributes. The whole tenor of Crescas' *Tratado* shows that he rejected Christian doctrines because of what he perceived as their underlying self-contradiction. The problem of attributes played a significant role in Crescas' general refutation of Christianity. Nevertheless, one would be mistaken to assume that Crescas' own theory of attributes was a major cause of his rejection of Christianity.

While Crescas was distinguishing between his own theory of essential attributes and the Christian Trinity, his contemporary Profiat Duran was arguing from a different point of view. According to Duran, acceptable divine attributes were those of relation, namely, attributes which expressed nothing about God's essence but only about His relation to the world. Though Maimonides had rejected such a theory of attributes,[218] Duran and a number of other thinkers still accepted it.[219]

Duran described the Christian belief as follows in his *Kelimat Ha-Goyim:*

They all agree that their assumption of a Trinity refers only to the attributes, which they call Persons.[220] These attributes are distinct, not just conceptually,[221] but *in actu.* There is one subject, the *suposit,*[222] which is the divine essence and which is one in utmost simplicity. Further, while the whole God became incarnate, only the attribute of the Son became incarnate.[223] Nevertheless, they think that they can combine absolute unity and absolute simplicity.[224]

Duran went on to explain the nature of these attributes or Persons.

They maintain that the Trinity is wisdom, power, and will. Theologians are required to accept these attributes in the Godhead because of their assumption

> that He is the Creator of the world, for it is impossible for there to be creation unless the Creator has these three attributes. (1) Wisdom, which is the intelligible order of action in the soul of the agent, and this they call the Son. (2) Power; this intelligible order in the essence of the Creator is sufficient for the agent because of his perfect intellectual conception; this does not happen with other agents. They call this perfection of conception the Father. (3) Will, which is also necessary for creation, for even if knowledge and power are present, unless they be conjoined to will, there will not be the existence of the work. They call this attribute the Holy Spirit. With these three, then, there is a sufficiency for creation of the world.[225]

Duran agreed that this description of the attributes would constitute "true philosophy" if the Christians had taught that the Persons were attributes of relation. "This, however, is not their intention."[226]

In his discussion of the Trinity, Duran also made an interesting observation, namely, that the Christians derived their doctrine from a misunderstanding of Kabbalah. Duran reported this opinion in the name of a German talmudical teacher, who had, in turn, heard it from certain mystics. These latter said that Jesus and his disciples had been mystics whose Kabbalah was distorted. This teacher added that Jesus' performance of miracles was a result of his theurgic use of the "left side, the side of impurity."[227]

When Duran himself came upon Christian works, he was able to confirm the words of his teacher. Indeed, he stated, the doctrine of the Trinity was very close to, though a corruption of, the kabbalistic theory of Sefirot, which was actually the philosophical theory of attributes.[228] Duran then proceeded with the distinction between attributes and Persons outlined above.[229]

In his rejection of the Christian distinct essential attributes, Duran did not state clearly what differentiated this unacceptable Christian doctrine from the philosophically acceptable divine attributes of relation or their equivalent, the kabbalistic Sefirot. It is likely, though, that he had in mind the fact that one attribute, the Son, was claimed to have become incarnate and was, thus, more than just an inseparable aspect of God as were the attributes of relation. That this was Duran's intention may be confirmed both by his definition of the Trinity cited above and by his almost immediate reference to the incarnation of the second Person.[230]

Fifteenth century. Not much was added to the discussion of attributes and the Trinity in the fifteenth century. Profiat Duran's treatment of this question was followed rather closely by both Shem Tov ibn Shapruṭ and Simon Duran. The former, in a supplement to *Even Boḥan* written in 1405,[231] merely paraphrased Duran's exposition of the attributes as power, wisdom, will, and explicitly quoted Duran's statement that these attributes were to be understood as attributes of relation.[232] Simon Duran, who accepted an Averroistic approach to attributes,[233] gave the incarnation as proof that the Christians held the attributes to be really distinct. He concluded that the Christians "reject the true unity and divert from the truth when they ascribe corporeality to the Son."[234]

Sixteenth century. Abraham Farissol also stressed that the Jewish philosophical doctrine of divine attributes was to be understood in the sense of attributes of relation.

> Their doctrine is not like our multiplicity of attributes, for even if we should believe that He, may He be blessed, has many attributes, still these are only in relation to the recipients of the actions which result from Him. Thus, even if the attributes be many or even contradictory, this does not necessitate any multiplicity in Him, God forbid. On the other hand, their Trinity necessitates a numerical multiplicity in Him.[235]

The author of *Kevod Elohim* offered one of the last polemical treatments of attributes and the Trinity. As was his fashion, he relied heavily on the arguments of earlier authors, in this case Saadia Gaon and Profiat Duran (in the paraphrase of Shem Tov ibn Shapruṭ). Borrowing from his Kalamic source, he said that the Christians "were mistaken and became heretical, while at the same time thinking that their belief in three [Persons] is based on speculation and subtlety of reasoning, and they came upon these three attributes, life, power, wisdom."[236] He then explained why a Creator needed life and wisdom, and answered the Christian arguments in much the same fashion as did Saadia.[237] Quoting Duran explicitly, the author explained the three attributes, power, wisdom, and will, as relational and not essential.[238]

Both the Aristotelian and Kalamic refutations of the Christian interpretation of the three Persons as essential attributes were effective in distinguishing Jewish and Christian doctrine. The Christians hoped to convince the Jews that just as a Trinity of essential attributes was possible, so too a Trinity of Persons in the Godhead was rationally acceptable. The Jewish polemicists, for their part, tried to reinforce the point that essential attributes were not inconsistent with God's absolute unity and simplicity because such attributes were not really distinct, as the Christians held the Persons to be.[239] The leap of faith from attributes to Persons was rejected by the Jewish philosopher.

GOD AS INTELLECT, INTELLECTUALLY COGNIZING SUBJECT, AND INTELLECTUALLY COGNIZED OBJECT (*SEKHEL, MASKIL, MUSKAL*).

As we have seen, the Jewish philosophical polemicists rejected any plurality in the divine essence, even if that plurality was expressed in terms of divine attributes. Their conception of God's unity implied that God was totally simple. At the same time, however, Jewish Aristotelians adopted a doctrine which appeared to be somewhat similar to the Christian trinitarian teaching. We refer to the doctrine that God is thinker, thinking, thought (*sekhel, maskil, muskal/'aql, 'āqil, ma'qūl/intellectus, intelligens, intelligibile*).[240] Though this formulation looked trinitarian, the Jewish Aristotelians took great pains to show how it differed from the Christian belief.

According to Aristotelian psychology, and as outlined by Maimonides, man is born with a potential intellect (*sekhel bekhoaḥ*). When he intellectually cognizes an object, e.g., when he perceives a tree and abstracts from it the form of the tree, his intellect has become actualized (*sekhel be-fo'al*). Since the Aristotelians taught that intellect *in actu* is nothing but the thing which is intellectually cognized (*muskal*), and the act of intellectual cognition (*maskil*) is the same as the intellect, it follows that in a person whose intellect is actualized, *sekhel, maskil,* and *muskal* are only one thing. Before the act of thought, there were three different things *in potentia*—a potential thinker, a potential act of thinking, and a potential object of thought; during cognition they are all one thing *in actu.* God, though, is an intellect who is eternally cognizing, always *in actu.*[241] Thus, God may appropriately be described as thinker, thinking, and thought without implying any plurality in His essence.[242]

Even if absolutely no diminution in God's unity was implied by such a description of God, still the Aristotelian Jewish polemicists were uneasy with its use. It appeared to be too close to the trinitarian doctrine, and thus was a source of disquiet. Indeed, Eastern Christians employed this Aristotelian doctrine as an analogy to the Trinity when they said that the Father was the intellect, the Son was the intellectually cognizing subject, and the Holy Spirit was the intellectually cognized object. Thinkers holding this doctrine included Yaḥya ben 'Adī (tenth century),[243] Abū 'Ali 'Isa Ibn Zar'aa (d. 1007),[244] Abū-l-Khair Ibn at-Tayyib (eleventh century),[245] Abū Isḥāq Ibn al-'Assāl (thirteenth century),[246] and Abū-l-Barakāt (d. ca.

1320–27).[247] It was also cited by the author of the anti-Christian polemical treatise attributed to Abū Ḥāmid al-Ghazālī.[248]

Western Christian Aristotelians, though they adopted this designation of God, did not generally connect it with the Trinity.[249] Nevertheless, Jewish polemicists repeatedly stressed that no relation existed between the acceptable Aristotelian doctrine and the unacceptable Christian Trinity. If the Christian philosophers were not teaching such an identification, why did the Jewish polemicists constantly deny it? The answer is provided by an examination of Christian polemical literature. A number of Christian polemicists, notably Abner of Burgos[250] and Raymund Lull,[251] explained the Trinity in terms of *sekhel, maskil, muskal.* It is obvious that the Christian debaters wished to convince Jews of the possibility of a Trinity by equating it with a common Jewish philosophical doctrine. The authoritative Christian theologians might not have considered the concept of God as thinker, thinking, thought to be analogous to the Trinity, but the Christian polemicists did. It was for this reason that the Jewish polemicists took care to distinguish between their own philosophically sound tenets and what they claimed was the illogical Christian belief.

In arguing against any identification between the Trinity and the Aristotelian doctrine, the Jewish polemicists made two points: (1) the Christian doctrine was a corruption of the Aristotelian teaching,[252] and (2) one could not accuse the Jews of trinitarianism because they held a doctrine which superficially looked similar to the Christian one.

1. The first point, namely, that the Trinity was a corruption of the doctrine that God is thinker, thinking, and thought, was made by Isaac Albalag (thirteenth century) and Simon Duran. In his commentary to al-Ghazālī's *Intentions of the Philosophers,* Albalag, the most radical of the Jewish Averroistic Aristotelians, said the following of the doctrine in question:

> Perhaps it is from here that there spread the faith in the Trinity held by the majority of the Gentiles. They heard it [sc. the correct doctrine] from their scholars, but understood it only in the way in which the majority is capable of understanding of such things. There is no doubt that this belief is good and true in itself. It is bad only in respect of the majority, who have erred grievously without hope of redress and have arrived at this corrupt belief.[253]

Albalag suggested that the ordinary people not be told this or any other potentially dangerous doctrine. This was why the sages did not reveal the complete truth in all matters.[254]

Simon Duran, after explaining the propriety of saying that God is thinker, thinking, thought, stated in like manner:

> Since the Christians heard the proof of the philosophers, they believed in the well-known Trinity and were further drawn into a belief in incarnation. Though they verbally negate multiplicity in God, they actually do assume it since they believe that He is both one and three.[255]

Albalag offered no refutation of the Trinity, and Duran's arguments against this doctrine were based on considerations other than Aristotelian psychology. Each simply made the comment that the Christians derived the Trinity from a misunderstanding of a correct philosophical doctrine.[256]

2. The denial of any identification between Jewish philosophical doctrine and the Christian belief was stressed by Moses ben Solomon of Salerno, Levi ben Abraham of Villefranche, Moses Narboni, Joseph Albo, Abraham Farissol, Judah Aryeh de Modena, and the author of *Kevod Elohim*.[257]

Moses ben Solomon portrayed "Philip the heretic from Tuscany" as having argued:

> Listen here, Hebrew. You have debated with Christians but have refused to humble yourself before them and have not believed in the Son of God. Now listen and understand that God has a Son. The philosophers have already explained that God is the thinker, the thinking, and the thought, and they are three—thinker, thinking, thought—and this is our Trinity. The thinker is the Father, the thinking is the Son, and the thought is the Spirit, and the three are one. If you do not [believe] in the Son of God, you deny that God cognizes Himself; you cannot, however, doubt this, because even your "Guide," Maimonides, of blessed memory, taught this in a separate chapter. In this chapter he thrice repeated these matters. The Trinity, therefore, is proven. Remember, do not forget![258]

Moses ben Solomon stated that it was necessary for him to discourse on this argument because certain friars, the *Praedicatores* (Dominicans), had sought to prove the Trinity by use of the philosophical doctrine.

> Every intelligent person surely knows that God, may He be blessed, cognizes Himself. Even though He cognizes Himself, it is impossible for Him to comprehend anything other than Himself, but certainly He comprehends. That which He comprehends is one form or one conception. This form which He cognizes is what we call the Son. The cognizing is the Father and the cognized is the Son, i.e., this form. This is the relation between the Father and the Son,

> and this form is called *verbo—principion era verbo*[259]— . . . and this is what took on flesh. It is known that just as a father loves his son and takes pleasure in him, so, too, God loves that which necessarily proceeded from Him. This love is mercy or will. Now you have three things—a cognizing substance, a cognized substance, i.e., the substance of the form that necessarily proceeded from Him, i.e., His cognition which He cognized, and the substance of love.[260]

Moses ben Solomon responded that no multiplicity was implied by the Aristotelian doctrine. If even in man cognizing *in actu* meant no multiplicity, certainly none was present in God. The Christians held that the three Persons were separate; this was not the case of thinker, thinking, and thought. This was known to all philosophers.[261] Furthermore, it was not true that as God cognized, He comprehended a form or conception which was the Son. God cognized only Himself, not anything external to Him. If He cognized another form outside Himself, He would not be thinking thought.[262]

Levi ben Abraham briefly rejected any connection between the Christian and Aristotelian doctrines.

> It is impossible to reconcile Trinity with unity since Trinity implies corporeality and multiplicity. One cannot compare it [the Trinity] with our statement that the Creator, may He be blessed, is thinker, thinking, thought and this is all one, because it [the Trinity] goes beyond unity and simplicity.[263]

In his commentary to Maimonides' *Guide of the Perplexed,* Moses Narboni twice referred to a possible link between the Trinity and the Aristotelian doctrine and rejected any such connection. As was stated above, Maimonides cited the trinitarian belief as an example of a theory which was self-contradictory. In his commentary to this passage in *Guide* I:50, Narboni said:

> This [the Trinity] is impossible unless two contradictories can both be true [at the same time]. As for us, when we say that God, may He be blessed, is the thinker, the thinking, and the thought, and they are all one, we are not saying He has in Him these three things and they are one. Rather, we say that a thing which is essentially one is called by three different names which are all His essence, since His intellectual cognition is by virtue of His intellectual self-cognition.[264] Therefore, since God intellectually cognizes Himself, and His object of intellectual cognition is Himself, and His essence is His intellectual cognition, then He is the simple, first intellect whose abstract essence is known to His pure essence. This is His true unity.[265]

To emphasize this point further, Narboni concluded his commentary to *Guide* I:68, the chapter in which Maimonides expounded the doctrine of God as *sekhel, maskil, muskal,* with the following statement: "The refutation of the trinitarians and the reaffirmation of God's unity has been hereby explained."[266]

Joseph Albo, in rejecting the denigration of the Torah because it did not teach the Trinity, pointed out the difference between the Aristotelian and Christian doctrines. He paraphrased Maimonides' exposition of the first of these theories and then went on to state:

> But that there should be in Him three distinct things, each one existing by itself, *distintos en personas* as they say, and that they should nevertheless be one, this is impossible, unless two contradictories can be true at the same time, which is opposed to the primary axioms and inconceivable by the mind.[267]

Albo thus accepted a threefold designation of God as long as there was no distinction between each term of this designation. The Christian trinitarian doctrine, on the other hand, did teach that the three persons were distinct. This was held to be unacceptable.

This point was made also by Abraham Farissol and Judah Aryeh de Modena. The former offered the following distinction between the Aristotelian and Christian doctrines:

> God knows everything and that which He knows (His intelligibles) is in Him and in His intellect, not external to Him. Therefore, in order to express His unity and simplicity, we call Him the thinker, the thinking, and the thought. These are not distinct in His essence making distinct *personae,* for all is one. This is not so when it comes to their propositions concerning the Trinity, such as the Father necessitating the Son, and from the Son there being necessitated the Holy Spirit; and every one of them having its own nature while still attached to essential unity. Rather, [they attribute] multiplicity to Him. In order to avoid this, the Torah states, "the Lord our God, the Lord is one" [Deut. 6:4].[268]

De Modena made a rather surprising statement, contending that the Trinity was not intrisically an incorrect belief.

> [The Christians] present the doctrine in the following manner. One cannot deny that God knows and intellectually cognizes Himself and generates from this an intellectually cognized object which He loves. Now the knower is the Father, what is generated from His intellectual cognition is the Son, and His

> love for it is the Holy Spirit.[269] None of these three things, His cognition, the result of His cognition, and His love, are accidental to God as they are to man, nor are they external to him. They are essential *[aẓmut]* to the Godhead, and therefore He is one in His substance *[be-aẓmo]* and His three attributes which they call *personae*. This is a wondrous doctrine and not impossible.[270]

Indeed, added de Modena, if the Christians really intended this doctrine to refer only to God's substance—the Persons being considered totally intradeical, not extradeical *(infra velo extra)*—then there would be no disagreement between Jews and Christians.

> We shall not deny that God knows and intellectually cognizes Himself and that which is generated from His intellectual cognition is that which loves Him, and everything is substance and not accident. Likewise the philosophers and the sages call Him thinker, thinking, thought. Their use of the terms Father, Son, and Spirit makes absolutely no difference.[271]

De Modena went so far as to say that the Jews would concede that the verses "Let us make man" (Gen. 1:26) and "In the image of God He created him" (v. 27), two typical "Christological" verses, could be interpreted according to Christian exegesis.[272]

What, then, distinguished the Jewish and Christian doctrines of God?

> When, however, they come and say that these three attributes are distinct, and external to Him, and go so far as to say that one of them can do or become something which the other ones will not do or become, e.g., their statement that the Son became incarnate, but not the Father or the Holy Spirit; then this is the difference which completely divides our opinion from theirs.[273]

For de Modena, verbal multiplicity, since it maintained essential unity, was permissible; real multiplicity was not allowed, for it effectively destroyed God's unity. That the Christians adopted the latter position was evident from their doctrine of incarnation.

Our examination of the above Kalamic and Aristotelian refutations of the Trinity leads us to the following conclusion. The basic disagreement between Jews and Christians was not whether God could be ascribed with attributes or other positive terms, e.g., as thinker, thinking, thought. Philosophers of both religions generally agreed that such attribution, even if it ostensibly implied a lack of absolute simplicity, was allowable. In addition, all concerned who ascribed essential attributes or who held the

Aristotelian doctrine believed that this did not in any way compromise divine unity. Some Jews were even willing to concede that the basic idea of Trinity was not only possible, but even conceivably meritorious. Nevertheless, for the Jewish polemicists, the difference between absolute unity and Trinity was seen in the Christian belief in the interrelations of the Persons. The Christian thinkers claimed that even though each Person was equal, and each was God, still, there was a seemingly causative relationship between the Father and the Son, and likewise, for Western Christians at least, between the Father and the Son, and the Spirit. Moreover, they contended that one Person, the Son, became incarnate in Jesus of Nazareth. It was obvious, the Jewish debaters stated, that the Christians held the attributes or Persons to be real and absolutely distinct. On the other hand, the positive attributes of Jewish philosophy were only verbally or conceptually distinct. There was no causative relation between them. In addition, no one attribute could possibly become incarnate. Hence, the Jewish polemicists argued, the Christian teaching of the Trinity actually implied multiplicity even though belief in the unity of God was stressed. Nevertheless, "belief is not the notion that is uttered, but the notion that is represented in the soul."[274]

Generation Disproves Unity

A number of Jewish philosophical arguments against the Trinity revolved on the issue of the Son's generation from the Father. According to Christian doctrine, the first Person of the Trinity generated the Son, and the Son became incarnate at a particular time.[275] Arguments directed specifically against incarnation will be treated in the next chapter; arguments against the Trinity stemming from either (1) the specific generation of Jesus, or (2) the belief in eternal generation of the Son, will be discussed here.

The Specific Generation of Jesus

The first type of argument against the Trinity, based on the concept of generation in the person of Jesus, was offered by the author of *Nestor Ha-Komer.* He asked whether Jesus was the son of God before his birth or after his birth. Perhaps he was not born, having been God's son who was called down from the heavens. If the Christians accepted this latter possibility, they must believe in two Gods. If they say that there were not two Gods, then they denied their own Scriptures. Jesus, having been born in time, could not have been God.[276]

Jacob ben Reuben proceeded along the same line of reasoning. After quoting the Christian doctrine of the Trinity, he asked:

> Was he called Son before he was born, or after he was born? If you say before he was born, this is not possible, because nothing in the world is called son before it is born. Only after birth is it called son. Therefore, your words are revealed as false, since you say that unity and Trinity are intrinsically connected. But, during the time before the Son was born from the maiden's womb, His unity was not a trinity but a duality, since the name Son was not yet attributed to Him. But God could not be composed of two, because the books of the philosophers testify[277] that if there were more than one Creator, there would be two possibilities: (1) either they have one essence, in which case the Creator, may He be blessed, is one; or (2) more than one, in which case the essences would be different. If the essences are different, they have some distinction; and every distinct thing is limited; and every limited thing has an end; and everything that has an end is composed; and every composed thing is created; and every created thing needs an external creator, since nothing creates itself, as stated above. All this is impossible to assert of the Creator, may He be blessed.[278]

Jacob ben Reuben's Christian interlocutor responded that one cannot compare God with His creatures. Whereas "son" normally refers to something which is born at a particular time, the Christian Person Son was not only Jesus, who was revealed at a certain time, but was also the eternally generated Son. Thus, the Trinity of Father, Son, and Holy Spirit was eternal.[279] The Jewish reply was that in refuting Christianity one was justified in comparing God with His creations, since the doctrine of incarnation taught that God was created and was subject to time and accident. Just as in the case of all other creations,

> the mouth cannot call something "son" unless the eye has seen it born and entered into the space of the world, so too in the case of this Creator, who, according to your statement was created and became like all the creations, one may not call Him son until He is born. Thus, your statement that God's unity and Trinity are intrinsically related is destroyed, "and the threefold cord is broken and the twofold rope is snapped" [cf. Eccles. 4:12, 12:6].[280]

Jacob ben Reuben's original argument was actually composed of two elements. The first part contended that before Jesus' birth, there was no Son. This reflected the opinion of Arius as quoted by Augustine: "If he is the son, he was born; if he was born, then there was a time when he was not the son."[281] Augustine's answer, which the Christian disputant here echoed, was to the effect that the Son's generation was from eternity, so that he was co-eternal with the Father.[282] Jacob ben Reuben refused to accept the notion that the name Son referred not only to the physical birth of Jesus, but also to the eternal relation of the second Person to the first, the Father. For him, there was no eternal generation of the Son, only a temporal generation of Jesus.

The second part of the argument, namely, the assertion that multiplicity implied creation, was actually an anti-dualist refutation. The Christians agreed that in God there was only one essence; their disagreement lay in their positing three Persons in the one essence.

Similar arguments were offered by Moses Ha-Kohen of Tordesillas[283] and Meshullam ben Uri, who argued that God could not have consulted with the Son before creating the world, for the Son himself was not created until a much later period.[284] The author of *Ḥerev Pifiyot* suggested that God might have spoken to the Holy Spirit.

> Now, if you say that the Holy Spirit was already born and only afterward became incarnate, it follows that the Holy One, blessed be He, is one thing and the Spirit of Jesus which became incarnate, is second to Him. How then can you say that the Trinity is both three and one, something which I do not understand, and you are unable to explain to me.[285]

All of these arguments tended to show that the polemicists did not adequately understand the Christian doctrine of the eternally generated Son. The fact that Jesus, the incarnated God, as it were, was born in time had no effect on the belief that there were three equal Persons of one God.

The Eternal Generation of the Son

Jewish refutations of the Trinity directed at the doctrine of eternal generation were more to the point. The author of *Nestor Ha-Komer,* having made the point that belief in Jesus as born and yet divine implied dualism, went on to criticize the Trinity. He stated that if the Christians believed that the Father, Son, and Holy Spirit were one substance *(qinyan),*[286] then either the Son was born from the Father or he was born with the Father. If he was with the Father, then the Christians denied his birth because in that case he could not have been born. If they agreed that he was not born, then they denied their statement that he was with the Father before he was born.[287]

The Christian doctrine, of course, claimed that the Son was both born and with the Father eternally; this the author ignored.

David Kimḥi, Meir ben Simeon of Narbonne, and Moses ben Solomon of Salerno offered similar arguments. Kimḥi wrote that if the Father generated the Son, he must have preceded him in time, since one cannot be called a father until there is a son, and the father always precedes the son in time. Now, since the Father must have preceded the Son, it followed that one part of God came before another part of Him. If this were not so, argued Kimḥi, then two parts of God should be called twin brothers,[288] not Father and Son, begetter and begotten, for no doubt the begetter preceded the begotten.[289]

Meir ben Simeon contended that there was no justification for ascribing to God a body, let alone three bodies, the Persons. One could further object to the Trinity on the basis of the Christian identification of the Father as power, the Son as wisdom, and the Holy Spirit as will.

> Why is this one called Father and this one Son because you admit that all [of God] is eternal without beginning and there is no power without wisdom and will and no wisdom without power and will. Since this is so, why is this one called Father, and this one Son, for the Son should be called Father. If neither has priority over the other, why is there a difference in names and what is their significance?[290]

Meir ben Simeon argued further that if the Christians said that the Son was not eternal, then the Father would have been at one time without wisdom.[291]

In his version of this argument, Moses ben Solomon made reference to the canons of logic. It is well known that according to logic, when two correlated things exist, both of them must be present at the same time. Thus, there is no master without a slave nor a father without a son. Similarly, one cannot be a master before there is a slave, nor a father before there is a son. Certainly, the father existed before the son, but he was not called father until the son was born. Now, if the "Son" were the Son of God, he could not be eternal because every father precedes his son and is not called father until the son is born. Since God the Father preceded the Son, the Son must have been created after nonexistence. But if he was not eternal, he was not God, for no created thing could be the Creator. Further, every son is an effect because if one calls him son, he must be the effect of his father, and every effect is from a cause. The Son, therefore, could not be God.[292] Even though God was omnipotent, he could not have created a Son who was God, because no created thing can be necessary of existence.[293]

Ḥasdai Crescas presented two arguments based on the Christian belief in generation. He stated first that generation contradicted the mutually agreed upon proposition that God was necessary of existence.[294] Yet if the Christians said that the Son was generated, it follows that God was generated, since the Christians claimed that each Person was God. But if God was generated, He was an effect of the generator, who was the cause of His existence. An effect could not be necessary of existence because it had dependence on something else.[295] Therefore, if God were a Trinity, God would not be the necessary of existence. The same argument applied to the Spirit, which, according to the Christians, proceeded from the other Persons.[296]

This argument reflects an objection to the Trinity mentioned by Thomas. He stated this difficulty as follows:

> Every generated thing accepts its existence from that which generates it. Therefore the existence of anything generated is something received. Yet no such existence subsists of itself. Since divine being subsists of itself . . . it follows that the existence of something generated can never be divine. There is, therefore, no generation within God.[297]

Thomas answered this argument by saying that since the Father and Son shared the same divine existence, one existence could not be distinguished from the other. This was not the case with creatures who received their existence from God and were other than God.[298]

Crescas' second argument was more complex. The Christians and the Jews both agreed that God had all perfections eternally.[299] Now, if the Father generated the Son, this was either in time or instantaneously. But if the Son were generated in time, there was a time when He did not exist, and thus he was not eternal. On the other hand, if one said the Son was generated in an instant, the same impossibility resulted.

> The only solution is that God generated him eternally in consecutive instants, and he is eternally existent from him without there being a first instant from which his existence began. Hence, the Father is always the agent of the eternally existent Son, and just as the Father is eternal, so too is the Son always eternal.[300]

This doctrine, argued Crescas, led to contradictions. First, one would have to assume that time was composed of instants. According to Crescas, the Christians held this belief despite Aristotle's refutations of it in the *Physics*.[301] Holding the doctrine that time was composed of instants was bad enough; it led, however, to an even greater impossibility, namely, that the Son was eternally corrupted. This can be demonstrated as follows. It was not possible that while a fully perfect Son existed another one would be generated. God eternally generated the Son; thus, there must be eternal corruption of the Son.[302]

From the doctrine of an eternally generated and corrupted Son derived an even greater impossibility, i.e., the Son existed and did not exist at the same moment. If the Son were to be corrupted in order for God to generate him anew, then he was corrupted eternally. At the very same instant that he was corrupted, he was generated again; he thus existed and did not exist at the same time.[303]

Further, it followed that the Son existing at this instant was not the same one who existed yesterday or even an instant ago, since that Son already had been corrupted, and another one was in his place.[304]

Finally, it followed that if the Son was caused, he was not perfect. Yet it was agreed that God had all perfections eternally. Thus the Son was not generated.[305] In addition, the Spirit could not have proceeded, since such emanation would cause all the same impossibilities which resulted from the doctrine of generation.[306]

The arguments cited above are not offered in the exact form given them by Crescas. This is because the translator of the *Tratado,* Joseph ben Shem Tov, was forced to "transgress the rules of translation" because of the writer's cryptic language.[307] Joseph ben Shem Tov also felt it necessary to comment on Crescas' refutation, because it appeared to contradict the latter's position in his *Or Ha-Shem.* In his philosophical work, Crescas cited and refuted an argument for creation which he took from Gersonides,[308] and which originally came from al-Ghazālī.[309] Crescas restated the proof as follows. If one said that the world was caused, it necessitated that it was created. Others contended, though, that causation did not mean creation because there might be eternal causation in the manner of rays of light emanating from their source constantly. Gersonides responded that this analogy held only for accidents which had no independent existence, e.g., motion or light. Something which had independent existence could not possibly be emanated eternally, because of the following impossibilities:

1. Something created out of nothing corrupts into nothing.
2. Time would be composed of instants.
3. The heavenly bodies would not always be *in actu* nor would their motion be continuous.

4. The spheres would have to corrupt immediately upon their creation.

5. The spheres would have to come into being and corrupt simultaneously.[310]

Joseph ben Shem Tov was obviously correct when he saw this as the origin of Crescas' argument against the Trinity. Yet he was also right in pointing out that Crescas himself refuted this very reasoning in his *Or Ha-Shem.*[311] Writing against Gersonides' proof, Crescas maintained that the assumption of continuous creations and corruptions would be untenable if one posited that the cause of the existence of the spheres also had a will which would maintain them eternally, and, indeed, did necessitate their continuous existence. If the ever emanating forms were continually impressed upon something ready to receive them, there was no reason for there to be constant creation and generation. The analogy of constantly emanating light was an acceptable one, since there was no real distinction between self-existent and non-self-existent things. Thus, all of the impossibilities which Gersonides claimed would occur if one understood causation of the world as eternal emanation did not really follow from such a claim.[312]

How can one reconcile the fact that Crescas employed against the Christian Trinity the very same argument he refuted when it was used to prove creation? Joseph ben Shem Tov, who believed that Gersonides' argument was so convincing that only "someone who does not know the nature of proof or one possessed of a great desire"[313] could possibly disagree with it, explained the contradiction as the result of evolution in Crescas' thought. He originally wrote *Or Ha-Shem* using a very weak counter-argument against Gersonides. He then realized his mistake when he understood the argument more correctly. At this point, he wrote the *Tratado,* employing this refutation of the Trinity.[314] Isaac Abravanel, following Joseph ben Shem Tov, arrived at the same conclusion.[315]

In truth, it is unnecessary to assume with Joseph ben Shem Tov that Crescas wrote the *Tratado* after a change of mind concerning this argument.[316] Most likely, this is just another example of Crescas' tactics in his polemical work. He used arguments that did not reflect his own opinion if he felt that they were useful. The purpose of this refutation of eternal generation was not to make a definitive statement on the concepts of time and creation. That Crescas did in his philosophical works. In the *Tratado* Crescas was concerned only with refuting the Christian position. He felt he had accomplished this by contending that eternal generation of the Son meant eternal corruption of the Son.

Other Jewish polemicists also argued against the doctrine of eternal generation. Shem Tov ibn Shapruṭ and Abraham Roman stated that if there be a father-son relationship between two Persons of the Trinity, then they had a coordinate relationship and are opposite to each other. Two opposites cannot be predicated on one subject, so the Father and Son must be different.[317] The author of *Makkot Li-Khesil Me'ah* asked how the Father and Son were equal if one caused the other.[318]

Syllogistic Logic Refutes the Trinity

Jewish polemicists stressed again and again the illogical nature of the Christian doctrine of the Trinity. We have noted a great number of proofs to this effect, but none of them referred explicitly to the science of logic. It was Profiat Duran who first introduced proofs based on logic as such.[319]

In his *Epistle* to the apostate David Bonjorn, Duran, adopting his sarcastic tone, urged him not to be like his fathers, who were persuaded by their intellect to accept the truth of philosophy. They had immersed themselves in the mathematical, physical, and metaphysical sciences. In addition, they investigated the various sorts of logical syllogisms in order to determine the best method of true proof. "This is the way of them that are foolish" (Ps. 49:14).[320]

Duran then suggested how the recipient of his letter could avoid the "mistakes" of his fathers.

> As for you, do not act in this manner. God forbid that you should believe that the conclusions of the first mood of the first figure of the figures of the syllogisms,[321] which is the foundation of the whole science of logic, will follow from the conditional predicated on the universal.[322] You will be led into a denial of the faith if you should say (A) The Father is God; (B) God is the Son; this should not "generate" the result that (C) The Father is the Son.[323]

As Joseph ben Shem Tov commented, Duran wrote in jest, since the conclusion would obviously follow from the premises.[324] What, however, did this syllogism prove? As it was presented by Duran, this syllogism was not a convincing argument against the Trinity. The Christians did not deny that both the Father and the Son were God; still, they maintained that the Persons were separate hypostases in God, though each was the essence of God. By demonstrating that the Father and the Son were both God (as was done in the syllogism), one proved only that the Father and Son had the same essence, not that they were actually identical. On its face, then, Duran's syllogistic argument against the Trinity does not appear too strong.

Joseph ben Shem Tov was aware of this possible objection, but he disclaimed it as being the result of paucity of knowledge.[325] The correct form of the syllogism, as understood in Duran's statement that the premises are conditionals predicated on the universal, ran as follows:

(A) All of the Father, and everything predicated on God, is God.

(B) All of God, and everything predicated on God, is the Son.

But (C) The Father is predicated on God (from A).

Therefore (D) The Father is the Son.[326]

Joseph ben Shem Tov also pointed out that the Christians agreed with both premises. The first premise (A) was acceptable to the Christians since they did not divide the Fatherhood, just as they did not divide the Godhood. The second premise (B) was likewise part of Christian doctrine, since the Christians said that God had no parts. If one asked whether, for instance, the Spirit was all of God or part of Him, they would say all, because God was totally simple. If the Christians were to deny that "everything predicated on God is the Son," they would have to agree with the contradictory proposition,[327] namely, "something predicated on God is not the Son." But then God would have parts. Therefore, "everything predicated on God is the Son." The conclusion naturally followed.[328]

By adopting this form of the syllogism, Joseph ben Shem Tov emphasized the unity of God against the Christian Trinity. Not just part of God, or an aspect or relation of God, could be called by the name Father, or Son, or Spirit. If the Christians wanted to use such terms, they would have to predicate them on all of God. Otherwise, one would be forced to assume that God was not totally simple. Once, however, the terms Father or Son were predicated on all of God, they had to be considered identical, and thus not distinct. If the Christians maintained that the Persons were distinct, they were upholding a logical contradiction, forced to admit that consequences did not follow from premises and that syllogistic reasoning was unreliable. Since syllogistic reasoning was the basis of all speculative knowledge, Duran and Joseph ben Shem Tov felt they were on firm ground in accusing the Christians of rejecting the dictates of reason and the conclusions of the sciences.

Joseph ben Shem Tov himself offered a similar logical argument against the Trinity. He stated that he used the following syllogistic reasoning in a disputation with "one of their greatest scholars." According to Aristotle, it is a first principle that a thing and its essence are identical.[329] With this the Christian would agree.[330] If this is so, then the Person of the Father is the essence of the Father. Further, the essence of the Father is the essence of the Son, since God has only one essence. It follows, then, that the Person of the Father is the same as the essence of the Son.[331]

Joseph then proceeded to another syllogism. If, as was now proven, the Person of the Father were the essence of the Son, and the essence of the Son were the Person of the Son, it followed that the Person of the Father was the same as the Person of the Son.[332] Nevertheless, the Christians held that the Persons were distinct.

This is obviously only a restatement of Duran's syllogism, subject to the same criticisms. The Christians claimed that the essence of the Father was the same as the essence of the Son. They denied, however, that the Father was identical with the Son. We have here the same conflict of the two different perceptions of unity which we have seen before. For the Jewish polemicist, arguing from Aristotelian logic, God's essential unity did not allow for individuals which partook of His essence but were distinct. For the Christian theologian, such individualization in the essence implied neither a multiplicity in God nor a complete identity of the Persons. It appears that Joseph ben Shem Tov was attempting a debating *tour de force* rather than a final convincing logical argument.

This is borne out by the fact that the Christians were not unaware of this type of objection to the Trinity. Thus, Thomas stated:

> It seems that the relations which are in God are not distinct in reality from each other. Because all things identical with one and the same thing are identical with one another. But every relation in God is identical in reality with the divine nature. Therefore divine relations are not distinct from each other in reality.[333]

Quoting Aristotle,[334] Thomas answered that this reasoning held only for things identical both in reality and in meaning. The Father and Son were identical in reality, but not in meaning since their proper meanings implied opposite relationships.[335] The problem with the syllogism, then, was that it disregarded the fact that according to the Christians, the Persons were the same, in the reality of their own nature, but were also distinct, in their relations. In their form, the logical arguments proffered by Duran and Joseph ben Shem Tov were correct; the two sides, however, interpreted the premises differently and, therefore, arrived at different conclusions.

Images of the Trinity

In attempting to explain the Trinity, Christian thinkers looked to the physical world to find various examples that could be seen as analogous to that concept. Though the Trinity was, in fact, held to be a mystery beyond full rational proof, the discovery of something corresponding to it in nature would make the doctrine more acceptable.[336] It could, therefore, be expected that Jewish polemics would to some extent focus upon the examples cited. For the Christians, these analogies were of secondary import, since the divine Trinity was a mystery beyond adequate explanation, even given the help of similes.[337] The Jewish polemicists appear to have taken these images more seriously; an examination of the polemical use of images of the Trinity will give us an idea why this is so.

Despite Christian disclaimers that images of the Trinity should not be taken too literally, they should be studied seriously, since it is apparent that the type of analogy employed is indicative of a particular theologian's concept of the Trinity. We discern this clearly in the anti-Christian work of Dawūd al-Muqammiẓ, who, as stated above, understood the Christians to hold God's triune oneness to be a unity of species. He cited the following Christian images of the Trinity: (1) Three individual men share one species, manhood. (2) Three gold coins are one in regard to their common mintage, size, and inscription. (3) Three colors, such as white, black, and green, share one essence of color, though they are three individuals.[338]

The doctrine that God was one in species, viz., that Godhood was the species of the three individual Persons, the Father, Son, and Holy Spirit, was well illustrated by the example of three men who all shared in the species humanity. In fact, this image was first employed by the Cappadocian Fathers, who originated the explanation of God's Trinity as oneness in species.[339] Gregory of Nyssa, for instance, explained the common substance *(ousia)* of the three Persons by the analogy of three individual men, and in reply to the objection that these three are called "men" and not "man," he argued that this was only according to custom and not by logic.[340] John of Damascus also made use of this analogy to indicate that the term God was the *ousia* of the hypostases Father, Son, and Holy Spirit, just as man was the *ousia* of the hypostases Peter and Paul. The individuals were Father, Son, Holy Spirit, Peter, and Paul.[341]

Al-Muqammiẓ's proximate source for this image was undoubtedly the works of his teacher Nonnus,[342] who in turn probably learned it from Abū Rā'iṭa[343] and Theordore Abū Qurra.[344] All three employed this analogy, even though they did not teach that God was one in species, despite the fact that al-Muqammiẓ so interpreted Nonnus.[345] Al-Muqammiẓ apparently realized that this image was meant to typify unity of species, and thus he cited it.

Al-Muqammiẓ did not offer a refutation of this image, concentrating instead on the analogy of the three coins. Undoubtedly, though, he would have agreed with Augustine, who rejected both the explanation of the Trinity as unity of species and the image of three men participating in the species humanity. Augustine argued to the effect that "if 'God' is the species of Father, Son, and Holy Spirit, just as 'man' is the species of Abraham, Isaac, and Jacob, then, just as Abraham, Isaac, and Jacob can be called three men, so the Father, Son, and Holy Spirit should be called three Gods."[346]

The image of the three gold coins was also from a Cappadocian source, as transmitted through al-Muqammiẓ's Christian teachers and modified by al-Muqammiẓ. This image can be understood in one of three ways. (1) Goldhood was the species of the gold coins, each being an individual exemplar of such goldhood. This was apparently its use by Gregory of Nyssa, who said that there is one gold no matter in how many different forms it appears.[347] (2) Gold was the substratum of the three coins, which all participated in the gold. In like manner, God was the substratum of the three Persons who participated in the substratum God. This explanation of the Trinity was the one favored by Augustine, who cited the example of three gold statues all sharing the substratum gold.[348] On the other hand, Basil rejected this image. He argued that if one cited an example of bronze as the substratum and coins made from it as the persons, one might be led to think that there were four Gods. Just as the common substratum and the individual coins added up to four things, so too the Godhead and the three hypostases could be seen as equaling four, not three.[349] (3) The three aspects of the coin, namely, its mintage, size, and inscription, were intrinsically part of the one God. This was the meaning of the image as employed by Jerome of Jerusalem (eighth century) in an anti-Jewish polemical work. He apparently was the first to mention not just the coins as exemplars of gold, but rather their particular characteristics, namely, the gold plus the king's image and the inscription.[350]

The more immediate sources of al-Muqammiẓ's citation of the images of three gold coins appear to have been Timothy,[351] Abū Qurra,[352] and Abū Rā'iṭa.[353] They presented the analogy of three pieces of gold participating in the substratum gold as an explanation of unity of substratum, not unity of species. In this they followed Augustine, even though Abū Qurra and Abū Rā'iṭa also proffered the example of three men participating in humanity, an image that Augustine rejected. Al-Muqammiẓ apparently followed this use of the image, i.e., as an example of unity of substratum. His own reference to the coins' mintage, size, and inscription, which was lacking in his source, was intended to make his counter-argument stronger.[354]

Al-Muqammiẓ's refutation of the gold-coin image is linked to his arguments against the Trinity. As was stated above, in al-Muqammiẓ's view the Christians held the Persons of the Trinity to be identical with the substance. If so, he asked, were the Persons exactly identical with the substance, or were they identical yet still something other than the substance? If the Persons were exactly identical with the substance, then nothing distinguished them.

Similarly, were the gold coins identical only with their substance, gold, or with their substance plus something else? The gold coins could not be identical merely with gold because they constituted not only pieces of gold, but also currency, as attested by their inscription.[355] Currency is something other than gold qua gold. Even more important, the coins could not be said to constitute one substance, since they were three. The only way, therefore, to say that the coins shared one essence was by reference to not only their common matter, but also their common shape and inscription. Thus, the example showed that the three individuals were identical with their substance/essence plus something else. This image was applicable, therefore, only in case one was willing to admit that the Persons of the Trinity equaled the substance plus something else.

What happened, however, in case one admitted that the three Persons of the Trinity were identical with the substance plus something else? This posed the problem of what that something else was. If that something else was a "property" which made each Person distinguishable, just as the mintage and the inscription of the coins made them into dinars, then one could ask whether these properties were substances or accidents. Al-Muqammiẓ proceeded to explain why this second alternative was not possible.[356] We see here that al-Muqammiẓ not only refuted the image itself, but also employed it, in its modified form, as part of his general argumentation against the Trinity. Not only did the image of three coins not prove the Trinity, he contended, but it also showed the impossibility of the trinitarian doctrine.[357]

The image of three colors all being exemplars of one essence, colorhood, appears also to have had a Cappadocian source. Basil cited the colors of the rainbow as an analogy of the Trinity. He warned, however, that this image was only a "shadow of truth."[358] Al-Muqammiẓ cited this example as an alternative to the image of three gold coins. This latter analogy might blur the distinction between Persons because each coin was identical with the other two. If, however, one referred to three different colors, a visible distinction between the individuals was assured.[359]

Al-Muqammiẓ stated that this substitution did not help the Christian argument any. True, the generic name "color" applied to white, black, and green as species of the genus color.[360] But colors were distinguished from each other by specific differences, including the fact that one color had its contrary in another color, the most notable example being black and white. This simile, then, could not apply to the Trinity, unless one was prepared to admit the same contrariety among the Persons as there was between black and white. Since the Christians denied this, the example fell apart.[361]

We may summarize al-Muqammiẓ's treatment of Trinity images as follows. The analogies which he cited had their origin in Christian Cappadocian teachings, though al-Muqammiẓ's immediate sources were the works of his Christian teachers. Like the Cappadocians and apparently unlike his teachers, al-Muqammiẓ understood these images as examples of unity of species, though they might apply to unity of substratum. Al-Muqammiẓ's refutation of the images was similar to his refutation of the Trinity. Either the Persons (the individuals of the analogy) were identical and, therefore, indistinguishable, or they were different and distinguishable, but not one. It was, hence, meaningless to say that God was "one substance, three Persons."[362]

Images of the Trinity were cited also in Western polemical literature, though they differed from those mentioned by al-Muqammiẓ. Instead of images composed of three individual exemplars of one species or substratum, we find the Western polemicists using the analogy of one substance with three necessarily intrinsic attributes. These images were meant to represent God as one substance with three necessarily intrinsic Persons. The first such image encountered in Jewish polemical literature is that of a burning coal composed of its matter, fire, and flame. This analogy was cited in the twelfth century by Jacob ben Reuben[363] and subsequently by Shem Tov ibn Shapruṭ,[364] Judah Aryeh de Modena,[365] Isaac Lupis, [366] and the anonymous author of *Kevod Elohim.*[367] Moses ben Solomon of Salerno apparently referred to this or a similar image when he mentioned Christian proofs from fire.[368]

It is possible that this image was actually Jewish in origin. In a discussion of fire, Philo said that "fire takes three forms: these are the live coal, the flame, and the firelight."[369] In describing the relationship between the Sefirot as in reality one, *Sefer Yeẓirah* used the simile of a flame connected to a coal.[370] In Christian sources, the analogy of fire also existed, first as an image of the mystery of generation, then as an example of the Trinity. Justin stated that the Son proceeded from the Father as fire from fire,[371] while Tatian gave the example of many fires or torches kindled by one torch.[372] Theodoret exemplified the two natures of Jesus with the image of the union of fire and iron.[373] Similarly, in a work attributed to Hugh of Saint Victor, the combination of God's Word and man was compared with the combination of coal and fire, which produces something which is neither coal nor fire.[374] An example much closer to the one used by Jacob ben Reuben was employed by Timothy, who stated that fire begets light and causes heat to proceed from it. In like manner, the Father is similar to fire, the Son is like light, and the Holy Spirit like heat.[375] Notice, though, that this is an image of one essence with two proceeding attributes, whereas in the example cited by Jacob ben Reuben, i.e., that of the coal, there is one essence composed of three attributes.

Jacob ben Reuben attacked the example of the coal from two sides. The first approach denied the validity of such images altogether, and the second undermined the very premises of the specific image cited. In refuting the validity of Trinity images, Jacob ben Reuben said:

> When you bring a proof from one of the several creatures that are one, but still three, you should also bring proof from one of the several creatures that is one but still five, or ten, or more. For instance, a man is one being, and when you mention the term "man," you immediately understand from that special term the fact that he has two hundred forty-eight limbs, for the term "man" refers only to something which has a mouth, eyes, ears, a body, and all other limbs. Now all of these two hundred forty-eight limbs still constitute the unity of the term "man," and the term "man" which is one still constitutes two hundred forty-eight limbs. Or take only the hand, which must have five fingers, and the five fingers, which must have one hand.[376] Therefore, instead of bringing an example of your God, which is one and still three, why do you not learn of your God from man, who is one and still two hundred and forty-eight limbs. Then your God could be as the number of limbs. Now, if you cannot worship all of them, bring an example from the hand, and there will be only five, or from any other of the multiple examples.[377]

This reply was obviously more flippant than serious. The Christian argument was not that the burning coal was the source of the belief in a triune God; rather, the coal was one way of understanding trinity in unity. That there were things which are five in one was irrelevant to the claim that God was three in one.

Jacob ben Reuben's second argument, which was somewhat more to the point, ran as follows. It was possible to find the various components of the image cited to be separate from each other, e.g., the flame without the coal, as in the "flame of a pan," or the coal without the flame, as in the "coal of a pot." He concluded: "Therefore have I spoken to you thus, since it is not possible for a wise man like you to speak such things."[378]

The point of this second argument was to the effect that according to the doctrine of the Trinity, the one essence and the three attributes were inextricably tied together. Thus, to be a true analogy, the coal and its three properties must always coexist with each other. This was not the case; the example fell.

This second argument was still rather weak. The Christian wished to prove only that trinity in unity is possible, not that the coal was exactly analogous to God. Perhaps it was this perceived weakness that caused Ibn Shapruṭ to add a third argument after quoting Jacob ben Reuben's first refutation.

> If you say that just as the coal is composed of three things, your God is composed of the Trinity, then composition is the cause of every composed body. Anything which has a cause for its composition is only possible of existence. Therefore, that which gives [the Trinity] its existence is God, not [the Trinity].[379]

This argument was based on the assumption that multiplicity implied composition, and God could not be composed, for He was uncaused. Similar arguments against the Trinity have already been discussed.

Moses Ha-Kohen of Tordesillas cited another Christian image of the Trinity.

> Athanasius adduced the following analogy at the beginning of his composition: In order to prove that God is three Persons *[temunot]* and one substance, I will bring you a concrete proof. We see that the sun has rays, light, and heat, and even though no two of these things are the same, still the sun has only one substance. Likewise is the case of God, for even though the Person of the Father is not that of the Son or Spirit, still they are one substance.[380]

This image, which Moses Ha-Kohen attributed to Athanasius (ca. 295–373), has a long history and a number of applications. In the form presented by Moses Ha-Kohen, and also Moses ben Solomon of Salerno[381] and Judah Aryeh de Modena,[382] it was an example of one substance (the sun) with three inextricably connected parts. This, of course, represented the one God with three Persons, Father, Son and Spirit. Originally, however, the image of the sun was used to denote the procession of the Son from the Father. Indeed, some Jewish polemicists, e.g., Azriel Alatino[383] and the author of *Makkot Li-Khesil Me'ah,*[384] cited this usage of the analogy.

Though the mentioning of the sun as analogous to God was of an early origin, it was not universally accepted by the Church Fathers. Objection to it was based on the denial of light according to Philo[385] and the pseudo-Aristotelian tractate *De Mundo.*[386] Justin Martyr, for instance, who must have had in mind this nominalistic conception of light, rejected such a comparison of the procession of the Son from the Father as light from the sun because this would lead one to deny the reality of the Son.[387] In fact, the heretic Sabellius had attributed to him the statement that the terms Father, Son, and Holy Spirit were but actions or names, comparable with "the light and the heat and the circular form in the sun."[388]

Despite the strictures by Justin, various analogies using the image of the sun and its light were common among other Church Fathers. For Hippolytus, the relation of the Father to the Logos was "only as light of light . . . or as a ray from the sun."[389] Similar images were used by Tertullian[390] and Lactantius.[391] It is with Athanasius, to whom Moses Ha-Kohen attributed this analogy, that the image of the sun became a major theme.

> So again we see that the radiance from the sun is proper to it, and the sun's essence is not divided or impaired. Its essence is whole and its radiance perfect and whole, yet without impairing the essence of light, but as a true offspring from it. We understand similarly that the Son is begotten not from without but from the Father; and while the Father remains whole, the expression of his subsistence has his being eternally.[392]

Though these and other Church Fathers accepted the imagery of the sun's light, they did caution, either implicitly or explicitly, against too literal an understanding of such analogies. Thus John of Damascus said, "Whereas light possesses no proper subsistence of its own, distinct from that of fire, the Son is a perfect subsistence inseparable from the Father's subsistence."[393]

Later Christian authors also employed the image of the sun and its light as analogous in some respects to God. Yaḥya ben 'Adī, trying to prove that causation of the Son by the Father did not prove the Father's priority in time, gave the examples of the sun shining and producing light or the knocking together of bodies to produce sound. Here were examples of one thing causing another, but their existence was simultaneous.[394] Referring to the Trinity, Timothy also cited the fact that the sun with its light and heat was not called three suns but one sun. "As light and heat are not separable from the sun, so also (the Word) and the Spirit are not separable from Him."[395] In an Arabic treatise known as "On the Trinune Nature of God," the author also attempted to prove the feasibility of a Trinity by comparing the relation between God, His Word, and His Spirit to the disk of the sun, its rays, and its heat.[396] Jerome of Jerusalem used a similar image.[397]

Western Christian thinkers generally cited the image of the sun in terms of three inextricably connected attributes as analogous to God and the three Persons. There were any number of such theologians from whose works Moses Ha-Kohen might have derived the image of the sun which he cited. Despite Abelard's objection to its use,[398] the analogy of one sun with three aspects was employed by Fulbert of Chartres (d. 1028),[399] Honorius Augustodunensis (twelfth century),[400] pseudo-Gilbert Crispin (twelfth century),[401] Alan of Lille,[402] and Peter of Blois.[403] The exact parallel of rays, heat, and light is found in the works of Roland Bandinelli (Pope Alexander III, d. 1181).[404]

How did Moses Ha-Kohen attempt to refute this widespread image of the Trinity? He offered two counter-arguments, the first of which was as follows:

> Now, you who are interested see that this analogy, which he adduced to support his faith, in fact contradicts it. We have already explained[405] that the unity which refers to the sun is not true unity, and this is apparent to every intelligent being, since anything which is composed of different things is not truly one. Since the sun's light is not its heat, when they are conjoined together, they are not truly one. It would be a great deficiency in the essence of the First Cause, may He be blessed, if His unity were as this unity. We would be doing great evil if we were to believe this type of belief, for that thing which men call one although it is composed of different, distinct things is greatly deficient since it cannot exist unless the parts of which it is composed have been conjoined.[406]

Moses Ha-Kohen went on to say that composed things need a cause for their existence, but God, as the necessary of existence, could have no cause nor composition. If God were composed, He would need something else to compose Him, and this would extend *ad infinitum*. Therefore, the First Cause must be one simple substance, God.[407]

The second approach consisted in criticizing the details of the example. Moses Ha-Kohen stated that one should ask the following questions about this analogy: Was the ray the essence of the light of the sun, in which case there would not be three forces? Was the light from the heat or the heat from the light? Were these three attributes really divided one from another? Were these attributes only accidentally in the sun's matter or were they the essence of the sun? Or were they the matter of the sun? Were they necessary for the sun? Or were they accidents deriving from the form of the sun? Moses Ha-Kohen only wished that he had been there to ask these questions of the originator of this image.[408]

The point of the above argument was that the symbolism did not hold. It was not just a case of the one essence of the sun being comprised of three separate, distinguishable, but inextricably tied attributes. The case was not so simple. We are not certain exactly how the sun is constituted, and therefore one should not use it as an example.

At the end of his account of the Disputation of Barcelona, Naḥmanides recalled that on the Sabbath following the end of the disputation, the Christian disputants and King James I gathered in the synagogue to preach to the Jews. After Naḥmanides rejected the explanation of the Trinity as the attributes power, wisdom, and will, the king was portrayed as saying: there are three things in wine, color and taste and fragrance, and these three constitute one thing. Naḥmanides described this as an analogy taught the king by "those who err."[409]

This was another image in which one substance, the wine, was analogous to God, and the three inextricable attributes, color, taste, and fragrance, were analogous to the Persons. Naḥmanides' answer was predictable.

> But this is entirely erroneous, since the redness and the taste and the fragrance in wine are three distinct things each of which might be present without the others. For there are red and white and other colors of wine. The same holds true in regard to taste and fragrance. Moreover the redness is not the wine, nor is the taste the wine, nor is the fragrance the wine. But the essence of the wine is the thing which fills the vessel, and is a body which bears three distinct accidents; a body in which there is no unity. And if (in regard to the Deity) we should proceed on this false analogy to calculate as has been done we would be compelled to affirm a quaternity.[410]

Simon Duran also cited this image, apparently taking it from Naḥmanides' work. He refuted the analogy by saying that the wine was but one substratum with three accidents, and one could not imagine God as a substratum of accidents, unless one believed either that God was corporeal or that God had multiple intellects. But Duran had already proved that this was impossible. In addition, Duran argued that there were not just three accidents in wine, but also a fourth, either lightness or heaviness. Thus the necessity of three being one and of one consisting of three did not hold.[411]

In his anti-Christian parody of the Passover Haggadah, Jonah Rappa stated that God was one, "but not like a thing which is composed and can be divided into its parts, like a candle that has in it light, wax, and wick."[412] We see here one more image of the Trinity, one that went back at least to Alan of Lille, who compared God to a candle which produced light which was composed of light, brightness, and flame.[413] This image was also used by Franciszek Antoni Kobielski (1679–1755), a Polish bishop, in public disputations in Brody, 1742–43. He said that God was one and three like a candle with tallow, wick, and flame. The Jews responded with a statement attributed to Aristotle: "Since He is perfect, God lacks distinctions, for if He had them, He would not be perfect."[414]

Four other images of the Trinity may be mentioned in passing. In addition to their citing briefly the analogies of the coal (fire) and the sun, Moses ben Solomon and Judah Aryeh de Modena also quoted Augustine's famous image of the Trinity, i.e., the soul with its intellect, memory, and will.[415] Moses ben Solomon stated that God, who was the true unity, could not be compared to the soul and its faculties.[416] De Modena did not object to the image per se; rather, he averred that a belief in the Trinity would be acceptable were it not for the concomitant doctrine of incarnation.[417]

Azriel Alatino stated that although the Christians claimed their beliefs to be mysteries, and therefore not amenable to intellectual proofs, still they tried to give a rational basis for their doctrines. Hence they attempted to make the Trinity more acceptable by comparing it to the rays of the sun or the branches of a tree, all coming from one source.[418] As we have seen, sun imagery was very common among Christian thinkers. In like manner, some theologians, including Tertullian,[419] Jerome of Jerusalem,[420] and the author of "On the Triune Nature of God,"[421] had used the tree as analogous to the Trinity.

Moses Ha-Kohen of Tordesillas mentioned a Christian exegesis of Canticles 2:3, "As an apple among the trees of the wood," to the effect that the just as the apple contains fragrance, color and taste, God consists of Father, Son, and Spirit.[422] This is reminiscent of an image adduced by Timothy.[423]

Yair ben Shabbetai cited one more Trinity image, namely, the three yods which Jews wrote in place of the Tetragrammaton.[424] This analogy was employed by Abner of Burgos in one of his anti-Jewish polemical works.[425]

As we have seen, the Jewish polemicists cited a large variety of images of the Trinity. Despite the Christian assertions that these analogies were not to be taken too literally, the Jews referred to them often in their polemics. Still, refutations of these images were only of minor importance in the overall Jewish polemic against the Trinity. Arguments which derived from logic or from a theory of attributes were much stronger than those directed against an imperfect approximation of the Trinity, as the Christians claimed the images to be. Why, then, did the Jewish polemicists recall them so often in their polemics?

The answer to this question becomes clear when we investigate the sources of Trinity imagery. These analogies rarely appeared in works of systematic theology devoted to Christian audiences. Rather, these images were employed mainly in polemical works, either anti-Jewish, anti-Muslim, or anti-heretical, Thus, we see that some of the most abundant use of images of the Trinity came in the anti-Jewish treatises of Jerome of Jerusalem, Alan of Lille, and Peter of Blois. These images may not have been of importance theologically; they were very important, or so it appears, polemically. The Jewish writers must have constantly heard these images from Christian antagonists; they therefore answered in kind.

There was also another element involved. The Jewish polemicists attempted to show the illogical nature of Christianity. Since, as even the Christians admitted, the images were not meant to be exact analogies, it was rather easy to refute them, thus adding further to the Jewish charge that Christianity was not rational. The refutation of a particular image would not undermine a Christian's faith, for his belief in the Trinity was separate from the analogies he may have adduced to exemplify it. For the Jew, the successful challenge of such an image was one more part, insignificant as it may have been in itself, of his general philosophical polemic against the Christian doctrine of the Trinity.

Conclusions

We have seen that Jewish philosophical polemicists expended much thought on their philosophical polemic against the Trinity. They marshaled a large variety of arguments, directing them at the weak points of the Christian doctrine. Many of these arguments were not original to the Jewish polemicists, and most were known to Christian theologians. Still, the Jewish thinkers employed them with great force, hoping thereby to defend the Jewish belief in God's absolute unity.

A number of conclusions emerge from the study of these arguments. First, it is apparent that the Jewish philosophical polemicists responded in their arguments to the doctrines espoused by the Christian polemicists. We have seen that the Jewish polemicists emphasized certain Christian beliefs, e.g., the relation between the Persons and the divine attributes or the images of the Trinity, which were not stressed by nonpolemical Christian thinkers. It was only in the Christian polemical literature that such notions were given prominence. The Jewish polemicists were not interested in Christian doctrine per se; on the whole, they took note only of those beliefs which were employed in Christian conversionary attempts.

Moreover, by comparing the Jewish philosophical criticisms to the Christian philosophical defense of the Trinity, it becomes clear that the differences between the polemicists were mainly theological, not philosophical. For instance, while Eastern Jewish thinkers were anti-attributist and their Christian colleagues were attributists, this divergence can be seen as a result, not the cause, of their concepts of God. In the West, Jewish and Christian Aristotelians agreed on basic philosophical issues, e.g., God's unity, simplicity, non-causedness, etc. Still, they were able to come to separate conclusions concerning God's unity or Trinity. The Jews used Aristotelian principles to prove that a Trinity was impossible. Christian philosophers attempted to show that the same Aristotelian principles were not incompatible with a triune God. We do not have here two separate philosophical movements. Rather, a common philosophy was employed for contradictory polemical purposes.

The medieval Jewish polemicists subjected the Christian doctrine of the Trinity to their most comprehensive philosophical polemic. Yet it was by no means the only Christian belief to be analyzed critically by this method of argumentation. We now turn to a discussion of the medieval Jewish philosophical polemic against incarnation, transubstantiation, and virgin birth.

CHAPTER FIVE

Incarnation

A casual glance at the extensive Jewish polemic against the Trinity might lead one to think that Jewish theologians rejected any notion of a triune God per se. As our detailed study of the arguments has shown, the idea that God had a number of different or specific aspects was not repudiated by them out of hand. Some polemicists stated explicitly that the Trinity, in itself, was not an unacceptable doctrine.[1] Yet the Christian Trinity was attacked with vehemence, and the Christian concept of a triune God was rejected as self-contradictory. The chief reason for this Jewish reaction lay in the Christian doctrine of incarnation, which was professed to be a concomitant of the belief in the Trinity.[2] According to Christian teaching, one Person of the Trinity, the Son, assumed flesh in Jesus of Nazareth. While Jewish theologians might accept the notion that God has a number of aspects, they totally rejected the possibility that one such aspect did, or even could, become human.[3] It was the doctrine of incarnation that most truly set apart the Jewish and Christian concepts of God.

Though there is no explicit statement in the New Testament claiming divinity for Jesus, and despite a number of verses which seem to disprove such a claim,[4] the Church Fathers adopted the belief that he was both God and man.[5] Those Christians who refused to accept this doctrine, such as the Ebionites or the Arians, who held that Jesus was only a man, were branded as heretics and excluded from the Church.[6] The Nicene Creed, which effectively established the belief in the Trinity, also made the acceptance of Jesus as both God and man obligatory for the orthodox.[7] Once this position was established, Christian thinkers found it necessary to explain how Jesus could be both God and man.[8] This, in turn, led to controversies. The orthodox doctrine, accepted universally in the West and by the Malkites in the East, was established by the decree of the Council of Chalcedon (451):

> Therefore, following the holy fathers, we all teach that with one accord we confess one and the same Son, the Lord Jesus Christ, the same perfect in

human nature, truly God and the same with a rational soul and a body truly man, consubstantial with the Father according to divinity, and consubstantial with us according to human nature, like unto us in all things except sin, [cf. Heb. 4:15]; indeed born of the Father before the ages according to divine nature, but in the last days the same born of the virgin Mary, Mother of God according to human nature; for us and for our deliverance, one and the same Christ only begotten Son, our Lord, acknowledged in two natures, without mingling, without change, indivisibly, undividedly, the distinction of the natures nowhere removed on account of the union but rather the peculiarity of each nature being kept, and uniting in one person and substance, not divided or separated into two persons, but one and the same Son only begotten God Word, Lord Jesus Christ, just as from the beginning the prophets taught about Him and the Lord Jesus Himself taught us, and the creed of our fathers has handed down to us.

Therefore, since these have been arranged by us with all possible care and diligence, the holy and ecumenical synod has declared that no one is allowed to profess or in any case to write up or to compose or to devise or to teach others a different faith.[9]

This formulation of the Council of Chalcedon taught a number of points concerning incarnation. First, Jesus was truly man because of his human nature consisting of body and rational soul,[10] thus being consubstantial with all men. Second, he was also consubstantial with God, since he had a divine nature. Third, the Son was born twice, once, according to his divine nature, from eternity, as the second Person of the Trinity, and again, according to his human nature, in time, as Jesus son of Mary. Fourth, the human and divine natures were united in the one person of Jesus, but this unity was "without mingling, without change, indivisible, undivided, the distinction of the natures [being] nowhere removed on account of the union."[11] Fifth, the purpose of the incarnation was the deliverance of mankind.[12]

There is very little in this statement with which the Jewish polemicists agreed. The only part acceptable to them was the claim that Jesus was truly man born in time as the son of Mary.[13] Otherwise, they rejected both the predication of divinity upon him and the doctrine that Jesus brought redemption. Since these beliefs lay at the heart of Christianity, it is natural that the Jewish polemicists directed a large number of arguments against them. It is to the philosophical aspects of the Jewish polemic that we now turn.

Two main features were apparent in the doctrine that Jesus was both God and man. The first was the soteriological, and the second was the Christological, having to do with the person of Jesus. Discussion of soteriology attempted to explain "why God became man," as is the title of Anselm's work on the subject, *Cur Deus Homo.*[14] Christology was intended to answer the question, How did God become man? Ḥasdai Crescas expressed these two aspects of incarnation as the final cause (why) and the formal cause (how).[15]

Why God became man was answered by the doctrine of original sin and its redemption. Adam sinned, causing all of his descendants, i.e., all humanity, to be in a state of original sin, and thus to owe a debt to God. Mankind, however, was not sufficient to pay this debt because of the debt's magnitude and mankind's limitation. Only God can redress the wrong, but God has no obligation to do so. Thus, there would exist a stalemate, were it not for God's love of humanity, which is expressed in His becoming a man. Only a God-man, and indeed a sacrificed one, could satisfy the debt which man owes to God.[16] According to the Christians, Jesus was this God-man who brought salvation to the world. In recognition of this fact, mankind was obligated to believe in Jesus and the Church he established.[17]

Jewish arguments against this doctrine can hardly be called philosophical in the way the term is being used here. The Jewish polemicists employed a wide range of contentions which stressed that this doctrine was not befitting God. They insisted that it was beneath God's dignity to enter into a woman's body, to be born into the world like other men, to live a worldly life in which He ate, drank, slept, etc., and finally was humiliated and suffered death.[18] Not only was such a course unbefitting God, but the reason for incarnation was also invalid. The Jewish polemicists rejected the Christian notion of original sin as inconsistent with God's justice, despite the fact that such a concept was not entirely foreign to Judaism.[19] The polemicists argued further that, even if all humanity were culpable as a result of the first man's sin, there would be no need for God to sacrifice Himself to redeem mankind. God had sufficient power to do as He willed, to forgive whom He wished to forgive, without being forced to take on human form.[20]

The Christians argued from a totally different perspective—that God became man was not unbefitting divinity; rather, it was a sign of God's great love for mankind. Only by becoming a man could God lift mankind up from its sins. "God was made man, that man might be made God."[21] Incarnation was not beneath God's dignity; it was wholly compatible with God's glory and greatness.[22] As for original sin, it was not unjust that all of Adam's descendants shared in his guilt. The first transgression was of such magnitude as to affect the rest of mankind. Satisfaction for sin could come only with the sacrifice of a God-man. God would not have become incarnate if He had not wanted to redeem mankind. Once He had determined to save the world, because of His love, incarnation became a necessity.[23]

From this brief sketch of the major arguments for and against the soteriological nature of the doctrine of incarnation, it becomes apparent that on the question of why God became man we are confronted with two entirely opposite views of man's nature. For the Jew, man's sin did not require redemption by means of a sacrifice of God. Moreover, it would be a diminution of God's dignity, a *lèse majesté,* for God to live as man among men and to suffer. For the Christian, however, incarnation did not imply a diminution of God's glory, but rather it indicated God's greatness, for He did not hesitate to become a man in order to bring men closer to Him.[24] If the Jewish polemicists were to present a philosophical critique of the soteriological aspects of incarnation, they would have had to demonstrate that this doctrine was inconsistent with fundamental speculative principles held by both Jewish and Christian thinkers. Since, however, there existed no such agreement concerning the presuppositions of soteriology, e.g., the nature of man, no Jewish philosophical critique was feasible. The Jewish polemicists restricted their contentions against Christian soteriology to exegetical, historical, and "common-sense" arguments.[25] Hence, this feature of the Jewish polemic against incarnation is outside the limits of the present study.

It is concerning the second aspect of incarnation, namely, Christology, that we discern arguments of a philosophical nature. Jews and Christians agreed here on certain philosophical presuppositions, e.g., God's unity, incorporeality, and immutability. Since the Christians accepted these principles, it was possible for the Jewish polemicists to criticize the notion of a God-man on the grounds that such a concept was incompatible with these mutually agreeable principles. If the Christians were to reject the logical consequences of their own initial presuppositions, the Jewish polemicists argued, then they were contradicting themselves. The Jewish philosophical critique of incarnation was based on this contention.

Three commonly held philosophical suppositions were seen as precluding God's taking on flesh. These were (1) God's incorporeality, (2) His immutability, and (3) His simple unity. In addition, the Jewish polemicists argued that (4) the assumption of a union of Divinity and humanity had certain impossible consequences.

God Is Incorporeal

The most fundamental Jewish objection to incarnation was based on the principle of God's incorporeality. Since God was immaterial, the Jews argued, how could Jesus, a human being composed of matter, be God? They contended further that God's incorporeality also implied His inability to be confined in one place. How, then, could the divinity be encompassed by a woman's womb or by Jesus' body?

God's Incorporeality Precludes Incarnation

Dāwūd al-Muqammiẓ began his critique of incarnation by stating that if the Christians maintained that the Son was eternally generated with neither end nor beginning, one should ask whether the Son walked around and changed places eternally. Most likely, he stated, the Christian would answer that walking around and changing places could be done only by physical things. Although the quotation of al-Muqammiẓ, which is found in Judah ben Barzilay's *Perush,* ends here, we can assume that in the sequel to the original text the question was posed: How could the Christians believe that God became human, walking around and changing places, if He was totally incorporeal?[26]

Saadia Gaon's arguments against incarnation were borrowed from his refutation of those who maintained that God created the world by emanation.[27] He stated that reason rejected the idea

> that an eternal being, that is subject to neither form nor quality nor dimension nor limit nor place nor time, can so be changed that a part of it becomes a body possessing form and dimension and qualities and place and time and other attributes belonging to corporeal beings. This is only most remotely conceivable.[28]

Saadia's other arguments in this context were based on the notion of the impossibility of God's desire to suffer needlessly.[29]

Joseph Kimḥi stated that God was invisible, having neither image nor form. How, then, could one believe that God entered a woman's womb and became incarnate?[30] The polemical treatise incorrectly attributed to Joseph Kimḥi's son David made the point that calling anyone the "Son of God" must be taken figuratively, since "the Creator, may He be blessed, is neither a body nor a power in a body."[31] Moses ben Solomon of Salerno, referring to Maimonides' proofs that God is neither a body nor a power in a body,[32] argued that if God became incarnate, He would have been a power in a body.[33] Likewise, Moses Ha-Kohen insisted that God was "fully spiritual and pure so that we are not able to predicate of Him any accident, physical thing, or change."[34] Since a body has generating and corrupting accidents, God, who was devoid of all accidents, could not possibly take on flesh.[35] Other Jewish thinkers offering similar arguments against incarnation were Simon Duran,[36] Isaac Abravanel,[37] Judah Aryeh de Modena,[38] and Isaac Lupis.[39]

In his anti-Christian polemical letter written before his conversion, Joshua Lorki questioned both the Trinity and incarnation. Even assuming that a concept of Trinity were possible, he argued,

> What would you say about their statement that he himself [Jesus] is the messiah of flesh and blood, eating and drinking, dying and living, and he himself is also the true God who is the cause of causes, from the overabundance of whose power the spheres move and from the emanation of whose existence the separate intellects, which are neither bodies nor powers in a body, and "whose dwelling place is not with flesh" [Dan. 2:11], come into existence? How could their existence remain and be continual [if it is derived] from one who is material in actuality? [That a physical being could eternally move the spheres] is one of the doctrines which the sages refer to when they say that "the impossible has a constant nature,"[40] such as God's causing His incarnation or His creation of another being equal to Him. The truth is that this is something that cannot be comprehended by the intellect, nor imagined by the heart, so as to render it [even] doubtful or to be perplexed by it in any way or to make it subject, finally, to God's power.[41]

If God were corporeal, argued Lorki, the world could not continually be in motion, since the separate intellects which move the spheres must themselves have derived from an incorporeal source.[42]

Joseph ben Shem Tov agreed with Lorki's conclusion.

> Would that I knew who it is that moves the heavens, with this great movement which you see, if, according to their opinion, God, who is the mover, is not incorporeal, but rather a bodily force with bodily existence there above the heavens [and who, therefore, as a bodily force, could not move the heavens eternally].[43]

Basing himself on Aristotle's *On the Soul*[44] and *Metaphysics*,[45] Joseph ben Shem Tov argued further:

> God, may He be blessed, comprehends because He is incorporeal, and He is living because He comprehends. According to the converse of the contrary proposition, it follows that anything which is a bodily power cannot comprehend an intellectual conception [as does God] nor can it live the special divine life.[46]

The above arguments served to demonstrate that the concept of a material God was rationally unacceptable. The Christian theologians themselves were well aware that the notion of incarnation was in apparent contradiction to the philosophical idea of God's incorporeality. They agreed with the Jewish polemicists that a corporeal God was impossible. How, then, did the Christians reconcile God's immateriality with His incarnation? Thomas Aquinas attempted to solve this problem by stating that God did not turn into material flesh. Instead, "for the sake of man's salvation, He united it to Himself."[47] Even though "it pertains to the dignity of God to be altogether separated from bodies," nevertheless, God's dignity was not lessened because God's nature remained distinct from the flesh of the incarnate Son.[48] Since God did not become a body, Thomas argued, there existed no incompatibility between divine incorporeality and incarnation.

This distinction was one which the Jewish polemicists did not accept. They argued that the statement "Jesus was God" could signify only a belief in God's corporeality. The Christians, however, maintained that their positing of a God-man did not necessitate God's having become material. The disagreement here was not whether God was corporeal; the real point of contention was whether or not incarnation implied corporeality. The Jewish philosophical polemicists insisted that it did. The Christian theologians answered that no such implication existed.

God Cannot Be Limited in Place

The argument against incarnation invoking the impossibility of circumscribing God in place had its origins in *Nestor Ha-Komer*. The author of this anonymous work wondered why the Christians were not embarrassed to say that Jesus was born or that he rode on a donkey. If "the heavens and the heavens of heavens cannot contain Him" (1 Kings 8:27), how could a woman's womb or a donkey receive God?[49] The same argument has been found in a Geniza fragment of an anti-Christian polemic written in Arabic.[50]

Jacob ben Reuben also employed this argument. After contending that there was no need for incarnation, he stated that if God was eternal, then He would be limitless. Jacob ben Reuben exhorted the Christian to accept this argument, "if he has a brain in his skull."

> Now settle your thoughts in the texture of your intellect, and delve your science into the depths of knowledge, perchance your thought will be able to understand what you are saying when you assert that the Creator, may He be blessed, just as He is, according to the way your mind is able to think about

Him, was completely enclosed in the recesses of the womb, and imprisoned in the darkness of the belly, and like a foetus that does not see light. This doctrine is one shameful to utter, to listen to it is sacrilegious, and God forbid that I sin with my tongue by even mentioning this doctrine with the opening of my mouth, or by saying these things brazenly in the face of heaven concerning the Creator. May He be blessed and may His name be excellent for ever and ever.[51]

Jacob ben Reuben's Christian interlocutor denied the correctness of the claim that God was confined to the impurity of the womb.

There is nought in your words; rather, being of an evil heart you wish to despise God, and things are not as you say. You disgrace your mouth, but I and Divinity are unblemished, for the Creator, may He be blessed, is unaffected by blemish and blasphemy. Language cannot in any way describe Him as "enclosed," for He is not enclosed nor does He enter into the secret places of darkness.[52]

The Christian offered an analogy to prove that God could not be considered to have been enclosed in the womb and to have acquired impurity. He illustrated it with the sun's rays, which might shine on refuse or dung without becoming unclean. Also, a ray might enter a small hole, but one cannot trap it by closing the entrance to the hole. Similarly, one cannot gather a ray with one's closed hand and bring it home. Now, if this is the case with one of God's smallest servants, should it not also be the case with God Himself?[53]

This image of the sun's retaining its purity was apparently originated by Athanasius.[54] We have evidence that it was also used specifically against Jewish objections to incarnation. For instance, Maximinus the Arian (ca. 451) answered the Jewish argument that God became impure through His birth by suggesting that the sun's brilliancy is not defiled by whatever it may touch.[55]

Jacob ben Reuben rejected this analogy. How can one compare, he asked, the sun's ray, which has neither matter nor form, with the allegedly created God, who, according to the Christians, has physical properties? The rays do not acquire impurity nor can they be enclosed because they lack materiality.

Why do you not look at what you are saying? Anything which can be felt by the hands can have something, whether pure or impure, attached to it. I have put your words through the furnace which purifies the truth, and all of them are dross, with no silver. Therefore, I advise you: "Put away from you crooked speech, and put devious talk far from you" [Prov. 4:24].[56]

Isaac Lupis, who repeated this argument verbatim, ended on a more cheerful note: "Even though you have sinned greatly, return to God for He is merciful and gracious, and He will have mercy upon you."[57]

Moses ben Solomon argued a number of times that the doctrine of incarnation necessarily implied that God was located in a limited place. If the Christians wished to claim that Jesus was truly God, then, he stated, they must also acknowledge that God was enclosed in his flesh.[58] Moses ben Solomon offered an explanation of this assertion.

> It is known that one special vessel of the human organs is the seat of man's soul. According to most, this is the heart, while others maintain that its seat is the head, even though the strength of its origin is in the heart. If Divinity became incarnate, it must, of course, have had a special limb as its seat. Let me ask you: which limb of "Ploni's"[59] body was God's seat?[60]

Since God was the dwelling place of the world, Moses ben Solomon concluded, how could a small thing become His place and seat?[61]

Abraham Farissol employed a number of arguments against incarnation, a doctrine which he said he had never understood and which no one could understand, since its possibility was excluded both in the intellect and outside it.[62] First, he asked how it was possible to ascribe to God matter and form, making Him incarnate and saying that the matter of their messiah's flesh and its six dimensions were God, thus assigning to Him a limit. This was against the commonly held principle.[63] Farissol then stated that incarnation implied two alternatives, i.e., either the matter of the messiah's flesh was God Himself, for God really became material, or the messiah's body was God through conjunction with something else, for God caused His glory to dwell with it, "encompassing it around all the day long" (Deut. 33:12), in which case Divinity and flesh remained distinct. Now, saying that God, in fact, became flesh was impossible, because it would mean that a substance became accident, the uncreated became created, the infinite became finite in six dimensions, and the whole became a part. Farissol said that the Christians agreed to the fact that this was impossible.[64]

What, then, of the second possibility, which the Christians accepted, namely, that Divinity and manhood remained distinct? If the Christians understood this as a union in the manner in which the divine emanation became connected with the prophets, then it would be acceptable.

> It is impossible and absurd, though, that Divinity could actually participate with flesh as the soul participates with the body of man, with the intellect and

> the matter being together.[65] This is because the created soul has a limit, since it is connected with all the parts of the flesh. It is a foolish doctrine to affirm a natural union after the fashion of man who is a union of flesh and soul with all their powers. The intellect cannot affirm this of God and flesh, whether their union be natural, or accidental, or willful, for "the impossible has a stable nature."[66] It can never be correct to say that flesh can be God because when the flesh of the messiah dies, it would be possible to say that God died with the flesh.[67]

Farissol's argument here is complex. He realized that the Christians did not teach that God turned into human flesh. Everyone agreed that this was logically impossible. He also appreciated that incarnation did not mean that Jesus, a man like other prophets, enjoyed divine inspiration. Christian doctrine held that manhood and Divinity united in the manner in which the soul and body of man unite. The analogy to man's union of body and soul was likewise rejected by Farissol for the reasons outlined above.

The Jewish argument that God could not possibly be circumscribed into a definite place, be it Mary's womb or Jesus' body, was repeated often in Christian polemical literature. Thus, Gilbert Crispin's Jewish disputant asked: "If God is immense, how could He be circumscribed by the paltry and small dimensions of the human body?"[68] The same question was asked by the Jew in the anonymous French polemical poem.[69] This problem, which was also cited by Thomas,[70] had been answered by Augustine. In replying to Faustus, this Church Father wrote that God was not so shut up in the virgin's womb as to cease to be elsewhere.[71] The Person of the Son assumed flesh; that does not mean that the flesh exclusively encompassed the Son. As Thomas said, the Son could assume another human nature at the same time since the Uncreated cannot be comprehended by any creature.[72]

God Is Immutable

Both Jews and Christians agreed that God was unchanging, for change needs an external cause. God, having no external causes, could not change. If God was immutable, argued the Jewish polemicists, how could He have become a man, since that means He changed from noncorporeality to corporeality. Similarly, God could not be said to have been created, for creation needs a creator previous to the act of creation, and nothing could create itself. In addition, flesh could not be seen as perfecting God because He had always been perfect.

The last point was made by the author of *Nestor Ha-Komer,* the first to argue along these lines. He stated that the Christians believed Jesus to have been fully God and fully man and that he was carried up to the heavens. Where did he find there food and water and other physical necessities, the polemicist asked. If the Christians said that Jesus was God and did not have bodily needs, then they contradicted their own statement that he was man. On the other hand, if they said that God released him from physical restraints, then they must agree that before this release from want, Jesus had a deficiency.[73] The point was made that Jesus could not be God if he at one time were lacking something and if he were perfected by an outside source.

Yūsuf al-Baṣīr argued that a belief in incarnation led to the conclusion that God was created. He had already shown that God was not a body, and therefore could exhibit no alternation. Further, He was not an accident; hence, one could not describe Him in terms of inherence/incarnation *(ḥulūl).* If one said that God inhered in the substratum man, it would follow that God was created, since inherence was a consequence of creation. The proof was as follows: Everything that inhered in something else depended on the latter thing for its existence. The substratum was the cause of the existence of the inherent, for if the substratum were to disappear, so too would the thing that inhered. Hence, the inherent thing must have been created. Since God, however, was not dependent on any other entity, it followed that He could not inhere; incarnation, therefore, was impossible.[74]

Drawing on the idea that God could neither be created nor acquire perfections, Jacob ben Reuben made the following argument. After citing the Christian belief that the Son became incarnate to redeem the world, he stated:

> All the philosophers and intelligent sages make fun of you, and they ask concerning this point: If the Creator, may He be blessed, was created, tell me if He was created before He existed or after He existed. If before He existed, you have contradicted your statement that He is the beginning of beginnings and first without beginning. If you say that after He already existed He became incarnate at the time He wished, then during that time, He was deficient on account of flesh, bones, and sinews which He received for the time you mentioned, and this cannot be right. Moreover, this would necessitate a distinction between the time He was without the form of flesh, and the latter time when He acquired shape and form. All the books of the philosophers[75] have already testified that everything distinct is limited; everything limited has an end; everything that has an end is composed; everything composed is created; everything created needs a creator external to it, for any intelligent person knows that nothing creates itself.[76]

This argument was also used by Shem Tov ibn Shapruṭ,[77] Isaac Lupis,[78] and the author of *Kevod Elohim.*[79]

According to Levi ben Abraham of Villefranche, incarnation was absurd since it implied corporeality and an addition to God's essence. It meant positing in God's essence a created thing, while it was clear to everyone that Divinity and createdness were incompatible, for everything created needed a cause, and all creation was an accident. God, of course, had no cause and was not subject to accidents. According to the Christians, God (viz., the second Person of the Trinity) was brought into being a long time after the creation of the world.[80]

In his polemic against incarnation, Meir ben Simeon of Narbonne employed the issue of God's possible mutability, not in terms of Jesus' birth but in respect to his death.

> It is well known that the Creator, may He be blessed, is without change, beginning or end. This is known by means of the intellect and reliable tradition. . . . In truth, anything which died underwent great change, and its years were ended. If they say that this [immutability] is said about God, not about the flesh He received, then they are not saying that the body's flesh is God and Creator, and they are not equating matter with its maker.[81]

Moses ben Solomon of Salerno reiterated a number of times that incarnation could not have been possible because it implied that God moved, changed, and was acted upon. For example, after quoting Maimonides' formulation of the kinds of motion,[82] he continued:

> If Divinity had participated with flesh, then you must admit that when the body moved so did Divinity move, as in the motion of a nail in a ship or the ship's mast. This is false. God, may He be blessed, has no motion, for all motion is change, as the sage [Maimonides] proposed in Proposition 5.[83]

A Christian responded that his religion did not teach that God enclosed Himself in flesh as the human soul is enclosed in man. If their faith were to teach this, the Christian would have to admit that God did move. Instead, they believed that Divinity remained where it was and did not enter flesh. The flesh became elevated and drew near the Divinity, thus becoming His son, God, and the Son of God.[84]

Again basing himself on Maimonides,[85] Moses ben Solomon replied that nothing could physically draw near or approach God because God was incorporeal. Furthermore, if one said that "that man's" soul or his intellect drew near God, then how could he have become God's son? He could not have been even God's grandson or great-grandson, for the intellects of both Moses and Elijah drew much nearer to God than did his soul, and yet they were not called sons of God.[86] If, on the other hand, the Christian insisted that the Divinity, indeed, became united with flesh, then:

> The Divinity in him had motion, and if it had motion, it had change, and everything that changes is divisible. This, God forbid, is impossible for God, may He be blessed. This [doctrine] is nothing other than blindness to your eyes.[87]

Moses ben Solomon also attacked incarnation on the grounds that such a doctrine implied that God was acted upon (affected). This was impossible, for, as Maimonides stated, "All affections entail change, and moreover the agent who effects those affections is undoubtedly not identical with him who is acted upon."[88] Since "Ploni" (Jesus) was acted upon when he received flesh, he could not have been God. One could not say that incarnation was not affection because great change was involved when an incorporeal power became a bodily power. Furthermore, how could an incorporeal power become a material power, since Aristotle had already stated that everything which changed must be proceeded in time by some potentiality.[89]

Another argument offered by Moses ben Solomon ran as follows: Since God is not a body or a power in a body, He cannot have motion, e.g., ascending, descending, coming, going, walking, standing, sitting, composition, separation, size, measure, border, or limit. God is like the air, which, though it fills the world, is not felt. God is everything, and everything, the upper and lower realms, i.e., the spheres and all that is in them, is in God, whose power and might bear them. How, then, could the Christians, by believing in incarnation, attribute motion to God?[90] In general, since God is the first cause and the necessary of existence, He is not subject to change, motion or affection, and He could not have become incarnate.[91]

In his *'Ezer Ha-Dat,* originally written in Spanish, Moses Ha-Kohen presented this objection in the following manner: After demonstrating that God must be incorporeal, since corporeality implied multiplicity, the polemicist recounted how he discussed this matter with Christian priests several times. Moses Ha-Kohen commenced his argument by saying that these priests agreed when he said that according to their doctrine God became incarnate in approximately 4000 A.M.[92] Now, everything which exists has a certain advantage and perfection, which it lacked before it existed, since its previous perfection was subject to doubt. There was doubt whether or not it would come into being; when, however, it passed from potentiality to actuality, there was no longer the same doubt. Hence, before the year 4000 their God (i.e., Jesus) did not have the same form he was to receive, and thus he had an imperfection. But God can have no imperfection.[93]

Moses Ha-Kohen proceeded further. A potential thing needs something actual to actualize it. Before incarnation, their God had human form only potentially. Who, then, was the agent *in actu* who could bring him into existence? Only God can actualize creatures, but if God were Himself only *in potentia*, who actualized Him?[94]

The Christians were portrayed as answering that God did not become incarnate sooner, either because of a lack of necessity for incarnation at an earlier time or because of the incapacity of matter to receive Him. Moses Ha-Kohen responded that according to Christian doctrine, incarnation became necessary immediately with Adam's sin. Further, if it were the inability of matter to receive God which prevented an earlier incarnation, then God was lacking in power, since He did not cause a change in nature so that He might become incarnate.[95]

The translator of this treatise, Meir ben Jacob, further explained this refutation of incarnation. If the Christians said that God was unable to arrive earlier because of the inability of matter to receive Him, then He should have caused a miracle (a change in nature) and prepared it for Himself. The Christians agreed that a number of miracles were attendant to incarnation (e.g., virgin birth); why, then, could God not have caused other changes in nature as He had done so many times in the past?[96]

Profiat Duran also used the argument that God's incorporeality and immutability precluded His becoming incarnate. Employing his sarcastic tone, Duran suggested to the recipient of his *Iggeret* that he not be like his fathers, who believed God to be totally incorporeal and immaterial. Basing themselves on rational speculation, they rejected the possibility that any mode of change could be attributed to God. Instead, they believed that God was a pure and simple intellect.

> As for you, do not be like this. Do not negate from Him materiality and corporeality. God forbid! Believe that with one of His attributes, but not all three, He became incarnate as He wished. His blood was poured out like water [Ps. 79:3] to atone for His people, and He was satisfied.[97]

Joseph ben Shem Tov, in his commentary on this section of the *Iggeret,* explained why immutability precluded incarnation. First, when Duran said that the Jews negated from God any of the modes of change, he meant in substance, in quality, in quantity, or in respect of locomotion.[98] None of these changes could be predicated upon God because, as Prime Mover and the necessary of existence, He was immaterial.[99] Matter was necessary for change,[100] because everything that changed was divisible.[101] The principle that everything that changed was divisible was based on two propositions. First, every change was from something to something else, and everything which was changing was partly at the starting point of change and partly at the goal of the change.[102] Second, everything which was partly at the starting point and partly at the goal must be divisible. Hence, everything that changed must be divisible.

Joseph ben Shem Tov continued to argue that one must also accept the contradictory converse of this principle, i.e., that which was indivisible was unchangeable. God was totally indivisible, both physically and conceptually, since He was the true one, being neither a body nor a force in a body. Therefore, God could not change. If God could not change, He could not become a man; incarnation was impossible.[103]

Abraham Farissol also argued against incarnation as being inconsistent with God's immutable nature.

> Attributing to God and His flesh this type of change [e.g., growth] implies an incapacity and deficiency in language, since the flesh is God. How can God be subject to change, such as growing, standing, descending, and other accidents which I do not even know [that would apply to God] if the flesh of the messiah were God?[104]

Farissol's argument here was to the effect that human flesh was subject to change; if Jesus' flesh were God, God, too, would be subject to change, something which was impossible.

Judah Aryeh de Modena phrased the objection in this manner: When God assumed flesh in order to suffer punishment, did He add perfection to Himself? If the Christians denied this, then God acted for no purpose, something He would not do. If they affirmed that God added a perfection in that He announced His humility and mercy and His ability to join His nature to human nature, this would still be impossible, for God could not add anything to Himself, even a perfection. If God were so to act, it would mean that He was previously deficient. In addition, incarnation was a new creation, and every creation was an accident. Therefore, incarnation could not be attributed to God.[105]

The Christians were well aware of the seeming incongruity of an unchanging, immutable God becoming a man. In fact, Cyril of Alexandria (fifth century), one of the major thinkers responsible for the orthodox formulation of incarnation, rejected the use of the word "became" as referring to God, since He was always unchanging.[106] Gilbert Crispin, in his anti-Jewish dialogue, had the Jew from Mayence ask how one could say that God, "with whom there is no variation or shadow due to change" (James 1:17), could become man. How could the Creator become a creature, the incorruptible one become corruptible? Crispin answered that God remained exactly as He always was; He merely assumed another nature. When one says that God became man, this was not by a transformation of Divinity into humanity; rather it was by the assumption of humanity by God.[107]

Thomas, too, discussed this problem. It would seem, he wrote, that the Word of God should not change into flesh, because God is immutable, but whatever was changed into another was manifestly mutable.[108] Further, it was not fitting that a divine Person assume a created nature, since it implied an addition to the Person, making it perfect. God, i.e., the essence and all three Persons, was already perfect.[109] Likewise, it seems that what belongs to human nature could not be said of God, for God is uncreated, immutable, and eternal, while man is the opposite.[110] Thomas also stated that one would think that the Person of Christ should not be composed because composition implied parts, and there were no parts in the divine nature.[111] Thomas answered these objections by stating that it was not the Word (the Son) that changed and became perfected. It was man who became perfected when the Son assumed flesh. Though the contraries, God and man, could not be predicated on the same subject in the same respects, they might be so predicated in different respects. One could not divide Jesus into divine and human parts, hence there was no composition in him; the union of the two natures was the greatest of all unions.[112] Though one could count two natures, that did not mean that there was composition in God.

The Christians were also cognizant of the objection that God, who is eternal, was seemingly created. In a work attributed to Hugh of Saint Victor, the question was asked whether, since Christ was a man, he was not created like all men. The answer given was that Christ was not created; a human nature was simply added on to him. A further objection was mentioned by this author: was not the result of Word made flesh a composite of Creator and creature? This composition must have been created, for it did not always exist. Since this composition had a divine part, it followed that the Creator would be part of something created. The author answered this objection by stating that the union of Word and flesh was not a physical mixture; it was more like the union of coal and fire. Together they made something which was more then either coal or fire, yet the two elements remained distinct. Likewise, Divinity remained distinct and uncreated in the incarnated Son.[113]

Thomas argued similarly that the union of Divinity and humanity did not mean that God was created. The union, which was undoubtedly created since it did not exist eternally, actually occurred in the human nature, not in the divine nature.[114] One cannot even say that "Christ is a creature," because of God's simple noncomposite nature.[115] On the other hand, one may say, "Christ as man is a creature."[116]

God's Simple Unity Precludes Incarnation

According to Christian doctrine, only one of God's three Persons, the Son, became incarnate in Jesus. Even though Jesus was "truly God," not all of God assumed the flesh. The Jewish polemicists argued that such a doctrine was logically contradictory. If Jesus were indeed God, then all of God would have become incarnate.

This argument was made first by the author of *Nestor Ha-Komer*. He stated:

> Now be careful with your words, for they are self-contradictory. You have testified that God is one and Jesus is the Son of God, and there is one God who created everything by His word. You have further stated that he descended from heaven without separation from the Father or the Holy Spirit. The Holy Spirit attached itself to the two natures *[nihugim],*[117] (1) the divine nature and divine governance, and (2) the human nature, and he became a complete man. Jesus, who was the son, was straight without sin, and one nature did in no wise become separate from the other nature. Now tell me: when you say that the substance *[qinyan]* of the Son [attached itself] to Mary, [do you mean] that he himself descended while the Father and Holy Spirit remained by themselves; then you have contradicted your own words that there are three [inseparable] natures *[nihugim]* in one substance *[qinyan],* for there is one divine nature and one human nature [not just three natures and one substance]. I see now that Jesus was of two substances, not [only] of the substance of the Father and Holy Spirit, part of him attached [to Divinity], and part did not. Your statement that no part of Divinity is separate from another part is found to be false.[118]

The author went on to say that if Jesus had been fully attached to the Godhead and the Holy Spirit, then his body would have had to fill all dimensions of space, while the historical Jesus did not differ from all other men on earth.[119] (The rest of the argument is difficult to establish, since the text is obviously defective.)

Jacob ben Reuben paraphrased *Nestor,* which he cited by name, though he changed the argument slightly.

> You have said that God is one and this your messiah is His son who descended from heaven without separation from the Father and Holy Spirit. In this son there were two natures, the divine nature and the human nature, which were never separated. Now, when you say that the substance of the Son descended to Mary's womb, tell me if the Father and Spirit attached themselves to him [in that descent], or he alone attached himself to her. If you say only the Son and Spirit attached themselves, then your statement that there are [two] natures in one substance, [viz.] a divine nature and a human nature, is false because the nature of the Father is not at all in him.[120] Now, if you say the messiah was of the substance of the Father, Son and Holy Spirit, part adhering and part not adhering, your words, i.e., that one part did not separate from another part, are false.[121]

This argument was also quoted by Simon Duran,[122] Judah Aryeh de Modena,[123] Isaac Lupis,[124] and in *Kevod Elohim.*[125]

A Christian answer to this objection has been preserved in Jewish literature. Shem Tov ibn Shapruț quoted Abner of Burgos (Alfonso de Valladolid) as responding to this argument cited by Jacob ben Reuben by stating: "The sun illuminates and heats simultaneously, while it does not heat in the same way as it illuminates."[126] The import of Abner's analogy becomes clear through a comparison with one of his possible sources, the anti-Jewish polemical *Dialogus* of another converted Jew, Peter Alfonsi. When the Jewish interlocutor of this work asserted that one Person could not become incarnate while the others were not, Alfonsi replied that God could be compared to fire, which illuminates and heats. Sometimes light without heat is present; at other times heat and not light exists. Likewise, Alfonsi contended, one Person might be incarnate at the same time that the other Persons remained unembodied.[127]

Ibn Shapruț rejected the analogy which he quoted in the name of Abner. The sun's many activities were the result of its composition. God, on the other hand, was a simple, incorporeal intellect which admitted no multiplicity or composition.[128]

The argument against incarnation originated by the author of *Nestor Ha-Komer* was employed several times by Moses ben Solomon. The Christians must say, he argued, either that all of God became incarnate or that only part of Him did so. If they said that only part of God took on flesh, they thereby divided God, who is indivisible.[129]

A Christian Friar named Philip answered that whereas all of God and not part of Him received flesh, there was one thing in Divinity, namely, one of the Persons, that received flesh.[130] Moses ben Solomon responded that the Christians held that even if the three Persons were one essence, they were separate. If, then, one of the Persons became incarnate, it must have separated itself from the Divinity. If this were so, the original objection stands—part of God remained as it always had been without matter, and part received matter.[131]

Furthermore, if the Christian said that the Person was not other than the essence and the essence was one, then only part of God received matter. The many who said that all of God became incarnate attributed a measure and limit to Him. In addition, if God was one essence, the Father must also have become incarnate as did the Son. Why, then, did the Christians state that only the Son became incarnate? Or if they believed that all of God was in Jesus but not all of God received matter, they still were forced to divide God and to say that only part of Him received matter. The previous objections remained valid.[132]

Moses ben Solomon also argued against incarnation by referring to the Christian doctrine identifying the Father with God's power, the Son with His wisdom, and the Holy Spirit with his will. The Christians must hold that God was divided, since they all say that only the wisdom, and not the power or will, became incarnate.[133] In addition, if only wisdom took on flesh, the incarnated being was devoid of power and will. But if it were without power and will, it was not God because God has power, wisdom, and will inseparably. It was also an evil doctrine to believe the Father remained without wisdom.[134]

Moses ben Solomon continued: The Christians may say that the Son is powerful, wise, and willful as are the Father and the Holy Spirit. If this were so, he responded, there would be nine Gods; otherwise, one must admit that all three attributes became incarnate.[135] The polemicist went on in this vein with further arguments against any real plurality in God based upon His three attributes.[136]

Employing another refutation of incarnation, Moses ben Solomon again stated that if only God's wisdom took on flesh, God must have been divided. If the Christians responded that God did not become divided, one may ask them: Which of them (the Persons) was the messenger and which the sender? If the Son was the messenger, as the Christians held,[137] then only the Son, and not the other Persons, became incarnate.[138]

The point of all these arguments was to the effect that one could not maintain simultaneously that the three Persons in God were inextricably tied, while only one Person became incarnate. Joseph ben Shem Tov, commenting on Profiat Duran's statement that God took on flesh in only one of His attributes,[139] put this contention into a syllogism.

(A) All the Godhead became incarnate.
(B) The three attributes (Persons), the Father, the Son, and the Holy Spirit, constitute the Godhead.
Therefore (C) The three attributes, the Father, the Son, and the Holy Spirit, all became incarnate.

This conclusion was also seen from the fact that there was no difference between the essence and the Persons, the essence of the Son being the same as the essence of the Father and the Spirit, and it was the essence of the Son that became incarnate.[140]

This argument was repeated by Joseph ben Shem Tov in his commentary on Ḥasdai Crescas' *Tratado.*

> How can they say the Son is the one who became incarnate, but the Father and Spirit remained in their divine force? For they say that the Godhead is indivisible; it follows, and they agree, that the Godhead received flesh. Therefore, the whole Godhead changed and lost its separate essence. Still, they say that the Father did not receive flesh and he is God. Look at this contradiction! They make Him one and many, divisible and indivisible. When you look at the aspects [of their doctrine] which allow Him to be one and many, divisible and indivisible, and you see what is necessarily consequent upon their root principles, you will see that these are words which are merely uttered, having neither intellectual representation nor reality.[141]

The upshot of these arguments is that incarnation for merely one Person was impossible, since there could be no real distinction between the Persons themselves. God's unity, even the Christian indivisible Trinity in unity, was incompatible with the belief that only one Person became incarnate.

Meshullam ben Uri made the same point when he asked how the Father and Son could become separate.[142] Judah Aryeh de Modena argued in like manner, copying both the refutation presented by *Nestor Ha-Komer* and Jacob ben Reuben, and the syllogism offered by Joseph ben Shem Tov.[143]

This type of argumentation was found not only in Jewish literature. The author of the work attributed to the Muslim al-Ghazālī discussed this proof against Jesus' divinity, also expressing it in a syllogism.

(A) The messiah was crucified.
(B) Nothing that is crucified is God.

Therefore (C) Nothing of the messiah is God.[144]

He based this reasoning on the Christian doctrine that only the human nature, not God, was crucified and died. For the Christians, however, the fact that God was not crucified did not mean that Jesus, who was crucified, was merely a man, not God. They held that although only his human part was crucified, Jesus still had a divine nature.

The Christians were well aware of these arguments. In fact, Roscelin (d. 1120) was quoted by Anselm of Canterbury as having said:

> If the three Persons are only one thing *[una res]* and not three things *[tres res]*, each separate in itself, like three angels or three souls—being one in such a way, however, that the three are wholly the same in will and power—then the Father and the Holy Spirit were incarnate with the Son.[145]

Anselm explained Roscelin's thinking in the following manner:

> If God is numerically one and the same thing, and this very same thing is both Father and Son, then when the Son became incarnate, how is it that the Father also was not incarnate? For where two different things are involved, there is no reason why something should not be affirmed of one thing, while at the same time denied of the other.[146]

Anselm answered that the unity of Godhood and manhood in Jesus was not a unity of nature, since the natures remained distinct, but rather a unity of person. In such a unity of person, only one Person of the Godhead, not the whole divine nature of the three Persons, could become incarnate.[147]

In an anti-Jewish polemical work falsely attributed to Gilbert Crispin, *Disputatio Ecclesiae et Synagogae* (ca. 1150), the synagogue is portrayed as saying: "Since the Father is God, the Son is God, the Holy Spirit is God, it seems to me that there are three incarnate, and three have taken flesh."[148] The author of the disputation answered simply that only the Son became perfect God and perfect man *(perfectus Deus, perfectus homo)*.[149]

Both Peter Lombard [150] and Thomas Aquinas [151] raised the same question as to how only one part of the Trinity could become incarnate. They both answered by distinguishing between the actual operation of the incarnation and the term *(terminus)* of the incarnation. The act was accomplished by all three Persons since "the works of the Trinity are inseparable."[152] The term of the act, however, was only one Person, the Son. By acting together, as they always invariably did, the three Persons caused one of the Persons to assume flesh.[153]

A Union of Divinity and Humanity Is Impossible

The Christian theologians contended that when the Son of God assumed human flesh, a divine nature united with a human nature producing the one person of Jesus Christ. The natures remained distinct, but their union was a true union which implied in God neither corporeality nor mutability. The Jewish polemicists, for their part, asserted that any assumption of a union of Divinity and humanity did have consequences incompatible with God's nature. In making this claim, they referred to (1) the types of physical union and (2) the person of Jesus, who, they argued, could not have been both man and God.

Types of Physical Union

Yūsuf al-Başīr offered the following refutation of incarnation:

> As to the statement of the Christians about union, our previous demonstration that He is incorporeal refutes their doctrine. This is because union is conceivable only with two bodies that mix one with the other and which combine forming one thing, because the parts cannot be distinguished. This is why they have illustrated His union with Jesus as the union of water with *nabīd* [date or raisin wine], or as fire with coal. It has, however, been explained to you that such [a mixture] is the attribute of bodies.[154]

Only bodies could unite; God was not a body. Therefore, God could not unite with flesh to make a God-man.

Moses ben Solomon of Salerno analyzed the question in the following manner: It is well known, he averred, that when any two things unite, the more powerful one compels the weaker one. Thus, when water is placed in blood, the blood forces it to become red. In like manner, water placed in wine also becomes red. If Divinity assumed flesh, it would compel the resultant union to become divine. This was not the case, however, with "Ploni" (Jesus), who was totally flesh with all the qualities of flesh. How, then, could Divinity have participated with him? This doctrine, he concluded, was but vanity and folly.[155]

The most comprehensive Jewish critical investigation of the Christian doctrine of the divine-human union was formulated by Ḥasdai Crescas. He offered a number of arguments showing why the Christian belief was deficient not only in terms of its final cause, i.e., why God became man, but also in respect to its formal cause, i.e., how God became man.

Ḥasdai Crescas stated the Christian belief as follows:

> Man was close to God before his sin and faithlessness. When he rebelled and transgressed His command, God, may He be blessed, became removed from him by an infinite distance. It was by God's grace and mercy that, by means of an infinite union of Divinity and manhood, man was to be restored to his previous state close to Him, may He be blessed, through redemption from that sin. Therefore, divine wisdom necessitated that God, the Son, would become flesh in the virgin's womb and be unified with man in an indivisible unity, even after his death, in an attachment even greater than the unity of the soul with the body, so that he would suffer death and afflictions in the redemption of the universal sin of man.[156]

Crescas began his refutation by stating that incarnation was impossible, since it was based on the doctrine of the Trinity, the falseness of which Crescas had already demonstrated. Even assuming that there was a Trinity, incarnation was not fitting in terms of its final cause, because if man were in sin and needed to be redeemed, it would be impossible for God to unite with him. God would have to remove man's sin before such a union could take place. It would be better to say simply that God would forgive man's sin without becoming incarnate.[157]

Turning to his discussion of the union of Divinity and humanity itself, Crescas said that man was finite and God was infinite. Since nothing could be more impossible than predicating two contradictories together, it followed that God did not unite with man; God had not the power to reconcile two contradictories.[158]

This reflects an objection mentioned by Thomas[159] and quoted from him by de Modena.[160] The argument contended that it was not fitting to unite things which were infinitely apart, and since God was most simple and flesh was most composite, they were infinitely apart. Thomas answered that according to its natural endowments, human flesh should not unite itself to God. God, however, out of His infinite goodness, united flesh to Himself.[161]

Crescas continued with a discussion of different types of union. If the doctrine of incarnation were correct, then the God-man was neither God nor man, but a *tertium quid* which was composed of the two natures. This was manifest from an investigation of the four categories of physical union: composition,[162] blending or mixture, e.g., water and oil,[163] juxtaposition of place,[164] and the union of matter and form.[165] God's union with flesh could not be by composition, because no separate, noncorporeal substance could mix with a body, let alone divine nature with human nature. Similarly, the union could not be by blending or juxtaposition in place, since God could not be in a place. Therefore, the union must have been formal, with man as matter and God as form. This, however, would mean that the resultant union was neither man nor God, but a *tertium quid,* for such a union of matter and form must have been different from its constituent elements. Further, a union of this type would have required that God be mutable, for by becoming the form of a man, He necessarily changed. Finally, since the product of this union was neither God nor man, it follows that it was not man who suffered death, and therefore redemption was not by means of a man.[166]

According to Joseph ben Shem Tov, this was the strongest argument one could offer against the Christian doctrine of incarnation. If the Christians did not admit that God was the form of the man Jesus, then,

> Why do you say that He united [with man] or took on flesh? This necessitates that He be corrupted and His Godhood be corrupted. This is because God is incorporeal, but when He becomes a material or human form, He already ceases to be immaterial, having been made a non-immaterial force. When He ceases to be incorporeal, then corruption of His Divinity and essence is necessitated. That which corrupts cannot preserve itself in being, and, hence, He cannot become a human or bodily form. Their scholars do not know what to answer to this objection, uttering with their mouths that He is immutable; nevertheless, their doctrine necessitates that He change.[167]

Joseph ben Shem Tov recognized a number of possible difficulties with this Jewish argument. First, Jewish philosophers denied that God could be the form of a body since He was immaterial. Yet they taught that God was the "form of the world."[168] Joseph ben Shem Tov responded to this seeming contradiction by claiming that saying God was the form of the world did not mean that God was a form adhering to matter. Rather, God maintained the world permanently, just as form maintained matter. The expression "form of the world" was not to be taken literally.[169]

Another possible objection was seen in Averroes' doctrine, shared by some Jewish philosophers, that God was the mover of the outermost sphere. This might imply that God may indeed be a power in a body, and thus incarnation might also be possible. Having already established that God could not have the same relationship to matter that the soul has to body, Joseph ben Shem Tov argued that God did not move the sphere in the way a soul moved a body. Even as the mover of the outermost sphere, God would not be physically encompassed by the sphere. Aristotle had already explained that God brought about the motion of the spheres by being the object of their desire and love.[170] Since God's movement of the spheres was not the result of physical contact, no analogy can be drawn between the Averroist doctrine that God was the mover of the spheres and the Christian belief that God became incarnate.[171]

Averroes also taught that the Agent Intellect, which was immaterial, was the form of human intellects causing each person's material intellect to become actualized.[172] If the immaterial Agent Intellect becomes incarnate, as it were, in every man, could not God have become incarnate in one man? This argument is almost identical with a contention advanced by Abner of Burgos. According to this converted Jew, the existence of the Agent Intellect in each human being was a form of incarnation. Though Abner denied that this type of incarnation was the true incarnation which brought salvation, it is clear that he was addressing Jewish philosophers on their own terms, turning their own doctrines into arguments for Christianity.[173]

It is likely that Joseph ben Shem Tov was well aware of Abner's argument here. Thus while Abner quoted Themistius as having said: "I am the Agent Intellect," Joseph ben Shem Tov stated: "it can never be rightfully said that we are the Agent Intellect." Likewise, one cannot say that the Agent Intellect could become a man or change into human form. The Christians, on the other hand, claimed that Jesus was God because God acquired human form.[174] Joseph ben Shem Tov rejected, then, any resemblance between acceptable philosophical doctrines and the Christian dogma of incarnation.

The problem of the type of union exhibited by the incarnate Son of God was also discussed by the Christians. Thomas, for instance, analyzed the issue in much the same way as Crescas, coming, of course, to a different conclusion. Thomas said that there was no possible type of union by which God could have become incarnate in His nature. There are three types of union: composition, e.g., a heap of stones; mixture of predominance, e.g., a drop of water in a bottle of wine; and imperfection, e.g., as man is made of body and soul. Composition was an impossible mode of incarnation because the resultant union was accidental and relative, not essential and absolute as was the union of Word and flesh. Incarnation could not have been by mixture, because this would mean that either the nature of God changed into something else, a patent impossibility, or that human nature was absorbed by the divine nature, contradicting the doctrine of Jesus' two natures. Similarly, Godhood and manhood could not combine as body and soul, because God could not be a material form. In addition, if the union of God and man were as body and soul, Jesus would exist neither in divine nor in human nature, for neither nature would remain as it was.[175]

Thomas, then, agreed with Crescas and Joseph ben Shem Tov that any of the proposed methods of union cannot be ascribed to God. Nevertheless, he upheld incarnation. This was accomplished by positing that the union of Godhood and manhood took place in the Person of the Son, not in the nature or essence of God. If there were a union of natures, as Eutyches (a Monophysite) claimed, then the resultant would not be God or man, but rather a *tertium quid.*[176] The divine nature could not combine with anything material; one Person, though, may have assumed flesh.[177] What, then, of the statement in the Athanasian Creed that "as the rational soul and the flesh together are one man, so God and man together are one Christ?"[178] This likeness, answered Thomas, was not in terms of unity of nature, but only in terms of unity of person.[179]

Either Crescas and Joseph ben Shem Tov were ignorant of this subtle distinction, or they chose to ignore it. Even though Christian dogmatists accepted the Jewish contentions, they still maintained a belief in incarnation. They agreed with Thomas that a union of God and man in the manner of the union of body and soul would entail impossible consequences. It would seem, then, of no avail for Crescas to insist that the Christians must believe the union to be as form and matter, because this is not what they maintained.[180] On the other hand, Crescas' contentions demonstrated that the normal categories of union could not apply to the mode of incarnation. If the Christians wished to maintain a philosophically respectable explanation of incarnation, they must posit an extraordinary type of union.

After his arguments derived from the different modes of union, Crescas proceeded with more refutations of incarnation. If Divinity and manhood did unite, the resultant being should exhibit indivisibility. The Christians claimed that the union of Divinity and humanity in Jesus was more intimate than the unity of soul and body. Since even in the lowliest creature union is indivisible, one should expect the greater unity to be all the more indivisible. But if this were so, all the arguments mentioned previously would apply.[181]

Further, if incarnation were possible, it would follow that the Son divided into two parts at the time of Jesus' death. Since the Christians held that at the time of Jesus' death, the Son remained attached to both the body and soul, they must also believe that there were really two substances, a God-soul and a God-body. There was, thus, not one incarnation, but two.[182] In addition, after Jesus' death God's attachment to the soulless body was no longer to be considered as a union of Divinity and humanity. Man without a soul was no longer a man.[183]

It can be shown, then, that this indivisible unity of Godhood and manhood was actually capable of division. When God was posited to be united with both the separated soul and the body, He was no longer incarnate as man. Therefore, God could not be said to be absolutely united with man. "Would that I knew what is that substance which results from the union of Godhood with the flesh of the dead person, and how such attachment is possible!"[184] Crescas concluded with exegetical arguments drawn from Isaiah 31:3 and John 2:4.

Joseph ben Shem Tov added one more reason why the doctrine that God remained incarnate in Jesus' dead body was impossible. If God were really attached to the body, it should not be dead. If the soul, which was devoid of the true, eternal (divine) life, could provide life to the body when they were connected, certainly God, who was the true life, would give life to any body to which He was attached. Since God provided the soul with life-giving ability, certainly He had the same ability Himself. Therefore, it was not possible for God to be incarnate in a dead body.[185]

Crescas' and Joseph ben Shem Tov's arguments are reminiscent of a number of contentions against incarnation advanced by Moses ben Solomon of Salerno.[186] This polemicist frequently pointed to Jesus' death as proof that he was not God. If God, who was the "life of the world" (Dan. 12:7), were incarnate in Jesus, Jesus could not have died. Some Christians answered that God was not the form of Jesus, as a soul was the form of a human body, and therefore Jesus could die. Moses ben Solomon responded that the only type of union God could have exhibited with flesh was the union of form and matter.[187] Further, if Jesus had been God even when he was dead, then the Christians believed that God was a dead body.[188] Since the Christians held that Jesus' soul was the intermediary between his Divinity and his humanity,[189] when he died and his soul left, his Divinity must also have departed.[190] All of these proofs indicated that Jesus was a created, mortal man. God, however, was not created nor could He die. Hence, Jesus could not have been God.[191]

The Christians were not unaware of the possible objections raised by their doctrine that the union of natures continued after Jesus' death. They contended that even after the crucifixion God remained incarnate in both Jesus' body and his soul. Although the body and soul were separated, nevertheless there was still only one person of Christ. As John of Damascus said: "When Christ died his soul separated from his body, but even so, the one hypostasis was not divided into two."[192]

The arguments advanced by Crescas, Joseph ben Shem Tov, and Moses ben Solomon demonstrated that the doctrine of incarnation involved more than just the positing of a God-man. According to the Christians, Jesus was both God and man; the Jewish polemicists argued that even if one admitted the possibility of incarnation, Jesus would still have been a *tertium quid,* neither God nor man. The idea of a union of two natures in one person, with each nature remaining distinct, was philosophically impossible if one nature were divine. Further, the Christians claimed that this unity of the divine and human natures was indivisible; Crescas and the others challenged this belief in light of the Christians' claim that even after Jesus' death, Divinity remained attached to both the body and the soul. The union of God and soulless body, they said, could not be considered a union of God and man. The Jewish polemicists contended, then, that what the Christians claimed about incarnation was neither philosophically possible nor internally consistent.

The Person of Jesus

A subject which engaged Christian theologians concerned whether Jesus had a human rational soul in addition to his Divinity. The orthodox answer was in the affirmative: Jesus' human nature consisted of both a body and a soul.[193] Concerning this, Joseph Kimḥi asked the following question:

> Was the Divinity which became incarnate in Mary's womb itself the soul of Jesus, or did he have another soul in the way of all men? If you say that he had no soul other than the Divinity which became incarnate, though there was in the flesh an animal soul apart from Divinity, i.e. the blood which is [also] in beasts and fowl, then Divinity did not enter a man but an animal. Furthermore, since he had no rational soul apart from Divinity, to whom did Divinity cry when he shouted: My God, my God, why have you forsaken me (Ps. 22:2)? How is it that he could not save himself and that he cried to another? If you say that he had like other men a spirit which ascends upward and after this being the case, Divinity entered, then Jesus is like any other man in his body and soul. He is neither God nor the son of God but the Divinity adhered to him.[194]

Joseph ben Shem Tov suggested a similar method of refuting the doctrine of incarnation. One should ask the Christians whether Jesus possessed the primary axioms of truth *in potentia* or *in actu,* or both at the same time. If the Christian responded *in potentia* and *in actu,* this was impossible, for these were two contradictories. If he said that Jesus possessed them always *in potentia,* except for periods of isolation and speculation, then he was simply a man like all other wise men. If he answered, always *in actu,* never having been *in potentia,* because God, with whom the primary axioms were always *in actu,* was his form, then Jesus was both God and animal, and not man and God, since man could not possess the primary axioms eternally.[195] De Modena repeated this argument verbatim.[196]

Christian theologians were aware of the question of Jesus' knowledge. To solve this problem, they posited that he had actually two kinds of knowledge, divine and human. As God he knew everything eternally; as man his knowledge increased and changed.[197] By teaching such a doctrine, they tried to avoid the difficulty raised by Joseph ben Shem Tov, who assumed that one person had only one knowledge, not two.

As noted previously, the Christian position as articulated by Anselm of Canterbury was to the effect that only a God-man could give satisfaction for man's sin. Man by himself was too insignificant to achieve atonement, while God had no reason to offer Himself as satisfaction for man's transgression. Accordingly, only a God-man could bring redemption. By this self-sacrifice, Jesus, as both God and man, atoned for the sins of all men. Some Jewish polemicists argued that this cannot be so. Solomon ibn Verga phrased the objection as follows:

> If God became incarnate in order to receive an infinite punishment for the sin of Adam who sinned against the Infinite, who received this punishment? If we say the divine part, this is impossible, for He cannot die. If it was the flesh part, it is well known that flesh is limited. How can we say, then, that he received an infinite punishment.[198]

Joseph ben Shem Tov also asked whether it was God or man who suffered and, thereby, redeemed man. First, he inquired whether the redemption was a result of grace or justice. If it was by means of grace, what grace was there in God's being dishonored and put to death? If the redemption was by means of justice, what justice was there in God's being punished for man's sin? Did Scripture not say: "Every man shall be put to death for his own sin"? The Christians might respond that only the human nature, not the divine nature, was punished. In that case, why should this one human be punished for Adam's sin, especially since Jesus, according to the Christians, was born without original sin? Further, if only the human nature was punished, how could this man's death be sufficient to atone for the universal sin of the human species? If one said that it was not God who died, what purpose was there to incarnation altogether? Joseph ben Shem Tov concluded that despite the denial by Christians that God Himself was crucified, one could still interpret their doctrine to imply that He was. In the case of a thieving merchant who was executed, one may justifiably state that the merchant was executed, even though he was not punished as a merchant but as a thief.[199]

Conclusions

As was the case with the philosophical critique of the Trinity, the Jewish refutation of incarnation consisted of arguments well familiar to the Christians. The speculative principles which underlay this critique were common to believers of both faiths. Their disagreement was not on the rationally derived philosophical conception of God; both the Jewish and Christian thinkers contended that, given the commonly accepted philosophical principles, God could not have become a man. They did disagree, however, on the implications of incarnation. The Jewish polemicists argued that this Christian doctrine did imply philosophical absurdities, such as God's becoming a man. The Christian theologians taught that God merely assumed human flesh, the result being a God-man. The Jewish polemicists rejected such a theory. In their view, the Christians tried to maintain two contradictory doctrines at the same time. The Christian theologians, who were aware of these seeming contradictions, made the claim that their belief was not incompatible with reason.

The Jewish arguments, then, were not sufficient to convince the Christians that their belief was illogical. They did, however, play an important role in highlighting the real differences between Judaism and Christianity. The philosophical doctrines held by the adherents of both faiths were generally in accord, but the theological beliefs were divergent. Once again we find that philosophy was used as a handmaiden of theology. The Jewish polemicists employed it as a means of attacking their opponents' beliefs, hoping thereby to demonstrate logical flaws in the Christian faith. Christians, for their part, tried to show that their doctrines were not incompatible with reason. Theology, then, not philosophy, was the major consideration of the theologians.

CHAPTER SIX

Transubstantiation

One topic of discussion that arose frequently in the Jewish-Christian debates of the Middle Ages was the relative value of two ceremonial rituals, the Jewish animal sacrifices[1] and the Christian Eucharist. Some of the arguments centered around both the appropriateness and the efficacy of the two modes of worship. Thus, a Christian was quoted as saying:

> Your modes of worship are polluted with the burning of meat and fats, and the sprinkling of blood. But our worship is clean, using bread and wine, and completely atones for all our sins when we eat the bread of our God, for we become holy. And he, whose God is in him, will not fear any evil thing.[2]

The Jewish polemicists usually answered the claim of the efficacy of the mass by citing the true usefulness of animal sacrifices, as recorded in the Bible, contrasted to the unverifiable Christian belief concerning the Eucharist. The sacrifices had resulted in the miraculous descent of fire from heaven, the resting of God's presence on Israel, and the priest's oracular ability with the Urim and Thummim.

> Nothing like this can be cited in all the offerings of the Christians. They cannot show a single continuous and public sign, well known to all, as in the sacrifices.[3] Their statement that their offerings benefit the soul, is one which is not testified to by the senses nor proved by the intellect. The rabbis say in reference to such a statement, if one desires to lie let him cite witnesses which are far away.[4]

After giving a similar answer, Shem Tov ibn Shapruṭ responded to the charge that the Jewish sacrifices were "polluted" and Christian sacrifices were clean.

Something that shows no such properties attached to it cannot be compared to that which has the wonderful properties. Should we say that silver is more fitting to be a nutrient because it is cleaner than meat?[5]

The Jewish polemicists were not content simply to compare the efficacy of the animal sacrifices to the uselessness of the mass, whose results were not apparent. They went further and disputed the very foundation of the Christian reenactment of the Lord's Supper. This reenactment was based on the dogma that the bread and wine used in the mass actually became the body and blood of Christ. This doctrine is called transubstantiation. It is the philosophical arguments against transubstantiation that will interest us here.

The Jewish polemicists had a rather clear picture of the doctrine of transubstantiation. Profiat Duran, for instance, relied heavily on Peter Lombard's *Sententiae* in giving the following account:[6]

One of the principles of their religion, which the "misleaders"[7] established, was that Jesus, in the same quantity in which he was crucified,[8] will come and apply himself to any quantity whatsoever of bread made from wheat.[9] The bread will cast off its substantial form of bread[10] and will receive the whole body of Jesus, while at the same time the accidents of the bread, such as quality and quantity and others, will remain without a subject.[11] It is he himself who, sitting in the heavens, comes to the altar even though he remains there [in the heavens]. It is he himself who is one in different places.[12] It is he himself who moves on the altar in different places while he is in heaven, and no matter how the bread is divided,[13] he stills exists in the same quantity in which he was crucified, such as a broken mirror in which the form of the person looking into it is seen fully in each part of it.[14] Similarly, he also exists in the wine pressed from grapes offered on the altar.[15] When one eats this bread and drinks this wine, the body of Jesus will unite with the body of the eater and the drinker.[16] It will remain, thus, kept inside his stomach, until the accidents of the bread, remaining after the corruption of their form, themselves become corrupted. According to them, this happens to the bread and wine after certain words are recited by the officiant priest designated for this rite, may he be old or young, wise or ignorant, righteous or evil, for the pope, Jesus' substitute on earth, has the power to confer this authority upon any priest.[17] This is so since the formula itself has the power to call down the body of Jesus from the heavenly heights[18] and to bring it through an eight-thousand-year journey[19] to an infinite number of altars while it remains in heaven quietly and peacefully.[20]

Joseph Albo summarized this doctrine much more succinctly.

For they say that the body of Jesus, which is in heaven and is of very great extension and magnitude, comes to the altar and clothes itself in the bread and wine as soon as the priest has pronounced the word—no matter who the priest is—a good man or a bad—and the whole becomes one with the body of the messiah, who comes down from heaven instantaneously. And after the bread and wine have been consumed, he goes up to the heaven again where he was before. This takes place at every altar.[21]

A survey of other Jewish formulations of the transubstantiation doctrine shows a similar, if not as detailed, knowledge of the Christian doctrine. Such descriptions were given by Ḥasdai Crescas,[22] Shem Tov ibn Shapruṭ,[23] Simon Duran,[24] Don David Nasi,[25] Elijah Ḥayyim ben Benjamin of Genazzano,[26] Abraham Farissol,[27] Yair ben Shabbetai of Correggio,[28] Isaac Lupis,[29] Jonah Rappa,[30] Joshua Segré,[31] and the authors of *Kevod Elohim*[32] and *Makkot Li-Khesil Me'ah.*[33] The Jewish polemicists, then, had a rather clear picture of the Christian doctrine of transubstantiation.

For many Christians, the sacrament of the Eucharist and the doctrine of transubstantiation were mysteries that were not amenable to rational investigation. "A mystery of the faith can be believed healthfully, but it cannot be investigated healthfully."[34] Gabriel Biel (d. 1495) suggested that one should not be too curious concerning the problems of transubstantiation, for God, "who created the world out of nothing and is able to return the world to nothing when He pleases," certainly is capable of anything.[35]

The Jewish polemicists were not unaware that Christians considered the mystery of the Eucharist beyond rational proof. Duran, for instance, in *Kelimat Ha-Goyim,* stated the Christian belief that since Jesus established the Eucharistic rite, it cannot be questioned.[36] He proceeded, then, to analyze the New Testament sources to prove that, in fact, Jesus had no intention of establishing the practice of the mass.[37] Duran was followed in this method by Ibn Shapruṭ[38] and Farissol,[39] both of whom were largely dependent upon him.

Yet the fact that mysteries were not rationally provable did not mean that Christian thinkers refrained from trying to give a philosophical underpinning to this doctrine.

Although, of course, the divine power operates with a greater sublimity and secrecy in this sacrament than a man's inquiry can search out, nonetheless, lest the teaching of the Church regarding this sacrament appear impossible to unbelievers, one must make the endeavor to exclude every impossibility.[40]

Since the Jews knew that Christians were using rational arguments to uphold transubstantiation, despite its essential mystery, it was only natural that they countered with their own philosophical contentions. And, as we shall see, the Jewish arguments were often taken from the Christian works themselves.

The orthodox Catholic doctrine of the Eucharist and transubstantiation, as first definitively established by the Fourth Lateran Council,[41] and later reestablished by the Council of Trent against the reformers (1547),[42] was not uniformly accepted by all Christians. In fact, two parallel patristic traditions on the subject were kept alive in the early Middle Ages. The Neoplatonic Augustinian tradition,[43] which was finally repudiated, was carried on by John Scotus Erigena, Ratramnus, Rabanus Maurus, and the chief heresiarch, Berengarius of Tours.[44] This rejected doctrine held that the presence of Christ in the Eucharist was not physically real but was only symbolic. The second tradition, that of Ambrose,[45] became dominant; it was supported by Paschasius Radbertus, Lanfranc, Guitmond of Aversa, Alger of Liège, Lombard, Thomas, and many others. These thinkers taught that the presence of Christ on the altar was real, in that the bread and the wine changed substantially into the body and blood of the messiah. Transubstantiation, a term first used in the early twelfth century, was the process by which the bread and wine became converted into the real presence.[46]

Despite the defeat of Berengarius in the eleventh century, and the codification of the Ambrosian "real-presence" theory in the thirteenth, opposition in the Church remained. The definition of the Fourth Lateran Council was directed against the Albigensians.[47] Transubstantiation was again upheld in 1341 against the figurative belief of the Armenians.[48] Further objections to the interpretation of the Eucharist in terms of transubstantiation were expressed by John Wyclif (ca. 1329–84), the followers of John Huss, and, of course, by the Protestant reformers of the sixteenth century, Martin Luther, Ulrich Zwingli, John Calvin, and many others.[49] It might be said that internal Christian opposition to the doctrine of transubstantiation was an ongoing, though somewhat suppressed, movement in the Middle Ages. As we shall see, the Jews were very aware of this movement and its argumentation.

The Jewish use of specifically philosophical arguments against transubstantiation, though, came surprisingly late. Whereas Berengarius (1000–1088) was the first Christian to employ such methodology against the "real-presence" theory,[50] we do not find Jewish polemicists employing rational proofs against transubstantiation until three hundred years later.[51] This is even more surprising considering the fact that the centuries between Berengarius and Profiat Duran, the first Jew to use such arguments, were full of philosophical expositions of transubstantiation by Christians. Still, Jewish polemicists did not use philosophical arguments until the end of the fourteenth century.

A number of reasons can be suggested for this late appearance of philosophical anti-Eucharistic polemics. Could it be that the full implication of this doctrine was just not understood by the Jews until then, whether from lack of interest or from underestimating the importance of the mass? Was this interest in the Eucharist brought about by the growing popularity of host adoration as expressed in the exposition of the host and the Feast of the Corpus Christi?[52] Or was there a connection between Jewish arguments against transubstantiation in late-fourteenth-century Spain and the host desecration libel of Barcelona, 1367, in which Ḥasdai Crescas was one of those arrested and detained?[53] This question needs further research.

Whatever the reason for the late appearance of Jewish philosophical arguments against transubstantiation, it is certain that by the time of their appearance, some Jews already had a good idea of the internal Christian objections to the real presence. This fact is evident not only from the arguments themselves, but also from specific statements in the polemics. Thus, Profiat Duran, citing texts from the New Testament as proof that Jesus had no intention of establishing the Eucharistic doctrine, stated that the traditional Christian interpretation was very weak, and "already some of them have realized its weakness."[54] Joseph ben Shem Tov described the Christian doctrine and stated: "They have no doubt about this and do not interpret it figuratively;[55] rather, they believe it literally, and he who raises rational objections to it is labeled a heretic."[56] We see, then, that Jewish cognizance of Christian opposition to transubstantiation was acknowledged.

We have now established that some of the Jewish polemicists had a very good understanding of the doctrine of transubstantiation and the internal Christian criticism of it. The Jewish critique, using the Christian arguments, began late in the fourteenth century. It is now time to turn to specific Jewish philosophical arguments.

The first Jewish polemicist to offer a comprehensive, philosophical critique of the doctrine of transubstantiation was Profiat Duran in his *Iggeret Al Tehi Ke–'Avotekha.*[57] Duran claimed that the whole idea of transubstantiation ran counter to the principles of the rational sciences. Thus, writing in his satirical manner to David Bonet Bonjorn, Duran stated: "Be not like your fathers who were obliged by the foundations of the intellect to accept the speculative principles, those of mathematics, physics, and metaphysics."[58] The scientific principles which were rejected by the proponents of transubstantiation were then enumerated, each science in turn.

Other Jewish polemicists, though relying upon Duran's arguments, used different frameworks to present their contentions. Thus, Joseph Albo divided his critique into an examination of those Christian principles that were in conflict with first principles and those in conflict with sense perception.[59] Elijah Ḥayyim ben Benjamin was content merely to say that this doctrine was against first principles,[60] while Elijah del Medigo said that it contradicted sense perception.[61] It is possible that these distinctions also go back to Duran, who stated in *Kelimat Ha-Goyim* that transubstantiation was based on principles which "contradict the nature of existence, refute sense perception, and contradict first principles."[62] Farissol contended that this doctrine was against reason, against what is self-evident and commonly accepted, and against the truth.[63] Other polemicists listed the various arguments against transubstantiation in no discernible order.[64]

The philosophical arguments to be discussed here have been drawn from the various sources and will be divided into five categories: (1) the interpenetrability of bodies; (2) the concepts of number and place; (3) the concept of motion; (4) the problem of accidents; and (5) miscellaneous arguments.

The Interpenetrability of Bodies

The impossibility of one body entering another body, without the displacement of the latter, was stated by Aristotle. We know that place exists because "what now contains air formerly contained water, so that clearly the place or space into which and out of which they passed was something different from both."[65] Water and air cannot exist together in the same place. Further, an argument against vacuums was based on the idea that if the void existed, one body could enter another body.[66] The impossibility of two bodies being in one place was also a consideration when trying to understand how plants grow.[67] Put succinctly, if one body could enter another, "the whole world could enter into a grain of mustard seed."[68]

The Jewish polemicists, accepting this principle, saw three basic contradictions in transubstantiation that related to the problem of the interpenetrability of bodies. (1) How could the body of Jesus enter into another body, that of the bread? (2) Assuming that Jesus could enter the bread, how could his large body fit into the smaller dimensions of the bread? (3) Even if one assumed the entrance into the bread, how could Jesus pass through the body of the heavens to the altars without causing damage to the heavens?

How Could the Body of Jesus Enter Bread?

If one body cannot enter another without the latter's displacement, how could Jesus' body enter into the sacramental bread, while the bread remained where it was? Joseph Albo stated:

> They say that the flesh and the blood which comes into being at the particular moment from the substance of the bread and the wine, which is finite and limited, is the very body of the messiah, who existed from eternity, and does not thereby increase or diminish in quantity. This leads to belief in the interpenetration of bodies.[69]

How Could Jesus' Large Body Fit into Smaller Dimensions?

A second ramification of this principle is involved, namely, the impossibility of a larger body entering into a smaller body. Duran pointed out that according to the principles of mathematics, the large and the small are different, and, as such, one cannot become the other. How, then, could the large body of Jesus become the small wafer of bread?[70]

This argument is a paraphrase of an objection raised by Thomas.

> A larger sized body cannot be completely contained under similar dimensions. Yet the dimensions of the consecrated bread and wine are much less than the dimensions of Christ's body. Hence, it cannot be that the whole body of Christ is under this sacrament.[71]

Thomas answered this objection by stating that it was the substance of Christ, not the dimensions of the body and blood, which was in the sacrament, by means of the sacramental sign. "The whole specific nature of a substance is as truly contained by small as by large dimensions."[72] Still, Duran used the same argument against transubstantiation, and Shem Tov ibn Shapruṭ[73] and Simon Duran[74] followed his lead.

How Could Jesus Pass Through the Heavens Without Damaging Them?

The third problem was how the body of Christ traveled from the heavens to the altars without damaging either itself or the heavens. Duran, and after him Crescas, gave two possibilities.

1. First, one could reject the physical truth that the body of the heavens had only circular motion. This principle, claimed by Aristotle,[75] meant that the motion of the heavens was uniform and continuous, allowing no tearing or rending. But, argued Duran:

> The body of the messiah, in ascending and descending perpetually every day, cannot help but have caused the body of the heavens to become full of passages and orifices.[76] Since it is now nearly thirteen hundred sixty years since Jesus' ascent to heaven, the heavens must now be like a sieve, or solely by his will or his speech, Jesus must be able to cure them without drugs.[77]

Duran's implication was that such a description of Jesus' ascent and descent was ridiculous. Crescas[78] and Albo[79] made similar arguments.

2. The belief in an alternative method of descent was founded on the belief that one body was able to penetrate another body; but this was impossible, as has been shown. What Duran most probably meant by this alternative method becomes clear from a statement by Crescas. According to Crescas, the alternative to one's having to assume a rending of the heavens is the belief in a body *glorificado,* which could enter the heavens without tearing the heavenly bodies, since it was presumed to be an ethereal body which occupied no space and had no dimensions.[80] Joseph ben Shem Tov also understood Duran to be referring to a *corpo glorificado.*[81]

What did a "glorified body" signify? The reference here was to the theory of transubstantiation offered by William of Auvergne (d. 1249). This thinker explained instantaneous presence in terms of the glorified body of Christ, whose agility permitted this otherwise impossible feat.[82] Bonaventure also stated that the glorified body of Christ might be able to be together with the bread.[83] Albertus Magnus referred to the opinion that the body of Christ was a "glorious body capable of co-existing with another body in the same place."[84] The term "glorified body" was used also to describe the state of the body of the faithful at resurrection.[85] Joseph ben Shem Tov knew this belief, too. He stated that the Christians expected that "even after their resurrection they will all merit that their bodies be after this fashion."[86]

Crescas' objection to a solution of this kind was that the glorified body was "a pure figment of the imagination that has no real existence."[87] He based this claim on his examination of the theory of the glorified body in relation to the dogma of the virgin birth.[88] Crescas argued that the glorified body must have extension, since if it did not, it would be a body and not a body at the same time.[89] But if it did have extension, it would not be able to pass out of the virgin's womb. Nor could the glorified body enter into another body because both bodies would have dimensions, which would prevent their interpenetrability. If, indeed, one body could enter another body, then two cubits could be one cubit, the part could be like the whole, and the whole world could enter into a mustard seed.[90] Joseph ben Shem Tov offered a similar argument against the doctrine of the glorified body, also stressing that if the glorified body were a body, it must have had dimensions, and if it had dimensions, it could not interpenetrate another body with dimensions.[91]

Abraham Farissol raised another objection to this Christian doctrine. If transubstantiation occurred, then there would be a real composition of a divine glorified body with a nonglorified body.

> Either the nonglorified body would become a divine glorified body, or the divine glorified body would become nonglorified, since the bread made of flour and water always remains real and material. Thus, if together they form one God, the priest eats this glorified body with parts of the bread's accidents.[92]

It would follow, then, that the priest would not be eating merely the divine glorified body of Christ, as Christians claimed, but a mixture of a glorified and a nonglorified body.

For the Jewish polemicists, then, the faith in Jesus' descent from heaven required that one accept either the rending of the heavens or a special glorified body. Duran suggested to his Christian correspondent that he take the alternative which went against reason and nature most.[93]

The Concepts of Number and Place

Two different kinds of arguments can be distinguished in this category. (1) How could there be only one messiah if his body were found on many altars simultaneously? (2) How could one body be in more than one place at the same time?

Simultaneity of Jesus' Body on Many Altars Remaining One

According to Aristotle, a number is a plurality of units.[94] But the Christians believed that even if the body of Christ were to be found on many altars at the same time, one could not add up all the different appearances and come up with more than one body of Christ. For Duran, this belief obviously contradicted the mathematical principle just enounced, since according to the doctrine of transubstantiation, the plurality of units did not make up a number, but only a single unit, one. Accordingly, ten, one hundred, and one thousand would all be equal to each other.[95] Shem Tov ibn Shapruṭ presented the same argument.[96]

This argument goes back to Berengarius, who said that if the body of Christ were actually on the altar, there would be a million bodies of Christ at the same time.[97]

Simultaneity of Jesus' Body Being in Many Places

Joseph ben Shem Tov related the mathematical argument just stated to a physical argument found in both Crescas and Albo, namely, the impossibility that one body could be in two places at the same time. This argument had two applications. Crescas saw the inconsistency in the circumstance that:

> At the same time as God, the Son, is in the heavens, he is also in the hand of the priest; it follows from this that he would be in many different places at the same time. Just as we see him at thousands and tens of thousands (and hundreds) of altars,[98] there either would be many gods or one body would be substantially present at many places at one time.[99]

The other aspect of the problem was the simultaneity of existence on many altars at the same time. "It requires belief in the simultaneous presence of one body in two or more places; for the body of the messiah is present on different altars at the same time."[100] Similarly, Farissol asked how it was possible that at one time one individual substance became collected in several different substances in different places.[101]

This argument may draw its impetus from Maimonides. In proving that God was incorporeal, Maimonides quoted Deuteronomy 4:39: "The Lord is God in heaven above and on the earth below." Since God was both in heaven and earth, He could not be corporeal, for no body could be in two places at the same time.[102]

The Christians were aware of such arguments deriving from the impossibility of one body being in more than one place at the same time, whether that body be both in heaven and on earth, or in many places on earth. Thus, for instance, Thomas mentioned the following objection:

> No body can be in several places at once. Not even an angel has that power; if he had he could be everywhere. But the body of Christ is a real body and it is in heaven. Therefore, it seems that it cannot be in the sacrament of the altar in very truth, but only as in its sign.[103]

Regarding the simultaneity of presence at many altars, Thomas noted the objection that:

> It is further impossible that one body should exist in many places. But, manifestly, this sacrament is celebrated in many places. Therefore, it seems impossible that the body of Christ is truthfully contained in this sacrament—unless one says, perhaps, that the body is contained in one of its particles here, and in another there.[104]

Thomas, of course, provided answers to these objections, but this did not prevent the Jewish polemicists from repeating them.

A striking Christian rebuttal to these Jewish contentions has also been preserved. Some Christian polemicists asked how the Jews could deny the simultaneous presence of Christ on many altars, when they themselves believed in Elijah's appearance at every circumcision, even if two or more were held at the same time in different places. The Jewish answer simply distinguished between the symbolic aspects of "Elijah's chair" and the Christian belief in the real presence.[105]

The Concept of Motion

The Jewish polemicists offered two arguments against transubstantiation using the concept of motion. (1) Motion in no time was impossible, and (2) a body could not be both in motion and at rest at the same time.

Motion in No Time Is Impossible

The change in the elements of the Eucharist into the body of Christ was held to take place instantaneously.[106] Assuming that the body of Christ descended from the heavens and entered the bread and wine at the exact moment of consecration, then it must have reached the altar in no time. But Aristotle had proved that all motion was in time.[107] Therefore, Jesus' descent from heaven, especially through a distance normally involving an eight-thousand-year journey, could not have been instantaneous; and so it was impossible that the body of Jesus entered the elements of the Eucharist from the outside. This argument was made by Duran,[108] Crescas,[109] and Albo.[110] Crescas also stated that the only alternative to entrance from the outside through instantaneous motion was the creation of the body of Jesus in the dimensions of the bread. "It is not possible that it be created there since that would necessitate that God is created and corrupted, along with many other impossibilities."[111]

Thomas agreed that if the body of Christ were to enter the bread by local motion, such motion would have to be instantaneous. Since, however, instantaneous motion was impossible, the change was effected by transubstantiation (conversion), not by local motion.[112]

One Body Cannot Be in Motion and Rest at the Same Time

Profiat Duran twice argued that transubstantiation was impossible because one body could not be in motion and at rest at the same time. The first time that Duran suggested this argument, he phrased it as a physical proof,[113] basing himself on Aristotle's conclusion that one body could not be both in motion and at rest at the same time.[114] Turning to metaphysical proofs, Duran repeated[115] Aristotle's principle that a thing could not at the same time be and not be.[116] Thus, a thing could not both be in motion and not be in motion, i.e., at rest. If the body of Jesus really entered into the bread as it remained in the heavens, it would follow that the body of Jesus was at rest (in the heavens) and in motion (on the altar) at the same time. Thus, transubstantiation was not possible, from both physical and metaphysical considerations. This same argument was repeated by Ibn Shapruṭ[117] and Simon Duran.[118]

Thomas agreed with this argument: "You cannot have something in movement and at rest at the same time; that would be to affirm contraries of the same thing. Now the body of Christ in heaven is at rest. Therefore, it is not in movement in this sacrament."[119] According to Thomas, then, the body of Christ was always at rest; when the host was moved on the altar, then the body of Christ moved only accidentally.[120]

The Problem of Accidents

A major problem that faced the Christian thinkers, as they sought to explain transubstantiation, was the seeming impossibility of accidents subsisting without a subject. Whereas the substances of the bread and wine were replaced by a different substance, namely, that of Christ, their accidents, such as color, size, weight, taste, etc., remained without a subject. This was the main issue on which Berengarius rejected the real substantial presence of Christ in the sacrament.[121] Wyclif, who also rejected transubstantiation, often referred to the problem of accidents.[122] The Christians, then, were well aware of the difficulties caused by the question of the accidents.

As the Jewish polemicists approached this problem, they divided their criticism into three recognizable categories. (1) How could accidents be without subjects? (2) The senses must not be deceived by what they perceive. (3) Substance could not become accident, nor accident substance.

How Can Accidents Be Without Subjects?

One of Aristotle's definitions of substance was that which was "the ultimate substratum, which cannot be further predicated of something else."[123] Accidents, however, were predicated of subjects.[124] Thus, substance came before accidents; if the substance departed, the accidents could not remain.[125] But, argued Duran, with the completion of the sacramental formula, the substance of bread could no longer be present at all, and therefore the accidents would have to remain in themselves, not in a subject.[126] This was repeated by Crescas: "It would be necessary that as he ascends to heaven, the accidents of the bread, i.e., its qualities, its color, its smell, its form, its taste, etc., subsist in themselves without a subject which is contrary to all nature and possibility."[127] Simon Duran gave the same argument, stating that this type of belief was a Mu'tazilite one.[128] Ibn Shapruṭ[129] and Albo[130] also repeated this argument.

Thomas knew of this problem, which he stated in a number of ways. First, he considered the objection that the accidents could not remain because the substance of bread no longer remained.[131] Since, however, the accidents did remain, it was necessary to find a subject for them. "For accidents to be without a subject is against the natural order of things for which God is responsible."[132] Since the subject of the accidents could not be either the body of Christ or the surrounding air or they themselves, and in order to be individuated they must have a subject, it appeared that the substance of the bread and wine remained.[133] Thomas solved this problem by positing the dimensive quantity of the bread and wine as the subject for the other accidents.[134] If this were so, then the substances of bread and wine would disappear after all.

The Senses Must Not Be Deceived

Profiat Duran stated that a principle of the science of optics was that "the sense of sight is not mistaken in that which it perceives, as long as the organ is healthy and the medium is fitting."[135] Therefore, when one saw the accidents remaining, and did not see God ascend from the host, one would have to conclude that nothing in the bread and wine had changed. This argument was also used by Ibn Shapruṭ[136] and by Albo, who cited it as proof that the Christian doctrine was in conflict with sense perception.[137] Elijah del Medigo, who cited this sacrament as one example of the unreasonable nature of Christianity, said that the Eucharistic belief presupposed that the senses of all people at all times were mistaken about a specific, sensible object.[138] We do not accept Christianity, he averred, because it contradicted sense perception, as one sees from their sacrifice.[139]

The Christians were well aware that the senses testified to the permanence of the appearance of bread. Thus, Ambrose stated: "But perhaps you say: 'I do not see the appearance of blood.'"[140] Berengarius, referring to Ambrose, agreed that with one's physical eyes one saw only bread and wine. The body and blood could be seen only with the spiritual eyes, and therefore the body of Christ was in the sacrament only figuratively.[141] Ambrose was also quoted by Lombard, who said that the senses must be believed in this sacrament.[142] Wyclif, rejecting transubstantiation, appealed to the testimony of the senses that the body of Christ was not seen in the host.[143]

Thomas agreed that according to the judgment of the senses the bread remained after the sacramental words, and that it was not befitting a sacrament that the senses be deceived thereby. Moreover, human reason also judged that the bread remained, because the accidents remained, and it was not fitting that human reason be deceived.[144] Besides, the senses were never deceived about their proper sensible objects.[145] Still, the orthodox Christian belief, which Thomas upheld, was that the substances of the bread and wine were changed into the substance of the body and blood of Christ, and the accidents remained, the dimensive quantity being their subject. There was no deception because the perceived accidents were actually there.

Substance Cannot Become Accident, nor Accident Substance

The impossibility of substance becoming accident or accident becoming substance was based on the principle that when two things were essentially opposed, one of them could never become the other.[146] Substance and accident were essentially different.[147] Therefore, substance and accident could not become each other. This conclusion had two applications to the transubstantiation polemic.

1. According to Profiat Duran, before the pronouncement of the sacramental formula, the bread was the substance of bread. After the formula was recited, all that was left of the bread were its accidents. It followed, then, that the substance had turned into accidents.[148]

2. The accidents should not become substance. But if the bread were eaten, nourished the priest, and then changed into an organ of the priest, it followed that either the substance of the bread was still in the consecrated Eucharist or that these accidents became a substance.[149] Crescas,[150] Ibn Shapruṭ,[151] and Simon Duran[152] repeated this argument in the same form, but Albo changed it slightly. He said that the Christians claimed that these accidents did not nourish, but sense perception informed us that indeed they did.[153] Del Medigo also objected to the idea that accidents became substances.[154] Farissol, however, combined the two aspects of the problem, asking: "How is it possible that the substance becomes accident and the accident becomes substance?"[155]

Thomas agreed that when two things were diverse, one never became the other. This raised the question how one substance, that of the bread, became another diverse substance, that of the body of Christ.[156] Though Thomas explained that such a conversion was possible, Del Medigo stated that it was impossible that one substance become another without generation and corruption.[157]

Thomas was also aware that since the sacramental species (the accidents) were not substance, they should not nourish.[158] This problem was solved by the conclusion that the sacramental species could be converted into a substance generated from them. Therefore, they could nourish.[159] In this case, as in those enumerated above, as far as the Jewish polemicists were concerned, the solutions offered by Thomas did not solve the problems that he himself had raised.

Miscellaneous Arguments

1. According to the Christians, no matter how many times the host was divided, the whole body of Christ was still present in each and every piece. It followed, then, that the host could be divided infinitely and each little piece *(portiuncula)* would still contain the whole of Christ. If this were so, then the whole bread was the whole body, and each part of the bread was also the whole body. Therefore, a part would be equal to the whole. This was logically impossible. This argument was made by Profiat[160] and Simon Duran,[161] Ibn Shapruṭ,[162] and Farissol.[163]

2. According to Maimonides, "the impossible has a permanent nature."[164] If one were to admit the possibility of transubstantiation, then it followed that anything imaginable, illogical as it might be, could exist. This, indeed, was a principle of the Kalam, which Maimonides refuted.[165] It is for this reason also that Profiat Duran objected to transubstantiation.[166] Del Medigo also used this argument.

> Should someone say: Do you, too, not say that God is omnipotent and, therefore, some of these things [incarnation, transubstantiation] are possible, we answer that we religionists do not say that God can be predicated as having powers over contradictory and contrary matters; rather, we say, He has no desire for them at all.[167]

3. Crescas argued that if one agreed to transubstantiation, then the son of God could be created and destroyed everywhere. Since it was part of the nature of God not to come into being or to be destroyed, transubstantiation was not possible.[168]

Conclusions

These are the Jewish philosophical arguments against transubstantiation. We have seen that the Jewish polemicists used a large range of philosophical arguments against this doctrine, most of which were already found in Christian sources. It was Profiat Duran who put the Christian criticism into a Jewish framework, and it was from his works that later Jewish polemicists borrowed. Given the fact that most of the arguments were originally Christian, we may ask whether there was anything specifically Jewish in the Jewish polemic against transubstantiation.

What distinguished the Jewish arguments from those of their Christian predecessors was their purpose. The Jewish polemicists were not interested in proving that Christ's presence in the Eucharist was figurative and not substantial, as was the heterodox Christian view. Instead, they sought to show that Christianity was irrational and in contradiction to science. Hence, they chose for criticism those doctrines that seemed to evidence this point most clearly. From the Jewish perspective, transubstantiation served as a telling example of irrationality.

For Christian believers, however, conformity with rationality was not the only criterion of truth. Certain beliefs were considered mysteries, beyond the grasp of reason. If a dogma did not conform to philosophy, that was no reason to dispense with it. The Jewish polemicists showed little evidence of appreciating this attitude. Thus, they adduced rational proof after rational proof to undermine a belief not founded on rational proofs. And so, though they were well founded and rationally sound from an Aristotelian viewpoint, the Jewish philosophical arguments did not address themselves to the mystery aspects of the Eucharist. On the other hand, they did appear to show, as did the rational objections voiced by the Christian themselves, that the doctrine of transubstantiation was not in total conformity with the dictates of reason. For the Jewish philosophical polemicists this was sufficient to invalidate it, for, as we have seen, many of them held that while religion did not have to be demonstrated by reason, it must not be in conflict with reason.

CHAPTER SEVEN

Virgin Birth

The Christian dogma of virgin birth teaches that Mary, the mother of Jesus, remained a virgin, i.e., a *virgo intacta,* her entire life, before, during, and after the birth of her son. "The Christian belief is that Mary's virginity was never broken, neither at the time of the birth *[in partu]* nor before *[ante partum],* nor after *[post partum].*"[1] The Jewish polemicists challenged this assertion on all three points.

The doctrine of the virgin conception was not attacked per se. The possibility that a woman might conceive with her virginity intact, though by means of normal fertilization, is an occurrence which is conceded in the Talmud.[2] Nevertheless, the Jewish polemicists rejected the notion that God could become incarnate by impregnating a virgin and fathering an offspring who was, according to Christian doctrine, God Himself. Hence, the Jewish thinkers rarely offered arguments against the doctrine of Mary's virginity *ante partum* without reference to incarnation. Abraham Farissol expressed it this way:

> We cannot deny the possibility that God, may He be blessed, could create a creation in a virgin, even one whom no man has known, for He created everything out of nothing. Rather, we deny that there was a need for incarnation.[3]

The denial of incarnation was sufficient justification for rejection of the doctrine of Mary's virgin conception of Jesus.

The maintenance of the doctrine of Mary's virginity after Jesus' birth, assuming that she had remained a virgin *ante partum* and *in partu,* was more an exegetical than a philosophical problem. Jewish polemicists, following the example of Christian dissenters,[4] pointed out various New Testament passages which seemed to indicate that, after Jesus' birth, Mary lived a normal married life, one that included sexual relations and the bearing of children.[5] Since exegesis and not philosophical considerations was the major issue here, in the context of this study we may disregard the debate over Mary's virginity *post partum.*

One topic remains, then, that of the doctrine of virginity *in partu,* during the actual birth of Jesus. This belief was not taught explicitly in the New Testament, and it was not unanimously supported by the Church Fathers. By the time the Jewish polemicists criticized it, the perpetual virginity of Mary was a well-established doctrine; this, however, had not always been the case.[6]

The chief patristic opponents of virginity *in partu* were Tertullian,[7] Origen,[8] and Athanasius.[9] The first argued that whereas conception caused no damage to Mary's virginity, Jesus' exit did. Tertullian held that it made no difference whether a *virgo intacta* lost her virginity by a male's entering her or by his leaving her.[10] The maintenance of the belief in Jesus' normal birth was especially important to some early Christians, since they wished to refute the doctrine of the Docetists, who taught that the body of Jesus lacked reality.[11] Whether Tertullian would have maintained virginity *in partu* were it not for the Docetists, as some authors would like to think,[12] is difficult to determine. It is certain, though, that one stream of early Christian thought denied Mary's virginity *in partu.*

The other viewpoint, which claimed that Jesus' birth as well as his conception was miraculous, was expressed in both apocryphal and patristic literature. The former included the Odes of Solomon 19:6–10,[13] the Protoevangelium of James 19–20,[14] and the Ascension of Isaiah 11:8–9.[15] The first of these works recounted the painless birth of Jesus, while the latter two specifically taught that Mary was still a virgin immediately after Jesus' birth.

The major patristic defenders of virginity *in partu* were Basil,[16] Gregory of Nyssa,[17] Jerome,[18] Ambrose,[19] and Augustine.[20] They made little effort to explain this doctrine philosophically; most of their arguments revolved around the exegesis of scriptural passages.[21] The doctrine of Mary's perpetual virginity became codified by the First Lateran Council (649): "She incorruptibly bore, her virginity remaining indestructible even after his birth."[22]

As various other doctrines concerning Mary, e.g., immaculate conception, developed in the Middle Ages, belief in Mary's perpetual virginity, and, specifically, her virginity *in partu,* remained comparatively unchallenged. There were, however, both those who challenged the virginity *in partu,* saying that Jesus was born like any other human baby, and others who asserted that Jesus' birth was totally miraculous, not having occurred through the normal reproductive organs. When Ratramnus (d. after 868), for instance, heard that certain people in Germany were spreading the belief in such a miraculous birth, he wrote a treatise defending its normality. He insisted, however, that virginity *in partu* was maintained.[23] At about the same time, Paschasius Radbertus (d. ca. 860) wrote a treatise emphasizing the supernatural aspects of the birth, not ruling out a totally miraculous birth. This appears to be in reaction to those who rejected virginity *in partu*.[24] The latter were also the target of Geoffrey of Vendome (d. 1132), who said that some people accepted virginity *ante* and *post partum*, but denied it *in partu*. He concluded that such a belief is both insane and profane.[25]

In the fourteenth century, Durandus of Saint-Pourçain (1275?–1334), a nominalist, offered the theory that, at the moment of birth, Mary's reproductive organs expanded and dilated so that Jesus could be born with no damage to his mother's virginity.[26] He took this view in order not to contradict the principle "that two bodies of separate quantities cannot be in the same place at the same time."[27] This view was not accepted, and Durandus was greatly criticized for it.[28]

It seems, then, that during the Middle Ages the orthodox Christian dogma of the virgin birth *in partu* was relatively unchallenged. There was, however, a recognition of the philosophical problems that this belief entails.

The Jewish polemicists were cognizant of the fact that the doctrine of virgin birth *in partu* raised a number of philosophical questions. In their critique of this Christian belief, they argued (1) that the impossibility of the interpenetrability of bodies precluded virgin birth, and (2) that the various images of virgin birth cited by the Christians were not convincing.

The Interpenetrability of Bodies

Just as Durandus realized that the doctrine of virgin birth might have contradicted the principle that two bodies cannot be in the same place at the same time, so, too, did the Jewish polemicists think that this physical law precluded a virgin birth *in partu*. The basic Jewish argument against the Christian belief can be summed up in the principle, "the interpenetrability of bodies is impossible."[29] This rule, quoted by Profiat Duran anonymously, was stated by Joseph ben Shem Tov[30] and Judah Aryeh de Modena[31] to have been derived from Aristotle's *Physics*[32] and *On Generation and Corruption*.[33] Repeating a statement made in connection with the debate over transubstantiation, some Jewish polemicists averred that if one body could enter another, then "the whole world could enter into a mustard seed."[34] This was a first principle.[35] Virgin birth *in partu,* which meant the entrance of one body into another, was, therefore, impossible.[36]

Ḥasdai Crescas saw the basis of this principle in the very nature of bodies. The definition of a body, as Aristotle stated in *On the Heavens,*[37] was that which had all three dimensions: length, width, and depth.[38] It followed, then, that since the sides of a virgin's womb adhered to each other, they had no dimensions (space) between them. If a body were to go through these sides, the dimensions of that body would be present between these sides. But it had already been assumed that there were no dimensions between them. Therefore, virgin birth was an impossible contradiction.[39]

This argumentation was known to Thomas, who at first stated that it seems that there was no virgin birth. "In the mysteries of Christ nothing should happen which would make his body seem unreal.[40] But that happens when it passes through a blocked passage, since two bodies cannot be in the same place at the same time."[41] It followed, then, that Jesus, who had a real body, could not have maintained Mary's virginity intact.[42] Thomas simply answered that Jesus, in order to show the reality of his body, was born of a woman; to show he was really divine, he was born of a virgin. The problem of the simultaneous presence of two bodies was not dealt with.[43]

Just as in the case of transubstantiation, some Christians offered an alternative to the belief in the interpenetrability of bodies by positing a glorified body of Jesus which could pass through another body without any harm to the latter. As was already noted, Crescas argued against such a doctrine, saying that a body was either a body, i.e., with dimensions and, therefore, noninterpenetrable, or it was not a body. In the first case, there was no glorification; in the second, there was no body.[44] Glorified bodies, then, did not exist.

De Modena also referred to the doctrine of a glorified body[45] but did not consider it seriously because even Thomas had rejected it.[46] Thomas stated that whereas it was true that glorified bodies could pass through blocked passages, the body of Jesus, in its conception, was not glorified. It was a physical body like all other human bodies.[47] Therefore, Thomas dismissed the opinion of some *(quidam)* who said that Christ assumed some properties of a glorified body during his lifetime, i.e., subtlety upon his birth and agility when he walked upon the waters. Thomas held that such qualities applied only to glorified bodies, not to the body of Jesus during his lifetime.[48] Thomas concluded that the maintenance of Mary's virginity *in partu* "happened miraculously by divine power."[49] The Jewish polemicists did not accept this conclusion.

Images of Virgin Birth

Referring to Mary's virginity, Augustine stated: "If we could explain the miracle (rationally), it would not be a miracle; if we were to find other examples, it would not be unique."[50] This teaching was reaffirmed by the Eleventh Council of Toledo (675).[51] Whereas most Christian thinkers refrained from rational explanations of the virgin birth, many did not hesitate to cite examples of it. Their aim was to show that the virgin birth was possible, since it had parallels in nature.

We find a number of these images in Christian literature. Several Church Fathers, for instance, cited examples from the animal world. Lactantius, to support the possibility of virgin conception, offered the analogy of certain animals who could conceive by means of the wind and the air. If they could do it, certainly God could impregnate a virgin.[52] What kind of animals can these be? Basil stated that birds—for instance, vultures—can impregnate without copulating.[53] Ambrose also cited the vulture.[54] Evodius, in a letter to Augustine arguing against the latter's pronouncement quoted above, asked why one should not give examples if they exist. For his part, he mentioned the spiders *(aranea),* which can reproduce without sexual relations.[55]

An anti-Jewish polemic of the seventh century, *The Trophies of Damascus,* suggested an image of virginity *in partu.* The rays of the sun can pass through a glass vase full of water and cause a fire without thereby changing or polluting either the vase or the water or the sun. Similarly, Jesus was born without causing damage or pain to his mother, Mary, who remained a virgin.[56]

Timothy cited a large number of analogies, as was his custom. According to him, parallels to virgin birth in Scripture could be seen in the birth of Eve from Adam's side causing no rending or fracturing, and the ascent of Jesus to heaven without breaking the firmament. Nature provided us with the examples of the fruit born from trees, sight born from the eye, aromatic substances born from trees and plants, and rays born from the sun, all without any damage to the "parent." Besides, just as the virgin conceived without marital relations, so too could she give birth without breaking her "virginal seals."[57]

In the Middle Ages, a favorite image was of Mary as Star of the Sea *(Stella Maris).* Mary gave forth the light, her son Jesus, as stars give their light. Neither was diminished thereby.[58]

In Jewish polemical literature, one image was quoted often, that of light going through a transparent substance. The first polemicist to cite this image was Jacob ben Reuben in *Milḥamot Ha-Shem* (1170).[59] Later polemicists, Shem Tov ibn Shapruṭ,[60] Judah Aryeh De Modena,[61] the author of *Kevod Elohim,*[62] and Isaac Lupis,[63] copied Jacob ben Reuben, both by citing this example and by repeating his refutation of it.

The analogy is quite simple. If one were to take a white crystal[64] and put it under the rays of the sun, the sun would pass through the jewel without leaving any damage, such as a hole.[65] If the sun can do that, then certainly the master of the sun could pass through a virgin and not cause any damage.[66]

The immediate source of this image may very well be the same source that Alan of Lille had before him.[67] The latter explained the conception of Mary with the example of a ray of sun going through a glass window. Nothing is broken because of the subtlety of the ray.[68] It should be noted that Jacob ben Reuben quoted this image as an example of virginity *in partu,* not *ante partum.*

Jacob ben Reuben responded to this image by citing some counter-examples. For instance, if one were to take a lamp, cover it with parchment, and light the candle inside the lamp, one would be able to see the rays of the candle from far away. The reason for this is not the passage of the flame through the parchment, for the parchment was not burnt. Rather, the light can be seen because of the thinness and lightness of the parchment. Still, it is impenetrable. One could also hold a glass full of wine and see red light on his hands. Yet the glass is still whole and impenetrable. The color of the wine appears to go beyond the glass because of the glass' own brightness and transparency. Similarly, the action of the sun on the crystal is a result of the former's great strength (as in the case of the candle) and the latter's brightness (as in the glass cup). There is no question here of one body passing through another body as was claimed in the case of virgin birth. Besides, the comparison was not applicable anyway, since the rays of the sun are incorporeal but the body of Jesus was not.[69] The other Jewish polemicists offered basically the same, if not as full, answer.[70]

Conclusions

There were not many Jewish philosophical arguments against the Christian doctrine of virgin birth. After they cited the obvious philosophical contradictions between virgin birth and the impossibility of the interpenetrability of bodies, and rebutted the images of virgin birth adduced from nature, the polemicists employed no further rational arguments. As Isaac

Lupis stated: "What more can I add in order to refute this strange belief since it has absolutely no support, neither from reason nor from the intellect!"[71] The dogma of virgin birth, then, was one more Christian belief which the Jewish polemicists regarded as irrational; they attempted to demonstrate that irrationality through the use of philosophical arguments.

CHAPTER EIGHT

Conclusions

In the preceding four chapters, the medieval Jewish philosophical arguments against Trinity, incarnation, transubstantiation, and virgin birth have been discussed. In addition, an attempt was made to suggest possible sources of these arguments, to show how the Jewish criticisms fit into the overall philosophical outlook of the polemicists, and to review Christian acquaintance with, and reaction to, Jewish refutations of their doctrines. Further study of additional material will no doubt lead to an even greater understanding of the use of philosophy for polemical purposes. What has been presented, though, should be sufficient to demonstrate the wide range and variety of the medieval Jewish philosophical polemic against Christianity. On the basis of the sources examined, it is also possible to outline general conclusions about the nature of Jewish-Christian polemics and intellectual relations.

Jewish Knowledge of Christianity

It is clear from the discussion of philosophical arguments that those Jews who participated in anti-Christian polemics had a fairly good knowledge of the beliefs with which they disagreed. In their descriptions of Christian doctrines, Jewish polemicists often employed literal translations of the original Latin formulations.[1] Not only did general statements about these tenets accurately reflect the views of the Christians, but also the Jewish exposition of the details of these doctrines evidenced a high degree of familiarity with the criticized beliefs. Though some Jewish polemicists had a much greater knowledge of Christianity than others, most of those engaged in religious debates had a fairly good understanding of Christianity.

How did the Jewish polemicists acquire their knowledge of Christianity?

Did Jews read Christian theological treatises in order to understand the doctrines they were to refute? The answer is most likely in the negative. The Jewish polemicists apparently learned about Christian beliefs from frequent contact with Christian polemicists and missionaries. Being subjected to the conversionary attempts of the dominant religion's representatives, Jews no doubt became familiar with Christian doctrines. Jews did not study Christianity dispassionately in libraries; they became acquainted with it as a result of Christian missionizing attempts.[2] Had a knowledge of Christianity not been necessary for self-preservation, it is doubtful that Jews would have ever investigated those beliefs very closely.

The truth of this assumption may be confirmed by a closer look both at the Jewish exposition of Christian doctrines and at the philosophical arguments against them. Though the Jews did not distort Christianity as they presented its beliefs, and it is clear that they were aware of the details of particular doctrines, still, it is evident that the subtle intricacies of many tenets were unknown to the polemicists. For instance, these Jewish thinkers rarely took into account the philosophical defense of Christianity developed by Christian theologians. The very same arguments to which Christian philosophers had already offered counter-arguments were repeated over and over again by Jewish polemicists with little or no consideration of the Christian defense. One might expect that if Jews were familiar with the works of the Scholastics, for instance, their arguments would have been directed against specific Scholastic formulations. This, however, is not the case.

On the other hand, when Jewish arguments are compared with Christian polemical works, which, no doubt, either grew out of actual disputations or were meant as guides to Christian debaters, one sees a striking relationship. The Jewish polemicists seem to have been refuting the doctrines as presented in these Christian controversial works. It is not being suggested that Jews actually read Christian polemical tracts; rather, it is likely that these works contain the very same arguments which Jews heard from Christians who attempted to convert them. It is the Christian religion as presented in the polemical literature with which the Jews were familiar.

Some examples should help demonstrate this fact. As has been noted, Jewish philosophical polemicists referred quite often to the Christian explanation of the Trinity as the attributes power, wisdom, and will. While it is true that this interpretation of the Trinity was taught by some Christian theologians, it was never considered as important a doctrine as one would imagine from Jewish polemical literature.[3] Why, then, did so many Jewish polemicists argue against it? The likely answer, as supported by Christian anti-Jewish works,[4] is that the Christians often attempted to convince the

Jews that a concept of Trinity was acceptable by comparing the three Persons, which the Jews rejected, with three attributes, which the Jews accepted. In their rejection of any relation between Persons and attributes, Jewish polemicists were directing their arguments against the doctrines of the Christian polemicists, not those of nonpolemicizing theologians. In like manner, it was the polemicists, not the philosophers, who equated the Trinity with the Jewish notion of God as thinking, thinker, thought. As the Jews rejected any such relationship between the acceptable Aristotelian doctrine and the unacceptable trinitarian belief, they could be contending only against those Christians who had attempted to convert them by drawing this parallel.

This pattern is also evident when looking at Christian images of the Trinity which were employed mainly in polemical works. The Christians admitted that they did not take these analogies very seriously; thus, when theologians wrote for those who already believed in the Trinity, an imperfect image was superfluous. In debate with the Jews and other nonbelievers, though, such images were apparently used frequently in the hope of convincing skeptics that a Trinity was possible.[5] Jewish emphasis on these images of the Trinity is additional evidence that Jews were arguing against the Christianity presented to them by Christian polemicists.

If it is true that the Jewish polemicists were arguing specifically against the religion of the Christian polemicists, then it is easy to understand why a number of arguments appear to miss their mark. Compared with the Christianity espoused with philosophical rigor by such thinkers as Thomas and Anselm, the popular religion of the missionary was rarely so sophisticated. Jewish polemicists, interested not in academic argument but in actual defense of Jewish survival, paid little attention to the more developed forms of the Christian doctrines. They did not equip themselves for debate held on the highest level of discourse. Thus, we would be doing an injustice to the Jewish polemicists by comparing the quality of their arguments with those of the most advanced contemporary expositions of Christianity. Nonetheless, as we have seen, the Jewish contentions were not taken lightly by the Christian philosophers. Indeed, the range and variety of the Jewish philosophical critique of Christianity is in itself a tribute to the polemicists' speculative powers. Though we do not know the success of the Jewish critique of Christianity in stemming apostasy, the polemicists can no doubt be credited with a spirited defense of Judaism against the attack of the missionaries. If the Jewish controversial literature does not always evidence an appreciation for the subtleties of Christian doctrine, the Jewish polemicists are hardly to be faulted. Since the Christian polemicists themselves resorted to popular expositions of their religion, it is not surprising that their Jewish opponents employed the same tactic.[6]

The Sources of Jewish Arguments

From the present study, there emerges another feature of the medieval Jewish philosophical critique of Christianity, i.e., the fact that the Jewish arguments were rarely original. It is rather easy to find the sources of these contentions in Christian heretical literature, Muslim Kalam, or orthodox Christian works which were intended to answer heterodox objections. Most of the philosophical arguments found in the works of Jewish polemicists can also be discovered in various earlier sources. Though the wide scope and comprehensiveness of the Jewish polemic may be considered unique to the Jews, the arguments themselves apparently were not.

The question arises as to the manner in which Jewish polemicists learned of these arguments. Did they read Christian literature, and copy the suitable refutations of Christian doctrines? Were the Jews in covert contact with anti-Catholic groups? Did they learn of the heretical arguments from the anti-Jewish Christian polemicists? Or is any resemblance between Jewish and heretical arguments coincidental?

The answer to these questions cannot be provided with certainty. No doubt, some anti-Christian arguments were so obvious that there is no reason to assume Jewish polemicists had to rely on others to formulate their refutations. On the other hand, some parallels are so striking that it is difficult to imagine that there was no relationship between Jewish and heretical contentions. There is some evidence that Jewish polemicists were somewhat attuned to the anti-Catholic sentiments of the dissidents. Thus, the anonymous author of *Vikuaḥ Radaq* used specifically Catharist arguments against Catholics (and Catholic arguments against the Catharists),[7] while Joseph ben Shem Tov referred to those who did not believe in transubstantiation and were, therefore, considered heretics.[8] It appears, then, that the Jews, as the main target of Christian polemics, were aware of the position of other groups which also incurred orthodox wrath. Further study of the relationship between medieval Jewish polemicists and Christian heretics is a desideratum.[9]

It is also possible that Jewish polemicists did draw some of their arguments from orthodox Christian literature. As has been stated, the Jews generally did not read the theological works of the dominant religion in order to learn the subtleties of Christian doctrines. Nevertheless, it is possible that some more knowledgeable Jewish polemicists attempted to use this literature as a source for their own arguments. Judah Aryeh de Modena, for instance, often quoted the objections to certain doctrines which were mentioned by Thomas.[10] The extent to which Jews actually read orthodox (or even heterodox) literature in their search for anti-Christian arguments cannot as yet be determined exactly.[11]

Even if many Jewish arguments were borrowed from other sources, there is still much which is original in the Jewish polemical literature. First, the language of these arguments is not Greek, Latin, or Arabic; it is Hebrew. The Jewish polemicists were responsible for the creation of Hebrew terms to describe Christian doctrines.[12] Second, the Jews often gave original nuances to old arguments. As has been shown, the same refutation may take on new forms as it is repeated through the centuries.

There is a third unique aspect of the Jewish polemic against Christianity. While it is true that many arguments were taken from Christian heretics, the purposes of Jewish and heretical thinkers were extremely different. The anti-Catholic polemics were conducted by Christians who wished to change certain Christian beliefs. They did not question the basic truth of Christianity; they objected to the orthodox Catholic interpretation of the religion. The heretics were interested, then, in internal reform. On the other hand, the Jews sought solely to defend themselves against the conversionary attempts of the dominant religion. Hence, it was their goal to demonstrate to fellow Jews that Christianity was altogether a false religion.

It is for this reason that the Jewish criticisms were so wide-ranging. The Jewish polemicists were not concerned with reforming one or two doctrines; rather, they criticized the whole Christian religion as rationally untenable. The Jewish polemicists were not attempting to effect a change in Christianity; they were not trying to convert Christians. Their main goal was to prevent Jewish apostasy to Christianity.[13] The uniqueness, then, of the medieval Jewish philosophical polemic against Christianity lies not in specific arguments but in its overall range and purpose.

The Role of Philosophy in Jewish-Christian Polemics

During the Middle Ages, Jewish, Christian, and Muslim thinkers all discussed whether or not their own religion, which was considered revealed and thus true, was compatible with the principles of philosophy, which were the result of rational speculation and also accepted as true. In addition, polemicists of the various religions attempted to show that the other faiths were rejected by the dictates of reason. As this study has made clear, Jewish polemicists in particular went to great lengths to demonstrate that philosophy disapproved of Christian doctrines. While generally asserting that Judaism was not incompatible with reason, even if not supported by it, the Jewish debaters claimed that Christianity's main tenets were contradicted by mutually agreed upon philosophical principles.

For their part, Christian philosophers rejected this Jewish assertion. Though they basically accepted the same principles of philosophy as were held by Jewish thinkers, the Christians sought to demonstrate that their doctrines were not incompatible with reason. In the course of this Jewish-Christian controversy, philosophy, in its many different aspects, was used extensively. As has been shown, thinkers of both religions often employed philosophical reasoning in their arguments and counter-arguments. Still, care must be exercised not to overestimate the importance of philosophy as a decisive factor in medieval Jewish polemics.

A close look at the role of philosophy in these religious debates indicates that this branch of knowledge was but a tool in the hands of the polemicists. Reason was not employed dispassionately in the pursuit of truth; rather, reason was called upon as a witness either in the defense of a proposition already accepted or in prosecution of a belief which had already been rejected. Jews and Christians alike did not look to philosophy as an independent source of religious truth. Philosophy was but an *ancilla theologiae*, a handmaid of theology. As important a part as philosophy occupied in the polemics, it did not play a decisive role in the Jewish rejection of Christianity. It was merely one weapon in the polemicists' arsenal.

One may adduce a number of arguments to support this conclusion. First, the polemicists themselves often represented exegetical, historical, and philosophical arguments as being of equal stature. Thus, for instance, they greeted both the Christian inability to understand the Bible as they themselves did and the apparent Christian flouting of reason with equal dismay.[14] Though some polemicists relied on philosophy to a much greater extent than they did on exegesis or history, the overall conclusion emerges that no one method of argumentation was considered more important than the others. The reasons for the Jewish rejection of Christianity were diverse, and they were not necessarily epitomized by any series of arguments. Indeed, it appears that most arguments—exegetical, historical, or rational—were formulated after the basic decision to maintain allegiance to Judaism was taken.

Furthermore, we have seen that not every philosophical polemicist was entirely consistent. In their refutations of Christianity, some thinkers, notably Ḥasdai Crescas, employed philosophical principles with which they themselves were in disagreement. In other cases, for instance as concerns the various theories of attributes, a number of Jewish polemicists apparently accommodated their philosophical conclusions to polemical purposes rather than transfer an independently developed philosophy into the realm of religious debate. The Jewish theories of attributes, and the Muslim ones on which they were based, were a direct answer to the Christian doctrine of Trinity.[15] Hence, Jewish philosophers did not reject a triune God on the basis of a previously formulated alternate system of God's attributes. Philosophical principles, then, were not the guiding reason for Jewish nonacceptance of the Trinity. Once the Trinity was rejected on theological grounds, philosophy was employed to explain further why the Jews repudiated this doctrine. It would be incorrect, then, to assume, on the basis of the wide-ranging Jewish philosophical critique of Christianity, that Jewish resistance to conversionary attempts was founded upon philosophy. It would be truer to say that philosophy was called upon to reinforce this resistance, which came about as a result of many factors. No doubt, reason was one component in the Jewish rejection of Christianity; nevertheless, it was by no means the only such element.

On the other hand, one should not conclude that Jewish polemicists were cynical in their use of philosophy. It is not the case that they believed speculative reason could be used to support either religion and that they chose to employ it in defense of Judaism. There is little doubt that the Jews honestly believed that Christianity was rationally untenable and in conflict with evident philosophical principles. The plethora of philosophical arguments was intended to back up this claim. When the Jews asserted that Christianity contradicted reason, they no doubt meant it. Still, one cannot say that philosophy was the overriding factor behind the Jewish refusal to convert.

The Significance of the Medieval Jewish Philosophical Polemic Against Christianity

This study has concerned itself with a literature which grew out of an emotionally charged, highly antagonistic situation. The polemic was one of Judaism's few defense mechanisms against the attacks of Christianity, which, on many occasions, were more than just verbal forays. It is for this reason that medieval Jewish polemical literature quite often was strongly worded and expressed a deeply felt antagonism toward Judaism's opponents. Similarly, the conditions under which these polemical works were formed and written may account for the Jewish arguments' occasional misdirection. Refutations which are employed in the heat of debate rarely show the results of thoughtful reflection.

Despite these factors, the Jewish philosophical polemic against Christianity in the Middle Ages was a remarkable intellectual phenomenon. Arguments were assembled from the various areas of philosophy, and they were developed with great acumen in rebuttal of Christian claims. The Jewish philosophical arguments are evidence of the intellectual vitality of an oppressed and persecuted people which, despite frequent danger, insisted upon meeting the challenge of its adversaries on their own terms. Jews became quite conversant with Christian doctrines and criticized their weak points with an impressive repertoire of philosophical arguments. Though polemical literature in general tends not to be particularly original, and the philosophical arguments per se are no exception, the overall Jewish philosophical polemic against Christianity is a striking creation.

It is difficult to determine how successful Jewish polemical literature was in combating apostasy. There is no way of knowing whether more Jews would have converted to Christianity had there been no Jewish defense. Likewise, the specific impact of philosophical polemics upon Jewish survival cannot be measured. These polemics, however, do provide us with a fertile source for the history of Jewish-Christian intellectual relations. In this history, philosophy plays a significant role.

List of Abbreviations

Denz.	Henry Denzinger, *Enchiridion Symbolorum* (Freiburg, 1957)
EJ	*Encyclopedia Judaica* (Jerusalem, 1971)
HThR	*Harvard Theological Review*
HUCA	*Hebrew Union College Annual*
JAOS	*Journal of the American Oriental Society*
JJS	*Journal of Jewish Studies*
JQR	*Jewish Quarterly Review*
JThS	*Journal of Theological Studies*
JTSA	Jewish Theological Seminary of America
MGWJ	*Monatsschrift für Geschichte und Wissenschaft des Judentums*
PAAJR	*Proceedings of the American Academy for Jewish Research*
PG	Jacques Paul Migne, *Patrologiae Cursus Completus . . . Series Graeca* (Paris, 1844–65)
PL	Jacques Paul Migne, *Patrologiae Cursus Completus . . . Series Latina* (Paris, 1844–65)
REJ	*Revue des Etudes Juives*
SCG	Thomas Aquinas, *Summa Contra Gentiles* (Rome, 1934)
ST	Thomas Aquinas, *Summa Theologiae*

Notes

Chapter One

1. After the Muslim conquest of the East, the religious debate was also three-sided. Though attention will be given to this period, the greatest focus of the present study is on Jewish-Christian polemics in the Christian West, where the Jews were the chief target of the Christian attack.

2. With the spread of the Christian hegemony, numerous heretical sects arose. Whereas the Jews were the only non-Christians in Western Europe (excluding Spain), there were a number of Christian groups which were also the object of the orthodox polemical literature. The relationship between Jews and the heretical movements will be touched on in passing.

3. On the relationship between the early Church and Judaism, cf. Marcel Simon, *Verus Israel* (Paris, 1948). He deals with the Jewish-Christian polemics of 135–425 C.E. on pp. 165–238. The period between 430 and 1096 is treated by Bernhard Blumenkranz, *Juifs et Chrétiens dans le Monde Occidental, 430–1096* (Paris, 1960); Jewish-Christian polemics are discussed on pp. 213–89. For a review of the whole medieval period, cf. Peter Browe, *Die Judenmission im Mitteralter und die Päpste* (Rome, 1942). A. Lukyn William's *Adversus Judaeos* (Cambridge, 1935) offers a capsule review of many published anti-Jewish Christian polemics. Cf. also F. Vernet, "Juifs (Controverses avec les)," *Dictionnaire de Théologie Catholique,* VIII (Paris, 1924), pp. 1870–1914. Other major works on the subject are Blumenkranz, *Les Auteurs Chrétiens Latins du Moyen Age sur les Juifs et le Judaïsme* (Paris, 1963); idem, *Die Judenpredigt Augustins* (Basel, 1946); Jean Juster, *Les Juifs dans l'Empire Romain,* I (Paris, 1914), pp. 43–76, 290–337; James Parkes, *The Conflict of the Church and the Synagogue* (London, 1934). On Christian conversionary attempts and oppression of Jews, see, e.g., Salo W. Baron, *A Social and Religious History of the Jews,* IX (Philadelphia, 1965), pp. 3–96; Yitzḥak Baer, *A History of the Jews in Christian Spain* (Philadelphia, 1966), II, pp. 95–299; Heinrich Graetz, *History of the Jews* (Philadelphia, 1894), III, pp. 297–310, 347–57, 494–521, 563–650; IV, pp. 179–220, 308–56, and in passim. On the general attitude of medieval Christians toward Jews, see Joshua Trachtenberg, *The Devil and the Jews* (London, 1943).

4. Cf. R. Travers Herford, *Christianity in Talmud and Midrash* (London, 1903); Arthur Marmorstein, *Studies in Jewish Theology* (London, 1950), pp. 93–100.

5. For a discussion of Jewish refutations of Christianity in Muslim countries, see below, chap. 4.

6. E.g., the commentaries of Rashi (Rabbi Solomon ben Isaac, 1035–1105) are replete with anti-Christian references; cf. Judah Rosenthal, "Ha-Pulmus Ha-'Anṭi Noẓri Be-Rashi 'al Ha-Tanakh," *Rashi: Torato Ve-'Ishiyuto,* ed. Simon Federbusch (New York, 1958), pp. 45–59; reprinted, *Meḥkarim U-Mekorot,* I (Jerusalem, 1967), pp. 101–16; E. Shereshevsky, "Rashi's and Christian Interpretations," *JQR* 61

(1970): 76–86; Baer, "Rashi Ve-Ha-Meẓi'ut Ha-Historit Shel Zemano," *Tarbiẓ* 20 (5709 [1949]): 320–32.

7. The intensification of pressure came as a result of the Crusades (First Crusade, 1096) and the changes in Christian anti-Jewish polemics. Cf. Amos Funkenstein, "Ha-Temurot Be-Vikuaḥ Ha-Dat Ben Yehudim Le-Noẓrim Be-Me'ah Ha-Yod-Bet," *Ẓion* 33 (1968): 125–44. Joseph Kimḥi, whose *Sefer Ha-Berit* (1170) may be the first Western Jewish polemical work, wrote his treatise in order to satisfy the request of a student who wished to know how to meet the Christian challenge; cf. *Sefer Ha-Berit*, ed. Frank Talmage (Jerusalem, 1974), p. 21; trans. Talmage, *The Book of the Covenant* (Toronto, 1972), pp. 27–28.

8. Cf. Eliezer ben Yehuda, *A Complete Dictionary of Ancient and Modern Hebrew* (New York, 1960), II, p. 1267. For the biblical usage of the root וכח, cf. Francis Brown et al., *A Hebrew and English Lexicon of the Old Testament* (Oxford, 1962), pp. 406–7. A *vikuaḥ* originally referred to a public disputation, but the term was taken over for polemical literature in general; cf. Moritz Steinschneider, *Jewish Literature* (London, 1857), p. 317, n. 25.

9. J. Wagenseil, *Tela Ignea Satanae* (Altdorf, 1681), translated this term by *Liber Victoriae*, taking *niẓẓaḥon* to mean "victory." Steinschneider, ibid., has shown that *niẓẓuaḥ* or *niẓẓaḥon* is the equivalent of *vikuaḥ* and actually signifies a controversy.

10. The most complete list of Jewish polemical works is Rosenthal, "Sifrut Ha-Vikuaḥ Ha-'Anti-Noẓrit 'Ad Sof Ha-Me'ah Ha-Shemoneh-'Esreh," *Areshet* 2 (1960): 130–79; "Milu'im," 3 (1961): 433–39. See below, chap. 2, for a discussion of the sources of this work. On Jewish polemics in general, cf. Baron, op. cit., V (1957), pp. 82–137, IX, pp. 97–134; H. H. Ben-Sasson, "Disputations and Polemics," *EJ* VI, pp. 79–103; Isidore Loeb, *La Controverse Religieuse entre les Chrétiens et les Juifs au Moyen Age en France et en Espagne* (Paris, 1888); idem, "Polémistes Chrétiens et Juifs en France et en Espagne," *REJ* 18 (1889): 43–70, 219–42; J. B. De Rossi, *Bibliotheca Judaica Anti-Christiana* (Parma, 1800). On the Jewish attitude to Christians in the Middle Ages, cf. Jacob Katz, *Exclusiveness and Tolerance* (Oxford, 1961). Cf. also Talmage, "Judaism on Christianity: Christianity on Judaism," in *The Study of Judaism* (New York, 1972), pp. 81–112.

11. Adolf Posnanski's *Schiloh: Ein Beitrag zur Geschichte der Messiaslehre* (Leipzig, 1904) reviews solely the polemical treatment of Gen. 49:10. Similarly, A. D. Neubauer and S. R. Driver, *The Fifty-Third Chapter of Isaiah According to the Jewish Interpreters* (Oxford, 1876–77), records only the Jewish exegesis of the "Servant of the Lord." Both works are valuable, but their subject matters are so strictly confined that they cannot be used for drawing general conclusions about medieval polemics. Oliver S. Rankin, *Jewish Religious Polemic* (Edinburgh, 1956), and Morris Braude, *Conscience on Trial* (New York, 1952), offer merely translations of certain polemical works, though Rankin's introductions and notes are helpful. Hans J. Schoeps attempted to review the whole scope of the Jewish-Christian argument, in the book of that title (New York, 1963), but his sources are extremely limited. Judah Rosenthal discussed a few selected topics of the medieval Jewish-Christian debate in

"Hagganah Ve-Hatqafah Be-Sifrut Ha-Vikuaḥ Shel Yeme Ha-Benayim," *Fifth World Congress of Jewish Studies: Proceedings* (Jerusalem, 1971), Hebrew sec., pp. 345–58, but he goes into little detail. J. D. Eisenstein's *Oẓar Vikuḥim* (New York, 1928) contains interesting material, but his texts are not printed carefully and cannot be used reliably (cf. his reference to Saint Patrick's Cathedral, New York, 1927, in "Crescas' *Biṭṭul 'Iqqare Ha-Noẓrim,*" p. 293). To my knowledge, no work has attempted to trace a major theme through the entire range of Jewish polemical literature.

12. For instance, it is believed that a study of Jewish exegetical arguments should yield results similar to the ones produced here through an analysis of philosophical arguments.

13. Arthur C. McGiffert, *Dialogue between a Christian and a Jew . . . ,* (New York, 1889), p. 5. Funkenstein, op. cit., discussed the change in Christian polemics which occurred in the twelfth century. Until that time, anti-Jewish works were usually solely a collection of "testimonies" taken from the Hebrew Bible. The twelfth century saw the rise of rational arguments, attacks against the Talmud, and attempts to prove the truth of Christianity to Jews by means of talmudic texts. For these types of argumentation, see below. For another treatment of polemical methods to the eleventh century, see Blumenkranz, *Juifs et Chrétiens,* pp. 215–26.

14. E.g., Ps. 110(109):1. The Christians read "Dixit Dominus Domino meo—The Lord said to my Lord." The Jews insisted that the reading is "adoni—my lord," not "Adonai—my Lord." Cf. *Sefer Ha-Berit,* pp. 47–48, trans., Talmage, pp. 58–59, cf. nn. 64–66; David Kimḥi's *Commentary on Psalms* 110:1 (censored from most editions; ed. Talmage, *Sefer Ha-Berit,* pp. 77–78); Joseph ben Nathan Official, *Sefer Yosef Ha-Meqanneh,* ed. J. Rosenthal (Jerusalem, 1970), pp. 114–15; Naḥmanides, *Vikuaḥ Ramban,* ed. H. D. Chavel, *Kitve Ramban,* 4th ed. (Jerusalem, 1971), I, pp. 317–18. This interpretation predated Jerome; cf. Justin Martyr, *Dialogue with Trypho* 83, *PG* 6, 672–73; trans. Thomas B. Falls, *Writings of Saint Justin Martyr* (New York, 1948), pp. 280–81. Another example of differing Jewish-Christian readings is Isa. 9:5(6). The Vulgate reads "vocabitur—vayiqqare—he will be called," and the MT reads "vayiqra—he will call." Cf. *Sefer Ha-Berit,* p. 22, trans., p. 29, cf. n. 5; Jacob ben Reuben *Milḥamot Ha-Shem,* ed. J. Rosenthal (Jerusalem, 1963), p. 89; *Yosef Ha-Meqanneh,* pp. 76–77; Isaac Troki, *Ḥizzuk Emunah,* ed. David Deutsch (Breslau, 1873), I:21, p. 142, trans., *Faith Strengthened,* Moses Mocatto (London, 1850), reprinted, p. 106. On these two verses, see Herman Hailperin, *Rashi and the Christian Scholars* (Pittsburgh, 1963), pp. 55, 81–84, 169–71. For more information on the Jewish polemicists and their works, see below, chap. 2.

15. E.g., the Christian reading of Dan. 9:24. Cf. *Milḥamot Ha-Shem,* pp. 135–36, and cf. n. 1; *Sefer Ha-Berit,* pp. 39–43, trans. pp. 49–53, cf. n. 42; *Niẓẓaḥon Yashan,* ed. Johannes Wagenseil *Tela Ignea Satanae,* reprint ed. (Jerusalem, 5730 [1969–70]), p. 69.

16. Cf. Profiat Duran, *Kelimat Ha-Goyim,* ed. Adolf Posnanski, *Ha-Ẓofeh Me-*

'Ereẓ Hagar, 4, 5675 (1914–15), pp. 120–23; Justin Martyr, *Dialogue* 71–73, *PG* 6, 641–49, trans. pp. 262–65. Isaac Troki stated in *Ḥizzuk Emunah* I:21, p. 142, trans., p. 106: "We know well that Jerome has made a practice of accommodating Scripture to the notions of his own creed."

17. *Kelimat Ha-Goyim, Ha-Ẓofeh*, 4, p. 120: לבאר שיבושי גירונומו המשבש המעתיק ספרי הקדש מלשון עברית אל לשון לאטיני ובהבאת הראיה על כי הנמצא אצלינו מספרי הקדש הוא האמת המדוקדקת ועליו אין להוסיף וממנו אין לגרוע לעולם. Abraham Farissol, *Magen Avraham*, JTSA ms. 2433, fols. 31b–32a (chap. 29), also devoted a chapter to a discussion of what he considered were Jerome's mistakes.

18. *Kelimat Ha-Goyim*, pp. 121–22; cf. p. 121, n. 1, where Posnanski agreed with Duran's assessment.

19. Ibid., pp. 122–23. In addition to the *Kuzari* (*Kitāb al-Khazarī*, III:30–32, ed. Hartwig Hirschfeld [Leipzig, 1887], pp. 180–83), Duran also quoted Maimonides and Benjamin of Tudela; cf. p. 122, nn. 4–8.

20. Cf. *Sefer Ha-Berit*, pp. 37–39, trans., pp. 46–49, and cf. pp. 22–23; *Vikuaḥ* of Elijah Ḥayyim of Genazzano, ed. J. Rosenthal, *Meḥkarim*, p. 444; Meir ben Simeon, *Milḥemet Miẓvah*, Parma ms. 2749 (De Rossi 155), fol. 3b; cf. S. Stein, "A Disputation on Moneylending between Jews and Gentiles in Me'ir b. Simeon's *Milḥemeth Miṣwah* (Narbonne, 13th Cent.)," *JJS* 10 (1959): 51; Justin Martyr, *Dialogue* 14, *PG* 6, 504–5; Isidore of Seville, *Contra Judaeos* II:20, *PL* 83, 528–29; Peter Alfonsi, *Dialogus* I, *PL* 157, 541–67; "Ostendit quod Judaei verba prophetarum carnaliter intelligunt, et ea falso exponunt."

21. This dispute appeared in practically every polemic. The Christians supported the contention that the life of Jesus fulfilled the messianic prophecies of the Hebrew Bible through the presentation of verses called testimonies. A good example of this methodology is Isidore's *Contra Judaeos*, *PL* 83, 449–538. The Jews responded by pointing out messianic prophecies which they claimed had not as yet been fulfilled. Yair ben Shabbetai offered 100 such verses; cf. *Ḥerev Pifiyot*, ed. Rosenthal (Jerusalem, 1958), pp. 35–47.

22. Jerome's translated *'almah* as *virgo* on the basis of Matt. 1:23 and the Septuagint's translation, *parthenos*. The question of the correct interpretation of this word arose in almost every polemic. Cf. *Milḥamot Ha-Shem*, p. 87; *Sefer Ha-Berit*, pp. 43–45, trans., pp. 53–56; *Yosef Ha-Meqanneh*, pp. 75–76; Profiat Duran, *Iggeret Al Tehi Ke-'Avotekha*, National and University Library, Jerusalem ms. Heb. 8° 757 (Posnanski's critical edition), Jerusalem, 5730 (1969–70), p. 54; Solomon ben Moses ben Yekutiel, *'Edut Ha-Shem Ne'emanah*, ed. Rosenthal, *Meḥkarim*, pp. 417–19; *Ḥizzuk Emunah* I:21, pp. 132–33, trans. pp. 95–96; *Magen Avraham*, 50, fols. 44a–45b; Shem Tov ibn Shapruṭ, *Even Boḥan*, JTSA ms. 2426, fols. 78b–85a, and many other places. Among the Christian sources, cf., e.g., *Tractatus Adversus Judaeum* (Anonymous), *PL* 213, 807–8; Gilbert Crispin, *Disputatio Judaei cum Christiano de Fide Christiana*, ed. Blumenkranz (Utrecht, 1956), pp. 55, 59. Cf. also Blumenkranz, *Juifs et Chrétiens*, p. 238.

23. See Neubauer and Driver, op. cit.

24. This pun is originally talmudic. Cf. Tosef. *Shab.* 13:5, *Shab.* 116a; Marcus Jastrow, *Dictionary of the Targumim . . .*, (New York, 1950), s.v. גליון, און; *Ḥesronot Ha-Shas* (Tel Aviv, 1966), p. 5. The translations used here are Jastrow's.

25. The second-century pagan Celsus repeated Jewish defamations of the New Testament in his *True Account;* see Origen, *Contra Celsum* I:28, 32, *PG* 11, 713, 720–24.

26. Cf. Herford, op. cit.

27. See Samuel Krauss, *Das Leben Jesu nach juedischen Quellen* (Berlin, 1902). Though the earliest Hebrew recension of this work is not before the tenth century, the Aramaic original may be from the fifth century; cf. pp. 246–47.

28. It should be noted that the medieval Jews did not automatically reject the stories of Jesus' miracle-working as nonhistorical; they simply interpreted such actions as having been produced by magic, not by divine power. Similarly, they interpreted the Christian claim that Joseph was not the father of Jesus to mean that Jesus was illegitimate; cf. ibid., pp. 38–40, 64–66, 68–69.

29. E.g., the genealogies in Matt. 1:1–16 and Luke 3:23–38; cf. *Niẓẓaḥon Yashan*, pp. 94–96; *Ḥizzuk Emunah* I:1, II:1, pp. 31, 285–87, trans., pp. 6, 228–30.

30. *Yosef Ha-Meqanneh*, p. 137; *Ḥizzuk Emunah* I:47, p. 2 76 trans., pp. 221–22.

31. *Toledot Yeshu*, Krauss, op. cit., pp. 80–81, 120–21.

32. *Kelimat Ha-Goyim*, chap. 10, *Ha-Ẓofeh*, 4, pp. 47–48, 81–96.

33. Ibid.

34. Ibid., chap. 6, *Ha-Ẓofeh* 3 (5674 [1913–14]): 171–78.

35. Ibid., cf. introduction, pp. 102–4. For other examples of Jewish use of the New Testament as a means of attacking Christianity, cf. *Milḥamot Ha-Shem*, pp. 141–56; *Yosef Ha-Meqanneh*, pp. 125–38; *Niẓẓaḥon Yashan*, pp. 94–122; *Sefer Ha-Berit*, pp. 24–25, trans., p. 31; *Ḥizzuk Emunah* II, pp. 283–354, trans., pp. 227–95. Shem Tov ibn Shapruṭ translated the whole book of Matthew in order to polemicize against it; cf. *Even Boḥan* XIII (other recension XII), and Abraham Marx, "The Polemical Manuscripts in the Library of the Jewish Theological Seminary," *Studies in Jewish Bibliography and Related Subjects* (New York, 1921), app. 2, pp. 270–73.

36. Cf., e.g., *'Avodah Zarah* 2:1.

37. For the general Christian attitude toward the Talmud, 500–1248, cf. Ch. Merchavia, *Ha-Talmud Be-Re'i Ha-Noẓrut* (Jerusalem, 1970). Cf. also Funkenstein, op. cit., pp. 137–41. Justin Martyr, *Dialogue* 16–17, *PG* 6, 509–13, trans., pp. 171–74, was one of the first to accuse the Jews of cursing Christians in the synagogue. For a typical medieval denunciation of the Talmud, cf. Peter of Cluny, *Tractatus Adversus Judaeorum Inveteratam Duritiem*, *PL* 189, 602–50. For the passages about Jesus, see Herford, op. cit.

38. *Vikuaḥ R. Yeḥiel Mi-Paris*, ed. Reuben Margoliot (Lwow, n. d.); cf. also Rosenthal, "The Talmud on Trial," *JQR* 47 (1956): 58–76, 145–69, and Jacob Katz, op. cit., pp. 106–13. The question of the identity of the talmudic Jesus was a frequent issue after the Paris disputation. Jewish polemicists were divided as to whether the talmudic Jesus was, indeed, the Christian Jesus of Nazareth. The reason

for the disagreement stemmed from the fact that the talmudic Jesus was said to have been a student of Joshua ben Peraḥya (*Sanh.* 107b, cf. *Ḥesronot Ha-Shas,* p. 50), who lived approximately 100 years before Jesus of Nazareth. Modern scholars are still divided on this issue; cf. Herford, op. cit., and Jacob Z. Lauterbach, "Jesus in the Talmud," *Rabbinic Essays* (New York, 1973), pp. 473–570. Just as Christian attacks upon the Talmud did not appear until a relatively late period, so too did the Jewish defense take shape only at an advanced stage of the Jewish-Christian debate. Jacob ben Reuben, writing in 1170, did not mention the Christian attack on the Talmud, even though Peter Alfonsi (1062–1110) made use of this tactic. The former's imitators made up for this omission; cf. the works of Moses Ha-Kohen, Shem Tov ibn Shapruṭ, and Isaac Lupis.

39. Commonly cited passages which were adduced as rabbinic proof that Jesus was the messiah are: *Lam. Rabbati* 1, 57; *Derekh Ereẓ Zuta* 1 (Tos. *Yev.* 15:2); *Sanh.* 97a–b, 98a. Other rabbinic passages were cited to prove various Christian doctrines, such as Trinity and incarnation.

40. *De Fide Catholica contra Hareticos* III; *PL* 210, 399–422; cf. Funkenstein, op. cit., pp. 141–42; Merchavia, op. cit., pp. 214–17.

41. Cf. *Vikuaḥ Ramban.*

42. Cf. *Pugio Fidei,* ed. Carpzov (Leipzig, 1687). The literature on Martini and his "forgeries" is extensive; cf. Saul Lieberman, *Shkiin,* 2nd ed. (Jerusalem, 1970), pp. 43–91.

43. Cf. *Sefer Teshuvot La-Meḥaref,* Parma ms. 2440 (De Rossi 533). On Abner, see Baer, *History,* I, pp. 327–54.

44. Cf. *Vikuaḥ Ṭorṭosa,* ed. Kobak, *Jeshurun* 6 (1868): 45–55. Another version appears in Solomon ibn Verga's *Shevet Yehuda,* ed. Baer-Shoḥat (Jerusalem, 1947), pp. 94 ff. The Latin protocol was edited by Antonio Pacios Lopez, *La Disputa de Tortosa* (Madrid, 1957). Cf. also Geronimo's work *Hebraeomastix,* in *Bibliotheca Magna Veterum Patrum* (Lyons, 1677), XXVI, pp. 528–54.

45. Cf. ibid., and *Vikuaḥ Ramban.* The most comprehensive analysis of midrashim concerning the messiah is Abravanel's *Yeshu'ot Meshiḥo* (Koenigsberg, 1861). Cf. also Solomon ben Simon Duran's *Milḥemet Miẓvah,* printed with Simon Duran, *Keshet U-Magen,* (Livorno, 5523 [1762–63]), pp. 28–39 (reprinted, Jerusalem, 5730); Moses Ha-Kohen, *'Ezer Ha-'Emunah,* ed. Yehuda Shamir, *Rabbi Moses Ha-Kohen of Tordesillas and His Book, Ezer Ha-Emunah,* II (Coconut Grove, Fla., 1972), pp. 127–60; *Even Boḥan* XI; Isaac Lupis, *Kur Maẓref Ha-'Emunot U-Mar'eh Ha-'Emet,* ed. Isaac Altaris (Metz, 1847), chap. 11.

46. Among the thinkers quoted by Duran in his *Kelimat Ha-Goyim* were Peter Lombard, Nicholas de Lyra, and Vincent of Beauvais. The first two were quoted extensively. For other possible Christian sources, cf. Posnanski's notes.

47. De Modena quoted mainly Thomas Aquinas and Pietro Galatino; cf. *Magen Va-Ḥerev,* ed. S. Simonsohn (Jerusalem, 1960), index, p. 79.

48. E.g., Maimonides and Ibn Ezra were quoted in *Teshuvot La-Meḥaref.*

49. As noted, the Midrash was not considered authoritative; still, every effort

was made by the Jewish polemicists to expound the rabbinic texts in refutation of Christian arguments.

50. *Shevet Yehuda*, p. 64: והמציאות יוכיח, כי למה ישבו בגלות דחופים סחופים ממושכים ומורטים? כי אם לנקום דם ישו!

51. Cf. Isidore, *Contra Judaeos* II:9, *PL* 83, 514–15; *Altercatio Aecclesie Contra Synagogam*, ed. Blumenkranz, *Revue du Moyen Age Latin* (Strasbourg, 1954), pp. 140–42; Migne, "Index de Judaeis," IV, "De Scelere, caecitate et poena Judaeorum," *PL* 220, 996–1001; Blumenkranz, *Juifs et Chrétiens*, pp. 272–79. For a modern treatment of this issue, cf. Augustin Bea, *The Church and the Jewish People* (New York, 1966), pp. 67–68, 75.

52. Aphrahat (ca. 336–45) recorded that Jews argued that Christianity must be false since its practitioners were persecuted; cf. Jacob Neusner, *Aphrahat and Judaism* (Leiden, 1971), pp. 97–112. Cf. also Justin, *Dialogue* 34, 110, *PG* 6, 545–49, 729–32, trans., pp. 197–200, 317–19.

53. *Additions to Sefer Ha-Berit*, pp. 62–68, trans., pp. 74–81; Solomon ben Moses ben Yekutiel, *'Edut Ha-Shem Ne'emanah*, pp. 396–400; *Ḥizzuk Emunah* I:2, 6–8, pp. 38–40, 45–77, trans. pp. 14–17, 22–44; *Vikuaḥ* of Elijah Ḥayyim, pp. 447–48; *Zohar*, Pinḥas, IV, 220b–221b.

54. *Milḥemet Miẓvah*, fol. 14a, Yom Tov Lipmann Mühlhausen, *Sefer Niẓẓaḥon*, ed. Theodor Hackspan (Altdorf, 1644), p. 118; *Magen Avraham* 23, fol. 27a. This argument is reflected in the polemical treatise of Gennadius, written ca. 1455, two years after the fall of Constantinople to the Muslim Turks. The Jews pointed to Christian suffering as proof of Christianity's falseness. Turkish Jews, on the other hand, were well treated by the Ottoman Turks. Gennadius replied that the sufferings were only local in nature, and, besides, Christians willingly bore all things for Christ; cf. Williams, op. cit., p. 196. Cf. also *Ḥizzuk Emunah* I:3, p. 41, trans. pp. 17–18.

55. Cf. Stein, op. cit.; *Sefer Ha-Berit*, p. 27, trans., pp. 33–34; *'Edut Ha-Shem Ne'emanah*, p. 405; *Niẓẓaḥon Yashan*, pp. 70–71; and Rosenthal, "Ribbit Min Ha-Nokhri," *Meḥkarim*, pp. 253–323. Joseph Albo, *'Iqqarim* III:25, ed. Isaac Husik (Philadelphia, 1929), III, pp. 237–38, gave a different answer: since the life of an idolater is allowed to be taken, surely his money is permitted to the Jew.

56. Cf. *Sefer Ha-Berit*, pp. 25–28, trans., pp. 32–35; *Niẓẓaḥon Yashan*, pp. 22–23, 126–27. The theme of Christian immorality runs through the latter work. Cf. also *Milḥemet Miẓvah*, fol. 85b.

57. For all the various interpretations of this verse, see Posnanski, *Schiloh*.

58. Cf., e.g., *Vikuaḥ Ramban*, p. 311; *Ḥizzuk Emunah* I:1, pp. 30–38, trans., pp. 5–14. Some Christians were aware of this type of reasoning; cf. *Trophies of Damascus* (681), ed. Gustave Bardy, *Patrologia Orientalis* 15, 2 (1927): 220–21.

59. E.g., *Sefer Ha-Berit*, pp. 28–29, trans., pp. 36–37; *Niẓẓaḥon Yashan*, pp. 4–5, 21. Christians were aware of this type of argument; cf. Thomas, *ST* III, 31, 4.

60. See below, chap. 5, for a full discussion of the philosophical arguments against incarnation.

61. See below, chap. 6.

62. See below, chap. 5.

63. Such an argument is made by the anti-Marrano polemicist Machado. I owe this reference to Prof. Frank Talmage who is editing his work.

64. See below, chap. 3.

Chapter Two

1. Op. cit., pp. 22–26. It should be noted that the bibliographical information contained in the notes to chap. 1 will not be repeated here. See above and the bibliography at the end of this study.

2. On Jacob ben Reuben's Neoplatonism, cf. *Milḥamot Ha-Shem*, pp. 3–4. For his quoting of various philosophers, see ibid., pp. 164–65. On this work in general, see David Berger, "Gilbert Crispin, Alan of Lille, and Jacob ben Reuben: A Study in the Transmission of Medieval Polemic," *Speculum* 49 (1974): 34–47.

3. Cf. *'Ezer Ha-'Emunah*, pp. 6–7.

4. The first edition of this work was printed in *Milḥemet Ḥovah* (Constantinople, 1710), pp. 18b–38a. Cf. Louis I. Newman, "Joseph ben Isaac Kimchi as a Religious Controversialist," *Jewish Studies in Memory of Israel Abrahams* (New York, 1927), pp. 365–72.

5. Cf. Z. Kahn, "Étude sur le Livre de Joseph Le Zélateur," *REJ* 1 (1880): 222–46; 3 (1881): 1–38; Ephraim E. Urbach, "Étude sur la Littérature Polémique au Moyen-Age," *REJ* 100 (1935): 49–77.

6. Ed. Frank Talmage, *Sefer Ha-Berit*, pp. 71–79. The first edition was printed as an appendix to Mühlhausen's *Sefer Niẓẓaḥon* (no. 10), ed. Hackspan (Altdorf, 1644), pp. 196–200. It also appears in *Ḥesronot Ha-Shas*, pp. 87–92. Cf. also Talmage, "R. David Kimḥi as Polemicist," *HUCA* 38 (1967): 213–35.

7. Stein, op. cit., has promised an edition of this work, but it has not as yet appeared.

8. There are two main recensions of this work. Some of the textual problems were discussed by Marx, op. cit. On Ibn Shapruṭ, see José Mª Sanz Artibucilla, "Los Judios en Aragon y Navarra: Neuvos Datos Biograficos Relativos a Šem Ṭoḅ Ben Iṣḥaq Šaprut," *Sefarad* 5 (1945): 337–66.

9. Cf. Yehuda Kaufman (Even Shmuel), *R. Yom-Tov Lipmann Mühlhausen* (Hebrew) (New York, 1927).

10. JTSA ms. 2452.

11. National and University Library, Jerusalem, ms. Heb. 8° 787 (Posnanski ms.), published Jerusalem, 5730 (1969–70).

12. Cf. Williams, op. cit., pp. 408–15. For De Lyra's knowledge of Judaism, cf. Hailperin, op. cit.

13. Ed. Shlomo Ḥanokh Degel-Zahav, *Koveẓ 'Al Yad* 15 (1899).

14. Two recensions of this work exist. S. Löwinger published part of *Magen*

Avraham and discussed the textual problem in "Liquṭim Mi-*S. Magen Avraham*," *Ha-Ẓofeh Le-Ḥokhmat Yisrael,* 12 (1928): 277–97. Cf. idem, "Recherches sur l'oeuvre apologétique d'Abraham Farissol," *REJ* 105 (1939): 23–52.

15. First edition Wagenseil, *Tela;* reedited with vowels and stanzas, Israel Davidson, "The Author of the Poem *Zikheron Sefer Niẓẓaḥon, JQR* 18 (1927–28): 257–65; trans. Rankin, op. cit., pp. 60–68. On the identification of the author, see A. Kaminka, "Note on Meshullam ben Uri," ibid., p. 437; cf. also, Davidson, "Note on *Zikheron Sefer Niẓẓaḥon,*" *JQR* 19 (1928–29): 75–76.

16. See, e.g., A. Lukyn Williams, *A Manual of Christian Evidences for the Jewish People,* 2 vols. (London, 1911–19). On Troki, see M. Waysbaum, "Isaac of Troki and Christian Controversy in the XVI Century," *JJS* 3 (1952): 62–77.

17. The history of this polemical work, which exists in a number of recensions, is obscure. Cf. G. B. De Rossi, *Mss. Codices Hebraici* (Parma, 1803), no. 75, pp. 38–39; references in this study will be cited from Bodleian ms. 2175.

18. The first edition was published by Wagenseil in *Tela.* For other editions, cf. Chavel, op. cit., p. 301. On the Disputation of Barcelona, see Baer, "Le-Vikoret Ha-Vikuḥim Shel R. Yeḥiel Mi-Paris Ve-Shel R. Moshe Ben Naḥman," *Tarbiz* 2 (5691 [1930–31]): 172–87; Martin Cohen, "Reflections on the Text and Context of the Disputation of Barcelona," *HUCA* 35 (1964): 157–92; H. Denifle, "Quellen in Disputation Pablos Christiani . . . ," *Historisches Jahrbuch der Gorres-Gesellschaft* 8 (1887): 225–44; Loeb, "La Controverse de 1263 à Barcelone," *REJ* 16 (1887): 1–18; Cecil Roth, "The Disputation of Barcelona (1263)," *HThR* 43 (1950): 114–44.

19. On the Paris Disputation, see Baer, "Le-Vikoret"; Katz, op. cit., pp. 106–13; A. Lewin, "Die Religionsdisputation des R. Jechiel von Paris 1240 am Hofe Ludwigs des Heiligen, ihre Veranlassung und ihre Folgen," *MGWJ* 18 (1869): 97–110, 145–56, 193–210; Loeb, "La Controverse de 1240 sur le Talmud," *REJ* 1 (1880): 247–61; 2 (1881): 248–70; 3 (1882): 39–57; Rosenthal, "The Talmud on Trial."

20. See Baer, *History,* II, pp. 170–243; Posnanski, "La Colloque de Tortose et de San Mateo (7 février 1413–13 novembre 1414)," *REJ* 74 (1922): 17–39, 160–68; 75 (1922): 74–88, 187–204.

21. Ed. Eliezer Ashkenazi, *Divre Ḥakhamim* (Metz, 1849), pp. 41–46. The version cited here is L. Landau, *Das Apologetische Schreiben des Josua Lorki* (Antwerp, 1906).

22. Ed. Abraham Berliner (Altona, 1875). The Arabic texts associated with this work are the following: Leon Schlosberg, *Controverse d'un Evêque* (Vienna, 1880) (Arabic), (Versailles, 1888) (French); Richard Gottheil, "Some Geniza Gleanings," *Mélanges Hartwig Derenbourg* (Paris, 1909), pp. 84–101; S. Krauss, "Un Fragment Polémique de la Gueniza," *REJ* 63 (1912): 63–74.

23. Stanislaus Simon, ed., *Mose ben Salomo von Salerno und seine philosophischen Auseinandersetzungen mit den Lehren des Christentums* (Breslau, 1931). Simon published only the philosophical part of this work. On Moses ben

Solomon's Neoplatonism, see Simon's introduction, and Giuseppe Sermonetta, *Un Glossario Filosofico Ebraico-Italiano del XIII Secolo* (Rome, 1969).

24. Ed. Frank Talmage, *Sefer Ha-Berit,* 83–96. The first edition was in *Milḥemet Ḥovah,* pp. 13a–18b. On the authorship of this work and an English translation, see Talmage, "An Hebrew Polemical Treatise, Anti-Cathar and Anti-Orthodox," *HThR* 60 (1967): 323–48.

25. Ed. Moritz Steinschneider, *Jeshurun* (Kobak), 8 (1872): 1–13.

26. Published as an appendix in *'Ezer Ha-'Emunah,* pp. 163–81. The Hebrew translator was Meir ben Jacob.

27. Printed Frankfort, 1866.

28. Ed. Rosenthal, *Meḥkarim,* pp. 431–55. See J. Bergmann, "Deux Polémistes Juifs Italiens," *REJ* 40 (1900): 188–205.

29. JTSA ms. 2461. See Bergmann, ibid.

30. Ed. George Belasco (London, 1908).

31. JTSA ms. 2214.

32. Ed. Posnanski, *Ha-Ẓofeh Me-'Ereẓ Hagar* 3 (5674 [1913–14]): 99–113, 143–80; 4 (5675 [1914–15]): 37–48, 81–96, 115–32. See also R. W. Emery, "New Light on Profayt Duran *The Efodi,*" *JQR* 58 (1967–68): 328–37; M. Saenger, "Ueber den Verfasser des polemischen Werkes: *S. Ha-Kelimah* oder *Kelimat Ha-Goyim,*" *MGWJ* 3 (1854): 320–27.

33. The first edition is of unknown date and place (Salonika?, 1860?). It was also edited by Ephraim Deinard (Kearny, N.J., 1904). Both editions are replete with errors. The text used in the present study is JTSA ms. 2209.

34. See J. M. Millás-Vallicrosa, "Aspectos Filosoficos de la Polémica Judaica en Tiempos de Ḥasday Crescas," in *Harry A. Wolfson Jubilee Volume* (New York, 1965), II, pp. 561–75.

35. Cf. also Rosenthal, "Sifrut," nos. 42, 77; Rankin, op. cit., pp. 89–154; for the correspondence between Bodo-Eleazar and Paul Alvare, see Bernhard Blumenkranz, "Un Pamphlet Juif Médio-Latin de Polémique Antichrétienne," *Revue d'Histoire et de Philosophie Religieuses* 34 (1954): 401–13.

36. See Rosenthal, "Ha-Pulmus," Shereshevsky, op. cit., Baer, "Rashi," and Hailperin, op. cit.

37. Cf., e.g., Ibn Ezra's *Commentary on Genesis,* Introduction, The Third Way.

38. As noted, parts of Kimḥi's Psalm commentary have been extracted into a separate polemical work; see above. On the subject in general, see Erwin I. J. Rosenthal, "Anti-Christian Polemic in Medieval Bible Commentaries," *JJS* 11 (1960): 115–35.

39. See Joseph Blau, *The Christian Interpretation of the Cabala* (New York, 1944); Baer, "Torat Ha-Qabalah Be-Mishnato Ha-Qeristologit shel Avner Mi-Burgos," *Tarbiẓ* 27 (5718 [1957–58]): 278–89.

40. Cf. Wilhelm Bacher, "Judeo-Christian Polemics in the Zohar," *JQR* o.s. 3 (1891): 781–84. The passage "Berikh Shme," *Zohar,* Vayakhel, may have an anti-Christian nuance: "Lo 'al enash raḥiẓna ve-lo 'al bar elohin samikhna."

41. Cf. Daniel Goldstein, *Seder Ha-Seliḥot* (Jerusalem, 5725 [1964–65]), pp. 12–13; Rabbenu Gershom Meor Ha-Golah, *Seliḥot U-Fizmonim*, ed. A. M. Habermann (Jerusalem, 1944). Cf. also, e.g., Abraham ibn Ezra's poem *El Eḥad Bera'ani:* "Re'eh li-geveret emet, shifḥah no'emet, lo ki benekh ha-met, u-veni he-ḥai."

42. Cf. *The Book of Tradition (Sefer Ha-Qabbalah)*, ed. Gerson D. Cohen (Philadelphia, 1967), pp. 15–16, 30 (Heb.), 20–22, 39 (Eng.).

43. Though one could argue that this is not really a chronicle, the author presents it as one.

44. The history of the development of *halakhah* concerning Christians is told by Jacob Katz, op. cit.

45. *Sefer Shofṭim*, H. Melakhim, 11:4, in uncensored editions.

46. *Teshuvot Ha-Rashba*, 4, 187 (Salonika, 5575 [1814–15]), pp. 36b–37b.

47. For bibliographic treatment of al-Muqammiẓ's works, see below, chap. 4.

48. *Kitāb al-Amānāt wa'l-I'tiqādāt*, ed. S. Landauer (Leiden, 1880); trans. Samuel Rosenblatt, *The Book of Beliefs and Opinions* (New Haven, 1948).

49. *Kitāb al-Hidāya ila Farā'id al-Qulūb*, ed. A. S. Yahuda (Leiden, 1912); trans. Menahem Mansoor, *The Book of Direction to the Duties of the Heart* (London, 1973).

50. *Dalālat al-Ḥa'irīn*, ed. Solomon Munk (Jerusalem, 1929); trans. Shlomo Pines, *The Guide of the Perplexed* (Chicago, 1963).

51. *Or Ha-Shem* (Vienna, 1861), reprinted.

52. *Derekh Emunah* (Constantinople, 1522). The Jerusalem, 5730 (1969–70) reprint does not include much of the anti-Christian material. Such passages can be found in the Gregg Publishers (England, 1969) reprint.

53. Ed. Isaac Reggio (Vienna, 1833), reprinted. Reggio censored anti-Christian passages, which are supplied by Judah Briel, "Hashmaṭot Bi-Defuse *S. Beḥinat Ha-Dat*," *Ozar Tov (Magazin fur die Wissenschaft des Judenthums)* 4 (1898): 082–084, and Julius Guttmann, "Elia del Medigos Verhaltnis zu Averroes in seinem *Bechinat Ha-Dat*," *Jewish Studies in Memory of Israel Abrahams* (New York, 1927), pp. 192–208.

54. Cf. Williams, *Adversus Judaeos*.

55. Cf. Wolfgang Seiferth, *Synagogue and Church in the Middle Ages* (New York, 1970).

56. For instance, a Christian discussing the law as found in the Hebrew Bible would most likely make reference to the Jews, the people to whom the law was given. A Jew, however, when discussing the same topic, would have little reason to refer to Christianity.

Chapter Three

1. The exposition in this chapter will be based on the theories of the Jewish Averroists (thirteenth–seventeenth century). Much of what will be discussed, though, can

be seen as applicable to other Jewish philosophical polemicists.

2. The King had dreamt that an angel appeared to him and told him that his intentions were good but his religious actions were deficient. Were he to accept the philosopher's opinion, he would, in essence, deny that the dream had any significance. The King rejected philosophy, then, because it denied the veracity of his dream.

3. On the literary significance of the opening passage, see Eliezer Schweid, "Omanut Ha-Di'alog Be-Sefer *Ha-Kuzari* U-Mashma'utah Ha-'Iyunit," *Ṭa'am Va-Haqashah* (Ramat Gan, 1970), pp. 55–73.

4. *Kitāb al-Khazarī* I:5, pp. 10–12; adapted from Hirschfeld, *The Kuzari* (New York, 1964), p. 42 (emphasis added). This passage was quoted with approval by Simon Duran, who continued to say that reason should yield to sense perception and experience. In such case that there is neither sense perception nor experience, and reason rejects a doctrine, it is not to be maintained; cf. *Keshet U-Magen,* p. 3b.

5. Schweid, op. cit., pp. 60–61, made the observation that the King, who rejected philosophy as unsatisfactory, used the methodology of philosophy as the basis for his nonacceptance of Christianity and Islam. Halevi's point, which was made only implicitly, was to the effect that reason in itself was not sufficient justification for belief. On the other hand, a doctrine which was contradicted by reason was not to be maintained. This is also the position of the Jewish Averroists; see below.

6. *Vikuaḥ Ha-Ramban,* pp. 310–11; trans., Rankin, op. cit., p. 191 (emphasis added). The words in brackets are found only in some texts.

7. *Magen Va-Romaḥ,* p. 135: כל ספרים שבעולם לא יכניסו זה במוח המשכילים כלל ובפרט לאשר גדלו בתורה רחוקה מכל אלה האמונות... כי כל אמונתו מסכמת בשכל.

8. *Ḥizzuk Emunah,* p. 13: הסכימו חכמי הנוצרים עם כל עוצם חכמתם בחכמות האנושיות לאמונותיהם הזרות בשכל האנושי בלתי ראיות נוכחות מדברי הנביאים.

9. Ibid., pp. 29–30: אז נודע לי בלי ספק שאמונו׳ הזרו׳ והשיבושים ההם נשארו להם בירושה מקדמוניהם ויתעום כזביהם אשר הלכו אבותיהם והורגלו והתנהגו בהם מנעורותיהם ושבו להיות להם כדברים הטבעיים ולכן (צ״ל אין) נראין זרים בעיניהם כי ההרגל טבע שני.

This section is not in the translation. Troki was referring to such pagan/Christian beliefs as the virgin birth. Moses Mendelssohn made the same point as the medieval polemicists. In his first letter to Lavater, he stated that if Lavater found the arguments of Charles Bonnet's *Palingenesis* irrefutable while he himself were unconvinced, "It can only mean that one of us must be a remarkable example of the influence which prejudice and upbringing exert upon those who search for the truth with all their heart"; *Moses Mendelssohn Gesammelte Schriften,* Jubiläumsausgabe (Berlin, 1930), p. 16; trans. Alfred Jospe, *Jerusalem and Other Jewish Writings* (New York, 1969), p. 121.

With these Jewish thinkers there was another issue involved besides just an explanation of why Christians believed in certain doctrines. The polemicists were very aware of the fact that many Jews were converting to Christianity, and an adequate interpretation of this phenomenon was sought. By positing that only a person raised as a Christian could possibly believe in Christian doctrines, the Jewish polemicists implied that conversions were based on non-rational motives. This is evident in both Profiat Duran's *Iggeret* to the apostate David Bonjorn, and Joshua Lorki's *Nusaḥ Ha-Ketav* addressed to Paul of Burgos (though, at a later date, Lorki himself converted also). Some polemicists offered another reason for the success of Christianity, namely the fact that Emperor Constantine forced Christianity upon the Gentiles (cf., e.g., *Even Boḥan* I:12, fol. 52a). No doubt the Jews who mentioned this had the forced conversions of their own day in mind.

10. *Guide* III:15, p. 331: ללממתמע טביעה ת׳אבתה קאימה אלת׳באת. trans., Pines, p. 459.

11. Ibid., p. 332; trans., pp. 459–60.

12. Ibid.

13. Ibid., I:73:10, p. 144; trans., p. 206.

14. Maimonides discussed the difference between divine will and divine wisdom in III:13, 25, and 26, pp. 323–29, 365–71; trans., pp. 448–56, 502–10. At the end of I:73:10, Maimonides said that the Jews held that the world was a product of divine will; cf. below.

15. Ibid., I:73:10, p. 144; trans., p. 207.

16. Ibid., pp. 146–48; trans., pp. 209–12.

17. Ibid., p. 148; trans., p. 211 (emphasis added).

18. If the man were the size of a mountain, it would not be a man. An elephant the size of a flea is not an elephant. Earth is inherently heavy and, thus, at the center; fire is inherently light and, thus, far from the center.

19. This is the import of *Guide* II:13–30, pp. 196–252; trans., pp. 281–359.

20. Ibid., III:15, p. 332; trans., p. 460.

21. Ibid.; trans., p. 461.

22. Ibid.: פיא לית שערי; trans., p. 460.

23. Ibid., III:13, pp. 323–26: פלא בד צ׳רורה אן ינתהי אלאמר פי אַט׳א אלגאיה אלי כד׳א שא אללה או כד׳א אקתצ׳ת חכמתה; trans., pp. 448–52. Maimonides argued that whenever one found a reason for one thing, the question of purpose immediately was transferred to another thing.

24. Ibid., pp. 326–29: ואן שית קׄל באלחכמה אלאלאהיה; trans., pp. 452–56.

25. Ibid., I:73:10, p. 148: ומא הו אמר יבאד׳ר בדפע ג׳מיעה באלהוינא; trans., p. 212.

26. Ibid., III:15, p. 332; trans., pp. 460–61.

27. P. 75; trans., p. 111. Cf. also *Maqala fi Teḥiyyat Ha-Metim (Treatise on Resurrection),* ed. Joshua Finkel (New York, 1939), p. 1 (Hebrew and Arabic).

28. P. 183; trans., p. 263.

29. In uncensored editions.

30. *Epistle to Yemen,* ed. Abraham S. Halkin (trans. Boaz Cohen) (New York, 1952), pp. 12–15 (Heb. and Arab.), pp. iii–iv (Eng.).

31. *Maskiyot Kesef* on III:15, ed. S. Z. Werbluner, *Sheloshah Qadmone Mefarshe Ha-Moreh* (Jerusalem, 1961), pp. 125–26; see below.

32. *Magen Avot* I:5 in *Keshet U-Magen,* p. 26b.

33. Mendelssohn was of the impression that Maimonides had nothing at all to say about Christianity. See Alexander Altmann, *Moses Mendelssohn* (Philadelphia,

1973), pp. 205, 793, n. 21.

34. Ed. G. F. Hourani (Leiden, 1959). For the Hebrew translation, see N. Golb, "The Hebrew Translation of Averroes' *Faṣl al-Maqāl*," *PAAJR* 25 (1956): 91–113; 26 (1957): 41–64. Cf. also Ernst Renan, *Averroes et l'Averroïsme* (Paris, 1852), pp. 162–72.

35. See Y. Baer, *History*, pp. 244–99.

36. I:21, ed. Husik, pp. 177–78.

37. Ibid., I:22, p. 178.

38. Ibid., p. 179.

39. Ibid. Though he did not say so explicitly, this statement appears to have been directed against Christianity.

40. Ibid., p. 180.

41. Ibid., III:25, pp. 220–21. Isaac Lupis virtually repeated Joseph Albo's words verbatim when he agreed that there existed a difference between logical and natural impossibilities; see *Kur Maẓref*, p. 18b. Shem Tov ibn Shapruṭ (ca. 1385) taught a very similar doctrine and may have been one of Albo's sources; cf. *Even Boḥan* I:11, fol. 50b.

42. *Biṭṭul*, fol. 3a: א׳ שהאמונה לא תכריח השכל להאמין דבר שיבא אל סתירה, ב׳ שלא ידומה יכולת אלקי לסתור המושכלות הראשונות ולא לתולדות אשר התבארו במופתים המוחלטים, וזה מפני שהם כבר נולדו מהראשונות.

43. *Commentary on the Iggeret*, pp. 28–32.

44. *Beḥinat Ha-Dat*, pp. 12–16. The explicit anti-Christian nature of this passage is obscured by Reggio's self-censorship. See Julius Guttmann, op. cit., pp. 201–3.

45. *Beḥinat Ha-Dat*, p. 16.

46. Ibid., pp. 16–17: נשיב שאנחנו בעלי הדת לא נאמר שיתואר השם ביכולת על הסותרים ולא על החולפים אבל נאמר שלא יחפוץ בם כלל, גם לא נאמר שיתואר ביכולת על עצמו כאלו תאמר לשנות עצמו או תאר מתאריו המיוחדים לו אבל לא יחפוץ בו.
Del Medigo added that religions were not judged on their doctrines alone, but also according to their commandments.

47. *Vikuaḥ*, pp. 439–40: חלילה לנו להאמין באמונה שאינה מסכמת עם השכל מאד, ומה שהשכל יכזיבהו אין ראוי להקרא תורה, כי לא תבוא התורה לבטל השכל.

48. Ibid., p. 451: אנחנו העברים אין אנו אומרים שאין להאמין בדבר אלא מצד שהשכל יחייבהו דרך מופת. אבל אנחנו אומרים שאין להאמין בדברים שהשכל יכזיבם וידחה אותם מכל וכל עד שיראה מניעות מציאותם.

49. *Magen Va-Ḥerev*, pp. 22–24.

50. Ibid., p. 38: האמונה צריך שתהיה ממוצע בין המופת והסברא, כלו׳ שלא יהיה עליה מופת גמור. שא״כ לא היתה אמונה, אבל יהיה לה איזה צד בסברא, למען לא תהיה סכלות גמורה.
De Modena's definition of faith was taken from Thomas Aquinas (*ST* II–II, 1, 2): "Fides est media inter scientiam et opinionem." De Modena, giving his definition in the name of "the sage" *(he-ḥakham)*, changed Thomas' *opinio* to *sevara'*, in the sense of reason. This was evident when he said that faith needed some basis in *sevara'* so as not to be complete foolishness.

51. *Gesammelte Schriften,* p. 301; trans., p. 123.

52. Ibid.; trans., p. 124. Cf., however, Mendelssohn's statement in his *Jerusalem* that if Judaism were proven irrational, he would have to subordinate reason to the yoke of faith; see Altmann, *Mendelssohn,* p. 532.

53. Mendelssohn's affinity to medieval Averroism, and to Del Medigo in particular, can be seen in his statements about miracles. According to both Mendelssohn and Del Medigo, miracles proved nothing in terms of faith. Miracles could not force one to believe in irrational doctrines. For Mendelssohn, cf. *Schriften,* p. 301, and *Letter to Charles Bonnet,* February 9, 1770, in ibid., pp. 321–25; trans., pp. 130–32. For Del Medigo, cf. *Beḥinat Ha-Dat,* pp. 9–10.

54. *SCG* I, 7, p. 6; trans. Anton C. Pegis, *On the Truth of the Catholic Faith,* I, (New York, 1955), p. 74. (Vol. IV was translated by Charles J. O'Neil, New York, 1957.)

55. Ibid., p. 7; trans., p. 75.

The dialectical trend, of which Thomas was the most important representative, was not the only Christian school of thought in the Middle Ages. The dialecticians were interested in reconciling Christian doctrines with philosophy, though they did not believe that mysteries of the faith were derived from reason. Other thinkers held that such beliefs could not be reconciled with reason and for this very reason were to be believed. Tertullian, the most important representative of this trend, said: "Prorsus credibile est, quia ineptum est—it is to be believed because it is senseless," and "certum est, quia impossibile est—it is certain because it is impossible" (*De Carne Christi* 5). Anselm stood in the middle between the dialecticians and the anti-dialecticians. He used reason extensively, but taught that one must submit to established doctrine even if he cannot understand it (*Liber de Fide Trinitatis et de Incarnatione Verbi, PL* 158, 263). He also said: "Credo ut intelligam—I believe in order to understand" (*Proslogion* I, *PL* 158, 227). A third school of thought was that of the Christian Averroists, e.g., Siger of Brabant, who taught a double truth theory. Both religious and philosophical doctrines were true, even if they contradicted each other; see Renan, op. cit., and Pierre F. Mandonnet, *Siger de Brabant et l'Averroïsme latin au XIIIme Siècle* (Louvain, 1908–11). The Jewish polemicists, by and large, ignored the Christian Averroists, and only one Jewish philosopher, Isaac Albalag, adopted a double truth theory; see *Sefer Tiqqun Ha-De'ot,* ed. Georges Vajda (Jerusalem, 1973), and Vajda, *Isaac Albalag* (Paris, 1960). Since the Jewish philosophers considered their doctrines in accord with reason, a radical double truth theory was felt to be unnecessary.

Some Jewish polemicists were quite aware of the attitude of the Christian anti-dialecticians. A number of them, including Naḥmanides, Ibn Shapruṭ, Farrisol, Elijah Ḥayyim, Solomon ibn Verga, and Azriel Alatino, quoted Christians as saying that their doctrines were beyond reason, and therefore to be believed (or despite this to be believed). The Jews rejected this mode of thinking, insisting instead that true religious doctrines might not be rejected by reason.

It was basically against the dialecticians that the Jewish philosophical critique of

Christianity was directed. These thinkers claimed that they accepted reason and logic, yet according to the Jewish polemicists, their doctrines were contradicted by philosophical principles. Such Christians, who said that religion and reason were not incompatible, were a much better target of attack than those thinkers, either anti-dialecticians or Averroists, who agreed that reason and the Christian religion did contradict each other. For their part, Christian philosophers were aware of many seeming contradictions in their doctrines, and they labored hard to reconcile Christianity with reason. Many Jewish arguments may, in fact, have been taken from these Christian works, in which they were originally mentioned as objections that must be met. The best example of this is Judah Aryeh de Modena's *Magen Va-Ḥerev* in which anti-Christian arguments found in Christian works, mainly from Thomas, are quoted explicitly.

56. This was apparently a veiled attack on incarnation, a doctrine which taught that only one of God's attributes, the Son, took on flesh, while other attributes remained as they were.

57. *Beḥinat Ha-Dat*, pp. 16–27: אבל נאמר שיתואר ביכולת על כל הדברים אשר זולתו ולא נקפיד הפעם בזה כי הדבור בזה זר. See above for the remainder of the quotation.

58. *Guide* III:13; see above.

59. Isaac Reggio interpreted Del Medigo's statements to mean that certain doctrines were impossible because they taught an imperfection in God. This criterion of impossibility was a common one, as is about to be shown.

60. The idea that what is unbecoming to say about God may not be predicated on Him goes back to the presocratic Xenophanes. This doctrine was stressed by the Stoics, who used the term *θεοπρεπές* to denote that which is proper to say about God. Biblical anthropomorphisms were reinterpreted by religious philosophers in order to avoid saying about God anything unbecoming to Him. Cf. Philip Wheelwright, *The Presocratics* (New York, 1966), pp. 31–39; Werner Jaeger, *The Theology of the Early Greek Philosophers* (Oxford, 1967), pp. 38–54, esp. p. 50.

61. *Sefer Ha-Berit*, p. 29: על כן, איני מאמין אמונה זו שאתה מאמין; כי שכלי לא ייתן אותי להפחית גדולת השם יתעלה, כי לא המעיט כבודו יתעלה ולא חיסר יקרו יתנשא. ואם איני מאמין אמונה זו שאתה מאמין, איני אשם; trans., p. 37.

62. *Maskiyot Kesef*, p. 126: הנה זה אינו טענה, כי נשיב להם שאותן הדברים אשר נודה היות השם ית׳ יכול עליהם אינם חסרון, אבל מה שאתם אומרים הוא חסרון וחלילה שיהיה בעצמות השם כח ואפשרות לרע או חסרון ופחיתות.

63. *Evan Boḥan* I:12, fol. 51b: ...הפרש גדול יש בין הדברים אשר הם גנות וחסרון בעצם האל לשאר הענינים שאין בהם רק חסרון ידיעת טעמם.

64. Cf. *Guide* II:15.

65. *Derekh Emunah* (Constantinople, 1522), p. 99a:
תשוב׳ שאלתך היא בשני פנים. הראשון כי מופתי ארסטו על הקדמו׳ אינם מופתים אבל טענות כמו שקויים אצלנו אנחנו תלמידי הרמבם ואז כאשר נכפור אותם ונאמין החדוש לא נאמין נמנעות כי זאת הגזרה אפשרית אצל הידיעה. והשני כי ההמנעו׳ הראשון כאשר נאמינהו נתן חסרון בחק האלהו׳ וההמנעו׳ השני נתן שלמות בחק האלהות. הנה כשנאמר שהשם ית׳ התפעל ונתגשם ונהרג ומת זהו חסרון לאלהות ונשים האלוה שאינו

אלוה אבל נמצא אפשרי המציאו׳ ומצטרך אל זולתו ומתפעל מזולתו.
This page is missing from the Jerusalem, 5730 reprint, but appears in the London, 1969 reprint.

66. Ibid.:
וכשנאמר שהשם ית׳ פעל וחדש העולם יש מאין עם שיהיה נמנע בחק שום פועל כשנאמין זה נתן שלמות לאלוה היכול על כל הדברים אפילו על הדברים אשר יראה להיותם מנועים ואנחנו רוצים להאמין כל דבר שיתן שלמות לשם ית׳ והנותן חסרון אין אני רוצה להאמין אותו.
This argument was repeated by Solomon ibn Verga in *Shevet Yehudah,* p. 88. A good example of a non-Averroistic answer to a similar question is provided in the pseudepigraphic *Vikuaḥ Radaq,* p. 91, trans., Talmage, "An Hebrew," pp. 344–45. The author said that the Christians asked how Jews could accept the miracles in the Hebrew Scriptures but reject virgin birth. The Jew replied that if virgin birth were a fact, it would have occurred in a truly miraculous manner, such as in a little girl, not a woman of child-bearing age. That Mary was old enough to conceive proved that there was no miracle. This was pseudo-Radaq's answer. A philosophical response would have stated that virgin birth was rejected by reason and therefore not to be believed.

67. For a fuller discussion of this question, see below, chap. 5.

Chapter Four

1. The Nicene Council (325) established the trinitarian belief as obligatory for the orthodox. How this doctrine became accepted is told by Harry A. Wolfson in *The Philosophy of the Church Fathers,* I (Cambridge, Mass., 1964), pp. 141–54, 192–256, 305–63; cf. also Jaroslav Pelikan, *The Emergence of the Catholic Tradition (100–600)* (Chicago, 1971), pp. 172–225. That the Trinity is nowhere mentioned explicitly in the New Testament was a major Jewish argument against Christianity. Cf. Profiat Duran, *Kelimat Ha-Goyim,* chap. 2, *Ha-Ẓofeh,* 3, pp. 143–49. The two major anti-trinitarian heresies are usually known as Sabellianism and Arianism. The former held that the three Persons existed but were not distinct. God was totally simple. The latter held that the Son was created in time, not generated eternally, and that Jesus was not God. The Jews had at least some acquaintance with these doctrines; cf. Judah Aryeh de Modena, *Magen Va-Ḥerev,* pp. 22, 24.

2. The most notable orthodox differences in doctrine are evident in the varying positions of Western and Eastern Christendom. Though the Jewish polemicists were aware of the doctrines in a general way, they did not delve into their intricacies. Thus, the various East-West disputes, e.g., the *Filioque,* did not come up for discussion. Eastern Jews knew Eastern beliefs; Western Jews knew Western beliefs.

3. *Denz.,* no. 39; trans. *The Sources of Catholic Dogma,* Roy J. Deferrari (London, 1957), pp. 15–16. Though this creed was based on Western Christian teachings, it was also basically acceptable to the Eastern Church. Cf. Pelikan, *The*

Spirit of Eastern Christendom (600–1700) (Chicago, 1974), pp. 189–90. The Athanasian Creed is offered here as a source of comparison with the Jewish explanations of the Trinity.

4. The Athanasian Creed was not the only one that dealt with the Trinity, but it had the fullest and most representative rendering of the doctrine. The date of the Creed is unknown; it is definitely not by Athanasius.

5. *Guide* I:50. This is one of Maimonides' few explicit references to Christianity. He equated a belief in the Trinity with the Attributist position, a common contention, as we shall see.

6. *Kitāb al-Muḥtawī,* JTSA ms. 3391, fol. 52: פנאקצׄו פי אללפט ואלמעני. French trans., Georges Vajda, "La Démonstration de l'Unité Divine d'après Yūsuf al-Başīr," in *Studies in Mysticism and Religion Presented to Gershom G. Scholem,* ed. E. E. Urbach et al. (Jerusalem, 1967), p. 300.

7. *Iggeret,* p. 42: מה שאין הפה יכולה לדבר וכבדה האוזן משמוע. This phrase was quoted, sarcastically, from *Rosh Ha-Shanah* 27a.

8. *Kelimat Ha-Goyim, Ha-Ẓofeh,* 3, p. 147: והם ענינים נאמרים ולא מושכלים.

9. *Livyat Ḥen,* ed. Moritz Steinschneider, *Jeshurun* (Kobak), 8 (1875): 2: ולעולם לא יצוייר האחדות באמונתם והוא בכלל הדברים הנזכרים שהם מבוארי ההמנעות בעצמם.

10. *Guide* I:50.

11. *Magen Avot* I:2, printed in *Keshet U-Magen,* p. 26a: הוא ענין נאמר בפה בלי מצייר בנפש.

12. *'Iqqarim* III:25; Husik, p. 225.

13. *Magen Va-Ḥerev,* pp. 22–24.

14. *Kur Maẓref,* p. 18b.

15. JTSA ms. 2227, fol. 4b: דבר שאין אני מבין, וגם אתה אינך תוכל להסביר לי זה. This is not *Ḥerev Pifiyot* of Yair Ben Shabbetai. On the other hand, Solomon ben Moses ben Yekutiel of Rome said that God's oneness and attributes were something "the lips cannot explain and the hearts cannot conceive—השפתים לא יבארוהו והלבבות לא ישיגוהו" *'Edut Ha-Shem Ne'emanah,* p. 380. The distinction between the utterance of the mouth and the belief of the heart is also found in Christian literature, appearing first in Rom. 10:9. Photius (ca. 820–891) referred to Tritheists, who taught three Gods "if not in word, yet at least in thought"; *Bibliotheca* 230, *PG* 103, 1080. In the *Profession of Faith Prescribed for Durand of Osca and His Waldensian Companions* (1208), *Denz.,* nos. 420–24, Innocent III had the dissident say, "By the heart we believe and by the mouth we confess—corde credimus et ore confitemur." Servetus (1511–53), who was burned as a heretic, stated, "I set forth . . . and prove not only that the three beings cannot exist in one God, but that they cannot even be imagined, and that it is wholly impossible to have any notion of them—et non solum tres illas res in uno Deo stare non posse probo, sed etiam inimaginabiles esse, et de eis notitiam haberi omnino impossible, nam habens notitiam trinitatis, haberet notitias distinctas illarum trium rerum et sic staret habere notitiam unius, non habendo notitiam alterius, quod omnes negant." He further said that "you cherish a Quaternity in your mind, though you deny it in words—Immo quaternitatem intellectu

colis, licet verbe neges." Cf. *De Trinitatis Erroribus Libri Septem*, eighteenth-century forgery of 1531 ed., pp. 32, 33; trans. Earl M. Wilbur, *The Two Treatises of Servetus on the Trinity* (Cambridge, Mass., 1932), pp. 50, 51.

16. *PL* 42, 819; trans. A. W. Hadden, in Whitney J. Oates, ed., *Basic Writings of Saint Augustine* (New York, 1948), II, p. 667.

17. *SCG* IV, 10, p. 442.

18. *ST* I, 32, 1. Cf. also Anselm, *Monologium* 66–67, *PL* 158, 211–12.

19. There were two types of exegetical arguments against the Trinity, namely, those based on passages from the Hebrew Bible and those citing New Testament verses. The Jewish argument was that God's absolute unity was taught in the Hebrew Bible despite the Christian exegesis, while nowhere in the New Testament was there a reference to a Trinity. Almost every polemical work referred to at least one or two verses concerning God's unity (especially Deut. 6:4, the *Shema'*).

20. *Metaph.* 12, 8, 1074a, 33–34. The earliest Christian conceptualizers of the doctrine of the Trinity were aware of this problem; cf. Wolfson, *Church Fathers*, pp. 308–9. Maimonides employed this principle to prove that there can be only one God; cf. *Mishneh Torah*, S. Madda', H. Yesode Ha-Torah 1:7.

21. *Amānāt* II:5; cf. below for a full discussion of Saadia's refutation of the Trinity. Notice that not only Aristotelians used Aristotelian principles to argue their case.

22. *Commentary on Psalms* 2, in Frank Talmage, ed., *Sefer Ha-Berit* (Jerusalem, 1974), p. 71: ואמור להם כי לא ייתכן באלוהות אב ובן, כי האלוהות לא תיפרד כי אינה גוף שתיפרד, אלא האל אחד בכל צד אחדות לא ירבה ולא ימעט ולא ייחלק.

Kimḥi applied this principle also to angels, stating that they were not in themselves numerable because they were immaterial; cf. Commentary of *Ma'aseh Merkavah*, end of *Commentary on Ezekiel.*

23. *Livyat Ḥen*, p. 2.

24. *Magen Avot* I:5, p. 5a.

25. Bodleian ms. 2175, fol. 7a.

26. Cf. Baḥya, *Al-Hidāya*, I:7:4, 7, pp. 54–55, 57; Joseph Ibn Ẓaddiq, *Sefer Ha-'Olam Ha-Qatan*, ed. S. Horovitz (Breslau, 1903), p. 55, reprint ed. (n.p., n.d.), p. 57.

27. *Milḥamot Ha-Shem*, pp. 41–42:

אמרת שהם שלש פירשונאש, ומשמעות, פירשונאש דיסטינטאס ריאלמינטי טריש אין פירשונא איט אונה אין שושטאנסייאה, שהוא גוף בפני עצמו... ודבר זה שאמרת אינו יוצא מאחת משתי פנים, או כי הבורא הוא גרם וצורה ושאינו אחד, או יהיה אחד בלי גרם וצורה, ואם הם שלשה פרצופים פירשונאס וכל אחד מהם גוף בפני עצמו כבר יש ביניהם הפרש בינוני, ויש להם ראשית ואחרית, ונמצא לקיומם מדה וקצב, והרי כל אחד מהם מוגבל, והעידו הפילוסופים על כל מוגבל שהוא מופרש, וכל מופרש מחובר, וכל מחובר מחודש, וכל מחודש צריך למחדש אחר זולתו, ונפסדה אלהותו ממנו. ולכן אינו יכול להיות כי אם בורא אחד, אחד שיהיה אחד בלי גרם וצורה, ובלי מדה וקצב, ובלי שום פרור וחבור וחידוש בעולם, אך ראשון בלי ראשית ואחרון בלי אחרית, וקדמון בלי קדם, ובענין אחר אי אפשר להיות.

28. *Even Boḥan* II:4, fol. 64a.

29. P. 4b. Lupis added that if God were material, then He would be subject to composition. Everything composed needs a composer who is greater than it. God

could not, therefore, be a body, since He was not caused by anything outside of Him.

30. Fol. 7a.

31. *Metaph.* 12, 8, 1073b, 1–1074b, 14. For a discussion of this passage and some medieval interpretations of it, cf. Wolfson, "The Plurality of Immovable Movers in Aristotle, Averroes, and St. Thomas," *Studies in the History of Philosophy and Religion,* I (Cambridge, Mass., 1973), pp. 1–21.

32. *Guide* II: Introduction, 16.

33. *Ta'anot,* p. i:

ואין תאר נוסף על אמתת עצמו לבד אם מודה שהאב עלה והבן עלול ואם תודה שהבן עלול תתרחק מן האמת אז יותר ויותר כי לא יתכן אז שיהיה בן אלוה.

34. Ibid.:

וכבר הקשתי זה לפני החכם הנוצרי ניקולאב דיובינצה ואמ׳ הפלוסוף אינו אומ׳ שלא יהיה בו מנין אלא שלא יושכל בו מנין שאם היה בו מנין או מספר היה השכל רואה אותו מיד ומשכילו אכן מפני שאין בו לא יושכל בו והפלוסוף שאחז זה הלשון ר״ל שאמר לא יושכל בו מנין ולא אמר שאין בו מנין מפני שידע שיש בשכלים הנפרדים מנין מצד אחר והוא מצד עלות ועלולים אולם מדרך אחרת אין בהם מנין כי השכל מרחיק שיהיה מהם מנין מדרך אחרת.

35. Ibid.:

ועוד נראה לי שהחכם שתפש לשון ״לא יושכל״ מפני שהשכלים הנפרדים אי אפשר לו לאדם להשיגם אלא בשכל יתכן לא יוכל אדם למהותם אלא בשכל.

36. Cf. *Metaph.* 12, 8, 1073b, 1–1074b, 14.

37. *Ta'anot,* p. ii:

וכבר השיבני חכם א׳ ואמ׳ ״והלא אריסטוטיל כתב שהשכלים מנינם כך, וכך נמנין הגלגלים.״ גם אני השיבותי כן: אמת על ידי עלות ועלולים וא״כ יש לך להודות כי האב עלה והבן עלול ולא נוכל להשכיל בהם מנין רק ע״י התנועה כי השכלים הם המניעים את הגלגלים ומכח תנועתם יודע מספר השכלים ושהן עלות ועלולים וא״כ יש לך להודות כי האב עלה והבן עלול וכדרך זו מנין באלהיך.

38. 3, 4–8.

39. Cf. 2, 4, 415b, 7 and 2, 5, 417b, 22–23.

40. Joseph ben Shem Tov cited chap. 11, which was known as *lamed.* This is actually chap. 12.

41. *Iggeret* p. 52:

כשתחשוב במושכל הנבדל בשכלך ואפילו מן המושכלות ההיולאניות אשר נשימם אנחנו מושכל הנה לא תמצא בשכל הריבוי בו ואי איפשר לצייר ממנו יותר מאחד. דמיון זה שצורת האל״ף כשתקחה מופשטת מהחומר והמקרים בשכל כי זהו הציור השכלי כמו שהתבאר בספר הנפש הנה לא תמצא בשכל הנקי שתי אלפין כי האחת היא האחרת. אמנם בדמיון תמצא ריבוי כי תבדיל ביניהם במקרים כי זו גדולה וזו קטנה וזו שחורה וזו לבנה. וכן תמצא ריבויים חוץ לשכל במקריהם ובמשיגיהם ההיולאנים אבל בשכל אי איפשר הצייור יותר מאלף אחת. וכבר התבאר אמתת זה העניין במאמר השני מספר הנפש ולזה אמר ארסטו במה שאחר הטבע כי הריבוי באיש הוא מצד החומר. אמנם הדברים הנבדלים מהחומר אי איפשר בהם הריבוי אלא במהות כאלו תאמר כי מהות אל״ף המושכל זולת מהות הבי״ת המושכל וכי מחות מניע גלגל המזלות זולת ציור ומהות מניע גלגל שבתי. אבל שיהיה מהותם אחד מושכל ויהיה להם ריבוי באיש אי איפשר בשום פנים ומזה ביאר הפילוסוף באחד עשר ממה שאחר הטבע כי השמיים רבים במין הוא ומניעיהם רבים במין רוצה לומר במהות לא שיהיו כמו ראובן ושמעון שהם רבים באיש ויש להם מהות אחד מושכל.

42. Ibid., pp. 52–54:

ואחר שהתישב זה אומר שאם היה מהות אחד לאב ולבן ולרוח והם נמצאים שלשה נבדלים חוץ לשכל כמו

שהניחו יתחייב שיהיה להם שלשה גופים או חמרים בו תחלה הריבוי (אשר בהם חל הריבוי?) כי בדברים הנבדלים אי איפשר הריבוי בשום אופן מהאופנים כמו שיש לראובן ולבנו ולנינו שהם אחד במהות רבים באיש. ומפני שהם אמרו שהשלשה אחד מתאחדים אי איפשר מבלי שיתאחדו הגשמים האלה קצתם בקצת באופן שיאמר בהם אחד.

This proof was repeated almost verbatim by Isaac Lupis, *Kur Maẓref*, p. 1b.

43. Cf. Wolfson, "Immovable Movers"; Simon van den Bergh, *Averroes' Tahafut al-Tahafut (The Incoherence of the Incoherence)* (London, 1954), I, p. 28, II, p. 23; Thomas, *ST* I, 47, 1, where matter is said not to be the cause of the distinction of things; ibid., 50, 1, where Thomas said that angels could be distinct, though immaterial, according to the divine wisdom devising the various orders of immaterial substances. In ibid., A.4, Thomas argued that there were as many species of angels as there were individual angels. For Maimonides' explanation of numerical distinctions among the angels, cf. *Mishneh Torah, Sefer Madda'*, H. Yesode Ha-Torah, II:5.

44. Cf. Wolfson, *Church Fathers*, pp. 308–9.

45. *ST* I, 30, 1.

46. On the relationship of the Trinity and the philosophical attributes, see Wolfson, "Extradeical and Intradeical Interpretations of Platonic Ideas," *Religious Philosophy* (Cambridge, Mass., 1961), pp. 27–68.

47. For earlier, basically nonphilosophical Jewish objections to the Trinity, derived mainly from Christian polemical literature, cf. Blumenkranz, *Juifs et Chrétiens*, pp. 262–65; idem, "Die jüdischen Beweisgründe in Religionsgespräch mit den Christen in den christlichlateinischen Sonderschriften des 5. bis 11. Jahrhunderts," *Theologische Zeitschrift* 4 (1948): 144–45.

48. On Kalam, cf., e.g., Wolfson, *The Philosophy of the Kalam* (Cambridge, Mass., 1976); W. Montgomery Watt, *The Formative Period of Islamic Thought* (Edinburgh, 1973), esp. pp. 151–250; Shlomo Pines, *Beiträge zur Islamischen Atomenlehre* (Berlin, 1936); A. J. Wensinck, *The Muslim Creed* (Cambridge, 1932), pp. 58–101; R. J. McCarthy, *The Theology of al-Ash'ari* (Beirut, 1952); Isaac Husik, *A History of Medieval Jewish Philosophy* (Philadelphia, 1940), pp. xxi–xxvii; Martin Schreiner, *Der Kalam in der jüdischen Literatur* (Berlin, 1895).

49. On Muslim criticism of Christianity, cf., e.g., Erdmann Fritsch, *Islam und Christentum im Mittelalter* (Breslau, 1930); I. Goldziher, "Uber muhammedanische Polemik gegen Ahl-al-Kitab," *Zeitschrift der Deutschen Morgenländischen Gesellschaft* 32 (1878): 341–87; Moritz Steinschneider, *Polemische und apologetische Literatur in arabischer Sprache* (Leipzig, 1877); J. Windrow Sweetman, *Islam and Christian Theology*, II:1 (London, 1955), pp. 178–309; Laurence E. Browne, *The Eclipse of Christianity in Asia* (New York, 1967), pp. 109–25; Wolfson, *Kalam*, pp. 304–54.

50. Kalamic arguments against dualism revolved on the superfluity of a second supreme being; cf. Saadia, *Amānāt* II:1–2, Baḥya, *al-Hidāya* I:7. On the threat of dualism, see Baron, *Social and Religious History*, V, pp. 103–8.

51. Exceptions to this statement were Qirqisānī and Hadassi. See below.

52. According to Qirqisānī, al-Muqammiẓ was once a Christian. He studied un-

der Nānā (Nonnus), and was converted by him to Christianity, but turned against it, writing in refutation of its doctrines. It is not clear whether al-Muqammiẓ actually formally returned to Judaism, nor whether he was a Karaite or a Rabbanite. See Qirqisānī, *Kitāb al-Anwār wal-Marāqib,* ed. Leon Nemoy, I:8:5, p. 44 (New York, 1939–43); also Nemoy, "Al-Qirqisani's Account of the Jewish Sects and Christianity," *HUCA* 7 (1930): 366. Al-Muqammiẓ's main opus is entitled *'Ishrun Maqālāt, Twenty Treatises.* Treatise Eight has been published in French paraphrase and commentary by Georges Vajda in "Le Problème de l'Unité de Dieu d'après Dāwūd ibn Marwān al-Muqammiṣ," *Jewish Medieval and Renaissance Studies,* ed. Alexander Altmann (Cambridge, Mass., 1967), pp. 49–73. Treatise Nine has been published in the original Arabic, with an introduction, translation, and notes in Russian, by I. O. Ginzburg, *Zapiski Kollegii Vostokovêdov* 5 (1930): 481–506. A Hebrew translation of Treatises Nine and Ten appears in Judah ben Barzilay of Barcelona's *Perush Sefer Yeẓirah,* ed. S. J. Halberstam (Berlin, 1885), pp. 77–83. Treatise Twelve has been translated into French with commentary by Vajda, "La Finalité de la Création de l'Homme selon un Théologian Juif du IXe Siècle," *Oriens* 15 (1962): 61–85. Treatise Sixteen appears in Hebrew translation in *Perush,* pp. 151–54, with a French translation by Vajda in "A propos de la Perpétuité de la Rétribution d'Outre Tombe en Théologie Musulmane," *Studia Islamica* 11 (1959): 29–38. We shall be concerned here with Treatises Eight and Nine. It should be noted that al-Muqammiẓ's separate polemical treatise against Christianity has survived in only one small fragment; cf. Hirschfeld, "The Arabic Portion of the Cairo Geniza at Cambridge," *JQR* o.s. 15 (1903): 682, 688–89. On Karaite polemics against Christianity, see also Nemoy, "The Attitude of the Early Karaites towards Christianity," in *Salo W. Baron Jubilee Volume* (New York and London, 1975), II, pp. 697–716.

53. Cf. *Metaph.* 5, 6, 1015b, 16–1016b, 18; 10, 1, 1052a, 15–1053b, 8; Wolfson, *Church Fathers,* pp. 314–17.

54. Cf. Vajda, "Le Problème," p. 66, n. 36.

55. Ibid., pp. 61–62.

56. Cf. Wolfson, *Church Fathers,* pp. 323–27.

57. Augustin Périer, *Petits Traités Apologétiques de Yaḥyâ ben 'Adî* (Paris, 1920), p. 44. Ben 'Adi presented a number of other trinitarian formulae, as we shall see below. For Muslim acquaintance with trinitarian doctrine, see Wolfson, "The Muslim Attributes and the Christian Trinity," *HThR* 49 (1956): 1–18, and in *Kalam,* pp. 112–32.

58. On the Cappadocians, see E. Gilson, *History of Christian Philosophy in the Middle Ages* (New York, 1955), pp. 50–64; A. H. Armstrong, ed., *The Cambridge History of Later Greek and Early Medieval Philosophy* (London, 1967), pp. 432–56. For the particular Trinity doctrines, see Franz Nager, *Die Trinitätslehre des hl. Basilius des Grossen* (Paderborn, 1912); Michael G. de Castro, *Die Trinitätslehre des hl. Gregor von Nyssa* (Freiburg, 1938); and Joseph Hergenröther, *Die Lehre von der göttlichen Dreieinigkeit nach dem heiligen Gregor von Nazianz* (Regensburg, 1850).

59. He was opposed to such an interpretation, partially on the grounds that declaring the Persons to be three individuals of one species would lead people to believe that there were actually three Gods. See *De Trinitate* VII, 6, 11; *PL* 42, 944; *Enarratio in Psalmos* 68, 1, 5; *PL* 36, 844–45.

60. An anti-Christian treatise attributed to al-Kindi refuted the Trinity in the sense of unity of species. In response, Yaḥya ben 'Adī agreed with his adversary that such an explanation of the Trinity was not feasible, and therefore, he said, Christians had ceased using such terminology. Ben 'Adī's refutation of this treatise was published with French translation by Périer, "Un Traité de Yaḥyâ ben 'Adî, Défense de la Trinité contre les Objections d'al-Kindī," *Revue de l'Orient Chrétien* 22 (1920): 4–21. The passage in question is on p. 10, trans. pp. 18–19. A revised translation appears in *Petits Traités,* pp. 118–28, with this passage on p. 124. This treatise contains a number of trinitarian formulations which Ben 'Adī claimed were no longer in use because they led to false conclusions. Cf. Wolfson, *Kalam,* pp. 318–36.

61. Vajda, "Le Problème," pp. 66–69, based on Nonnus of Nisibis, *Traité Apologétique,* ed. A. van Roey (Louvain, 1948), pp. 3–4 (text), 37 (translation). Cf. Roey's introduction, pp. 47, 55–57.

62. The three images—men, gold coins, and colors—will be discussed below in a section devoted to these Trinity analogies.

63. Al-Muqammiẓ mentioned the Jacobites, for he was most familiar with their doctrines; his teacher, Nonnus, and the latter's teacher, Abū Rā'iṭa, were Jacobites. This was a Christian Monophysite sect whose name came from its founder, Jacob Baradai (sixth century). Monophysites, who held that there was but one nature (divine) in Jesus, not two (human and divine) as in the orthodox belief, were still to be considered orthodox in their conception of the Trinity. See Périer, *Petits Traités,* p. 55. Al-Muqammiẓ's refutation, then, would apply to orthodox doctrine, at least if it were expressed in terms of unity of species. The same arguments could, though, be used against Augustine's unity of substratum.

64. If A, B, and C are exactly identical with D, and there is no other feature of A, B, and C, they must be identical with each other (and with D).

65. Vajda, "Le Problème," pp. 62–64.

66. The Christians asserted that God was one unique and eternal substance (with, of course, three Persons). Any additional substances in God's nature would have to be noneternal.

67. All existents which are composed of substance and accident are considered created, since there must be a cause of their composition. Cf., e.g., Périer, "Un Traité," p. 4; Saadia, *Amānāt* I:1 (second and third proofs); Baḥya, *Al-Hidāya* I:7:4.

68. Vajda, "Le Problème," pp. 64–65.

69. Wolfson, "The Muslim Attributes."

70. Arabic, p. 493:
وذلك قول النصارى في اثبات التثليث اذ جعلوحى بحيوة هى روح القدس
وعالم بعلم (هو) الكلمة وهو الـ(ذي) سموه البن وهذا هو شرك الصرح .
Hebrew, p. 79.

71. Périer, *Petits Traités,* p. 37. Though this formulation was put in the mouth of the "adversary," Ben 'Adī did not challenge it. Ben 'Adī appeared to prefer the formula: the Father is goodness, the Son is wisdom, the Holy Spirit is power. See "Un Traité," p. 5.

72. L. Horst, *Des Metropolitan Elias von Nisibis Buch von Beweis der Wahrheit des Glaubens* (Colmar, 1886), p. 2. Cf. also Louis Cheikho, *Vingt Traités Théologiques* (Beirut, 1920), p. 126.

73. Cheikho, ibid., p. 20. Instead of knowledge for the Son, he equated the second Person with reason *(nuṭq);* al-Muqammiẓ used the term *kalima.* Both were translations of *logos.* Qirqisānī specifically stated that *nuṭq* and *'ilm* were the same for the Christians. See *al-Anwar* III: 2:7, p. 190.

74. On the difference between the semantic and ontological problems, see Wolfson, "Philosophical Implications of the Problem of Divine Attributes in the Kalam," *JAOS* 71 (1959): 73–80, and *Kalam,* pp. 205–34. Al-Muqammiẓ was certainly mistaken here. The doctrine of attributes was an answer to the Christian Trinity, not the Trinity a corruption of the attribute theory. If al-Muqammiẓ was serious here, it shows how the origin of the theory of attributes became lost very early after its inception.

75. The Jews in general were anti-Attributists, and they attacked the Ṣifātiyya as well as the Christians. See Wolfson, "The Muslim Attributes," on the origin of the Ṣifātiyya.

76. For the history of these formulations and al-Muqammiẓ's use of them, see Wolfson, "Philosophical Implications."

77. Al-Muqammiẓ offered this not as an actual Christian position, but more as a ridicule of incarnation. Therefore, he did not bother to give any answer.

78. Arabic, pp. 498–99:

واما النصارى فانا نقول لهم اذا كان عندكم محال فى القياس ان يكون الحى
حيا الا بحيوة وان يكون العالم عالما الا بعلم قياسا على ما شاهدا فلم لا
كان عندكم محال فى القياس ان يكون حيا بحيوة والموت جائز عليه ان
عالم بعلم والجهل جائز عليه قياسا على ما شاهدنا من الحى فان اجازو هذا
ان قالو به لزمهم ان ربهم حى بحيوة والموت جائز عليه وعالم يعلم والجهل
جائز عليه . فان ابو ذلك وقالو نحن وان كل حى وعالم شاهدنا حى بحيوة
وعالم بعلم فالموت والجهل جائز عليه فانا قد ادركنا قياسا ان حى عالم فى
الغائب هو الخالق (حى) بحيوة وعالم بعلم وليس الموت والجهل جائز عليه
قلنا لهم وكذلك يجب ان تجزون لنا ايضا اذا ق(ل)نا . . ا والم نكون شاهدنا
فى الشاهد حى وعالم وحيوة وحى بحيوة وعالم بعلم فانا قد ادركنا قياسا
ان حى عالم فى القياس وهو ال. . (خال)ق حى بلا حيوة كنحن وعالم لا يعلم
كنحن ولا (يكون) لهم فى هذا السوءال كما لم يكون للمثانية.

Hebrew, p. 81. All al-Muqammiẓ had shown here was that the Christian position was no stronger than his own. One must correlate his refutation of the Trinity with his theory of attributes to get the full proof. See below.

79. Al-Muqammiẓ ultimately suggested that negative attributes were the most fitting ones to ascribe to God. He based this conclusion on the saying of Aristotle. Cf. Arabic, p. 496; Hebrew, p. 80.

80. Saadia, *Amānāt* II; Landauer, pp. 73–112, Rosenblatt, pp. 87–136. For an analysis of Saadia's refutation of Christianity, see Wolfson, "Saadia on the Trinity and Incarnation," *Studies and Essays in Honor of Abraham A. Neumann,* ed. M. Ben-Horin et al. (Leiden, 1962), pp. 547–68; Jacob Guttmann, *Die Religionsphilosophie des Saadia* (Göttingen, 1882), pp. 101–13; David Kaufmann, *Geschichte der Attributenlehre* (Gotha, 1877), pp. 37–52. For Saadia's treatment of anthropormorphism, see Simon Rawidowicz, "Saadya's Purification of the Idea of God," *Saadya Studies,* ed. E. I. J. Rosenthal (Manchester, 1943), pp. 139–65; reprinted with condensations, S. Rawidowicz, *Studies in Jewish Thought,* ed. N. Glatzer (Philadelphia, 1974), pp. 246–68.

81. Cf. Wolfson, ibid., pp. 547–48. This conclusion is based on Périer, *Petits Traités,* pp. 44–45.

82. *Amānāt,* II:5, Landauer, p. 86:

وجاءوا الى هذه الثلث صفات فتعلقوا بها وقالوا لا يخلو الا شي حي عالم

فاعتقد واحيوته وعلمه شيئين غير ذاته فصارت عندهم ٣ .

The translation is Wolfson's, ibid., p. 558.

83. Wolfson, "Muslim Attributes," p. 8, *Kalam,* p. 121, seems to interpret Saadia's formulation in the same sense that life was the Son and knowledge was the Holy Spirit. There is no textual proof, however, that the order given the attributes can be used to determine the correlation between each attribute and Person. Shahrastānī reported that the attributes existence, life, and knowledge were the Father, Son, and Holy Spirit, but immediately said that God's knowledge became corporeal. See his *Kitāb al-Milal wal-Niḥal (Book of Religious and Philosophical Sects),* ed. William Cureton (London, 1842), p. 172; cf. pp. 173, 175. Cf. also Kaufmann, *Attributenlehre,* p. 42, n. 78.

84. *Amānāt* II:5, Landauer, p. 86; Rosenblatt, p. 103. The reference to Aristotle is *Metaphysics* 12, 8, 1074a, 33–34. See above for a fuller discussion of this principle and the Trinity. Cf. also Wolfson, "Saadia," p. 559, and *Church Fathers,* pp. 308, 338; also Altmann, *Saadya Gaon: Book of Doctrines and Beliefs,* in *Three Jewish Philosophers* (New York, 1972), p. 81, n. 7.

85. Saadia considered the use of one term in place of these three attributes. Yet this new, invented term could be explained only in reference to the three terms, so nothing would be gained. Cf. *Amānāt* II:4, Landauer, pp. 84–85; Rosenblatt, pp. 103–4.

86. Ibid., pp. 86–87, trans. p. 104.

87. On the difference between the semantic and ontological aspects, see Wolfson, "Philosophical Implications" and "Saadia on the Semantic Aspect of the Problem of

Attributes," in *Baron Jubilee Volume,* II, pp. 1009–21.

88. *'Ishrun Maqālāt* IX, Arabic, pp. 490–91:

فان قال قائل فهو حى نما نعقل من الاحياء وحكيم نما نعقل من الحكماء وسميع
بصير كما نفهم السميع البصير من منا وعندنا قلنا معاذ الله ان يكون الله حيا
كما نحن احياء ان نكون احياء كما ان الله حيا او ان يكون الله حكيما وسميع
وبصير كما نحن حكماء سمعاء بصراء او نكون نحن بذلك كهو وتفسير ذلك ان الله
(حى) لم يكون لا حى فحيا ولا اذ هو حى يصير الا ان يفقد الحيوة لانه لم
يزل حى ولم يزال حكيما ولا يزال حكيم لا يستفيد الحكمة ولا يزال حكمة ولا
ينقص فاما نحن فانا لم نكون احيا وصرنا احيا وياول بنا الاخر عند الموت ان
نصير لا احياء وكذلك كنا لا حكماء ثم نصير بالادب والاستفادة (حكماء و)
علماء وياول بنا الى ان تذهب حكمتنا وعلمنا مع ح(يو)تنا مع ✦ قد يتملك على
حكمتنا السهو والغلط والزيادة والنقصان والله عز وجل بخلاف ذلك هو الحي
الذى لا يموت الحكيم الذي لا يجهل والجواد الذي لا يبخل فتبارك وتقدس
وتعالا وتمجد .

Hebrew, p. 78.

89. It is not clear whether Saadia held that God's attributes were real positive essential attributes, or only attributes of action, or negative attributes. See Julius Guttmann, *Philosophies of Judaism,* trans. D. W. Silverman (New York, 1964), pp. 77–79.

90. *Amānāt* II:5, Landauer, p. 87, Rosenblatt, pp. 104–5:

وانما موهوا بهذا القول ليقيموا به ما قيل لهم .

This argument against the Trinity was quite common in Jewish polemical literature, as we shall see. It was also used by Muslims; cf. Wolfson, "Saadia," pp. 559–60.

91. *Amānāt* II:5–6, Landauer, pp. 87–90, Rosenblatt, pp. 105–18.

92. Op. cit., index, p. 056. *Kitāb al-Anwār* was written in 937, four years after Saadia's *al-Amānāt.* It is divided into thirteen treatises.

93. Qirqisānī's discussion of God's unity was in the form of a commentary on the Shema' (Deut. 6:4) in ibid., VI:3–4, pp. 569–70. No mention of Christianity is made in the fragments which have been preserved. It is not unlikely, though, that such references existed and have not survived. For a discussion of this passage, see Vajda, "Le Problème," pp. 71–73.

94. Ibid., III is devoted to this subject. In it, Qirqisānī criticized the following: Samaritans, Christians, Abū 'Isa al-Isfahānī, Muslims, Daniel al-Qūmisī, and the holders of various other beliefs, e.g., deniers of reward and punishment. Rabbanites were criticized throughout the work. The refutation of the Trinity is in III:2,4, pp. 187–90, 198–201. III:3 is a digression refuting the doctrine of the eternity of God's *logos (kalām),* which is directed against both Christians and Muslims. That it is not specifically against Christianity is seen by its conclusion, p. 198: "And now we return to our previous matter concerning the doctrine of the Christians." The order of the

books in *al-Anwār* is as follows: I. historical introduction (with an account of the various sects); II. philosophical and theological principles of jurisprudence; III. criticism of sectarian doctrines; IV. methods of construction and interpretation of law; V–XIII. exposition of Karaite law. For a summary of Qirqisānī's refutation of Christianity, see Nemoy, "The Attitude of the Early Karaites."

95. Ibid. I:8:1–2, p. 43. Cf. III:16:3, p. 303, where Paul is said to be the author of the trinitarian theory. Qirqisānī was not alone in considering Paul the originator of contemporary Christianity. See S. M. Stern, "'Abd al-Jabbār's Account of How Christ's Religion was Falsified by the Adoption of Roman Customs," *JThS,* n.s. 19 (1968): 128–86. 'Abd al-Jabbār wrote his work in 995.

96. Ibid. I:8:3, p. 43:

فاما دين النصارى الذي هم عليه الان فانه الحاد قائم وذلك انهم يزعمون
ان الباري ء جوهر واحد ثلثة اقانيم وانه واحد ثلثة وثلثة واحد لانه عندهم حي
عالم فالحياة والعلم صفتان للجوهر فالجوهر قنوم والصفتان قنومان فلذلك
صار ثلثة اقانيم وزعموا ان المسيح الذي بشرت به الانبياء ووعدت بمجيئه
هو ישוע وهو احد الاقانيم الثلثه وان الاقانيم الثلثه هي ابن واب وروح والابن
هو ישוע وهو لاهوتي ناسوتي لان الباري ء الذي هو الجوهر اتحد به فهذا
جملة ما يقولونه وهم المختلفين في التفصيل .

Translation is from Nemoy, "Al-Qirqisānī's Account," p. 365.

97. Cf. Saadia's assertion that God is not a substance, *al-Amānāt* II:9, Landauer, pp. 93–95, Rosenblatt, pp. 112–15. Note that Saadia did not cite the Christian formula: one substance, three Persons, and thus did not argue against the belief in God as substance in an anti-Christian context. Cf. also Abū Bakr al-Bāqillānī, *Kitāb al-Tamhīd,* ed. Richard J. McCarthy (Beirut, 1957), pp. 75–79. There is a great affinity between Qirqisānī's and al-Bāqillānī's refutations of the Trinity, and they may have used a common source.

98. Cf. Aristotle, *Metaphysics* 5, 8, 1017b, 10–26; *Categories* 5, 2a, 10–15. Qirqisānī stated that the Christians relied heavily on logic and used it as a source of truth. One may infer that this was not Qirqisānī's appraisal of how Christians really derived their doctrine.

99. For a discussion of this terminology, see Josef van Ess, "The Logical Structure of Islamic Theology," G. E. Von Grunebaum, *Logic in Classical Islamic Culture* (Wiesbaden, 1970), p. 39.

100. *Al-Anwār* III:2:1, p. 187:

قد كنا حكينا عنهم انهم يزعمون ان الباري ء تقدست اسماؤه جوهر واحد ثلثة
اقانيم فلنبتدى ء قبل مسالتهم والرد عليهم في الاقانيم والتثليث بمسالتهم
في اثباتهم له الجوهريه فيقال لهم ما الدليل على ان الباري ء جوهر وما الامر
الموجب له معنى الجوهريه فجوابهم في ذلك بان يقولوا لانه قائم بنفسه وكل
ما كان قائما بنفسه فهو جوهر لا محالة واعتمادهم في ذلك على الاوضاع المنطقية

از كان المنطق عندهم اصلا في استخراج الحقائق وان صاحب المنطق حد الجوهر بانه هو القائم بنفسه الذي لا يحتاج في قوامه الى غيره فلما كان هذا حد للجوهر وكان الحد هو الذي ينعكس على محدوده وهو بان كل جوهر قائم بنفسه وكل قائم بنفسه فهو جوهر وكان الباري ء قائم بنفسه ثبت انه جوهر.

101. Aristotle, *Categories* 5, 4a, 10–4b, 19. Christians would agree that God did not have contrary qualities in His essence.

102. Idem, *Metaphysics* 7, 3, 1028b, 33–1029b, 12.

103. Everyone agreed that God could not be subject to accidents.

104. *Al-Anwār* III:2:2, p. 187:

فيقال لهم ان كان المنطق اصلا يعتمد عليه واساسا يبنى عليه وكان سلما الى استخراج الحقائق فان صاحبه لما حد الجوهر لم يحده بما ذكرتموه فقط بل اضاف الى ذلك قولا اخر وهو قوله انه قابل لمتضادات في ذاته فان اوجبتم للباري ء جل ثناؤه معنى الجوهر لانه قائم بنفسه فاوجبوا له قبول المتضادات في ذاته اذ كان جوهرا وكل جوهر فهو قابل للمتضادات كما ان كل قابل للمتضادات جوهر على ما يوجبه العكس في الحد والمحدود وذلك انكم زعمتم على الاوضاع المنطقية انه لما كان حد الجوهر انه قائم بنفسه وان كل قائم بنفسه جوهر كما ان كل جوهر قائم بنفسه فكذلك لما كان كل قابل للاعراض فهو جوهر وجب ان يكون كل جوهر فهو قابل للاعراض فان كان الباري ء عز وجل جوهرا لم يلزمه حد الجوهر الذي هو قبول الاعراض فلم لا يكون قائما بنفسه وليس بجوهر وان كان كل قائم بنفسه جوهرا وهذا ليس لهم منه محيص ولا يقدرون فيه على فصل، ولو لم يكن عليهم سواه لكان فيه اقناع.

105. In the *Categories* Aristotle discussed quantity, quality, and relation as the first three categories.

106. For a discussion of these categories, see ibid.

107. *Al-Anwār* III:2:3, pp. 187–88:

على انهم في قولهم انه لا يجوز عليه قبول الاعراض كاذبون مناقضون اذ كانوا فيما يدعونه من الثلثة اقانيم قد الحقوا الاعراض التسعة به وذلك انهم اذا قالوا انه ثلثة اقانيم ادخلوه تحت العدد الذي هو الكمية واذا جعلوه حيا بحياة وعالما بعلم فقد اوجبوا له الصفة التي هي الكيفية واذا قالوا انه اب وابن فقد ادخلوه في باب المضاف فهذه الثلثة الاعراض البسيطة قد الحقوها به فاما سائر الستة الاخر المركبة فانهم الحقوها بالابن الذي هو احد الاقانيم وذلك انهم زعموا ان يسوع الذي هو الابن ظهر في زمان كذا وولد في وقت كذا فادخلوه تحت الزمان الذي هو متى وزعموا انه كان في بلد كذا فاطلقوا عليه الوجود في المكان وذلك معنى اين ثم زعموا انه كان يلبس ويركب فاوجبوا له القنية وقالوا انه قعد وقام ومشى وذلك هو النصبة وذكروا انه كان ياكل ويشرب ويبطش وياخذ ويعطي وذلك

هو الفعل واخر ذلك بانه قتل وصلب وذلك هو الانفعال والمفعول فاي شيء بقى
من الاعراض الا وقد الحقوه به ونسبوه الى قبوله .

Cf. Saadia's rejection of the categories being attributed to God; *al-Amānāt* II:9–12, Landauer, pp. 93–107, Rosenblatt, pp. 112–31.

108. *Al-Anwār* III:2:4, p. 188:

ثم نسالهم في الاقانيم التى هى العلم الذى هو عندهم الابن والحياة التى
هى عندهم الروح فيقال لهم ما دليلكم على ذلك فجوابهم فى ذلك ان قالوا
ان كل فاعل لا بد من ان يكون حيا بحياة وهى غيره وعالما بعلم هو سواه
فلما صح ان الباريء فاعل وجب انه حى بحياة وعالم بعلم فاذا كان ذلك كان
علمه وحياته قنومين والجوهر القنوم الثالث فلما كان العلم متولدا من العالم
كتولد الابن من الاب كان العلم ابنا له وكذلك لما كانت الحياة انما تكون
بالروح كانت حياته روحا له فوجب من ذلك انه ثلثة اقانيم اب وهو الجوهر
وعلم وهو الابن وروح وهو الحياة .

The equivalences of the Persons as seen here is the same as that found in al-Muqammiẓ. See above.

109. Ibid. III:2:5, pp. 188–89:

فيقال لهم انكم ايضا فى هذا الدليل انما عولتم على الفاعل المشاهد
المحسوس فان كان هذا هاكذا وكان البارئ يجب ان يكون حيا بحياة وعالما
بعلم لان كل فاعل محسوس هذه سبيله فقولوا ايضا انه لما كان كل فاعل مشاهد
هو جسم ذو جوارح والات وجب ان يكون البارئ جسما اذ كان فاعلا وان جاز ان
يكون البارئ فاعلا وليس بجسم ولا ذى جوارح والات بخلاف المشاهد فلم لا جاز
ان يكون فعالا حيا عالما بذاته وليس هناك علم ولا حياة بخلاف المشاهد ولا
فرق وكذلك يلزمهم ايضا ان يكون جسما لا طويلا ولا عريضا ولا عميقا وان كان
ليس فى المشاهد جسم يخلو من ذلك لما كان جوهرا ليس بقابل للاعراض وان
كان كل جوهر مشاهد فهو قابل للاعراض ولا فرق ومثل ذلك يلزمهم فى قولهم
(انه) حى وهو انه ان كان البارئ حيا بحياة هى غيره لان ليس فى المشاهد
حى الا ما هذه سبيله فكذلك يجب ان يكون حساسا متحركا اذ كان لا حى
فى المشاهد الا وهو حسوس مترحك ولا فرق فان كان البارئ حيا ليس بحساس ولا
متحرك بخلاف المشاهد فكذلك يكون حيا لا بحياة بخلاف المشاهد ولا فرق .

This argument is a variant of one used by al-Muqammiẓ. If God lived and knew by virtue of life and knowledge, like all other things that lived and knew, the latter argued, then He should also die and be ignorant. See above and cf. the terminology.

110. The analogy appears to be that while God was eternal, the Son was created. The Christians maintained that the Son was generated, but still eternal.

111. *Al-Anwār* III:2:6, pp. 189–90:

وقد يسالون ايضا فيقال لهم خبرونا عن الاب والابن والروح اذا قلتم هو واحد
في المعنى اتقولون ان الاب هو الابن وهو الروح فان قالوا ليس هو الابن ولا
هو الروح قيل لهم فما انكرتم ان لا تكون الثلثة هو واحد في المعنى لما لم يكن
كل واحد من الثلثة هو الثلثة في المعنى ويقال لهم خبرونا ايجوز ان تكون ثلثة
اب وابن وروح وهو واحد في المعنى فاذا قالوا نعم قيل لهم فما انكرتم
ان يكون اثنان قديم ومحدث واحد في المعنى فان قالوا ان ذلك جائز قيل
لهم فما انكرتم ان يكون القديم هو المحدث والمحدث هو القديم والقديم احدث
نفسه اذ كان المحدث هو القديم والقديم هو المحدث فان قالوا لا يجوز ان يكون
القديم والمحدث اثنين في العدد وواحدا في المعنى قيل لهم وكذلك لا يكون
الاب والابن والروح ثلثة في العدد وواحدا في المعنى .

112. Qirqisānī stated that the Christians considered God's knowledge *('ilm)* and his reason *(nuṭq)* to be the same thing. They both reflect the Greek *logos.*

113. It is also not clear whether more anti-trinitarian arguments were originally included in III:2.

114. *Al-Anwār* III:2:7, p. 190:

ثم يقال لهم اذا قلتم ان البارئ حي بحياة وناطق بنطق لان العلم عندهم
هو النطق فخبرونا عن حياته اهي قديمة فاذا قالوا نعم قيل لهم فتقولون ان
الحياة حي ناطق والنطق حي ناطق فان قالوا نعم قيل لهم فما انكرتم ان
يكون كل واحد من هذه الثلثة ثلثة ايضا اذ كان الاب انما وجب ان يكون معه
ابن وروح لانه حي ناطق وكذلك مع الروح فان قالوا ليس الروح بحي ولا ناطق
وكذلك النطق قيل لهم فخبرونا عن النطق اتقولون انه فاعل صانع فان قالوا
ليس النطق بفاعل ولا صانع يقال لهم فما انكرتم . . .

115. On the Muslim controversy as to whether God's word was eternal or created, cf. Wolfson, *Kalam,* pp. 235–303, and Wensinck, op. cit., pp. 77, 121, 127, 149, 189, etc.

116. Some Christians claimed that Moses did not reveal the doctrine of the Trinity because the people were intellectually unprepared for it. Cf. *Trophies of Damascus,* pp. 197–98; Anastasius of Sinai, *A Dissertation against the Jews* (ca. 1050), *PG* 89, 1277; Pseudo-Andronicus, *Dialogue of a Christian and a Jew against the Jews* (ca. 1310), *PG* 133, 804–5. Some Jews agreed that the Israelites coming out of Egypt were not intellectually prepared, but they drew different conclusions; cf. Maimonides, *Guide* III:24, 32.

117. *Al-Anwār* III:4:1, pp. 198–99:

فيقال لهم خبرونا هل من دليل على ان البارئ جوهر ذو ثلثة اقانيم ام لا فلا بد
لهم من القول ان لهم على ذلك دليل اذ كان لا يجوز اثبات ما لا دليل عليه
فاذ كانوا عند انفسهم قد يدلون على ذلك من المعقول والكتاب جميعا فيقال

لهم فقيام البرهان على ذلك ناقض لما تدعونه من ان من تقدم لم يوقفوا عليه وذلك انهم ان كانوا ذوي عقول ومعارف يعلمون الاشياء الغائبة مثل حدث العالم واثبات الصانع بالبراهين العقلية قد كان يجب ان يستدلوا على ما تدعونه من ان الباريء جوهر ذو ثلثة اقانيم بالبرهان الذي دلكم انتم على ذلك كما ثبت عندهم واستدلوا على حدث العالم واثبات الله الباريء جل ثناؤه ووحدانيته مما استدللنا نحن فانتم ان كان البرهان الذي تدعونه على ذلك هو انه حي عالم وقد كانوا هم عالمين بانه حي عالم كما ان الاجسام التي فيها امر التاليف والاعراض التي دلتنا على انها محدثة وان لها محدثا احدثها هي التي دلتكم على مثل ذلك. وان كانوا لم يكونوا عالمين بذلك بل انما كانوا سدى غير ذوي عقول ولا معارف فحسبنا بهذا القول وظهور فضيحة قائله وايضا فانكم تدعون البرهان على ما تقولونه من الكتاب ومن قول الانبياء المتقدمين فكيف يجوز ان يكونوا الانبياء المتقدمين قد قالوا اشياء تدل على ان الباريء جوهر ذو ثلثة اقانيم وهم لا يعلمون ان الذي قالوه يدل على ذلك وهل يكون في المحال والبهت والقحة اكثر من هذا.

118. That there may be more than three Persons was a common argument; cf. on Saadia, above; on others, cf. below.

119. *Al-Anwār* III:4:2, pp. 199–200:

ويقال لهم ايضا اليس حقيقة ذات الباريء انه جوهر واحد ثلثة اقانيم كان من تقدم من الناس قبل مجيء عيسى يعلمون انه جوهر ولا يعلمون انه اقانيم ثلثة ولم يكشف ذلك لهم لان عقولهم لم تكن تبلغه ولا تحتمله واذا قالوا نعم قيل لهم فما يؤمن ان تكون له صفات اخر واقانيم زائدة على هذه اما خمسة او عشرة لم تكشف لمن كان في عصر عيسى لان عقولهم لم تكن تحتمله وانما كشف لهم من ذلك ما بلغته عقولهم كما لم يكشف لمن كان في عصر موسى الا الوحدانية فقط ولم يكشف لهم امر الاقانيم لان عقولهم لم تكن تبلغه ولا تحتمله وانه قد يجوز ان يحدث قوم اخرون تحتمل عقولهم ذلك فيكشف لهم امر الاقانيم كما كشف لاصحاب عيسى امر الثلثة اقانيم وبعد فاذا كان الله هو الذي خلق الناس وخلق لهم العقول فلم خلق خلقا عظيما مذ لدن ادم الى ان جاء موسى لم يخلق لهم من العقول ما يبلغون بها معرفة حقيقة ذاته وفيهم انبياء كثيرة وهل هذا الا سخنة عين من القول او هل يخفى قبحه وفساده على البهائم فضلا عن ذوي العقول.

These last two arguments are not strictly philosophical, but contain philosophical elements.

120. Al-Başīr, in general, was very dependent upon the Kalam. See P. F. Frankl, *Ein Mu'tazilitischer Kalam aus dem 10 Jahrhundert* (Vienna, 1872).

121. *Kitāb al-Muḥtawī*, fols. 13–56. The refutation of Christianity begins on fol.

52. The most relevant portions of al-Basīr's work appear in a condensed French translation by Vajda, "La Démonstration," pp. 285–315. The refutation of Christianity begins on p. 299.

122. *Al-Muḥtawī,* fol. 56: גַֿעלו אקנום אלאבן הו כלמתה ואקנום רוח אלקדס חיאתה. Vajda, "La Démonstration," p. 306. Al-Başīr followed al-Muqammiẓ in identifying the Son with the Word and the Holy Spirit with the life.

123. Ibid., fol. 52: קאלו תלת אׄקאנים גֿוהר ואחד אלה ואחד. Trans., p. 300.

124. Ibid., fol. 52:
ואלנצארי יקולון אן אלאקאנים אלתלתה לא נקול אנהא מתגֿאירה ולא נקול אן אחדהא הו אלאכֿר פלא יקולון גֿירה ולא אלאב אקנום אנה אלאבן אקנום פי. Trans., Vajda, pp. 299–300.

125. *Epistola 101 ad Cledonium, PG* 37, 180; Gregory said one may use the term ἄλλος but not ἄλλο. Cf. Thomas, *ST* I, 32, 2. This teaching was reaffirmed by the Fourth Lateran Council, 1215; *Denz.*, 432.

126. On modes, see Maimonides, *Guide* I:51; Wolfson, *Kalam,* pp. 147–205, and "Philosophical Implications"; D. B. Macdonald, "Ḥāl," *Encyclopedia of Islam,* II (Leiden, 1927), p. 227; L. Gardet, "Al-Djubbai," *Encyclopedia of Islam,* new ed., II (Leiden, 1965), pp. 569–70.

127. Cf. Wolfson, "An Unknown Splinter Group of Nestorians," *Revue des Études Augustiennes* 6 (1960): 249–53, and *Kalam,* pp. 337–54.

128. Cf. ibid., p. 251, (*Kalam,* p. 339) quoting Shahrastānī, op. cit., p. 175. Shahrastānī stated that Nestorians, while orthodox in believing that God was one, possessing three hypostases, differed from the accepted doctrine by holding that "these hypostases are not additional to the essence [of God] nor are they identical with Him." Al-Başīr associated the Christians with Şifātiyya, not Kullābiyya (fols. 52, 56; Vajda, pp. 299, 305–6). This may be because of the Christian doctrine which taught that one of God's attributes (the Word) became incarnate. This implied a real existence for this attribute, and hence the doctrine of the Şifātiyya; but see also Wolfson, *Kalam,* pp. 345–47.

129. This was based on the principle that everything which was composed was caused and noneternal. God, being eternal and uncaused, could not have any composition in His nature. Cf. Vajda, "Le Problème," p. 64.

130. *Al-Muḥtawī,* fols. 55–56:
פאלתתלית אדן לא יצח למא בינּאה מן קבל מן אן קולנא תלתה אסם (אסם) לעדו בעצֿה גֿיר בעץֿ מע אסתחאלה כונה ת״ע דא אבעאץֿ פאלתגֿאיר אדן פיה לא יצח למא לם יכן מן אלגֿמל.
Vajda, "La Démonstration," p. 305. Al-Başīr's refutation was based on 'Abd al-Jabbār's *Kitāb al-Mughni.* Cf. also al-Başīr's refutation of the Şifātiyya, fols. 52–53, trans. pp. 300–301.

131. Wilhelm Bacher, "Inedited Chapters of Jehudah Hadassi's *Eshkol Hakkofer,*" *JQR,* o.s. 8 (1896): 432; reprinted at the end of *Eshkol Ha-Kofer,* Eupatoria ed., republished, 1971:
ואמרו כי הוא אב ובן ורוח הקדש והאב הוא כולל עיקר האלהות ודברו הוא הבן ולבש בשר כדרך בני האדם ורוח הקדש היא חכמתו ונבואת נביאיו והושוו שלשתם והם כאחד.

132. E.g., that God should exit from a womb or have to suckle, or should walk

on the earth like a man and be killed.

133. Hadassi followed al-Başīr here, as in other cases. Cf. Bacher's notes.

134. Bacher, p. 433. Cf. Alphabet 28, *Eshkol Ha-Kofer,* p. 19c, where God is described as living by virtue of Himself, powerful by virtue of Himself, etc.

135. Ibid., p. 437; cf. p. 439. These remarks were injected into Hadassi's discussion of the New Testament as side comments.

136. *Kitāb al-Hidāya* I:7, p. 58. Cf. also I:10, p. 89, and V:5, p. 234. These anti-Christian references are censored from the standard editions of Yehuda ibn Tibbon's translation. In I:7:4 (pp. 54–55), Baḥya stated that those who believed in more than one God either believed these divine beings to have one essence *(dhat)* or more than one. If they believed in one essence, then they believed in one God. This was obviously not meant as an adequate refutation of Christianity, though it was repeated by Jacob ben Reuben, *Milḥamot Ha-Shem,* pp. 9–10. Possibly, Baḥya had no clear concept of the doctrine of the Trinity, though he was somewhat influenced by Christian teachings; cf. Yahuda's introduction, pp. 77–82.

137. *Sefer Ha-Berit,* ed. Frank Talmage (Jerusalem, 1974), pp. 32–33; trans., p. 41. Kimḥi cited Baḥya's parable of a manuscript with a uniform script: We must assume at least one scribe, but since the handwriting is the same throughout, there is no reason to assume more than one scribe. Cf. *al-Hidāya* I:7:3. Kimḥi knew Baḥya's work well, since he translated part of it.

138. *Eẓ Ḥayyim* 67–73, ed. F. Delitzsch (Leipzig, 1841), pp. 81–91; trans. Moses Charner, *The Tree of Life by Aaron ben Elijah of Nicomedia* (New York, 1949), pp. 133–48. Aaron mentioned Christianity in passing, e.g., p. 4, trans. p. 7. For another Kalamic anti-Christian comment, cf. the commentary on *Sefer Yeẓirah* attributed to Dunash Ibn Tamim, in Leopold Dukes, *Shire Shelomo* (Hannover, 5618 [1857–58]), reprinted (Jerusalem, 5729 [1968–69]), pp. ii–viii.

139. Cf. Wolfson, "The Muslim Attributes," p. 8, *Kalam,* pp. 121–22. It should be noted that when the Father was considered "essence," there were only two essential attributes in addition.

140. *De Divisione Naturae, PL* 122, 455. Augustine compared the Trinity to the mind with its intellect, memory, and will. Cf. *De Trinitate* X, 11–12. This analogy was only an image of the Trinity and is not relevant in this context.

141. Erigena was condemned during his life, and his *De Divisione Naturae* was later condemned for pantheism, Paris, 1210, and burned in 1225. See Maïeul Cappuyns, *John Scot Erigène* (Brussels, 1964), pp. 121–27, 247–50. It appears that the similarity of trinitarian doctrines between Erigena and Abelard and the condemnation of both was coincidental.

142. *Theologia Christiana, PL* 178, 1113–1330 in passim, esp. 1125, 1126. Yaḥya ben 'Adī suggested the same three attributes, but stated that the Father was goodness and the Spirit was power. Cf. Périer, *Petits Traités,* p. 119.

143. *Denz.,* no. 368: "Quod Pater sit plena potentia, Filius quaedam potentia, Spiritus sanctus nulla potentia." This was not the only doctrine of Abelard to be condemned.

144. For the activity of Abelard's followers, see D. E. Luscombe, *The School of Peter Abelard* (Cambridge, 1969).

145. See William of Saint Thiery, *De Erroribus Guillelimi de Conchis, PL* 180, 333. George F. Moore thought that Naḥmanides' and Crescas' statement that the Holy Spirit was will *(ḥefeẓ, raẓon)* reflected a translation of *benignitas.* From this and following quotations, it is obvious that such an interpretation is unnecessary (though the confusion between "will" and "good will" appears to be Christian in origin). See Wolfson, "Crescas on the Problem of Divine Attributes," *JQR,* n.s. 7 (1916–17): 210, n. 117.

146. His work, *Sententie Hermanni,* was erroneously attributed to Abelard. See *Petri Abelardi Epitome Theologiae Christianae, PL* 178, 1716–17. For the identity of Hermann as the author, see Luscombe, op. cit., pp. 158–59.

147. *De Sacramentis* I, 3, 26–29, PL 176, 227–31; Eng. trans. Hugh of Saint Victor, *On the Sacraments of the Christian Faith,* trans. Roy J. Deferrari (Cambridge, Mass., 1951), pp. 53–57.

148. *Sententiae* I, 34, 6–8, *PL* 192, 616.

149. *ST* I, 39, 8. The commentators attributed it to Hugh of Saint Victor, not Augustine.

150. Cf. especially Hugh, Lombard, and Thomas.

151. Cf. Anselm of Canterbury (1033–1109), *Proslogion* 12, *PL* 158, 234. Also the "Confession of Faith in the Trinity" of the Council of Rheims, 1148 (*Denz.,* 389): "We believe that He is wise only by that wisdom which is God Himself." Also, cf. Peter Lombard, *Sententiae* I:22:6, *PL* 192, 582–83; also, Wolfson, "Extradeical and Intradeical," pp. 55–56.

152. *PL* 157, 606–7. Alfonsi was a contemporary of Abelard. He may have learned his trinitarian doctrine from Saadia's refutation; cf. Funkenstein, "Ha-Temurah," p. 135.

153. H. Pflaum, "Poems of Religious Disputations in the Middle Ages" (Hebrew), *Tarbiẓ* 2 (5691 [1930–31]): 472–74, ll. 305–67. For the date and sources of the poem, see Pflaum's introduction, pp. 447–58.

154. *Contra Perfidium Judaeorum, PL* 207, 834, where he described the Son as wisdom and the Holy Spirit as goodness but did not ascribe to the Father any attribute.

155. Cf. *Contra Judaeos probatio temporis incarnationis Christi,* in *Biblia Latina cum Postilla Nic. de Lyra* (Venice, 1481). This work appears at the end of the last volume and is unpaginated. The relevant sections appear on fols. 1d, 2c–d.

156. *Teshuvot La-Meḥaref,* fols. 15b–17a. Cf. Y. Baer, "Torat Ha-Qabbalah," pp. 279–86.

157. *Guide* I:50–60; the literature on this subject is extensive. For a survey and much of the relevant bibliography, see Altmann, "The Divine Attributes," in *Faith and Reason,* ed. R. Gordis and R. Waxman (New York, 1973), pp. 19–23.

158. Cf. Altmann, ibid., pp. 23–27; Wolfson, "Avicenna, Algazali, and Averroes on Divine Attributes," *Homenaje a Millás-Vallicrosa,* II (Barcelona, 1956), pp.

545–71; reprinted in Wolfson, *Studies*, pp. 143–69. Cf. also idem, "The Amphibolous Terms in Aristotle, Arabic Philosophy and Maimonides," *HThR* 31 (1938): 151–73, and *Studies*, pp. 455–77.

159. Maimonides mentioned the Christians in this connection only in passing; cf. *Guide* I:50. Of course, he did not live in a Christian environment.

160. Joseph ben Shem Tov referred to this question in the context of Crescas' theory of attributes. Cf. *Biṭṭul*, fols. 10b–11a, and see below. It should be noted that the terms "Maimonidean" and "Averroist" are not applicable in a rigorous sense. Thus, Crescas was anti-Aristotelian, yet close to Averroes in his theory of attributes. Some of the other polemicists who will now be considered cannot really be classified as belonging in any particular philosophical school.

161. *Tahafot at-Tahafot*, ed. Maurice Bouyges (Beirut, 1930), p. 301:

وهذا هو مذهب النصارى فى الاقانيم الثلاث وذلك انهم ليس يرون انها صفات زائدة على الذات وانما هى عندهم متكثرة بالحد وهى كثيرة بالقوة لا بالفعل ولذلك يقوّلون انه ثلاثة واحد اي واحد بالفعل ثلاثة بالقوه.

Averroes' Tahafut al-Tahafut, trans. Simon van den Bergh (London, 1954), p. 178. Cf. vol. 2, pp. 109–10. Cf. also *Tafsir ma ba'd at-Tabi'at*, ed. Bouyges, III (Beirut, 1948), p. 1623, where Averroes stated that the Trinity implied conceptual, not real, alternation *(taghayyur)* in God.

162. Ibid., p. 322: وليس يضعونها صفات ذاتية كما يضع ذلك النصارى .
Trans. p. 193; cf. *Tafsir*, p. 1620.

163. *Commentary on Guide* I:58, ed. J. Goldenthal (Vienna, 1852), p. 9b: והנראה לי כי התארים הג׳ בפועל אצל הנוצרים והעצם אחד לא שיהיו בכח כמו שאמר ב״ר.

164. In the section dealing with God as *sekhel, maskil, muskal.*

165. *Kitāb al-Kashf 'an Manāhij* . . . , in M. J. Müller, *Philosophie und Theologie von Averroës* (Munich, 1859), p. 56:

وهذا قول النصارى الذين زعموا ان الاقانيم ثلاثة اقانيم الوجود والحياة والعلم وقد قال تعالى في هذا لقد كفر الذين قالوا ان الله ثالث ثلاثة.

166. *Magen Avot* I:5, printed in *Keshet u-Magen* p. 27a. The reading חיות for חיוב of the printed edition is confirmed not only by the Averroan Arabic original, but also by the Bodleian ms. 1294, fol. 16a:
והנה ן׳ רשד בדברו בתארים אמר שאם יאמרו האומרים בתארים שכל א׳ עומד בעצמו הנה האלוהות רבים וזהו מאמר הנוצרים שחשבו שהעצמות הג׳ המציאות והחיות והידיעה זה לשונו אבל הנוצרים בזמנינו זה הם מאמינים בג׳ על היכולת והחכמה והרצון.

167. Pp. 121–23. Jacob ben Reuben, who appears to have been a Neoplatonist, knew Saadia from the same paraphrase of *al-Amānāt* that was used by Berakhya Ha-Nakdan. Cf. p. 157, n. 1.

168. *Milḥemet Miẓvah*, fol. 30a: גם מה יאמרו בכח הזה שנקרא בן היה בו הכח שנקרא האב אם לא אם יאמרו לא היה בו כח האב הנה בן זה חסר הכח והיכולת אם יאמרו כי היה בו הכח שנקרא האב הנה האב נולד כמו הבן ואם כן שניהם נולדים.

169. Ibid., fols. 107b–108a:

ועוד כי על זה השלוש כל ישראל וכל חכם לב אמיתי בעולם מודה (מודה) כי הבורא חכם ויכול וחפץ בלי ספק אך שאנו מרחיקים לומר שיהיו שלשה גופות אך הוא אחד אמתי שאין כאחדותו בלא גוף וגויה בכחו ובחכמתו ורצונו הכל אחד אחדות אמתי מאין ראשית ואחרית.

170. *Ta'anot*, p. vi:

עוד טענה גדולה: אמרת שה׳ אחד ושלשה אחד והנה לפי דבריך צריך אתה לומ׳ שיהיה ענין א׳ ביניהם שיכלול השלשה להיות אחד וענין אחד הוא שיפרידם לשלשה עכשיו איזה ענין הוא שיכלול הטירניטאד להיות אחד? השיב: העצם הוא שיכלול הג׳ להיות אחד. אמרתי: ארבעה הם ג׳ תארים והעצם שכוללם והיאך אתה קורא טירניטאט יש לך לקרוא קוארטיטאט. השיב הנוצרי: לא כן כי אם הפירצונה ענין א׳ מהעצם ואינם כי אם שלשה. אמר העברי: כי אין הפירשונה — התואר ענין אחד מהעצם הרי גם הפירשונה התואר האחד אינו ענין א׳ [אחר] מהשני כי העצם אח׳ והשלשה אשר מנית טעות ושגיאה והנה אין שם טירניטאט.

171. Ibid.:

ואם כדבריך שהשם עצם אחד ויש עליו תארים נושאים אין הסבה הראשונה אחד אמיתית אלא מורכבת מענינים רבים עצם ותוארים נשואים עליו והוא כלל אחד וכל כלל צריך לכולל כאשר התבאר למטה. ל״א אם התאר הוא ענין מהעצם ואם תאמ׳ שהוא ענין הרי אלהיך מוחלק לחלקים ולפלגות ראובן [הש׳ שופטים ה׳ ט״ו]. ואם תאמ׳ שאינו ענין אחד א״כ התואר האחד אינו ענין אחר מן התאר השני והטריניטט שלך אינה כלום.

172. Ibid.:

ה׳ אצלכם מורכב משלשה ענינים ונודע מכח הקדמות אלו שקדמו שכל מורכב ההרכבה ההיא היא סבת מציאותו ואם כן צריך לסבה שימציאהו ואיננו מחוייב המציאות בעצמו.

173. Ibid., p. xii:

וכבר שאלתי לחכמיהם על ענין אחר הנמשך בזה אם יכולת ה׳ הוא ענין אחר מחכמת ה׳ וחכמתו ענין אחר מרצונו כי ידוע שחכמת בני אדם ויכולת הם ענינים שונים. אמנם אצל ה׳ איך הם?

174. Ibid., p. xiii:

והשיבו קצתם כי יכולת ה׳ וחכמתו אחת היא. וטענתי עליהם: אם כה הוא הטירניטאט שלכם בטולה. ואחרים השיבני: ״זה אחר מזה ומוחלק כל אחד מחבירו.״ וטענתי עליהם עוד: א״כ הוא שתואר זה מובדל מזה ומובדל מזה יש שם כביכול הפך ואין הדעת סובלת שיש בשם דיבירסידאד חלילה לאל׳ חלילה. והיה משני פנים הללו ואמונתם הבל המה. וכן מצות עשה ולא תעשה קורין הנוצרים פרימטיבי וינגאטיבי וההגמון הודה שה׳ אחד יחוד גמור בלי הרכבה בו והיכולת והחכמה והרצון הכל אחד עם העצם ואין תאר זה מובדל מזה.

175. *Vikuaḥ*, p. 320:

אחרי כן קם פראי רמון דיפנייא פורטי ודרש בענין השילוש ואמר שהוא חכמה וחפץ ויכלת. ואמר בבית כנסת: וגם המאישטרי הודה בזה בגירונא לדברי פראי פול.

176. Ibid.:

עמדתי על רגלי ואמרתי: האזינו ושמעו קולי, יהודים וגוים. שאלני פראי פול בגירונא: אם אני מאמין בשילוש. אמרתי לו מהו השלוש, שיהיו שלשה גופים גסים כבני אדם האלוהות. אמר: לא. ושיהיו שלשה (דברים) דקים כגון נשמות או שלשה מלאכים. אמר: לא. או שיהיה דבר אחד נמזג משלשה, כגון הגופים הנמזגים מד׳ יסודות. אמר: לא. אם כן מהו השלוש. אמר: החכמה, והחפץ, והיכולת. ואמרתי שאני מודה שהאלוה חכם ולא טפש, וחפץ בלא הרגשה, ויכול ולא חלש. אבל לשון שלוש טעות גמורה, שאין החכמה בבורא מקרה, אבל הוא וחכמתו אחד והוא וחפצו אחד והוא ויכלתו אחד. אם כן החכמה והחפץ והיכולת הכל אחד. וגם אם היה מקרים בו, אין הדבר שהוא אלהות שלשה אבל הוא אחד נושא מקרים שלשה.

This portion is not in the Latin protocol. The translation is adapted from Rankin, p. 209.

177. Ibid.:

ועוד יש לכם לומר חמוש, כי הוא חי, והחיות בו כמו החכמה. ויהיה גדרו: חי חכם חפץ יכול ועצם האלהות חמשה. כל זה טעות מבואר.

The example of wine and its three attributes will be discussed below. Note that Naḥmanides took power, wisdom, and will from the European tradition and added life and essence from the Eastern tradition, which he knew, no doubt, from Saadia's work.

178. *Theologia Christiana* III, *PL* 178, 1259–60.

179. *ST* I, 27, 3.

180. *ST* I, 27, 5.

181. So argued Farissol, *Magen Avraham,* fol. 22b, and the author of *Makkot Li-Khesil Me'ah,* p. 2a, in commentary.

182. *Ma'amar Elohi,* Bodleian ms. 1324.5, fol. 121b:

ולמה שחשבו אנשים שאלה התארים נבדלים במספר אמרו בשלוש עם אחדות העצמות.

Though Ḥasdai Crescas quoted Ha-Levi approvingly, very little is known about this author. Cf. Altmann, "Moses Ben Joseph Ha-Levi," *EJ,* 12, pp. 421–22; Steinschneider, *Die Hebräischen Ubersetzungen des Mittelalters und die Juden als Dolmetscher,* Berlin, 1893, no. 239, p. 410; Wolfson, "Crescas on the Problem," pp. 40–44; Crescas, *Or Ha-Shem* I:3:3, Vienna ed., pp. 25b–26a. The copyist of ms. 1324 considered Ha-Levi to have had heretical ideas *(yoẓe' mi-kelal ha-dat)* about attributes. He included critical marginal comments throughout.

183. *'Ezer Ha-'Emunah,* p. 20:

וא״ת שהשלוש הרי הרצון והיכולת והחכמה, ושלשתם הם בבורא מה שאין כן בשאר הנבראי׳, ושהבורא נתיעץ עם אלו הג׳ בבריאת העולם, ואתה קורא אותם טריני״אד, הנה קצרת וחסרת בהכרח בזה כח ומהלל הבורא ית׳, שהרי דֹעֹה אמר ״לך ה׳ הגדולה והגבורה והתפארת״ וכו׳, וכתי׳ ״והעושר והכבוד מלפניך״ וכו׳ והלא בפסוק הראשון הם ה׳ מלבד האחרי׳ שבפסוק שלאחריו. הנה לך ראיות ברורות להוציאך מכלל השלוש בבריאת העולם.

184. *Or Ha-Shem* I:3:3, p. 25b:

כי כמו שלא יצוייר היות העצם בזולת מציאותו ולא מציאותו בזולת העצם כן לא יצוייר מציאות התאר בזולת המתואר ולא המתואר בזולת התאר ויכללם הטוב המוחלט שהוא כולל כל מיני השלמיות.

Trans. by Wolfson, "Crescas on the Problem," p. 209. (Corrections on this and following quotations are on the basis of JTSA ms. 2514.) It is possible that the passage in *Sefer Yeẓirah* was the source of the image of the Trinity as a burning coal. See below. On Crescas' theory of attributes, see Wolfson, ibid.; Altmann, "The Divine Attributes," pp. 56–57; Eliezer Schweid, "'To'ar 'Azmi' be-Mishnat Ha-Rav Ḥasdai Crescas," *Ṭa'am Va-Haqashah* (Ramat Gan, 1970), pp. 149–71.

185. *Or Ha-Shem* I:3:3, pp. 25a–b:

ואחר שהמובן מושג אצלנו הנה הידיעה איננו יכולת ורצון והם אם כן ג׳ עניינים מתחלפים ולפי שעצמותו ית׳ אחד מכל פנים אם הם עצמותו או חלק מעצמותו יהיה כמאמר האומר הוא אחד אבל הוא הג׳ והג׳ אחד.

186. This differs from the Kalam doctrine, which maintained that the attributes were conceptually one, verbally three (or many).

187. Joseph ben Shem Tov's philological note is correct. *Persona,* originally meaning "mask," is the Latin translation of the Greek *prosopon,* the origin of the Hebrew *parẓof.* The point Joseph ben Shem Tov made was that the essence takes on

the masks, *personae/parẓofim,* of the Persons. See Marcus Jastrow, *Dictionary,* s.v. *parẓof.*

188. *Biṭṭul,* fol. 10b:

והוצרכתי להעירך עליו יען ראיתי קצת משכילים ישיבו על סברת החכם בהאמינו התוארים העצמיים קצת מאלה הבטולים והיה זה סבה לבלתי יעמדו על אמתת דעתו והבדל הסברות ואשר הטעה אותם הו׳ מלת תואר אשר הועתק מפרישונה ואינה העתקה אמיתית ואחרים העתיקו פרצוף כלו׳ רוצים שהאב מתראה בעצמותו זה וכן הבן והרוח ובכלל אין מובנם א׳ וזה הטעאה למאשימים לבעלי סברת התוארים וכן הטעם אומרם שהפריסונס הם יכולת חכמה רצון ובעבור שהאומרים בתוארים יאמרו שבו יכולת חכמה ורצון חשבו שהמובן א׳ ואינו כן.

Cf. Wolfson, "Crescas on the Problem," pp. 210–12.

189. *Biṭṭul,* fol. 2b:

א׳ שהנצרי אומ׳ שיש באל ית׳ ג׳ תארים נבדלים ובלשונם פירסונה...ב׳ שהנצרי מאמין שיש באל ית׳ תאר נק׳ בן נולד מהאב... ג׳ שהנצרי מאמין שיש באל ית׳ תואר נאצל מהאב והבן נק׳ רוח.

190. Ibid., fol. 6b:

האמונה הנצרית מנחת שהעצם האלקי יכלול (אל?) ג׳ תארים בלשונם פירסונס אב בן ורוח הקדש יכולת חכמה ורצון האב מוליד הבן ומאהבת שניהם הרוח הקדש הוא נאצל מהאב הוא היכולת מהבן החכמה מהרוח הרצון והג׳ במהות הם אל א׳ הם נבדלים אבל בתארים , וכל א׳ מהם הוא אלהים.

191. See below.

192. Cf. *ST* I, 4 on God's perfection, and *ST* I, 10, 14, 18, 19, 25, for a discussion of God's eternity, wisdom, life, will, and power.

193. *Biṭṭul,* fol. 9a:

ובהקדמה השלישית והיא שהמהות האלקי בו חיים נצחיים יכולת חכמה ורצון ומעלות אחרות רבות אומ׳ שאם יכולת חכמה ורצון הניחו אותם לג׳ תארים נבדלים ר״ל פירשונס על מה זה לא נניח החיות לתואר אחר, וכן יתחייב שתהיינה יותר מעלות ויהיו התוארים רבים לא שלשה נקראים פירשונס לבד או יתחייב להם שלא יהיו בו זולת אלו ולא יהיה חי והוא הפך מה שהונח שבו חיים נצחיים.

194. On Crescas' interpretation of the principle that one infinite cannot be greater than another one, see Wolfson, *Crescas' Critique of Aristotle* (Cambridge, Mass., 1929), pp. 63–64, 191, 423–24. This was a very commonplace notion; cf. Wolfson, *The Philosophy of Spinoza* (Cambridge, Mass., 1961), pp. 286–95.

195. Cf. Augustine, *De Trinitate* VI, 4–9, *PL* 42, 927–29; the declaration of the Fourth Lateran Council, 1215, *Denz.,* no. 428: "God's essence, substance, or nature is entirely simple *(simplex omnino)*"; and *ST* I, 3, 7. That one infinite may not be greater than another, see, e.g., Nicolas Cusanus (Nicholas of Cusa), *Of Learned Ignorance,* trans. Germain Heron (London, 1954), p. 36.

196. *Biṭṭul,* fols. 9a–b:

בהקדמה הד׳ האומרת שהוא ית׳ פשוט פשיטות בב״ת ופשיטות בב״ת יאמ׳ אותו פשיטות שא״א שידומה פשיטות יותר גדול ממנו שא״א בב״ת גדול מבב״ת אבל הפשיטות הזה אשר הניחו אפשר שידומה פשיטות יותר גדול ממנו וזה מבואר שכבר אפשר שידומה שלא יהיה בו רבוי בתאר ושלא יהיה תואר א׳ אלהים ותואר אחר אלהים יתחייב א״כ שאינו בתכלית הפשיטות ועוד כאש׳ היה המהות מתחלף לתואר וזה מבואר להנחתם שהמהות הוא אחד והתוארים רבים יתחייב שיהיו בו ד׳ דברים מהות א׳ ושלש תוארים לא שלש לבד וזה נגד ההקדמה האומרת שהו׳ בתכלית הפשיטות.

197. Cf. *ST* I, 3, 7: "quia omne compositum causam habet: quae enim secundum se diversa sunt, non conveniunt in aliquod unum, nisi per aliquam causam

adunantem ipsa. Deus autem non habet causem, ut supra ostensum est, cum sit prima causa efficiens."

198. Cf. the teaching of the Fourth Lateran Council, *Denz.* 432: "And that reality [the essence] is not generating, nor generated, nor proceeding, but it is the Father who generates, the Son who is generated, and the Holy Spirit who proceeds."

199. *Biṭṭul,* fol. 9b:

בה׳ האומרת שאין באל ית׳ הרכבה אומ׳ למה שהוא מבואר שהתואר והמהות הם מתחלפים לפי מה שזכרנו והוא מבואר ג״כ שהתוא׳ או יוליד או יאציל שהאב מוליד הבן שניהם מאצילים הרוח והמהות אינו מוליד ואינו מאציל א״כ הוא מורכב מדברי׳ מתחלפים ממהות ותוארים נושא ונשוא והוא הפך מה שהונח בזאת ההקדמה.

200. *Ta'anot,* p. vi.

201. *'Ezer Ha-'Emunah,* p. 170.

202. *Sefer Niẓẓaḥon* 128, pp. 83–84.

203. *Commentary on the Iggeret,* pp. 46–50.

204. *Magen Avraham,* fol. 22b.

205. *Ḥizzuk Emunah* I:10, pp. 83–84.

206. Fols. 5a–b.

207. Cf. *SCG* IV, 14, 8, pp. 454–55.

208. *Ḥilluf* is internal change or distinction between parts: *diversitas, differentia* (Jacob Klatzkin, *Oẓar Ha-Munaḥim Ha-Filosofiim,* Berlin, 1928–33, I, p. 301). Crescas was perhaps reading too much into Christian acceptance of God's simplicity. The Christians agreed that God was not composed and was totally simple; still, they admitted internal distinctions in God in terms of relation. Cf. *ST* I, 28, 3: "Unde oportet quod in Deo sit realis distinctio, non quidem secundum rem absolutam quae est essentia, in qua est summa unitas et simplicitas, sed secundum rem relativum." Cf. also ibid., 31:2, where Thomas said that when referring to God, one may not use the terms *diversitas* or *differentia,* but may employ *distinctio.* Similarly, William Ockham rejected any distinction in God, except for the Trinity. Cf. Matthew C. Menges, *The Concept of Univocity Regarding the Predication of God and Creature According to William Ockham* (St. Bonaventure, N.Y., 1952), p. 157.

209. *Biṭṭul,* fol. 10a:

אמנם בששית האומרת שאין בו ית׳ חלוף אומ׳ שאם היה כמו שהניחו היה בו חלוף בהכרח וחלופים רבים גם יתחלפו לבב״ת ראשונה יתחלפו שהמהות הוא בלי רבוי והתוארי׳ יש בהם רבוי יתחלפו עוד שהאב יוליד הבן והבן לא יוליד יתחלפו עוד שהאב והבן הם מאצילים הרוח והרוח ולא אחד מהם לבדו יאציל וכן לא יוכלו להאציל אל בב״ת אם כן הם מתחלפים בב״ת.

Crescas meant to say that God's essence, though infinite, could not emanate beyond the Spirit. Hence, there was an infinite difference between essence and its capacity.

210. *SCG* IV, 10, 9, p. 444: trans. O'Neill, p. 79.

211. Ibid., 14, 15, pp. 452–55.

212. *Denz.,* 391: "Credimus (et confitemur) solum deum Patrem et Filium et Spiritum Sanctum aeternum esse, nec aliquas omnino res, sive relationes, sive proprietates, sive singularitates vel unitates dicantur, et huiusmodi alia, adesse Deo, quae sint ab aeterno, quae non sint Deus." Cf. also Lombard, *Sententiae* I:8:9; *ST* I,

3, 3; 27, 3.

213. *Biṭṭul,* fols. 10a–b:
אמנם ההקדמה הז׳ שאין דבר באל שלא יהיה אלהים אומר אם האל הוא מהות א׳ וג׳ תוארים יתחייב שלא יהיה א׳ מהן לבדו אלהים וזה מבואר שאם כן יצטרך שיהיה כל א׳ מהם מהות א׳ וג׳ תוארים וזהו יתחייב ג״כ בכל א׳ מן הג׳ תוארים וכן אל בב״ת יתחייב א״כ שלא יהיה כל א׳ מהם אלהים והוא נגד ההקדמה השביעית.
This recalls Qirqisānī's truncated argument that God's life and reason would each require a life and reason. See above.

214. *ST* I, 30, 2. Anselm was also aware of a similar problem. Cf. *Monologium* 60–62, *PL* 158, 206–8.

215. Cf. below on Crescas' arguments against the Trinity based on eternal generation.

216. Al-Ghazālī apparently followed a similar pattern in his *Tahāfut al-Falasifa.*

217. *Biṭṭul,* fol. 10b:
ראוִי שתדע שהמקיים התארים העצמיים באל ית׳ איננו תחת זה הסוג ... וזה מבוא׳ שהם אמרו שהאב הוליד הבן ומי שמניח שבו ית׳ יכולת וחכמה לא יחשוב חלילה שהיכולת יפעל לחכמה ולא שהיכולת אלהים והחכמה אלהים וכן המציאות והאחדות למי שמניח אותם דברים עצמיים למהות ואינם עצם המהות כמו שהניח זה הרב ז״ל. ולכן לא תשיג לזאת ההנחה א׳ מאלה הבטולים המתחייבים לאמונת הנצרים ולא יאמרו שהם א׳ והם ג׳.

218. *Guide* I:52.

219. Joseph ben Shem Tov, *Iggeret,* p. 48, interpreted Duran's reference to attributes of relation, *to'are ha-ẓeruf,* as attributes of action, which Maimonides accepted. It is evident from some of the following citations that at least some of the polemicists were referring to attributes of relation.

220. I.e., there was not a Trinity of substances or essences.

221. *Lo ba-beḥinot;* cf. Klatzkin, *Oẓar,* I, pp. 81–82; Albo, *'Iqqarim* II:13, ed. Husik, p. 73.

222. "Substance," in Catalan. The correct reading and its interpretation are by Prof. Talmage, who is editing this work.

223. Jesus was "both God and man" and "truly God" (Council of Ephesus, 431, *Denz.,* 114, 117). Cf. also the decree of the Council of Chalcedon, 451 (*Denz.,* 148). Duran's statement was based on the following considerations: "God" referred to the essence of God. Jesus was truly God; therefore, the one essence of God, which was indivisible, became incarnate; still, only the Person of the Son did so. By using such a formulation, Duran implied a possible refutation. Cf. *Iggeret,* pp. 54, 78.

224. *Kelimat Ha-Goyim, Ha-Ẓofeh,* 3, p. 147:
והסכימו גם כן על שזה השילוש אשר הניחוהו הוא בתארים לבד אשר יקראום פירשונאש וגם כי אלה התארים נבדלים ולא בבחינות אבל בפועל וכי הנושא אחד הוא שופושיט והיא המהות האלהית אשר היא אחת בתכלית הפשיטות וכי האלהות בכללה קיבלה בשר והיתה אדם ובתאריו לא היה בשר כי אם הבן לבדו וחשבו בכל זה לקבץ בין האחדות הגמורה והרבוי הגמור.

225. Ibid., p. 148:
ואמרו בשילוש הזה שהם החכמה והיכולת והרצון וכי אמנם הוכרחו בעלי התורות להניח אלה התארים באלהות בעבור מה שיניחוהו מחדש העולם לפי שהחידוש אי אפשר שישלם אם לא יימצאו במחדש אלה שלשה התארים: החכמה והוא הסידור המושכל אשר בנפש הפועל מהפעול ההוא וקראו לזה בן, והיכולת והוא היות הסידור המושכל הזה אשר בעצם הבורא מספיק אל הפועל הפעול לשלימות הציור ההוא מה שאיננו כן

בשאר הפועלים וקראו לשלימות הציור ההוא אב, והרצון אשר הוא גם כן הכרחי בבריאה לפי שכבר יימצאו החכמה והיכולת ולא יחוייב המצא הפעול אם לא יתחבר אליו הרצון, וקראו לזה התואר רוח הקודש, ובאלה השלשה די בחידוש העולם.

226. Ibid: ואלה העניינים כולם פילוסופייאה אמיתית כשיונחו אלה התארים צרופיים ואין זאת כוונתם.

227. Ibid., p. 143; the kabbalistic doctrine taught that the "left side" was the source of ėvil. Cf. Gershom Scholem, *Kabbalah* (New York, 1974), pp. 55, 123–25.

228. This is, of course, inaccurate. Both the theory of Sefirot and the doctrine of divine attributes postdated the belief in the Trinity, and the Sefirot were not the same as attributes.

229. *Kelimat Ha-Goyim,* pp. 143–44. Cf. also Judah Aryeh de Modena, *Magen Va-Ḥerev,* p. 21. It is inappropriate here to enter into a major discussion concerning the relation of Kabbalah and Christianity. A number of Christians, notably Pico della Mirandola and Johann Rittangel, saw the Kabbalah as a confirmation of their belief. It is also true that the kabbalists resorted to the same type of explanations of the Sefirot as were used by the Christians to explain the Trinity. One example of this was the use of images to express the relationship between God and the Persons or Sefirot. Cf. A. Jellinek, "Christlicher Einfluss auf die Kabbalah," *Beiträge zur Geschichte der Kabbala,* II (Leipzig, 1857), pp. 51–56; Joseph L. Blau, op. cit.; Rankin, op. cit., pp. 89–154; Yitzḥak Baer, "Torat ha-Qabbalah"; Scholem, *Kabbalah,* pp. 196–201.

230. *Kelimat Ha-Goyim,* p. 149.

231. The work, incorporated into *Even Boḥan* as either chap. XII or XVI, was based almost entirely on Duran's works.

232. *Even Boḥan* XII (XVI):3, fol. 155a.

233. *Magen Avot* I:5, pp. 6a–8a.

234. *Magen Avot* I:5, printed in *Keshet U-Magen,* p. 27a:
ע״כ הם מכחישים האחדות האמתית וכן הם נוטים מהאמת במה שמאמינים הגשמות אל הבן עם היותו אלוה.
Don David Nasi also followed Profiat Duran in citing the Persons as wisdom, power, and will, remarking that some say that the Persons were living, powerful, wise. He offered exegetical refutations; cf. *Hoda'at Ba'al Din,* pp. 22–23.

235. *Magen Avraham,* fol. 22b:
ואין הענין הזה אצלם כענין רבוי התוארי׳ אצלנו כי גם שנאמין היות רבוי התוארים בו ית׳ הנה המה יהיו בערך המקבל הפעולות הנמשכות ממנו ואם רבות תהיינה והפכיות מ״מ לא תתחייבנה הרבוי בו חלילה, אמנם ענין השלוש אצלם הוא רבוי מספרי מחוייב בו.
Farissol's other arguments showed why such a numerical multiplicity was necessitated.

236. Fol. 5b: טעו הנוצרים ויצאו לכפירה וחושבים שהם מאמינים בשלשה בעיון ובדקות תבונה ובאו אל אלו המדות שהוא חי יכול וחכם.

237. The author apparently confused Saadia's three essential attributes, life, wisdom, power, with Saadia's exposition of the Christian Trinity as essence, life, wisdom. The author argued: (1) in order to have distinction and alternation between Persons, God must be corporeal; (2) anyone who has external life and wisdom must have been created; and (3) all attributes are really one, but man does not have the

one word to express it; see fols. 5b–6a.

238. Ibid., fols. 5a–b. Duran is *he-ḥakham ha-nizkar.* This latter passage was taken verbatim from Ibn Shapruṭ's *Even Boḥan.* The above arguments also appear in an untitled polemical work, JTSA ms. 2207, fols. 4a–5b.

239. Thomas stated that the difference between the attributes, which provided no basis for distinguishing Persons, and relations, which did, was that the attributes were not opposed to each other as the relations were. According to Thomas, Persons really derived from the relations, not from the attributes; cf. *ST* I, 30, 1.

240. This doctrine was originated by Alfarābī, deriving it from Aristotle's *Metaphysics* 12, 7, 1072b, 20 and *On the Soul* 3, 5, 430a, 20 and 7, 431b, 16. Cf. F. Dieterici, *Alfarabi's philosophische Abhandlungen* (1890), p. 58 (Arabic), (1892), p. 95 (German); Altmann, "Ma'amar be-Yiḥud ha-Bore'," *Tarbiẓ* 27 (5718 [1957–58]): 302. Other terms used for this formula are *madda', yode'a, yadu'a/'ilm, 'ālim, ma'alūm.* The translation, "intellect, intellectually cognizing subject, intellectually cognized object," is taken from S. Pines' translation of Maimonides' *Guide,* p. 163.

241. If God were to have changed from potentiality to actuality, He would have needed a cause for this change. God, however, is totally uncaused, and thus totally *in actu.*

242. *Guide* I:68; cf. Munk's notes in *Le Guide des Égarés* (Paris, 1856), pp. 301–12. Maimonides' commentators pointed out a number of contradictions in his theory. First, Maimonides negated from God all positive attributes (*Guide* I:50–60). He then stated that God was the thinker, the thinking, and the thought, seemingly a positive ascription. Second, Maimonides said that there existed no comparison or similitude between man and God (ibid.). Now, he said that man's intellect *in actu* and God's intellect operated in the same manner. Third, if God were identical with the objects of His cognition and He cognized the forms of the natural universe, then He must be identical with these forms, i.e., with the laws of nature. Cf. the traditional commentators ad loc., Altmann, "Ma'amar," and Pines, op. cit., pp. xcvii–xcviii, cxv.

243. Périer, *Petits Traités,* pp. 18ff. Cf. G. Graf, *Die Philosophie und Gotteslehre des Jaḥjâ ibn 'Adî und Spateren Autoren* (Munster, 1910), pp. 26–27.

244. Paul Sbath, *Vingt Traités Philosophiques et Apologétiques d'Auteurs Arabes Chrétiens du IXe au XIVe Siècle* (Cairo, 1929), pp. 9, 68–75.

245. Ibid., pp. 176–77.

246. Graf, op. cit., p. 69; also, Al-Ghazālī, *Réfutation Excellente de la Divinité de Jésus-Christ d'après les Evangiles,* ed. and trans. Robert Chidiac (Paris, 1939), p. 26.

247. "La Lampe des Ténèbres," ed. L. Villecourt et al., *Patrologia Orientalis,* 20 (1929): 637, 638–40.

248. Op. cit., p. 44 (text). Cf. also Franz-Elmar Wilms, *Al-Ghazālī's Schrift Wider die Gottheit Jesu* (Leiden, 1966), pp. 48, 209–12.

249. Cf. Thomas, *ST* I, 14, 2–6; 28, 4. The Christians did, however, give the example of the action of the intellect as parallel to the procession of the Son. Cf. ibid., I, 27, 1. Augustine compared the Trinity to love, loving, and the loved; cf. *De Trin.*

IX, 2, 2, *PL* 42, 961–62.

250. *Teshuvot La-Meḥaref*, fol. 16b; Baer, "Torat Ha-Qabbalah," p. 281.

251. *El "Liber Predicationis Contra Judeos,"* ed. José Mª Millás-Vallicrosa (Madrid-Barcelona, 1957), p. 94: "Sequitur ergo quod sit beatissima Trinitas in Deo sicut in suo intellectu, in quo est intelligens, intellectus, et intelligere." Cf. also pp. 78, 84.

252. This is obviously an anachronism. The Aristotelian doctrine was first put in this form by Alfarābī (ninth century).

253. *Sefer Tiqqun Ha-De'ot*, p. 69:

ושמא מכאן התפשטה אמונת המון הגוים בשלוש החוזר לאחד כששמעו אותו מן החכמים שבהם והם לא הבינו ממנו אלא מה שבכח ההמון להבין מן הענינים האלה. ואין ספק כי האמונה הזאת טובה ואמיתית בעצמה ואינה רעה כי אם בערך אל ההמון אשר נכשלו בה מכשול שאין לו תקומה ויצאו ממנו למה שיצאו מן האמונה הנפסדת.

On Albalag, see Vajda, *Isaac Albalag*, cf. pp. 88–90.

254. *Tiqqun*, p. 69. Albalag reflected a common Averroistic position that only religious and not philosophical truths should be revealed to the masses. For them, (Averroists), this explained why rabbinical literature was devoid of explicit Aristotelian teachings; the rabbis were reluctant to teach the true doctrine publicly.

255. *Magen Avot* I:5, p. 6b, continued in *Keshet U-Magen*, p. 26b:

ולפי ששמעו הנוצרים מופת הפלוסו׳ האמינו בשלוש המפורסם ונמשכו בו עד שהאמינו בהגשמה וישוללו מא״י הרבוי בדבור והניחו עניינו שהוא א׳ והוא ג׳.

Cf. also I:2 (*Keshet U-Magen*, p. 26a).

256. Albalag apparently mentioned this not because of an interest in Christianity but more as another reason for not divulging philosophy to the masses.

257. Fol. 11b; this was apparently copied from Levi ben Abraham's *Livyat Ḥen*. No refutation was offered.

258. *Ta'anot*, pp. xviii–xix:

אמר פליפו המין מטושקאנה: ״שמע נא עברי: הנה עם הנוצרים נתוכחת ולענות מפניהם מאנת והבן אלוה לא האמנת ועתה שמע נא והבן כי יש לאלוה בן; כי כבר בארו הפלוסופים שה׳ הוא השכל והוא השכיל והוא המושכל והם שלשה: שכל ומשכיל ומושכל והוא הטירניטאט שלנו: השכל הוא האב והמשכיל הוא הבן והמושכל הוא הרוח ושלשתן אחד ואם לא בבן אלוה תכחיש שה׳ (אינו) משכיל את עצמו ובזה לא תוכל לפקפק כי ג״כ הביאו המורה שלכם הרמב״ם ז״ל פרק בפני עצמו וכפל שם הדברים באותו פרק פעם ופעמים ושלש. והנה השלוש נוכח זכור ואל תשכח״.

259. John 1:1 (Italian).

260. *Ta'anot*, p. xix:

הוצרכתי אני העברי לחזור ולכתוב על זאת הטענה של זה כי קמו האחים הנקראים פידריקאדוריש להוכיח השלשה מדרך זו שאמרו הפילוסופים, שהשי״ת שכל ומשכיל ומושכל זה דרכם כסל למו: ״אמת ידוע אצל כל משכיל, שהשי״ת משכיל עצמו ואם הוא ישכיל עצמו אי אפש׳ שלא ישיג עם עצמו דבר אלא בודאי משיג; והדבר אשר ישיג הוא כעין צורה אחת או שאפיציאה א׳. והצורה הזאת אשר ישכיל הוא הבן שאנו קוראים. הנה משכיל הוא האב והמושכל הוא הבן ר״ל הצורה הנ״ל — כעין ההצטרפות שיש בין האב״ן — האב והבן — דילאציון (צ״ל רילאציון) בלעז והצורה הזאת היא הנקרא בירבו — פירניציפיון אירא בירבו —...והוא הוא שקבל הבשר וידוע שהאב אוהב את הבן ומשתעשע בו כך ה׳ אוהב את זה שנתחייב ממנו והאהבה הזאת היא הרחמנות או הרצון. הרי לך שלשה עצם המשכיל ועצם המושכל ר״ל עצם הצורה שנתחייבה ממנו כלומ׳ השכלתו שהשכיל ועצם האהבה״.

261. Ibid.:

שלשה אלו אינם עושים רבוי כלל כל עקר והנה אפי׳ באדם כשמשכיל בפועל אינו עושה רבוי, כ״ש בבורא ית׳ ואין שם רבוי עצמם ר״ל שאין עושים פירצוני נבדלים לא שלשה ולא שנים; וידוע שהאמונה של נוצרים היא שיש בבורא שלשה פירשוני נפרדים זה מזה שאינו עושה השכל והמשכיל והמושכל כי שלש אלו אפי׳ באדם הוא אחד כאשר אמרנו בשכלינו בפועל ואין שם רבוי כלל כ״ש בשי״ת. וכבר התבאר זה בספרי המעולים מן הפלוסופים והוא ידוע אצל כל משכיל ואין מן הפלוסופים שיחלוק עליו.

262. Ibid., pp. xix–xx:

אמרת בשהשם משיג צורה אחת או אישפיציאה אחת והוא הבן, אמרת הבל ורעות רוח כי ה׳ לא ישכיל רק עצמו ית׳ לא דבר אחר ר״ל לא צורה ולא שפיציאה ולא פירשונה מובדלת שאם היה משכיל צורה או ענין אחר, ל״א, אם היה משכיל על עצמו צורה אחרת לא היה משכיל מושכל.

263. *Livyat Ḥen,* p. 6:

לא יתכן להסכים השלוש עם האחדות כי השלוש מביא לגשמות ולרבוי ואין לדמותו לאמרנו על הבורא ית׳ שהוא השכל והמשכיל והמושכל והכל אחד, כי זה הפלגה באחדות והפשיטות.

264. I.e., God's intellectual cognition was not by virtue of anything external to Him, therefore causing multiplicity. According to Narboni, there was no distinction between God and His cognition, and hence God's unity was not incompatible with the doctrine of God's cognition.

265. *Commentary on Guide* I:50, p. 5b:

וזה נמנע אם לא שצדקו שני הסותרים ואנו שאומרים שכל משכיל ומושכל באל יתברך ושהכל אחד אין אנו אומרים שבו אלו השלשה דברים ושהשלשה אחד אבל נאמר שהדבר האחד בעצמו נקרא באלה השלשה שמות והוא עצמותו והמשכיל מצד השכילו עצמו כי האל הוא השכל הראשון הפשוט אשר עצמותו המופשט גלוי לעצמותו הנקי כי ישכיל עצמו מצד שעצמו מושכל לעצמו ואמתתו הוא השכלתו וזאת היא אחדותו האמיתית.

Cf. also *Commentary* ad I:68. Shem Tov ibn Shapruṭ quoted this statement almost verbatim (without attribution) in *Even Boḥan,* fol. 187b.

266. *Commentary,* p. 14a:

וכי בזה יתבאר בטול מאמיני השלוש וקיום האחדות ית׳ אין כמוה יתונה לזולתו.

Joseph ben Shem Tov also saw a connection between *Guide* I:68 and a refutation of the Trinity. This was stated in a work which was devoted solely to explication of this chapter. While not saying so explicitly, his son, Shem Tov ben Joseph, citing his father's work, also implied that this may have been the intention of the chapter. Cf. M. Steinschneider, *Heb. Über.,* no. 108, pp. 206–7; Shem Tov's *Commentary on Guide,* ad loc., Warsaw ed., I, p. 99a; *Commentary on the Iggeret,* p. 48, where Joseph ben Shem Tov equated ascribing God with attributes of action with saying that He was intellect, intellectually cognizing subject, and intellectually cognized object; Altmann, "Ma'amar," pp. 301–2.

267. *'Iqqarim* III:25, ed. Husik, p. 225:

ואבל שיהיו בו שלשה דברים נבדלים נמצאים כל אחד עומד בעצמו, כמו שהם אומרים דישטינטו״ש אי״ן פירשונא״ש ושיהיו אחד, זה אי אפשר אם לא יצדקו שני הסותרים יחד, שהוא דבר כנגד המושכלות הראשונות שאי אפשר לשכל לצייר מציאותו.

268. *Magen Avraham,* chap. 18, fol. 22b:

והוא יודע הכל ומושכליו בו ובשכלו ולא חוץ ממנו על כן להורות אחדותו ופשיטותו נק׳ כי הוא שכל משכיל ומושכל ולא יפרדו בעצם לעשות פירסוני נפרדות כי הכל א׳ הוא מה שאין כן בהקדמות דרכי השלוש להם שהאב יח(ו)ייב הבן ומהבן יחוייב הרה״ק. וכל א׳ וא׳ טבע לבדו דבק באחדות עצם א׳ והרבוי בו, ולברוח מזה אמרה תורה ה׳ אלקינו ה׳ אחד.

269. For the details of the procession of the Son and Spirit, cf. *ST* I, 27. Abraham Ger of Cordova cited the same trinitarian formula in his *Ẓeriaḥ Bet El*, JTSA ms. 2296, fol. 54b. This work was translated from Spanish into Hebrew by Mordecai Luzzato, 1774.

270. *Magen Va-Ḥerev*, p. 25:
ויציעו הדבר באופן זה, כי אין לכחד שהאלוק׳ יודע ומשכיל את עצמו ומוליד מזה מושכל ואוהב אותו שהיותו יודע הוא האב, ומה שמוליד מהשכלתו הוא הבן, ואהבתו לו הוא רוח הקדש. השכלתו, ומשכלו, ואהבתו אין כל א׳ מאלו בה׳ מקרה, כמו שהוא באדם, ולא דבר חוץ מעצמו, כי הם עצמות באלוקות, א״כ הוא אחד בעצמו ושלש בתואריו, שקראו פירסוני, ונמצא שאמונה זו נפלאת היא, ולא רחוקה היא כמו שאמרנו.
Joseph Kaspi also agreed that the Trinity was not intrinsically incorrect, and that, indeed, the Torah taught a trinitarian doctrine of God as Father, with the agent intellect (Son) and the Holy Spirit proceeding from Him. Cf. Ernst Renan, *Les Écrivains Juifs Français du XIVe Siècle, Histoire Littéraire de la France*, 31 (Paris, 1893), p. 183 (529), quoting Kaspi's *Gevi'e Kesef*, question 5. Cf. also Steinschneider, *Al-Farabi* (St. Petersburg, 1869), p. 242.

271. *Magen va-Ḥerev*, p. 25:
על דברים אלה נאמר, שאם היתה כונתם בכך בעצמות האלוק׳, שהם קוראים א״כ הם מבפנים ולא מבחוץ, אינפרה ולא איקשטרה, לא היה בינינו מחלוקת. כי היותו ית׳ יודע ומשכיל את עצמו, והנולד מהשכלתו זאת אוהב אותו, ושהכל בו עצם ולא מקרה, אנחנו לא נכחיש זה. וכן קראוהו הפילוסופים והחכמים שכל משכיל ומושכל. וקריאתם להם שמות, אב, ובן, ורוח לא יעלה ולא יוריד.

272. Ibid.; namely, implying that there was some plurality in God's soul or essence.

273. Ibid., pp. 25–26:
אך בבאם לומר, שאלה הג׳ תוארים נבדלים, והם חוצה לה עד שנא׳ שהא׳ יפעל ויהיה כמה שלא יפעל ויהיה חבירו, באמרם שהבן הוא שנתגשם, ולא האב ולא רוח הקדש, זהו ההפרש המפריד לגמרי בין דעתנו לדעתם.

274. *Guide* I:50; Pines, p. 111.

275. For the origins of the doctrine of generation, cf. Wolfson, *Church Fathers*, pp. 287–304.

276. *Sefer Nestor Ha-Komer*, p. 3:
ועתה הבן ממני את אשר אני משיבך מתוך דבריך אמור לי עתה מתי היה ישו בן אלוה קודם שילדו האב או לאחר שילדו או היה בנו ולא ילדו או קראו מן השמים לחברו וא״ת כן הנה נמצאת כופר באלהים כי שמת אותם שנים וא״ת שאינם שנים תכזיב את הספר כי כן כתוב בו.

277. The latter part of this argument is a paraphrase of Baḥya, *al-Hidāya* I:7:4, Yahuda, pp. 54–55. Baḥya's argument was also obviously irrelevant for the Christian belief in one essence, three Persons.

278. *Milḥamot Ha-Shem*, pp. 9–10:
אם נקרא בן קודם שנולד, או אחר שנולד? אם תאמר קודם שנולד, זה לא יתכן, שאין דבר בעולם שיקרא עליו שם בן קודם שנולד, אך לאחר שנולד נקרא בן. ואם כן נמצאו דבריך שאינם אמתיים, שאמרת שאין האיחוד יוצא מידי שלוש, והנה בפעם הזאת על כרחך אותו הזמן שעמד קודם שנולד מבטן העלמה, לא היה איחודו בכלל השילוש, כי אם בכלל השנים, שעדיין שם הבן לא נולד עליו. גם משנים אי אפשר להיות, שכן העידו ספרי הפילוסופים, אם הבורא יתברך יותר מאחד, אינו יוצא משתי פנים, או שעצם שניהם אחד, או יותר מאחד, ואם הוא אחד, הנה הבורא יתברך אחד הוא, ואם יותר מאחד, הנה הוא מתחלף, ואם העצם מתחלף, הנה יש ביניהם הפרש בינוני, וכל מופרש מוגבל, וכל מוגבל יש לו סוף, וכל מה שיש לו סוף מחובר, וכל

מחובר מחודש, וכל מחודש צריך למחדש אחר זולתו, לפי שאין דבר מחדש עצמו כאשר אמרתי למעלה, וכל זה נמנע מהבורא יתברך.

This argument was copied, almost verbatim, by Isaac Lupis, *Kur Maẓref*, pp. 1a–b.

279. Ibid., p. 11.

280. Ibid., p. 12:

וכמו שמצד נבראים, אין הפה יכול לקרוא שם בן אלא במה שהעין רואה נולד ויצא לאויר העולם, כן בזה הבורא אחרי אשר אמרת שנברא ובא בכלל הנבראים, דין הוא שלא יקרא עליו שם בן אלא לאחר שנולד. ונמצא שנהרסו דבריך שאמרת שאין איחודו יוצא מכלל שילוש, והנה החוט המשולש ינתק וחבל השנים ירתק.

281. *De Trin.* VI:1, *PL* 42, 923: "Si filius est, natus est; si natus est, erat tempus quando non erat filius."

282. Ibid.

283. *'Ezer Ha-'Emunah*, p. 20.

284. *Zikheron Sefer Niẓẓaḥon*, p. 260.

285. Fol. 4b:

וא"ת שרוח הקדש כבר היה נולד ואח"כ לבשו מן ב"ו, א"כ הקב"ה הוא א' ורוח של יש"ו שנתלבש שני לו, ואיך אתם אומרים שהשלוש הם שלשה והם א' דבר שאין אני מבין, וגם אתה אינך תוכל להסביר לי זה.

286. This unusual term for "substance" reflects the underlying Arabic *qunūm*, which, of course, means "Person," not "substance." Cf. Schlosberg, *Controverse*, Arabic, p. 4, French, p. 6, where *qunūm* is also used as "substance."

287. *Nestor*, p. 3:

ואשר הזכרת והעדת כי האב והבן ורוח הקדש קנין אחד הם אמור לי עתה נולד מן האב או עם האב נולד א"ת כי עם האב היה וקודם שנולד הי' כבר בטלת הילדה כי לא יולד. ואם תאמר כי לא ילדו בטלת דבריך הראשונים כי היה עם האב קודם שיולד.

288. This may be derived from Jacob ben Reuben's statement that if Gen. 1:26 ("Let us make man") implied that there were more than one divinity, it should refer to two brothers or a brother and a sister. Cf. *Milḥamot Ha-Shem*, p. 44.

289. *Commentary on Psalms* 2, printed in *Sefer Ha-Berit*, ed. Talmage, p. 71:

האב קודם לבן בזמן ומכוח האב יצא הבן. ואף־על־פי שלא ייתכן זה מבלי זה בקריאת השמות, כי לא ייקרא אב עד שיהיה לו בן ולא ייקרא בן אם לא יהיה לו אב, מכל מקום אותו שייקרא אב, כשיהיה הבן, היה קודם בזמן בלי ספק. ואם כן האלוה שאתם אומרים ואתם קוראים לו אב ובן ורוח הקודש, החלק שאתם קוראים לו אב קודם לחלק האחר שאתם קוראים בן. כי אם היו כל זמן שניהם כאחד היו קוראים להם אחים תאומים, ולא תקראו להם אב ובן, ולא יולד וילוד; כי היולד קדם לילוד בלי ספק.

This was more or less copied in *Kevod Elohim*, fol. 7a.

290. *Milḥemet Miẓvah*, fols. 49b–50a:

אין ראוי לומ' אצל הבורא ית' שיהיה גוף כל שכן שאין ראוי לומ' בו שיהיה בשלש גופות . . . ומה שנוכל להקשות עליכם על מה שהם קוראים לכח אב ולחכמה בן ולחפץ רוח הקודש ומפני מה נקרא זה אב וזה בן אחר שאתם מודים שהכל קדמון מאין התחלה ו(א)שאין היכולת בלא חכמה וחפץ ולא החכמה בלא יכולת וחפץ וכיון שכ(י)ן למה יקרא זה אב וזה בן כי הבן ראוי שיקרא לו האב ואחר שאין קדמות לזה על זה מה ענין הבדל אלו השמות ומשמעותם.

291. Ibid., fol. 30a: ואם יאמרו שאינו קדמון אם כן היה האב בלא חכמה.

292. *Ta'anot*, p. ix:

כבר ידוע מה שאמור בספר ההגיון כי מסגלת שני המצטרפים שהם נמצאים יחד בטבע וכשעלה האחד יעלה האחר בהצטרפות האדון לעבד והאב לבן כי לא יקרא אדון מבלי עבד ולא אב מבלי בן וכן מראשית אין קדימת

שניהם יחד כי אפשר לקדום האדון לעבד והעבד לאדון או אפשר שיהיו בזמן אחד וזה לא היה אדונו של זה וזה לא היה עבדו של זה. אמנם קדם לבן בלי ספק כל אותו הזמן שלא ילדו קדם לו אך לא נקרא אב רק אחר הולידו את בנו. ואחרי זאת ההקדמה יש לסתור אמונתך מעיקרה כי הבן אשר אתה מתאר לשם אם הוא בנו כאשר אתה אומ׳ לא היה קדמון כמוהו כי כל אב קודם לבן כאשר הקדמנו בהקדמתנו וכן לא יקרא אב רק אחר הלידה והנה ה׳ קדם לבן אשר אתה מאמין מתאר לו. ואם קדם האב הרי הבן נברא אחר ההעדר ר״ל אחר שלא היה; ואם איננו קדמון איננו אלוה כי כל נברא אינו בורא וכל בן הוא עלול כי מאחר שהוא בן ר״ל מאחר שקורין אותו בן בעל כרחך צריך לומ׳ שהוא עלול לאביו וכל עלול [מ]עלה.

293. Ibid., p. xii.

294. This designation of God originated from Avicenna and was adopted by almost all subsequent Aristotelians. Cf. *ST* I, 2, 3.

295. Since it has a cause, it is only possible of existence, not necessary.

296. *Biṭṭul,* fols. 6b–7a:

וראשונה זאת האמונה סותרת ההקדמה הראשונה שאומרת שהאל ית׳ מחוייב המציאות וזה כשנאמר אם הבן הוא נולד האלהים הוא נולד, וזה יתחייב מאמרך שכל א׳ מהם הוא אלהים ואם היה האל נולד, א״כ הוא עלול ומסובב, זה מבואר שהמוליד סבת מציאותו, אבל מי שהוא עלול אינו מחוייב המציאות וזה מבואר שיש לו התלות, א״כ יתחייב שהאל אינו מחוייב המציאות. דומה לראיה הזאת נעשה ברוח הקדש כשנאמ׳ שהרוח הקדש נאצל א״כ האלהים עלול ומסובב, וא״כ אינו מחוייב המציאות ולפי אלה השתי הקדמות האמונה הזאת סותרת ההקדמה הראשונה אשר הסכימו עליה.

297. *ST* I, 27, 2, trans. Ceslaus Velecky, *The Trinity* (*Summa Theologiae,* 6), (London, 1965), p. 9.

298. Ibid.

299. *ST* I, 4.

300. *Biṭṭul,* fol. 7a:

לא נשאר א״כ אלא שהאב יולידהו תמיד בעתות רצופות והוא תמיד נמצא ממנו מבלי שיהיה שם עת ראשון ממנו התחיל מציאותו ולכן יהיה האב פועל הבן תמיד בכל עת לנצח וכמו שהאב נצחי הבן הנמצא ממנו נצחי בכל עת ועת יולידהו.

301. 4, 10–14; 6, 2, 232b, 20–233a, 32. For Crescas' own theory of time, cf. Wolfson, *Crescas' Critique,* pp. 93–98, 282–91, 633–64.

302. *Biṭṭul,* fols. 7a–b:

ראשונה שיהיה הזמן מחובר מעתות ורגעים אחר שהוא נאצל ממנו תמיד בכל עת ועת וכבר התבאר המנע זה בד׳ ובו׳ מספר השמע במופתים מוחלטים, ר״ל שהזמן הוא מדובק ושאינו מחובר ממה שלא יתחלק ולכן לא יהיה מחובר מרגעים אבל הוא מתחלק אל בלתי תכלית בכח החלוקה כמשפט כל מתדבק, וראוי שתדע שהנצרים מאמינים בזאת החלוקה האחרונה ר״ל שהו׳ נולד תמיד והאב מוליד את בנו תמיד וכמו שאין ראשית והתחלה לאב אין התחלה וראשית לפעולתו שהו׳ בנו זה והוא ממציא אותו תמיד אשר יתחייב ממנו שיהיה הזמן מחובר מעתות אחר שלא יולידהו בזמן מדובק אבל בעתה והוא נמצא ממנו תמיד בכל עת ועת ולכן יהיה הזמן מחובר מאלה העתות. ויתחייב עוד בטול גדול יותר לזאת ההנחה והוא שיהיה הבן נפסד על התמידות וזה מפני ששמוהו נמצא מהאב ומתחייב ממנו בכל העתות על התמידות ואם היה מוליד אותו בעת א׳ ונשלם מציאותו אי אפשר שימציא ויוליד אותו פעם שנית כי הדבר השלם והדבר הנמצא בפועל א״א שימציאוהו פעם אחרת מזולת שיהיה מציאותו נפסד ואחר שיפסד יתהוה או יהיה נולד פעם אחרת ואחר ששמת שהבן נולד תמיד ומתחייב מהאב תמיד הנה הוא מחוייב שיפסד תמיד בכל עת ואחר יתהוה ואחר יפסד וכן אל בלתי תכלית לנצח.

303. Ibid., fol. 7b:

ויתחייב מזה בטול יותר גדול והוא שיפסד וימצא בכל עת באופן שבעת א׳ יהיה נמצא ונפסד ממנו תמיד וזה כי

הדבר הנמצא לא יולידהו עד שיפסד והוא מוליד אותו בכל עת א״כ בכל עת יהיה נפסד שאם יהיה נשאר שום עת א״כ לא יולידהו תמיד כי אותו העת שנשאר שוה במציאותו לא יהיה נולד אחר שהנמצא לא יתהוה ולא יפעלוהו בעודו נמצא א״כ מחוייב הוא שיהיה נפסד בכל עת באופן יקבל מציאותו בכל עת וכאשר היה זה מבואר שהוא יהיה בכל עת הווה ונפסד נמצא ונעדר וזה מבואר השקרות.

304. Ibid.: ויתחייב ג״כ שהאלהים הבן אשר הוא עתה איננו אשר היה הוא אתמול ולא העת שעבר אחר שכבר נפסד אותו הבן ונמצא זה.

305. Ibid.: שאחר שהאלהים הבן עלול מהאב הוא בלתי שלם הפך מה שהונח בהקדמה שבו כל השלמויות לנצח.

306. Ibid.

307. Ibid.: עברתי חק ההעתקה.

308. *Milḥamot Ha-Shem* VI:7 (Riva di Trento, 1560), pp. 51b–52a.

309. Cf. *Tahāfut al-Falasifah*, ed. Bouyges (Beirut, 1927), pp. 49–51; trans. Sabih A. Kamali, *Al-Ghazali's Tahafut al-Falasifah* (Lahore, 1958), pp. 34–35.

310. *Or Ha-Shem* III:1:3, p. 63b. Joseph ben Shem Tov also summarized the argument in *Biṭṭul*, fols. 8a–b.

311. *Biṭṭul*, fol. 8b.

312. *Or Ha-Shem* III:1:4, pp. 67a–b.

313. *Biṭṭul*, fol. 8b: ואין לו ראיה זולתי למי שלא ידע טבע המופתים או בעל תאוה גדולה.

314. Ibid.; Joseph said that he had already demonstrated the weakness of Crescas' arguments in a special treatise on the subject.

315. Cf. Wolfson, *Crescas' Critique*, pp. 16–17, nn. 59–60. Abravanel believed that the deciding factor was Crescas' reading of al-Ghazālī's *Tahāfut* or Averroes' *Tahāfut at-Tahāfut.*

316. The *Tratado* is usually dated around 1398, twenty years after the papal schism mentioned in chap. 8, fol. 17a. *Or Ha-Shem* was completed in 1410 but consists of earlier parts. Cf. Wolfson, ibid., pp. 17–18.

317. *Even Boḥan* XII (XVI):2, fol. 154b; Roman, *Sela' Ha-Maḥloket*, in *Milḥemet Ḥovah* (Constantinople, 1710), p. 6 (unpaginated).

318. Fol. 2a. The commentary on the poem (by the same author?) asked why the Father did not always generate more Sons.

319. He was copied by Shem Tov ibn Shapruṭ, *Even Boḥan* XII (XVI):2, fol. 154b; Don David Nasi, *Hoda'at Ba'al Din*, p. 19; Judah Aryeh de Modena, *Magen Va-Ḥerev*, p. 21. Some Church Fathers attributed the Arian heresy to the use of Aristotelian syllogistic reasoning. Cf. Wolfson, "Philosophical Implications of Arianism and Apollinarianism," *Religious Philosophy* (Cambridge, Mass., 1961), pp. 126–27.

320. *Iggeret*, p. 78. After proceeding to show how the Trinity contradicted logic, Duran showed that the doctrine of transubstantiation was inconsistent with mathematics, physics, and metaphysics. See chap. 6 on transubstantiation below.

321. According to Aristotelian logic, there are three figures of the syllogism, the first and second of which have four moods and the third has six. In the first figure, the middle term is the subject of one of the premises and the predicate of the other. Thus, in the syllogism: (A) Every man is an animal; (B) Every animal is sentient;

therefore (C) Every man is sentient; animal is the middle term. This syllogism is an example of the first figure. In the first mood of the first figure, the two premises and the conclusion are universal affirmatives, e.g., "Every man is an animal," "Every animal is sentient," and "Every man is sentient." Aristotle stated that syllogisms of all three figures can be reduced to universal syllogisms in the first figure. Cf. Aristotle, *Prior Analytics* 1, 4–26; Nabel Shehaby, *The Propositional Logic of Avicenna* (Dordrecht, Holland, 1973), pp. 91–100; Moses ben Maimon, *Maimonides' Treatise on Logic (Maḳālah Fi-Ṣināʿat Al-Manṭiḳ),* ed. Israel Efros (New York, 1936), pp. 14–17 (Arabic), 34–39 (Hebrew), 41–47 (English). In Duran's syllogism, both premises and the conclusion are universal affirmatives, and this, Joseph ben Shem Tov noted, "is the most well known and most respected mood of conclusion, and the most fitting proof"; cf. *Iggeret,* p. 82.

322. Joseph ben Shem Tov, following Averroes' *Commentary* on Aristotle's *Prior Analytics,* offered the following difference between (1) a universal affirmative and (2) a conditional predicated on the universal. One may understand the proposition "all men walk" in two ways: (1) Everything which is a man, walks; or (2) Every man, and everything predicated on man, walks. The latter is a conditional predicated on the universal. This distinction will be important for understanding Duran's syllogism; cf. *Iggeret,* p. 82, and notes, p. 81.

323. Ibid., p. 78:

ואתה לא כן חלילה לך לא תאמין שיוליד המין הראשון מהתמונה הראשונה מתמונות ההיקש אשר הוא יסוד כל חכמת ההגיון כפי תנאי הנאמר על הכל כי תצא מזה לכפירה בחוזק (צ״ל בחוק) האמונה אם תאמר זה האב הוא האל וזה האל הוא הבן לא יוליד אם כן זה האב הוא זה הבן.

Duran was saying that, despite Christian teaching that the Father was God and God was the Son, the Christians did not draw the logical inference that the Father was the Son.

324. Ibid., p. 82.

325. Ibid., p. 84.

326. Ibid.:

ונחזור לבאר אמתת צורת ההקש והוא מבואר שכאשר היה אצלנו שכל האב הוא האלוה (לצודק?) ועוד נשא על כל זה הנשוא ועל כל מה שיתואר בו נשוא אחר והוא אמרנו וכל האלוה וכל מי שיתואר באלוה הוא הבן וכבר היה לנו שהאב הוא מתואר באלוה יתחייב בהכרח שהאב הוא הבן.

327. Cf. *Maimonides' Treatise,* pp. 10 (Arabic), 29 (Heb.), 38 (Eng.).

328. *Iggeret,* pp. 82–84.

329. *Metaphysics* 7, 6, 1031a, 15–1032a, 11; cf. *On the Soul* 2, 4, 415b, 12–14.

330. Cf. *ST* I, 3, 3, where Thomas stated that God was the same as His essence or nature, and ibid. 39, 1, where he said that the Persons were identical with God's essence.

331. *Commentary on Iggeret,* p. 50:

ועתה ראיתי לכתוב פה ויכוח אחד קצר נתווכחתי עם אחד מגדולי חכמיהם על זה הדרוש. הנחתי הקדמה אמרה ארסטו בשבעה ממה שאחר הטבע אין בה ספק כי הדבר ומהותה דבר אחד על כי ראובן אינו ראובן זולת מהותו וזה מושכל ראשון. אמרתי אם תאר האב הוא מהות האב או זולתו. השיב מהות האב הוא תאר האב. אמרתי עוד מהות האב הוא מהות הבן. ואמר כן מהות האב הוא מהות הבן והרוח כי לכולם מהות אחד. אמרתי

יתחייב מזה שתאמר שתאר האב הוא מהות הבן.
Anselm stated that it was more appropriate to call the Son the essence of the Father than the Father the essence of the Son. Cf. *Monologium* 45, *PL* 158, 197–98.

332. *Iggeret*, p. 50:
אמרתי עוד נקח זאת התולדה ונעשה ממנה התחלה מופת אחר וזה דרך הגיונינו נאמר תאר האב הוא מהות הבן וכל מהות הבן הוא תאר הבן אם כן תאר האב הוא תאר הבן.
Cf. also Joseph ben Shem Tov's commentary on *Biṭṭul*, fols. 9a–10b. This argument was employed also by Lupis, *Kur Maẓref*, p. 1b.

333. *ST* I, 28, 3; trans. Velecky, op. cit., p. 33. Cf. also *SCG* IV, 10, 5, p. 443.

334. *Physics* 3, 4, 202b, 10.

335. *ST* I, 28, 3.

336. Cf. Wolfson, *Church Fathers*, pp. 305–63; Wolfson speaks of the Trinity images in passim, esp. pp. 359–61.

337. Cf. A. Mingana, "The Apology of Timothy the Patriarch before Caliph Mahdi," *Woodbrooke Studies*, fasc. 3, *Bulletin of the John Rylands Library* 12, 1 (1928): 207: "I made use of such similes solely for the purpose of uplifting my mind from the created things to God. All the things that we have with us compare very imperfectly with the things of God." Note also John of Damascus, *De Fide Orthodoxa*, *PG* 94, 821.

338. Vajda, "Le Problème," pp. 62–63.

339. See above.

340. *Quod Non Sit Tres Dii, ad Ablabium*, *PG* 45, 132; cf. also *De Communibus Notionibus*, *PG* 45, 175–86; Basil, *Epistola* 38, 2, *PG* 32, 325–28; Gregory Nazianzus, *Oratio* 31, 19, *PG* 36, 153.

341. *De Fide Orthodoxa* III, 4, *PG* 94, 997.

342. *Traité*, pp. 4, 5 (text), 38–39 (trans.).

343. G. Graf, *Die Schriften des Jakobiten Ḥabīb ibn Ḥidma Abū Rāi'ṭa*, Scriptores Arabici, 14–15 (Louvain, 1951), pp. 24 (text), 29 (trans.).

344. Idem, *Die Arabischen Schriften des Theodor Abū Qurra* (Paderborn, 1910), pp. 144–47; *Varia Opuscula* II, *PG* 97, 1476–77; Constantin Bacha, *Les Oeuvres Arabes de Théodore Aboucara* (Beirut, 1904), pp. 33–35.

345. See above, and Vajda, "Le Problème," pp. 66–69. For another use of the image of three men despite the author's rejection of unity of species, see Périer, "Un Traité," pp. 13, 20.

346. Wolfson, *Church Fathers*, p. 351, based on *De Trin.* VII, 6, 11, *PL* 42, 943–44; *Enarratio in Psalmos* 68, 1, 5, *PL* 36, 845.

347. *Quod Non Sint Tres Dii*, *PG* 45, 132.

348. *De Trin.* VII, 6, 11, *PL* 42, 944–45; *Enarratio in Psalmos* 68, 1, 5, *PL* 36, 844–45.

349. *Epistola* 52, *PG* 32, 393. This argument reveals the weakness of Basil's own theory of unity of species. In order to avoid a quaternity, one would have to deny that Godhood (the *ousia* of the three Persons) had real existence.

350. *Dialogus de Sancta Trinitate*, *PG* 40, 852; this is an anti-Jewish polemic.

351. "Apology," p. 205.

352. Bacha, op. cit., p. 37; Graf, *Die Arabischen Schriften*, p. 148; *Opuscula, PG* 97, 1480.

353. Graf, *Die Schriften*, pp. 24–25 (text), 28 (trans.).

354. Vajda, "Le Problème," p. 70. One could say, though, that just as Abū Rā'iṭa saw these two images as parallel and representing unity of substratum, al-Muqammiẓ also believed they were interchangeable and represented unity of species. It is also possible that al-Muqammiẓ knew the work of Jerome of Jerusalem (or someone else who mentioned the three aspects of the coins). He did not, however, draw the same inference from the three aspects of the coins as did Jerome.

355. Notice the importance to al-Muqammiẓ of stressing the characteristics of the coins, instead of merely pointing out three indistinguishable pieces of gold.

356. Vajda, "Le Problème," pp. 62–64. See above for a complete discussion of al-Muqammiẓ's refutation.

357. Vajda, ibid., p. 70, makes the point that even if al-Muqammiẓ had quoted the image as he found it in his source, he would not have been convinced by it.

358. *Epistola* 38, 5, *PG* 32, 333–36.

359. Vajda, "Le Problème," p. 63.

360. Colorhood is actually the genus, and white, black, and green are the individual species. Al-Muqammiẓ was apparently none too rigorous with his analogies, since he was more interested in offering refutations than in presenting Christian thought systematically.

361. Vajda, "Le Problème," p. 64.

362. For Muslim refutations of images of the Trinity, cf. Fritsch, op. cit., pp. 110–11.

363. *Milḥamot Ha-Shem*, p. 8.

364. *Even Boḥan* II:1, fol. 60a.

365. *Magen Va-Ḥerev*, p. 24.

366. *Kur Maẓref*, pp. 1a–b.

367. Fols. 6b–7a.

368. *Ta'anot*, p. xi.

369. *De Aeternitate Mundi* 17, 88; trans. F. H. Colson, *Philo*, IX, Loeb Classical Library (Cambridge, Mass., 1961), p. 245.

370. *Shalhevet ha-qeshurah be-gaḥelet*, I:7.

371. *Dialogue with Trypho* 61, 128, *PG* 6, 613–16, 773–76.

372. *Oratio adversus Graecos* 5, *PG* 6, 817.

373. Dialogue II "Inconfusus," *Later Treatises of St. Athanasius . . . and an Appendix on S. Cyril of Alexandria and Theodoret*, trans. William Bright (Oxford, 1881), p. 204. Cf. *Epistola* 145, *PG* 83, 1383 (example of red-hot gold).

374. *Apologia de Verbe Incarnata, PL* 177, 305.

375. *Apology*, p. 215.

376. Peter of Blois referred to the raising of the thumb, index, and middle fingers and the subsequent making of the sign of the cross as a signification of the Trinity's

excellence. Perhaps Jacob ben Reuben had this image in mind when he mentioned the hand. See *Contra Perfidium Judaeorum, PL* 207, 833.

377. *Milḥamot Ha-Shem,* p. 10:

בעוד שאתה מביא ראיה מאחד הנבראים האחדים שהוא אחד ואינו יוצא מכלל שלשה, הבא ראיה מאחד מהנבראים האחרים שהוא אחד ואינו יוצא מכלל חמשה או מכלל עשרה, או יותר. כגון אדם שהוא אחד, וכשיעלה על דעתך לזכור אדם, מיד הבינו רעיוניך מאותו שם המיוחד שהזכרת שנכללו בו כל אבריו שהם רמ״ח, שאין שם אדם מתקיים כי אם בפה ועינים ואזנים וגויה וכל האיברים כאשר הם. וכל האיברים שהם רמ״ח אינם יוצאים מכלל איחוד שם האדם, ושם האדם שהוא אחד אינו יוצא מכלל רמ״ח איברים, או כעין היד לבדה שאינה יוצאת מכלל חמש אצבעות, וחמש אצבעות אינן יוצאות מכלל היד שהיא מיוחדת, על כן בהביאך ראיות לאלהותך מאחד מן הנבראים שהוא אחד ואינו יוצא מכלל שלשה, יתברר לך האלהות מהאדם שהוא אחד ואינו יוצא מכלל רמ״ח איברים, ויהיו אלהיך כמספר איבריך, ואם לא תוכל לעבוד את כולם, הבא ראיה מהיד ויהיו חמשה, או מאחרים כי רבים כמו אלה.

This was based on the common argument as to why there were not more than three Persons.

A similar retort is found in Benjamin ben Moses' *Teshuvot Ha-Noẓrim* 21, p. 10. Objecting that Christians used the Scriptures to prove that God had three Persons, he argued that they should ascribe Him with thirteen Persons (the thirteen attributes of Exod. 34:6–7). Further, Benjamin stated that if creator, word, and spirit were hypostasized to Persons, so should God's other features, e.g., hearing and seeing. Also, if God had become incarnate as Jesus, He should have had the ten aspects of a human being, e.g., flesh, blood, bones, etc. And finally, in an apparent reference to images of the Trinity, he stated: There are a number of things in the world with three aspects, e.g., citron, watermelon, peaches, and many other fruits, whose three aspects are skin, middle, and seed; these, however, are shameful and disgraceful things. Therefore, there is no reality to their words, for the Creator has many innumerable good qualities.

378. *Milḥamot Ha-Shem,* p. 10:

ועוד שאני מוצא להב שאינו על הגחל, וגחל שאין בו להב, כגון להב מחבת, וכגון גחל מרחשת. על כן דברתי אליך, שלא יתכן לאדם חכם כמוך לדבר כדברים האלה.

379. *Even Boḥan* II:1, fol. 60b.

אם כדברך כמו שהגחלת מורכבת משלשה ענינים גם אלקיך הוא מורכב מהשלוש וכל מורכב הרכבתו היא סבתו ומה שיש למציאם סבה הוא אפשר המציאות א״כ הנותן לו מציאות הוא האלוה לא הוא.

380. *'Ezer Ha-Dat* in *'Ezer Ha-'Emunah,* p. 170:

ואותו משל מביא אטאנאשיאו הנז׳ בתחלת חבורו, וזה לשונו; כדי לאמת שהאל הוא שלשה תמונות ועצם אחד אביא לך ראיה מגושם אחד. אנו רואים שהשמש יש לו נצוץ ואורה וחמימות ואלו הג׳ עניני׳ אפי׳ שהאחד אינו האחר מ״מ לא נחלקו מהיות עצם אחת מהשמש. וכן באלוה, אפי׳ שתמונת האב אינה אותה של הבן ואינה אותה של רוח, אפי׳ הכי אינם נחלקי׳ מהיות עצם אחת.

381. *Ta'anot,* p. xi. Moses ben Solomon argued that the analogy was specious because the sun was material and not truly one.

382. *Magen Va-Ḥerev,* p. 24. He offered no refutation of the image.

383. *Vikuaḥ,* fol. 2b.

384. Fol. 2a, in the commentary.

385. *De Aeternitate Mundi* 17, 88; 18, 92.

386. 4, 395a, 29–31, cited by Wolfson, *Church Fathers*, p. 300, n. 81.

387. *Dialogue with Trypho* 128, *PG* 6, 776; Justin cited the image of the setting sun, apparently taking it from Philo, *De Aeternitate Mundi* 17, 88.

388. Epiphanius, *Adversus Haereses Panarium* LXII, 1, *PG* 41, 1052; Sabellius believed that the Persons were not separate, distinct subsistences; cf. Wolfson, *Church Fathers*, pp. 583–84, 594–98.

389. *Contra Haeresin Noeti* 11, *PG* 10, 817.

390. *Adversus Praxeam* 8, *PL* 2, 163–64.

391. *Divinae Institutiones* IV, 29, *PL* 6, 539.

392. *Orationes contra Arianos* II:33, *PG* 26, 217; trans. Pelikan, *The Light of the World* (New York, 1962), p. 68. Pelikan shows the importance of light imagery in Athanasius' thought. On the development of the sun-and-radiance metaphor, see G. L. Prestige, *God in Patristic Thought* (London, 1959), p. 298. Cf. also Athanasius' *De Decretis* 23, *PG* 25, 456–57.

Though the exact form of the image as mentioned by Moses Ha-Kohen was apparently not originally Athanasian, still this Church Father did employ similar imagery. It is possible, however, that Moses Ha-Kohen may actually have been referring to the doctrine of the Athanasian (Quicumque) Creed, which was well illustrated by the image of the sun, rather than to Athanasius himself.

393. *De Fide Orth.* I:8, *PG* 94, 821; trans. Wolfson, *Church Fathers*, p. 301; cf. ibid., p. 360.

394. Périer, "Un Traité," pp. 8, 17–18.

395. "Apology," pp. 158–59.

396. Margaret D. Gibson, ed., *Studia Sinaitica* 7 (1899): 76(Arabic), 4(English). The title of this work has been postulated by Gibson.

397. *Dialogus de Sancte Trinitate*, *PG* 40, 852.

398. *Theologia* 4, *PL* 178, 1287; *Introductio ad Theologiam* 2, 13, *PL* 178, 1071.

399. *Sermo* 1, *PL* 141, 317.

400. *Elucidarium*, *PL* 172, 1110–11.

401. *Disputatio Ecclesiae et Synagogae*, in E. Martène and U. Durand, *Thesauras Novus Anecdotum* (Paris, 5, 1717), p. 1505.

402. *Contra Haereticos*, *PL* 210, 407.

403. *Contra Perfidium Judaeorum*, *PL* 207, 834.

404. *Die Sentenzen Rolands nachmals Papstes Alexander III*, ed. Ambrosius M. Gietl (Freiburg, 1891), p. 26. For a modern use of the image of the sun and its light as analogous to the Trinity, cf. Thomas Newberry, *Solar Light as Illustrating Trinity in Unity* (Glasgow, 18??). Cf. also Williams, op. cit., p. 110.

405. *'Ezer Ha-Dat*, p. 169.

406. Ibid., pp. 170–71:

ועתה ראה אתה המעיין, שזה המשל שהביא לסיוע אמונתם הוא כנגדם, כי כבר ביארנו, שהאחד שנקרא בו השמש אינו אחד אמתי, וזה נראה לכל בעל שכל, לפי שכל הדברי׳ המורכבי׳ מעניני׳ שוני׳ אינם אחת באמת. ומאחר שאור השמש אינו החמימות שלו, כשנתקבצו יחד אינם אחד באמת. וחסרון גדול היה בחוק סבה ראשונה ית׳ אם יחודו היה ביחוד כזה ואנחנו היינו עושי׳ רעה גדולה אלו היינו מאמיני׳ אמונה כזאת, שהדבר

שקורין אותו האנשי׳ אחד שיהיה מחובר מדברי׳ שוני׳ ומחולקי׳ שזהו חסרון גדול, לפי שאין יכול להיות מצאותו ולא אחר שנתקבצו אותם הדברי׳ שמהם נמצא.

407. Ibid., p. 171:

ואנחנו רואי׳ ויודעי׳ כפי מה שזכרנו, שמציאות השי״ת היא מחוייבת ואינה צריכה לדברי׳ אחרים להיותה נמצא בהם, כי היה הוא צריך לנמצאיו, ואינו כן, כי כל הנמצאי׳ הם צריכי׳ אליו והיו בחכמתו הגדולה קודם שנעשו, אבל הוא אינו צריך להם. ומי הוא שהיה מחבר באלוה העניני׳ הנחלקי׳ והמתחלפי׳. בהכרח הוא שצריכים לזולתם שיקבצם, שמ(י)ן השוא שיקבצו הם לעצמם קודם שהיו. א״כ המחבר הראשון לכל העניני׳ וקבצם לא קבצהו אחר, שאם ה״כ שיהיה אחר שיקבצנו, ואותו אחר אחר, וזה לא ילך לאין תכלית, בהכרה הוא שיעמוד למקבץ ראשון, שלא היה צריך לזולתו ולא היה דומה לאחרי׳, אלא עצם פשוט, והוא הש״י.

408. Ibid.:

ואם תעיין הטב תוכל לשאול להם על משל של השמש, שהביאו בו ראיה, אם אותו נצוץ הוא עצם אור השמש, וא״כ הוא אין בו שלשה כחות, ואם זאת האורה הוא מחמימות השמש או החמימות מהאורה, ואם אלו הג׳ נחלקי׳ זה מזה, ואם הם במקרה בחומר השמש או אם הם עצמם, או אם הם חומר השמש, או אם הם צורך לשמש, או אם הם מקרי׳ באי׳ מצורת השמש. ומי יתנני שם בשעה שהיו אלו השאלות נשאלי׳ להם לראות מה ישיב עליהם.

409. *Vikuaḥ*, p. 320:

ואדוננו המלך אמר בכאן משל שלמדוהו הטועים. אמר: כי ביין ג׳ דברים, גוון וטעם וריח, והוא דבר אחד.

Rankin, p. 209.

410. Ibid.:

וזה טעות גמורה, כי האודם והטעם והריח ביין דברים חלוקים ימצא זה בלא זה, כי יש אודם ולבן וגוונים אחרים, כן בטעם והריח. ועוד כי האודם אינו היין ולא הטעם ולא הריח, אבל עצם היין הוא הדבר הממלא את הכלי. והנה הוא גוף נושא שלשה מקרים חלוקים שאין בו שום אחדות. ואם נמנה כן בטעות, על כרחנו נאמר רבוע.

Trans. adapted from Rankin, p. 209. Could this be a covert argument against transubstantiation? The Christians said the accidents remained while the substance of wine changed into the blood of Jesus. Naḥmanides might have been referring to this when he said that it was the substance of the wine that filled the vessel.

411. *Magen Avot* I:5, in *Keshet U-Magen*, pp. 26b–27a.

412. *Pilpul*, ed. George Belasco (London, 1908), p. 22:

ולא כא׳ מורכב אשר יחלק לאחדים רבים כגון הנר שיש בו אור ושעוה ופתילה.

413. *Contra Haereticos* III, *PL* 210, 406. According to Alan, both God and the Father are *lux*, the Son is *splendor*, and the Holy Spirit is *flamma*.

414. N. M. Gelber, "Die Taufbewegung unter den polnischen Juden in XVIII Jahrhundert," *MGWJ* 68 (1924): 233: "Deus caret distinctione propter excepit perfectionis, sin secus non esset perfectus."

415. Cf., e.g., *De Trin.* XV, 21, 40–22, 43, *PL* 42, 1088–91.

416. *Ta'anot*, p. xi.

417. *Magen Va-Ḥerev*, p. 25; see above.

418. *Vikuaḥ*, fol. 2b:

גם הראיה השנית שהבאת ממה שמנחת דעות ואמונות שא״א לשכל לצייר מציאותם אינה סודרת לזה שהרי אתם משתדלים בכל תוקף לקרב דעות ואמונות אלו אל השכל באמרכם שהשלוש הוא כמו ניצוצי השמש או כמו ענפי אילן שהכל בא ממקור א׳ ומעצמות א׳.

419. *Adversus Praxeam* 4, *PL* 2, 163–64.

420. *Dialogus, PG* 40, 852.

421. P. 76 (Arabic), p. 4 (trans.).

422. *'Ezer Ha-'Emunah,* p. 123. Joseph ben Shem Tov also made use of this image, but for quite a different purpose. In attempting to explain that man had but one soul despite its different aspects (vegetative, animal, and rational), he gave the example of an apple with its taste, fragrance, and color. See Joseph ben Shem Tov, *Commentary on Aristotle's Ethics,* Paris, Bibliothèque National ms. 996, fol. 51a.

423. *Apology,* p. 162.

424. *Ḥerev Pifiyot,* p. 52. Cf. Jacob Z. Lauterbach, "Substitutes for the Tetragrammaton," *PAAJR* 2 (1930–31): 39–67. For the three yods, see pp. 52–55, nos. 31–61.

425. *Teshuvot La-Meḥaref,* fol. 21a; cf. Baer, "Torat Ha-Qabbalah," p. 287. For the sake of completeness, the following Trinity images apparently not cited in Jewish polemical literature should be mentioned: (1) three lamps lighting a dark room (Abū Qurra); (2) three men singing one song (idem); (3) mirrors reflecting each other (Yaḥya ben 'Adī); (4) water in spring, river, and lake (Anselm, Roland, Nicholas of Cusa, and many others); (5) a seal (Abelard, Roland); (6) one cloth folded three times (Peter of Blois); (7) a cithara (Roland); (8) a triangular stone (idem); (9) a finger (Jerome of Jerusalem); (10) an eye (idem., *Triune*); (11) a hand (idem); (12) the burning bush (idem); (13) a furnace (idem); (14) three pearls (Timothy); (15) three stars (idem); (16) one person, three characteristics (Yaḥya ben 'Adī, *Triune*). This list, of course, is not complete. It does, however, give some idea of the variety of images adduced to represent the Trinity.

Chapter Five

1. E.g., Joseph Kaspi and Judah Aryeh de Modena; cf. above. Joshua Lorki, who later became a Christian, admitted in his anti-Christian polemical letter to Paul of Burgos (Solomon Ha-Levi) that a Trinity was possible, "though the members of the covenant of Abraham do not believe in it." Cf. *Nusaḥ Ha-Ketav,* p. 15. This statement is, of course, suspect, since Lorki may well have been on his way to convert.

2. De Modena pointed out that it often happened that when one adopted an impossible doctrine, he was forced to accept more impossible doctrines in order to justify the first one.

3. Cf., e.g., the refutations of the Trinity based on a theory of attributes. The objection was not to the positing of distinctions in God, but rather to the Christian assumption that the distinctions were real. One determinant of real distinctions was the doctrine of incarnation.

4. Jewish exegetical arguments did not fail to point out this fact. Cf. Profiat Duran, *Kelimat Ha-Goyim* I, *Ha-Ẓofeh,* 3, pp. 104–13.

5. The doctrine of incarnation was adopted when the Christians began to iden-

tify the *Logos* not only with Jesus, but also with God. Cf. Wolfson, *Church Fathers,* pp. 364–493.

6. Cf. ibid., pp. 587–94.

7. *Denz.,* 54.

8. Pelikan, *The Emergence,* pp. 226–28.

9. *Denz.,* 148. Dissenters to this decree were the Nestorians and the Monophysites (Jacobites). Whereas orthodoxy taught one person of Christ with two natures (human and divine), Nestorians held two natures and two persons (God and man), and Monophysites believed in one person and one nature (divine).

10. Apollinarius taught that Jesus had a human body but no rational soul; cf. Wolfson, *Church Fathers,* pp. 433–44.

11. On the significance of these terms, see ibid., pp. 372–418.

12. The literature on Chalcedon is extensive. Cf., e.g., Aloys Grillmeier and Heinrich Bacht, eds., *Das Konzil von Chalcedon,* 3 vols. (Würzburg, 1951–54); Robert V. Sellers, *The Council of Chalcedon* (London, 1953).

13. Medieval Jews did not deny Jesus' historicity. Most believed him to have been a magician or sorcerer. Cf. R. Travers Herford, op. cit.; Samuel Krauss, *Das Leben Jesu.*

14. *PL* 158, 359–432; Eng. *Why God Became Man . . . ,* trans. Joseph M. Colleran (Albany, N.Y., 1969), pp. 59–163. This work presented one of the most important theoretical conceptualizations of mankind's need for incarnation.

15. *Biṭṭul,* fol. 11b.

16. The Christians debated the question whether God would have become incarnate without original sin. Cf. *ST* III, 1, 3.

17. This is the explanation of incarnation given by Anselm and generally followed by later thinkers; cf. *Cur Deus Homo.* The proof-texts quoted from the New Testament were Rom. 3:24, Heb. 9:12, etc. On the necessity of Jesus' death for salvation, cf. Thomas, *ST* III, 46, 1–3. Arguments of this type were offered in the following anti-Jewish polemical works: Odo, Bishop of Cambrai (d. 1135), *Disputatio Contra Judaeum Leonem Nomin de Adventu Christi Filii Dei, PL* 160, 1103–12; William of Champeaux (attributed), *Dialogus inter Christianum et Judaeum, PL* 163, 1050–54; cf. also Gregory of Tours (ca. 538–93), *Historiae Francorum Libri Decem* 6:5, *PL* 71, 373–75.

18. For Jewish arguments of this kind, see Joseph Kimḥi, *Sefer Ha-Berit,* pp. 28–29; Levi ben Abraham, *Livyat Ḥen,* pp. 4–5; Ḥasdai Crescas, *Biṭṭul,* fols. 5b–6b; Joseph ben Shem Tov, *Commentary on the Iggeret,* pp. 64–66, *Commentary on Biṭṭul,* fol. 13a; Abraham Farissol, *Magen Avraham,* chap. 15, fols. 18b–21a; Judah Aryeh de Modena, *Magen Va-Ḥerev,* pp. 37–38. Cf. also above, chap. 3.

19. Certain kabbalists taught a doctrine of original sin in that Adam's transgression gave evil an active existence in the world. The entire creation became flawed by this first sin. Unlike the Christians, however, the kabbalists taught that every man had the power to overcome the state of corruption by his own efforts with divine aid. There was no implication here, as there was in Christianity, that salvation could be

achieved only by the sacrifice of a God-man; cf. Scholem, *Kabbalah*, p. 154.

20. These and similar arguments are found in *Sefer Ha-Berit* (Additions), pp. 60–62; *Biṭṭul*, fols. 3b–5a; *Commentary on the Iggeret*, p. 66; *Magen Avraham*, chap. 14; and *Magen Va-Ḥerev*, pp. 7–20.

21. Augustine, *Sermo XIII de Tempore*, *PL* 39, 1997: "Factus est Deus homo ut homo fierit Deus."

22. This was a rather common argument. For two representative discussions of it, see Anselm, *Cur Deus Homo*, and Thomas, *ST* III, 1.

23. The Christian doctrine of original sin had its source in the New Testament; cf. Rom. 5:12, and F. R. Tennant, *The Sources of the Doctrine of the Fall and Original Sin* (New York, 1968). Its chief theoretician among the Church Fathers was Augustine, who, in the Pelagian controversy, established original sin as the orthodox belief; cf. Nicholas Merlin, *Saint Augustin et les Dogmes du Péché Original et de la Grâce* (Paris, 1931); Norman P. Williams, *The Ideas of the Fall and of Original Sin* (London, 1927). Anselm presented a justification of original sin in *De Conceptu Virginali et de Peccato Originali*, *PL* 158, 431–64. Thomas' exposition of the subject is in *ST* I–II, 81–83. For other Christian literature on original sin, cf. J. Migne, *Indices*, s. Peccatum Originale, *PL* 220, 803–8. Cf. also Henri Rondet, *Original Sin* (Shannon, 1972), and Ch. Baumgartner, *Le Péché Originel* (Paris, 1969).

24. Even though Christians taught that it was not unbefitting God to assume human flesh, they did agree that it was not proper to say that God Himself suffered. Jesus' humanity alone died on the cross. Cf. *ST* III, 46, 12.

25. The most common exegetical arguments were based on Gen. 3, the story of Adam and Eve. The Jews maintained that nothing in that account implied a doctrine of original sin. Jews further pointed to Deut. 24:16: "The fathers shall not be put to death for the children, nor shall the children be put to death for the fathers; every man shall be put to death for his own sin," as proof against original sin. Mention was already made of Jewish arguments against Jesus' divinity drawn from the New Testament. The most frequent historical argument against the Christian doctrine of redemption was to the effect that the visible signs of Adam and Eve's punishment, e.g., pain in childbirth and the need to toil to eat one's bread, have not disappeared. As Naḥmanides said (*Vikuaḥ* p. 310), "He who wishes to lie, let him call upon witnesses who are far away." "Common-sense" arguments were the ones cited above. For a discussion of various theological schemes, see *Types of Redemption*, ed. R. J. Zwi Werblowsky and C. Jouco Bleeker (Leiden, 1970).

26. Treatise Ten in *Perush*, pp. 82–83:
הבן שאתם אומרים הודיעונו עליו הלא כבר היה נולד לעולמים אשר היו לפנינו וכן יהיה נולד לעולמים אשר יהיה אחרינו עד אשר תאמרו עליו כי אין ללדתו ראשית ואין ללדתו אחרית והם אומרים בודאי על השאלה הזאת הן וכשהן משיבים אותנו כך אנו אומרים להן היש לו תחלה או סוף והם אומרים אין לו תחלה ולא סוף כי כן הם ראוים לומר. ואנו אומרים להם אם כן למה לא אמרתם עליו שהוא מתהלך וסובב ומחלף מקומותיו ותאמרו שכבר היה מתהלך ולעד יהיה מתהלך ואין להלוכו סוף ולא תחלה ולא ראשית ולא אחרית כמו שאתם אומרים עליו שהיה נולד והוא נולד ויהיה נולד ואין ללידתו ראשית ולא אחרית ולא תחלה ולא תכלית ואם הם משיבין אותם ואומרים לא נכון לנו לשום לו הילוך וחילוף מקומות מפני שההילוך והחילוף עקום מסימני בעלי הגוף והגולם.

27. On the identification of the holders of this theory, see Altmann, *Book of Doctrines,* p. 66, n. 3.

28. *Amānāt* I:3, p. 46; trans. p. 56:
تغير معنى الازلي الذى لا صورة له ولا حال ولا مقدار ولا حد ولا مكان ولا زمان حتى صار بعضه جسما له صورة ومقدار واحوال ومكان وزمان وسائر ما انطوت عليه الموجودات وما اخطار هذا بالبال الا فى بعد البعد .

29. Ibid., pp. 46–48; trans. pp. 56–58. Saadia stated that these arguments were directed against the holders of the first and third doctrines of incarnation, which Wolfson has identified with the Jacobites and the Nestorians. It appears that Saadia realized that, according to the orthodox, Malkite doctrine, God was not the flesh itself, which was material and suffered. It is doubtful, though, that this was the Jacobite or the Nestorian theory either. In any case, if Saadia refrained from directing these arguments against orthodoxy because of his understanding of it, he apparently showed a much more sophisticated knowledge of Christianity than other Jewish polemicists evidenced. Cf. *Amānāt,* pp. 90–91; trans. pp. 109–10; Wolfson, "Saadia on the Trinity," pp. 561–68.

30. *Sefer Ha-Berit,* p. 29; trans. pp. 36–37:
ואני תמה ואיני יכול להאמין דבר זה, כי [הוא] אל גדול ונורא אשר עין לא ראתה; ואין לו דמות ואין לו צורה... ואיך אאמין באל הגדול, נעלם ונכסה, שנכנס בבטן אישה.

31. *Vikuaḥ Radaq,* printed in *Sefer Ha-Berit,* p. 96: הבורא יתברך אינו גוף ולא כוח בגוף.

32. *Guide* II:2.

33. *Ta'anot,* pp. iv–v:
כתב רבינו משה ז״ל בפ׳ שני בחלק שני ממאמרו היקר כי אריסטוטיל הוכיח מכח מופתים מבוארים מציאות הסבה הא׳ ועוד הוכיח שהסבה הראשונה שהוא השי״ת איננה גוף ולא כח בגוף ר״ל לא כח מתפשט בגוף...וזה שאם ה׳ בא וקבל בשר הרי שב מכח נבדל להיות בגוף והוא שנוי גדו׳ מאד ובשי״ת אין שנוי חלילה.

34. *'Ezer Ha-'Emunah,* p. 27: והרי הבורא כלו רוחני וטהור, ולא נוכל לשום בו מקרה ולא שום דבר גופני ולא שום שנוי.

35. Ibid., pp. 42–43.

36. *Magen Avot* I:3 in *Keshet U-Magen,* pp. 26a–b; *Keshet U-Magen,* p. 20a.

37. *Yeshu'ot Meshiḥo,* p. 15b.

38. *Magen Va-Ḥerev,* p. 36.

39. *Kur Maẓref,* p. 1b.

40. Maimonides, *Guide* III:15.

41. *Nusaḥ Ha-Ketav,* p. 15:
אבל מה תאמר נפשך על אמרם שהוא הוא המשיח בשר ודם יאכל וישתה ימות ויחיה והוא הוא עצמו האלה האמיתי אשר הוא סבת הסבות ועלת העלות אשר משפע כחו יתנועעו הגלגלים ומאצילות מציאתו ימצאו השכלים הנבדלים אשר אינם גוף ולא כח בגוף ודי מדורהון עם בשרא לא איתוהי. איך ימשך ויותמד מציאותם מאשר הוא גשם וחומר בפועל מתמיד והרי הוא אחד מהענינים אשר החכמים מקיימים בו [בטבע] הנמנע קיים ואומרים שהוא כמו הגשמת האל לעצמו או היציאו נמצא שוה לו. והאמת כי זה הוא ענין לא יכילהו השכל ולא יעלה על לב לשומו מסופק ולהיות נבוך בו בשום צד ולא להשאיר יכולת לאל עליו.

42. Cf. Aristotle, *Physics,* 8, 10; Maimonides, *Guide* II:1 (1).

43. *Biṭṭul*, fol. 13a:

ומי יתן ידעתי מי הוא זה אשר יניע השמים בזאת ההנעה הגדולה אשר אתה רואה אחרי שהאלהים שמניע אינו נבדל אבל כח גופני והוא שם קיים קיום גשמי על השמים לפי דעתם.

44. 3, 4–8.

45. 12, 7, 1072b, 14–1073a, 12; 9, 1074b, 15–1075a, 11.

46. *Biṭṭul*, fol. 14a:

וכבר התבאר אמתת זה הצייור בג׳ מספר הנפש וביארו ארסוט״ו במאמ׳ הי״א ממה שאחר הטבע שהאל ית׳ משיג להיותו נבדל, ושהו׳ חי להיות משיג, ולפי הפך הסותר יתחייב כי מי שהוא כח גופני לא יצייר צייור שכלי ולזה אינו חי החיים המיוחדי׳ לאלקות, ובזה הדבקות היה מת כי היה שם דבק במדרגת אחד מכוחות היסודות אשר הם כחות גשמיות.

47. Thomas, *ST* III, 1, 1.

48. Ibid., 5, 1.

49. P. 13:

ותמה אני ממך איך לא תתבייש... והשם יתברך שמו גדול ועצום שמי השמים לא יכלכלוהו ואתה אומר כי האלהים נקטן שנשא אותו מרים ט׳ חדשים בבטנה... ואיך נשאתו מרים או אמונתו על ידיה או חמור על גביו.

50. Krauss, "Fragment Polémique," pp. 72, 74.

51. *Milḥamot Ha-Shem*, p. 13:

ואתה כמו כן תודה ותאמין לכל דברי, אם יש מוח בקדקדך. ועתה השב רעיוניך במסכת שכלך, והעמק מדעך במעמקי הדעת, אולי תהי מחשבתך נוגע להשכיל את דבריך, באמרך שהבורא יתברך כאשר הוא, מכל צד שהמחשבה והלב יכולים להרהר עליו, כולו נסגר במחשכי הרחם, ונכלא באפלת הבטן, ויהי כעוללים לא ראו אור. והדבר הזה גנאי הוא לאמרו, ועון פלילי לשמעו, ואנכי חלילה לי מחטא לי״י בלשוני, מהעלות הדבר הזה על דל שפתי, ולדבר דברים כאלה כלפי מעלה לענין הבורא יתברך ויתעלה זכרו לעד ולנצח.

52. Ibid., p. 15:

אין בדבריך כלום, אך שאתה ברוע לבבך תבקש להבזות האלהות, ואינו כן. כי אתה תנבל את פיך, ואני והאלהות נקיים, כי בענין הבורא יתברך אין שום ניבול ודופי יכול להדבק בו, ואין הלשון יכולה לקרוא עליו שום הסגר, כי הוא לא נסגר ולא בא במסתרי חושך.

53. Ibid.:

ויש לי ראייה אמיתית על דבר זה שאין להשיב עליה, שהרי הילת השמש תעבור על האשפה ותעמוד על הצואה, ולא תדבק בה שום טנופת ודופי. וגם ההילה הזאת תוכל להכנס בעד נקב קטן, ואחרי אשר תכנס בה, לא תוכל להסגירה שם, שאם תסגור הנקב, לא תמצאנה שם, גם לא תאסוף אותה בחפניך להביאה הביתה, ובראותך זה באחד מקטני עבדיו, תוכל להבין נפלאות הבורא כמה וכמה הן.

54. *Oratio de Incarnatio Verbi* 17, *PG* 25, 125. Cf. Pelikan, *Light of World*, p. 70.

55. *Tractatus V Contra Judaeos, PL* 57, 797. Cf. also Peter of Cluny, *Tractatus*, *PL* 189, 532; Williams, op. cit., p. 121.

56. *Milḥamot Ha-Shem*, p. 17:

ואיך לא תתבונן במוצא שפתיך שכל דבר שיש יכולת ביד למשמש בו, ראוי הוא להדבק בו כל דיבוק נקי ושאינו נקי? ועל כל אלה הבאתי דבריך בכור מצרף האמת, והנה כולם סיגים וכסף אין! על כן יעצתיך לאמר, הסר ממך עקשות פה ולזות שפתים הרחק ממך.

57. *Kur Maẓref*, p. 3b: ואע״פי שהרבית לפשוע שוב עד ה׳ כי רחום וחנון הוא וירחמך.

58. *Ta'anot*, pp. xvii–xviii, xx.

59. This term, meaning "a specified person," was a term of derision for Jesus. Moses ben Solomon avoided explicit reference to Jesus throughout his work. On "Ploni," cf. Jastrow, op. cit., p. 1178.

60. *Ta'anot,* pp. vii–viii:
ידוע שיש לנפש האדם כלי מיוחד מאברי האדם שהוא מושבה וכסא שלה והוא הלב על דעת רבים וי״א שהראש מושבה וכסאה ואע״פ שכח שרשה בלב: ואם האלהות קבלה בשר צריך כמובן שיהא לה אבר מיוחד וכסא. אשאלך איזה אבר מהגוף ר״ל מגוף פלוני היה מושב האל.

61. Ibid.

62. *Magen Avraham* 18, fol. 23a: את אלה לא בינותי מעולם ולא יבינהו איש בהיות נמנע אפשרותו בשכל ואף חרץ לשכל.

63. Ibid. 13, fol. 16b:
איך יעשו ממנו י״ת וי״ת שמו חומר וצורה ויגשימוהו לאמר כי חומר הבשר מהמשיח שלהם וששת רחבי צדדיו הוא האלוק ויתנו לו גבול אשר זה הפך עקר הכל.

64. Ibid. 18, fol. 23a:
ולא ימנע מחלוקה זו אם שגשם בשר המשיח היה האל ממש מצד שהאל נתגשם בעצמותו ולבש צורת בשר, או שהגוף מהמשיח היה האל בשתוף מה כי שכן אתו כבוד ה׳ חופף עליו כל היום והיה אלקותו לבד ובשרו לבד, ואם נאמר שהאל נתגשם ממש, ושב עצם האלקות בשר וזה נמנע לכל להאמין ואף להם לפי שההגשמה נמנעת בעצמות האלוקות שיהיה משנה (צ״ל משתנה) העצם למקרה, והבלתי נברא מעצמו להיות נברא, והבב״ת להיות ב״ת ושש רחבים והכל להיות חלק.

65. This analogy is derived from the Athanasian (Quicumque) Creed. See below for a fuller discussion of the types of union considered for incarnation.

66. *Guide* III:15.

67. *Magen Avraham* 18, fol. 23a:
אמנם נמנעת וכוזבת היא ההקדמה שישתתף האלקות אם הבשר בשתוף הנפש עם הגוף האדם שכל וחמר יחדיו לפי שהנפש הנבראת בעלת גבול הנקשרת עם כל חלקי הבשר, זה דרכה כסל לה בחייוב שתוף טבעי בהמצאת האדם כי כן הוא בשר ונשמה יחדיו עם כל כחותיהם מה שלא יחייבו השכל באלוק עם הבשר שישתתפו יחדיו בשתוף טבעי ולא מקרי ולא רצוני כי לנמנע טבע קיים שלא יצדק לעולם לומר שהבשר יהיה אלוק לפי שנוכל לומר במיתת הבשר מהמשיח כאשר מת שהאלוק מת אם הבשר הוא אלוק והבן זה.

68. *Disputatio Judei et Christiani,* p. 43: "Si deus est immensus, quomodo uili et parua humanorum dimensione membrorum potuit dimensus circumscribi?"

69. Pflaum, op. cit., pp. 461–62, ll. 41–78; cf. p. 450.

70. *ST* III, 1, 1, 31, 4. De Modena (*Magen Va-Ḥerev,* p. 38) quoted this objection from 1, 1.

71. *Contra Faustum* 23, 10, *PL* 42, 472.

72. *ST* III, 3, 7. Anselm disagreed with this statement; see below.

73. P. 3:
ואם תאמר אלהים לא יאכל ולא ישתה יפסדו דבריך הראשונים אשר אמרת לא נחסר מנהוגו כלום. ואם תאמר הוסיף האלהים בו כח שלא יאכל ולא ישתה הנה תשימנו חסר כי חסר היה מקודם עד שהוסיף בו השם כח לסבול.

74. *Kitāb al-Muḥtawī,* fol. 56:
ומא קאלתה אלנצארי מן אלאתחאד באטל במא תקדם מן אנה ת״ע ליס בגֿסם פתצח עליה אלמגֿאירה וליס בערץֿ פיצח עליה אלחלול ולו צח עליה אלחלול לוגֿב אן יכון מחדתא לאן אלחלול תאבע ללחדות וקד בינא פי אול הדֿה אלכתאב מא ידל עלי צחה דֿלך ממא חדדנא בה אלחלול ובינא חקיקתה והוא וגֿודה תאבע למחלה חתי וגֿב עדמה בעדמה ויציר פי חכם אלמנתקל פי אלגֿהאת בחסב אנתקאלה ודֿלך יקתצֿי אן וגֿוד אלמחל יצחה וגֿוד מא יחל פיה ודֿלך לא יצח פי אלקדים ת״ע מע וגֿודה לם מסתגֿניא ען סאיר אלדואת.
Cf. Vajda, "La Démonstration," pp. 305–6.

75. Cf. Baḥya, *al-Hidāya,* I:7:4, pp. 54–55; Joseph Ibn Ẓaddiq, *Sefer Ha-'Olam Ha-Qaṭan,* p. 55 (57); Al-Muqammiẓ, *Perush Sefer Yeẓirah,* p. 74.

76. *Milḥamot Ha-Shem,* pp. 8–9:

וכל הפילוסופים וחכמי השכל מלעיגים עליך, ושואלים על הדבר הזה: אם הבורא יתברך נברא, הודיעני אם נברא קודם היותו או לאחר היותו? ואם קודם היותו סתרת את דבריך, שאמרת שהוא תחילת כל תחילות וראשון בלי ראשית? ואם תאמר לאחר היותו נצטייר בצורת בשר לזמן רצונו, אם כן באותו זמן היה חסר מהבשר והעצמות והגידים שקבל לזמן שאמרת וזה אינו נכון. ועוד שהיה הפרש בין אותו זמן ראשון שעמד בלי צורת בשר, ובין אותו זמן אחרון שקיבל תבנית וצורה. וכבר העידו כל ספרי הפילוסופים שכל מופרש מוגבל, וכל מוגבל יש לו סוף, וכל מה שיש לו סוף הוא מחובר, וכל מחובר מחודש, וכל מחודש צריך למחדש אחר זולתו, לפי שנתברר לכל מבין שאין הדבר עושה את עצמו.

77. *Even Boḥan* II:1, fol. 60a.

78. *Kur Maẓref,* pp. 1a–b.

79. Fol. 6b.

80. *Livyat Ḥen,* p. 1:

אמונת (האמונה?) הידועה יש בה מן הרחקה מה שנודע בו עם היותם נותנים לאל גשמות ודבר נוסף. הנה ימציאו החידוש בעצמו ודבר ברור לכל שאין ראוי אלהות לדבר מחודש כי יש לו סבה בהכרח וכל חדוש מקרה וכל שכן שלא יקרה ליחס לו בריאה והמצאה שהרי שמותו (שמוהו?) מחודש זמן ארוך אחר הבריאה.

81. *Milḥemet Miẓvah,* fol. 101a:

ידוע הוא כי הבורא יתברך הוא מאין שנוי וראשית ואחרית וזה נודע מדרך השכל והקבלה האמתית... ובאמת כל מי שמת נשתנה שנוי רב ותמו שניו ואם יאמרו כי על האלהות נאמר זה לא על הבשר שקבל אם כן לא יאמרו שהבשר הגוף הוא אל עם הבורא ולא ישוו החומר ליוצרו.

82. *Guide* II: Introduction, 6.

83. *Ta'anot,* p. ii:

אם האלהות השתתפ' בגשם צריך אתה להודות שכמו שהתנועע הגוף התנועע האלהות כתנועת המסמר בספינה או כתנועת התרן אשר בה וזה פאלשידאד, כי לשם ית' אין תנועה כי כל תנועה שנוי כמו שהקדים החכם בהקדמה ה'.

84. Ibid.:

ובזה השיבני הנוצרי ואמ': "חס ושלום שאמונתנו היא שנסגר האלהות בתוך בשר כהסגרת הנפש בו כי אם היתה אמונתנו כך היינו צריכים להודות שיש שם תנועה לאלהות כמו לבשר שכל אמונתנו שהאלהות לא התנועע אלא על עמדו עמד ולא [בא] בקרב בשר רק הבשר שנתעלה ונתקרב אל האלהות ונעשה בנו, אלוה, ובן אלוה".

85. *Guide* I:18.

86. *Ta'anot,* pp. ii–iii:

לא יקרב אל האלהות דבר כאשר הוכיח החכם בפרק מן החלק הראשון...ואם תאמ' הנפש באותו האיש אשר הוא שכלו נתקרב אל ה' ונעשה בנו כי מפני זה ר"ל מפני קרוב זה נעשה כך? וכך איננו אפי' נכדו ולא [בן] נכדו שהרי משה ואליהו נתקרב שכלם אל ה' ית' יותר ויותר ממנו ולא מפני כן נקראו בני אלהים.

87. Ibid., p. iii:

ואם "כל כך" נתיחד האלהות בו בעל כרחך היה לאלהות שבו תנועה ואם היה לו תנועה היה לו שנוי וכל משתנה מתחלק מה שאי אפשר בשם ית' חלילה ואין זה כי אם עורות לעיניכם.

88. *Guide* I:55.

89. *Ta'anot,* pp. viii–ix:

שקר הוא אמונתך כי פלוני אלהיך בעת שקבל גשם נתפעל וא"כ אינו אלוה כי האלהות אי אפש' להתפעל ופלוני זולתו הוא שפעל בו ושינהו. ולא תוכל לומ' שאין קבלת גשם הפעלות כי הפעלות ושנוי רב הוא מי

שהוא כח נבדל לשוב כח בגוף. ל״א: מי שהוא שכל נבדל שב להיות שכל בחומר? ואין צריך להאריך עוד בו וכדבר כתב אריסטוטיל כל משתנה אפשרות קודמת לה בזמן וכו׳.

Cf. *Metaphysics* 5, 11 and 9, 1–6.

90. *Ta'anot*, pp. xvii–xviii:

כבר כתבנו למעלה שהשי״ת אינו גוף ולא כח בגוף ולכן לא תכשר עליו תנועה כי אין תנועה אלא לגוף ולא יאות לו שנוי גם הפעלות. ולפיכך לא תכשר עליו לא עליה ולא ירידה לא ביאה ולא יציאה ולא הליכה ולא עמידה ולא ישיבה לא חבור ולא פירוד לא שיעור ולא מדה לא גבול ולא תכלית... ודוגמת זה הדבר כאשר העולם מלא מהאויר והכל נכנסים בתוך האויר אינם מרגישים ממנו כך השי״ת הוא הכל והכל בו עליונים ותחתונים ר״ל הגלגלים וכל מה שבתוכם הכל הם בה׳ ובכח ה׳ ובגבורתו סובל את כלם. ואחר שכן הוא איך יהיה לו תנועה, עלייה או ירידה, יציאה, וביאה?

91. Ibid., pp. iv, xii.

92. 1 C.E. = 3760 A.M.

93. *'Ezer Ha-'Emunah*, p. 172:

וכמה פעמי׳ נשאתי ונתתי עם כומרי הנוצרי׳ בזה הענין. והייתי טוען כנגדם: כן אתם הנוצרי׳ אומרי׳, שבד׳ אלפי׳ לבריאת העולם רצה האל לעשות דבר כדי שיכירוהו ברואיו, ויקבל צורה אנושית בבטן אשה. אמרו לי: כן. אח״כ הייתי טוען כנגדם כן: ידוע כי כל הדברי׳ שהם עתה ובזמן שעבר לא היה יש להם יתרון ושלמות עתה שהם, כי השלימות שהיה להם קודם שהיו היתה מסופקת, או יהיו או לא יהיו, ועתה שהם חוץ מן הספק ויצאו מן הכח אל הפועל, א״כ אלהיכם קודם הזמן שזכרנו של הד׳ אלפי׳ לא היה באותה צורה שאח״כ קבל, א״כ קודם שקבלה היה חסר בערך זה הזמן שעתה קבל זאת הצורה, וחלילה מאל מהחסרון.

94. Ibid.:

וער׳ הייתי או׳ להם כי כל הדברי׳ שהם בכח אם יהיו אם לא צריכי׳ לזולתם שיהיה בפועל שיוציאם מאותו כח ומאותו ספק לפועל. א״כ אלוהיכם קודם שקבל צורת האנוש היה בכח אם יקבלוהו אם לאו. א״כ מי הוא זה שהיה בפועל והוציאו מן הכח אל הפועל והוציאו מזה הספק, כי אם האל ית׳ שהוציא אני וכל הנמצאי׳ שהיו ויש להם להיות.

95. Ibid., p. 173:

יראה מדבריהם שצורך הביאה וחסרון הכנת החומר האם עיכבו ביאת האיש שהם אומרי׳ ראשונה כמה שהם אומ׳ שצורך הביאה עיכבהו שלא בא עד אותו זמן אינם אומרי׳ כלום, שלפי דבריהם מזמן חטא אדם הראשון היו בניו הבאי׳ אחריו מסורי׳ ביד השטן, א״כ מאותו זמן היתה צריכה ביאתו, אחר שהיה לו להושיעם. ואם החומר עיכב — הוא חסרון בחקו, אחר שהיתה כ״כ צריכה ביאתו, והוא אלוה — היה לו לשנות הטבע ולהקדימו.

96. Ibid.:

שהם מאמיני׳ שביאותו בבטן האשה היה שינוי טבע וגם לידתו ועוד היא בתולה היה שנוי טבע, א״כ ג״כ היה לו לשנות הטבע לביאתו קודם זמנו ולהכינו מיד אחר החטא, למה שינה בזה ולא בזה.

97. *Iggeret*, p. 54:

אל תהי כאבותיך אשר האמינוהו בלתי משתנה באחד מאוֹפני השינוי. וטעו באמרו אני י״י לא שניתי ששללו ממנו הגשמות והגופיות במוֹחלט. והרחיקו ממנו השינוי בכל מאמצי כח עיונם. נתנוהו שכל פשוט ונקי להמשכם אחרי העייון ברב המונם ושאונם... ואתה לא כן. לא תשלול ממנו הגשמות והגופיות חלילה לך אך האמן בו שנתלבש בשר באחד מתאריו. ואל השלשה לא בא. כאשר רצה — ונשפך כמים דמו לכפר על עמו ונרצה.

98. Aristotle, *Physics* 3, 1, 201a, 4–8; cf. Maimonides, *Guide* II: Introduction, 6.

99. *Physics* 8, 10, 267b, 25–27.

100. *Metaph.* 12, 2, 1069b, 3–27.

101. *Physics* 6, 4, 234b, 10–25; cf. *Guide* II: Introduction, 7.

102. If it were totally in one or the other, then its motion would not have started

yet or would have already been completed.

103. *Commentary on the Iggeret,* pp. 56–58:
כבר התבאר במופת שהשם יתעלה בלתי משתנה. וגם התבאר במופת בראשון מספר השמע כי ההיולי סיבת השינוי. ואמרו "באחד מאופני השינוי" ראוי שתדע שארסטו זכר במאמר השלישי מספר השמע כי השינוי אשר הוא סוג לתנועה נאמר לפי הפרסום בארבעה מאמרות: בעצם בכמה באיך באנה... ואמרו "ששללו ממנו הגשמות והגופיות במוחלט" ירצה שהשם יתעלה אינו גשם כי מחוייב המציאות אי איפשר שיהיה גשם כי לא יהיה אחד אמתי והמניע הראשון כבר התבאר במופת בסוף המאמר השמיני מספר השמע שאינו גשם ולא כח בגשם. ואמרו "בכל מאמצי כח עיונם" ירצה שהביאם אל זה העיון רוצה לומר לשלול ממנו השינוי. והמופת אשר הקימו על זה הוא בנוי על הקדמה אחת התבאר אמתתה ביאור שאין בו ספק בששי מהשמע והיא שכל משתנה מתחלק. וארסטו הניח להקדמה הזאת שתי הקדמות אחרות יתחייב מהם זה. האחת שכל משתנה קצתו במה שממנו התנועה וקצתו במה שאליו התנועה כי הדבר בהיותו במה שממנו לא יתנועע עדיין וכשהוא במה שאליו כבר התנועע התחייב שבעת השינוי שיהיה קצתו במה שממנו וקצתו במה שאליו. וההקדמה השנייה שכל מה שקצתו במה שממנו וקצתו במה שאליו מתחלק בהכרח התחייב בהכרח שכל משתנה מתחלק. ויתחייב מהיפוך הסותר שמה שלא יתחלק לא ישתנה והשם יתעלה בלתי מתחלק כלל...כי הוא אחד אמתי אינו גשם ולא כח בגשם יתחייב שלא ישתנה.

This argument is copied by de Modena, *Magen Va-Ḥerev,* p. 35.

104. *Magen Avraham* 28, fols. 31a–b:
ההשתנות הזה הוא לאות וחסרון בדבור ליחס אל האלוק ובבשרו אחרי שה(ה)בשר הוא אלוק איך יפול תחת ההשתנות בגידול עמידה וירידה ומקרים אחרים לא ידעתים בו אם בשר המשיח הוא אלוק.

This passage was quoted by S. Löwinger, "Recherches," p. 43.

105. *Magen Va-Ḥerev,* p. 41:
אחר כל אלה אשאלה מהם שאלה, יורוני יאמרו לי, אם האל ית׳ נוסף בו דבר ממה שהיה בו קודם בלבשו בשר עד קבלת ייסורין ומיתה, אם הוסיף שלמות בזה. אם יאמרו לא, א"כ היה פועל זה לבטלה, ופועל גדול ונורא לא נשמע כמהו. ואם יאמרו הן, כאשר ראיתי אומרים ממחבריהם, וכאשר אמרנו לעיל אמרם, שבזה הודיע עצמו ענו ורחמן ויכול להתחבר טבעו לטבע האנושי. זה א"א שיתוסף בו דבר עת זולת עת, ואפי׳ שום שלמות. שא"כ הוצרכנו לומר, שהיה חסר קודם, וההגשמה חדוש, וכל חדוש מקרה, א"כ א"א לתתו באלקות.

106. *Deux Dialogues Christologiques,* in G. M. de Durand, ed., *Sources Chrétiennes* no. 97 (Paris, 1964), pp. 208, 312–14.

107. *Disputatio,* pp. 43, 46–47. The same questions were discussed in Crispin's *Disputatio Christiani cum gentili,* ed. Clement C. J. Webb, *Mediaeval and Renaissance Studies* 3 (1954): 61–62. Cf. also R. W. Southern, "St. Anselm and Gilbert Crispin, Abbot of Westminster," ibid., pp. 82–84.

108. *SCG* IV, 31, p. 479.

109. *ST* III, 1, 1; 3, 1. De Modena (*Magen Va-Ḥerev,* p. 38) quoted this objection from the first passage.

110. *ST* III, 16, 4.

111. Ibid., 2, 4.

112. Ibid., 2, 9.

113. *Apologia, PL* 177, 302–5.

114. *ST* III, 2, 7.

115. Ibid., 16, 8.

116. Ibid., 10.

117. Cf. Matt. 1:20; Jesus was conceived of the Holy Spirit. The unusual term

nihug apparently was not used consistently by the polemicists. Here, it seems to connote nature.

118. P. 3:

ועתה הזהר בדבריך שסותרים זה את זה. ואשר העדת כי האלהים א׳ וישו בן האלהים הוא וי׳ אחד אשר ברא את הכל בדברו ואמרת כי ירד מן השמים בלי פירוד מן האב ור״ה וידבק ר״ה באלה השני ניהוגים ניהוג האלהות ושליטות האלהים והניהוג ניהוג באישות והיה איש שלם וישו הוא הבן היה ישר בלי חטא ולא נפרד הניהוג אל הניהוג כלום. הודיעני עתה באמרך כי קנין הבן הי׳ על מרים ירד עצמו והאב ור״ה הם לבדם נסתרו עליך דברים אשר אמרת כי ג׳ ניהוגים בקנין א׳ היו ניהוג האלהות וניהוג האישות אראה עתה כי ישו הי׳ משני קנינים ולא מקנין האב ור״ה במקצתו נדבק ובמקצתו לא נדבק נפסדו עליך דבריך אשר אמרת כי לא נפרד קצתו מן קצתו.

119. Ibid., pp. 3–4:

וא״ת היה בכל האלהות ובר״ה נדבק הודיענו ברדתו המשיח בארץ אנה היה בשרו ודמו בשמים או בארץ בים או בהרים בצפון או בדרום במזרח או במערב כי לא היתה קומת המשיח כל כך גדולה כי אם ככל אדם אשר על הארץ. ואם תאמר כי לא היתה עמו כדבריך נראה כי לא הי׳ שלם בכל ר״ה. ואם תאמר כי היה שם מקצת אלהות דע כי פגמת מקצתו על קצתו.

120. I.e., if the Son and Holy Spirit became separated from the Father.

121. *Milḥamot Ha-Shem*, p. 154:

הנה אמרתם כי הקב״ה הוא אחד וזה משיחכם הוא בנו וירד מן השמים בלי פירוד מן האב ורוח הקדש.,וזה הבן היו בו שני נהוגין, נהוג האלהות ונהוג האישות ולא נפרד נהוג האלהות מנהוג האישות כלל. עתה באמרך כי קנין הבן ירד בבטן מרים הודיעני אם נדבק בו האב והרוח או נדבק הוא לבדו עמה. אם תאמר שנדבקו הבן והרוח לבדם נפסדו דבריך אשר אמרת כי נהוגים בקנין אחד נהוג האלהות ונהוג האישות שעתה לא היה בו מנהוג האב כלום. ואם תאמר שהיה המשיח מקנין האב והבן והרוח הקדש מקצתו נדבק ומקצתו אינו נדבק נפסדו עליך דבריך אשר אמרת לא נפרד קצתו מקצתו.

122. *Keshet U-Magen*, p. 7b.

123. *Magen Va-Ḥerev*, p. 34.

124. *Kur Maẓref*, p. 1b (in much abbreviated form).

125. Fols. 7a–7b.

126. *Even Boḥan* XIV (XVI):1, fol. 186a:

ע״כ מדבריו נראה שלא הבין נסתור ענין הקניינים האלה כי הנה השמש מאיר ומחמם יחד ואינו מאיר מצד שהוא מחמם.

127. *Dialogus*, *PL* 157, 617–18.

128. *Even Boḥan*, fol. 186b:

כי התחלפות פעולות השמש הוא מצד היותו מורכב כי הוא תאיר בספיריות נצוציו ומחמם בהם [ב]הפכותם מצד תנועתם החזקה אמנם הש״י שכל נבדל פשוט בתכלית הפשיטות לא יפול בו שום רבוי והרכבה.

Cf. also *Kevod Elohim*, fol. 7b. Ibn Shapruṭ rejected the Christian analogy despite Maimonides' use of the image of fire as analogous to God's multiple activities. Cf. *Guide* I:53. For another Christian treatment of Nestor's argument, cf. *Milḥamot Ha-Shem*, pp. 154–55, n. 49, quoting Nicholas de Lyra, and Williams, *Adversus Judaeos*, p. 415.

129. *Ta'anot*, p. v:

הודיעני כל האלהות קבל׳ גשם או קצתו... ואם תאמ׳ קצת האלהות קבל׳ בשר נמצא׳ משים חלוק ופרוד בדבר שלא יתפרד ולא יקבל חלוקה.

130. Ibid.:

ועל טענתי זאת השיב אח קטן שמו אח פליפ׳ ואמ׳ אמת כי כל האלהות קבל׳ בשר ולא קצת האלהות אבל יש דבר באלהות שקבל גשם והוא אחד מן הפירצונה.

131. Ibid.:

וטענתי עוד עליו הרי אתה אומ׳ שה[ש]לשה מוחלקים בענין אע״פ שהם בעצם אחד והעצם אחד. ואם אחד מהפירשונה קבלה גשם הרי יש פרוד וחלוקה כי הפירצונה מן האלהות הוא כפי דבריך והדרן קושיא לדוכתיה שקצת האלהות עמד מפני עצמו כמו שהיה מאז ומלפנים בלי גשם וקצתה קבלה גשם.

132. Ibid.:

ל״א הרי אתה אומ׳ שאין הפירצונה ענין א׳ [אחר] מהעצם העצם הוא אחד ואחר שהעצם הוא אחד צריך אתה לומ׳ בעל כרחך שקצת האלהות קבל גשם ועדין הארגומינטו שלי עומד במקומו. ורבים אמרו שכל האלהות היה שם כשקבל גשם והנה ישימו מדה וגבול לשם. ופרכא אחרת שא״כ הוא האב קבל בשר כמו הבן ולמה יאמרו שהבן קבל בשר ולא האלהות האב.

Cf. also pp. iii, x–xi.

133. Ibid., p. xiv:

והנני מוכיח עליך שענין קבלת הבשר היה פירוד וחלוק שהרי שגור בפי כל נוצרי שהחכמה היא שקבלה גשם לא היכלת והרצון ואם אין בענין פירוד, איך יתכן שקבלה זו בלא זו.

134. Ibid., p. xv:

גם באמרך שהחכמה לבדה היא שקבלה גשם, נמצא שהמקבל הזה היה בלי יכולת ורצון כי אחד מהשלשה תארים היה שקבל ואחר שהוא בלי יכולת ורצון אינו אלוה הואיל ואין בו שלשתן כי האלהות כן הוא לפי דעתך יכולת חכמה ורצון כלל׳ אחד מוכלל משלשתן אחר שהוא חסר משני תארים נכבדים אי אפש׳ להיותו אלוה. וגם זו רעה חולה שהאב נשאר בלי חכמה ודעת.

135. Ibid.:

וא״ת שאפילו הבן יכול וחכם ורוצה כמו האב וכן רוח הקדש א״כ צריך שיהיה כל אחד שלשה ויהיו לך תשעה אלהות; או צריך אתה לומ׳ שלא לבד החכמה קבלה גשם רק קצת האלהות שהיה בו יכולת וחכמה ורצון נפרד וקבל גשם.

136. Ibid., pp. xv–xvi.

137. Cf. *ST* I, 43.

138. *Ta'anot*, p. xiv:

אמרו שהחכמה לבדה היא שקבלה גשם לא היכלת והרצון הרי שדבריך סותרים זה את זה...שאם קבל הבן ולא קבל האב נמצא פירוד וחלוק בענין, תחזור ותאמ׳ אז: אין פירוד שם כי כמו שקבל הבן קבל האב כי אינם עומדים שיחלקו כי אחד הם. וכשאשוב ואקשה לך: איזה מהם היה שליח ואיזה מהם היה שולח, תסתור דבריך ותהפכם, שהבן הוא השליח. ואם הבן הוא השליח נמצא שהבן לבדו הוא שקבל גשם ונגלה ענין הבירור.

139. *Iggeret*, p. 54.

140. Ibid., p. 60:

ויסודר ההיקש כן: כל האלהות נתלבש והתארים השלשה שהם אב ורוח ובן כל האלהות אם כן כל התארים השלשה שהם אב בן ורוח נתלבשו. עוד שמהות הבן נתלבש והוא מהות האב והרוח המהות הוא התאר.

141. *Biṭṭul*, fols. 13a–b:

ואין להם שיאמרו שהבן הו׳ אשר נתגשם אבל האב והרוח נשארו בכח אלקותם כי הם אומרי׳ כי האלקות בלתי מתחלק, ולזה יתחייב והם מודים בו שהאלקות קבל הבשר, ולכן האלקות כלו נשתנה והפסיד עצמותו הנבדל עם שיאמרו שהאב לא קבל הבשר ושהוא אלהים, ראה זאת הסתיר׳ איך עשו אותו א׳ והרבה, מתחלק ובלתי מתחלק, וכאשר תעיין אל הבחינות אשר יאמרו אשר מצדם יהיה א׳ ורבים, ומשתנה ובלתי משתנה ותעיין מה שיתחייב לשרשיהם תראה כי הם דברים נאמרים אין להם ציור ולא מציאות.

142. *Zikheron Sefer Niẓẓaḥon,* p. 260:
למה גוים רגשו עת למשפט נגשו שהאב מתייעץ עם בנו בבריאות עולם איך נפרדו לפי דבריהם שנצמדו עד בית שני לבניינו אחרי הפרד מעמו.

143. *Magen Va-Ḥerev,* p. 34.

144. *Réfutation Excellente,* p. 33 (Arabic):
المسيح صلب ولا شيء مما صلب بالـه ولا شيء من المسيح بالـه.

145. *Liber de Fide Trinitatis et de Incarnatione Verbi, PL* 158, 262: "Si in Deo tres personae sunt una tantum res et non sit tres res unaquaeque per se separatim, sicut tres angeli, aut tres animae: ita tamen ut potentia et voluntate omnino sint idem: ergo Pater et Spiritus sanctus cum Filio est incarnatus." Trans. Jasper Hopkins and Herbert Richardson, ed., Anselm of Canterbury, *Trinity, Incarnation, and Redemption* (New York, 1970), p. 11.

146. Ibid., 268–69; trans. p. 15.

147. Ibid., pp. 274–75. Thomas disagreed that the incarnation of one Person rendered impossible the simultaneous incarnation of other Persons or even of the same Person; cf. *ST* III, 3, 4.

148. Martène and Durand, *Thesauras,* cols. 1506B–C: "Cum autem Pater est Deus, Filius est Deus, Spiritus Sanctus est Deus, videtur mihi quod tres sint incarnati, et quod tres carnem acceperunt."

149. Ibid. Cf. also Raymund Lull, "Disputatio Fidelis et Infidelis," *Raymundus Lullus Opera,* IV (Mainz, 1737; reprinted Frankfurt/Main, 1965), p. 29 (405): "quia si in Deo sunt Pater et Filius et Sanctus Spiritus existentes una Deitas, Unus Deus et incarnatio est, convenit, quod omnes tres Personae sunt incarnatae."

150. *Sententiae* III, 1, 4, *PL* 192, 758–59.

151. *ST* III, 3, 2 and 4.

152. Augustine, *Enchiridion ad Laurentium* 38, *PL* 40, 251.

153. This terminology was Thomas', but the concept was shared by both Thomas and Lombard.

154. *Al-Muḥtawī,* fol. 55:
פאמא קול אלנצארי באלאתחאד פמא קדמנאה מן אנה ת״ע גיר גִסם יבטל קולהם מן חית אן אלתחאד (צ״ל אלאתחאד) לא יעקל אלא פי גִסמין יכטלט (יכתלט?) אחדהמה בצאחבה וימתזג בה פיציראן פי חכם אלשי אלואחד לאסתחאלה תמייזהמא ולדלך מתלו אתחאדה ת״ע בעיסי באתחאד אלמא באלנביד ואלנאר באלכחס פקד באן לך אן הדה מן צפאת אלאגִסאם.
Cf. Vajda, "La Démonstration," p. 305.

155. *Ta'anot,* pp. xvi–xviii:
ידוע הוא כי כל שני דברים שמשתתפים זה עם זה יחד והא׳ חזק מחבירו צריך שהחזק יכריח את החלש. ואתן לך משל: דע שאם אדם משים מים בתוך דם, הדם יכריח את המים וישובו המים אדומים כדמות דם. וכן אם תשים מים בתוך יין אדום היין מכריח את המים וישובו כדמות יין. ואחרי המשל הזה תדע שאם קבל האלהות בשר לפי דבריך כאשר היא אמונת הנצרים היה צריך שיכריח האלהות את כחות הבשר וישוב הכל אלהות. והנה ראינו בפלוני אלהיך כל זה להפך כי כח הבשר הכריח את האלוה וכל טבע הבשר היה בו ולא נשאר אחד שלא היה בו ואיך נשתתפה בו האלהות? אין זה כי אם ריקנות מח וחסרון דעת.

156. *Biṭṭul,* fol. 11a:

למה שהיה האדם טרם חטאו ומעלו קרוב אל האלקים וכאשר מרד ועבר מצותו, רחק ממנו ית׳ רוחק בב״ת, היה מחסד ה׳ ורחמנותו אשר באמצעות אחדות בב״ת מאלוקות והאינושות ישוב האדם לאיתנו ולהיות קרוב אליו ית׳ עם גאולה מאותו חטא ולכן חייבה החכמה מהאלהים הבן שהוא קבל הבשר בבטן הבתולה ונתאחד עם אדם אחדות בלתי מתחלקת ואף אחרי מותו דבקות יותר גדול מאחדות הנפש עם הבשר, באופן יסבול המות והיסורים בגאולת חטא אדם הכולל.

157. Ibid., fol. 11b; Crescas referred to chap. 2 of his work in which he presented his arguments against the Christian doctrine of redemption.

158. Ibid., fol. 11b:
או׳ שהאחדות עם אל הוא נמנע שיביא אל סתירה, וזה מבואר שהאדם הוא ב״ת והאל ית׳ הוא בב״ת וא״כ אינו דבר יותר נמנע מלא׳ חייוב עם שלילה, וכבר זכרנו שהדברים המחייבים סתירה אינו יכול עליהם.
See above in chap. 3 on the use of reason for a discussion of the limits to God's powers. Shem Tov ibn Shapruṭ also used the argument that since Godhood and manhood were opposites, they could not apply to the same subject; cf. *Even Boḥan,* I:11, fol. 50b.

159. *ST* III, 1, 1.

160. *Magen Va-Ḥerev,* p. 38.

161. *ST* III, 1, 1.

162. *On Generation and Corruption* 1, 10, 327b, 34–328a, 9.

163. *Metaph.* 8, 2, 1042b, 16.

164. Ibid., 19.

165. Such as in the case of the body and the soul; cf. *On the Soul* 2, 1, 412a, 16–21.

166. *Biṭṭul,* fols. 11b–12a, 14a:
שנית אם היה זה האחדות אפשרי יתחייב שזה האיש אשר יתאחדו בו לא יהיה אלהים ולא יהיה אדם אבל יהיה עצם א׳ מורכב משני אלה הטבעים וזה יתבאר בשתי ראיות, הא׳ נאמ׳ זה האחדות או היה מזגיי או מקומיי או שכני או צוריי, ר״ל מהדברים המתחלפים כשיתאחדו או יהיה ע״ד המזג כיסודות בנמזג או ע״ד שכנות כיין והשמן, או שהם דבקים במקום אחד או ע״ד צורה, כאלו תאמ׳ שהחומר והצורה הם דבקים ושם דבקות צוריי, וא״א שיהיה מזגיי שהנבדל לא יתמזג עם הגוף כ״ש טבע אלקי עם טבע אנושי, ולא ג״כ ע״ד שכנות ולא במקום א׳ שהאלקים לא יהיה במקום, ישאר א״כ שיהיה צוריית, וזה יהיה א״כ שהאדם יהיה שם מעמד החומר והאלהים מעמד הצורה, ויתחייב א״כ בהכרח שזה המורכב א׳ שיהיה מתחלף במין לחומר ולצורה, כי הדברים הרבים כשיתאחדו ויעשו א׳ זה האחד הוא זולת כל א׳ מהם וזה לא יהיה לא אל ולא אדם אבל יהיה א׳ מורכב מאנושות ואלוקות, וזה מבואר למי ששימש החכמה הטבעית ויתחייב מזה בטולים אחרים ר״ל שיתחייב שהעצם האלקי נשתנה באחר וזה כי כאשר היה צורה לאדם כבר נשתנה בהכרח וזה שגגה גדולה... ויתחייב עוד אם זה אינו אדם ולא אל שלא סבל אדם מיתה ויסורין ולכן הגאולה לא היתה ע״י אדם.
Crescas' account of the types of union was not very comprehensive, nor did he follow Aristotle closely. Cf. *On Gen. and Corr.* 1, 10, 327a, 29–328b, 25; Wolfson *Church Fathers,* pp. 372–86.

167. *Biṭṭul,* fols. 12a–b:
ואם לא למה תאמ׳ נתאחד או קבל הבשר ויחוייב בהכרח שיפסיד עצמו ויפסיד מהיותו אלהים וזה שהאלהים הו׳ נבדל וכאשר שב צורה גשמית או אנושית כבר שב מהיותו נבדל, ונעשה כח גופני בלתי נבדל, וכאשר הפסיד היותו נבדל הוא מחוייב ר״ל זה ההפסד מחוייב לאלקותו ולאמיתתו ומהותו והנפסד לא יתהוה את עצמו ולכן לא יוכל אחרי כן להיות צורה אנושית ולא גשמית, וחכמיהם בורחים ואינם יודעים מה שיענו אבל אומרים בפיהם שלא נשתנה, והו׳ מחוייב להם בהכרח שישתנה.

168. *Guide* I:69; *Metaph.* 12, 10, 1075a, 11–24.

169. *Commentary on the Iggeret*, p. 62:
נקרא צורת העולם לא צורה דבקה שהוא מעמיד העולם כדין הצורה המעמידה לדבר אשר הוא לו צורה.
De Modena copied this argument in *Magen Va-Ḥerev*, p. 35.

170. Cf. *Metaph.* 12, 8: *Tahāfut al-Tahāfut*, ed. van den Bergh, II, pp. 20, 91. Cf. also *ST* I, 105, 2.

171. *Commentary on the Iggeret*, p. 62:
ואף לדברי אבן רשד שאמר במה שאחר הטבע שהשם יתעלה מניע לגלגל הראשון...לא רצה שיניעהו על צד שתניע הנפש לגוף חלילה אבל על צד שיניע החשוק והנכסף הציור השכלי כמו שביאר ארסטו במאמר הלמ״ד.
De Modena copied this argument in *Magen Va-Ḥerev*, p. 35.

172. Joseph ben Shem Tov quoted this opinion from Averroes' commentary on Aristotle's *On the Soul* 3. Cf. Husik, *History*, p. 334, Gersonides, *Milḥamot Ha-Shem* V:3:11.

173. Cf. *Teshuvot La-Meḥaref*, fols. 21b–25b; cf. Y. Baer, *History*, I, pp. 344–45.

174. *Biṭṭul*, fol. 12b:
ואף לדברי ן׳ רשד שאומ׳ שהשכל הפועל צורה לנו ושהו׳ מלובש בהכנה ושמצד עצמו ידע את אשר שם ומצד דבקותו בנו ילמד את אשר היה יודע כבר כמו שביאר בג׳ מספר הנפש אין זה הדבקות אשר הונח באל אפשרי, כי אנחנו לא יצדק בנו בשום עת שאנחנו השכל הפועל ולא עליו שהו׳ אדם ולא שהו׳ נשתנה ושב צורה אנושית כמו שיאמרו שיצדק על יש״ו שהוא אלהים אמתי אשר ברא שמים וארץ.

175. *ST* III, 2, 1; cf. *SCG* IV; 32, p. 480 in which Thomas argued that Jesus must have had a rational soul because, without such a soul, God would have had to be the form of the body, which He could not be.

176. *SCG* IV; 35, p. 488; cf. Thomas' discussion here of the various modes of union.

177. This explained how one Person could become incarnate while the others did not.

178. *Denz.*, 40.

179. *ST* III, 2, 1.

180. This most likely demonstrates that the Jews did not have a clear understanding of the intricacies of the Christian doctrines. They apparently were more aware of the image in the Athanasian Creed of body and soul than they were of Thomas' exposition of the modes of union.

181. *Biṭṭul*, fol. 14a:
אם מדבקות הנפש בגוף נעשה עצם א׳ בלתי מתחלק, דבקות האלהים בבשר שאומרים שהו׳ בדבקות יותר גדול מהנפש עם הגוף ראוי שיעשו ממנו עצם א׳ בלתי מתחלק וזה מבואר כי מה שיתחייב מהדבקות היותר קטן ראוי שיתחייב מהדבקות היותר גדול, ויתחייבו מזה כל הבטולים הנזכרים.

182. Ibid.:
אם היה האחדות אפשרי יתחייב שהבן ישתנה אל שתי עצמיות בעת א׳ בעת המות, כאשר נתאחד עם הנפש ועם הבשר המת, וכל א׳ מאלה הב׳ דבקיות יעשה עצם א׳ והוא נמנע שהעצמות המתהוה מאחדות האלוקות עם הנפש יהיה אותו עצמות אשר יהיה מאחדות עם הבשר.

183. Ibid., fols. 14a–b:

האחדות אשר היה עם הבשר בעת המות לא היה אחדות אלקי עם אדם, שהבשר כאשר נפרד הנפש ממנו ומת לא יצדק עליה שם אדם ולא גדרו שהוא חי מדבר.

184. Ibid., fol. 14b:
שכבר היה זה האחדות אשר שמוהו בלתי מתחלק נבדל ומתחלק וזה אחר שמת כי אז לא היה שם דבקות האלוקות עם אנושות כי אעפ״י שיאמרו שנשאר דבק עם הנפש לבדה ועם הגוף לבדו כבר נבדל האחדות ר״ל אחדות האל עם אדם שהדברים כיצדקו מורכבים לא יצדקו נפרדים, ואחדות אלהים עם אדם יהיה כאש׳ יתייחד עמו בהיותו חי והיו הנפש והבשר ביחד, אמנם כאשר נפרדו בעת המות לא יצדק עליהם שם אדם ולזה לא נשאר דבק עם אדם ולכן נבדל הדבקות האלקי מהטבע האנושי, הפך מה שהניחו באמרם כי בשום זמן לא נבדל הדבקות, ומי יתן וידעתי מה הוא זה העצמות אשר יהיה מדבקות האלקות עם בשר המת ואיך אפשר זה הדבקות.

185. Ibid., fol. 13b:
אמרו שהאלקות נשאר דבק עם בשר המת כאשר היה על העץ ומתאחד בו באופן יצדק האלהים מת ואם היה הדבקות הזה באלקות והיה שם האלקות באלקותו הנה יש״ו חי. וזה מבואר מאד שהנפש עם היותה דבקה אל הגוף הנה הוא חי עם שאין לה החיים האמתיי׳ הנצחיים אשר לאלקות...ואם הנפש בדבקותה אל הגוף נותנת לו חיים, החיים האמתיים שהוא האל יתברך יותר ראוי שיתן חיים לגוף עם היותו דבק עמו כי המשים דבר בתואר מה הוא יותר אמתי באותו תואר ממנו.

186. The relationship between Crescas and Moses ben Solomon is difficult to determine. Though the latter preceded Crescas by 150 years, the fact that no manuscripts of his work remain might indicate that he was not a very influential polemicist. Still, a number of arguments in Crescas' *Biṭṭul* are very similar to ones in Moses ben Solomon's *Ta'anot*.

187. *Ta'anot*, pp. iii–iv:
איך לא תבוש מלדבר כזה והלא ידוע שהשי״ת הוא חיי העולם בכללו הן מדרך חכמה הן מדרך נבואה שנאמ׳ ״וישבע בחי העולם״ כלומ׳ נשבע בה׳ שהוא חיים של עולם ואומ׳ ״ואתה מחיה את כלם״. ואם היתה האלהות דבוקה בו לא היתה בו אפשרות מיתה...ואחרים השיבו: לא היה האלהות בו בדרך פורמא צורה כעין הנפש באדם על כן היה אפשר למות. ותשובתי זו היא: אם קבלת הבשר אינה כדרך צורה פורמא בלעז כלמ׳ לא כח בגוף ולא דבוק ולא שתוף א״כ לא נשארה שם דרך לקבלת הבשר והנה הכל הבל ורעות רוח.

188. Ibid., p. vi:
הרי אתה אומ׳ שפלוני אלהיך מת ועמד משוחתו ג׳ ימים מיום ששי עד יום ראשון. עכשיו, אותם הימים שעמד שם נקרא אלוה אצלכם או לא? אם תאמ׳ שהיה אלהיך וכי היאמ׳ אלוה אל גוף מת.

189. Cf. *ST* III, 6, 1, 50, 2.

190. *Ta'anot*, p. vii:
הודו לי חכמי הנוצרים שהנפש היא שהיתה אמצעית בין האלהות והבשר. ואחרי זאת ההצעה אוכיח איך שכמו שנפרדה הנפש מעל פלוני אלהיך כך נפרדה האלהות ממנו ומעליו כי ידוע שכל שני דברים שעמידתם וקיומם על ידי אמצעי בהסתלק האמצעי מבטל עמידתם. ואם כן הוא האלהות נסתלקה מעל אלהיך כאשר נפרדה נפשו ממנו ונשאר פגר מת.

191. Ibid., pp. vi–vii, x.

192. *De Fide Orth.* III, 27, *PG* 94, 1097; quoted by Thomas, *ST* III, 50, 3; cf. AA. 1–3, for the full exposition of the issue.

193. As we have seen, this assertion was made against Apollinarius, who denied that Jesus had a rational soul. Cf. the decree of the Council of Chalcedon, 451, quoted above.

194. *Sefer Ha-Berit*, pp. 30–31:

האלוהות אשר לקח הבשר בבטן מרים היא עצמה הייתה נשמתו של ישו או הייתה לו נשמה אחרת כדרך כל בני־אדם? אם תאמר, ולא הייתה לו נשמה אחרת כי אם האלוהות שלקח הבשר, אבל הייתה בבשר זולת האלוהות נפש חיות—והוא הדם כמו שיש בבהמה ובעופות —, הרי לא נכנס האלוהות באדם כי אם בבהמה. ועוד, כי בשעה שהיה צועק "אלי אלי למה עזבתני", האלוהות למי היה צועק? כי לא הייתה לו נפש מדברת זולתי האלוהות. ואיך לא היה יכול להושיע עצמו והיה צועק לזולתו? ואם אתה אומר, כי רוח אחרת הייתה לו כדרך בני־אדם העולה היא למעלה ואחר שכן בא האלוהות, הרי ישו ככל אדם בגופו ונשמתו ואינו אלוה ולא בן אלוה.

Trans., Talmage, pp. 38–39. Cf. also *Nestor Ha-Komer,* p. 10.

195. *Commentary on the Iggeret,* p. 60:

אם המשיח הזה היו אצלו המושכלות הראשונות בכח או בפועל או בשניהם אם יאמרו בכח ובפועל זה אי אפשר שהם סותרים. אם יאמרו שתמיד היו בכח אצלו זולתי בעת ההתבודדות והעיון הנה נאמר אם כן היה אדם לבד כי זה דין כל חכם לב. ואם יאמרו בפועל תמיד ולא היו אצלו מעולם בכח בעבור שהיתה צורתו הקרובה השם יתעלה ואצלו המושכלות בפועל תמיד אם כן היה בעל חי והאלוה לא אדם ואל.

196. *Magen Va-Ḥerev,* p. 35. Cf. also the Geniza fragment published by Richard Gottheil, op. cit., pp. 85, 87. The author of this text, which shows affinity with *Nestor Ha-Komer,* asked how it was possible for Jesus to acquire knowledge.

197. *ST* III, 9, 1; cf. also 3, 4 and 10–12. In III, 15, 3, Thomas said that Jesus had no ignorance in him.

198. *Shevet Yehudah* 32, p. 88:

ועוד, שאם נתלבש בבשר לקבל עונש בלתי בעל תכלית על עון אדם שחטא כנגד הבלתי בעל תכלית, עונש זה מי קבלו? אם נאמר החלק האלהי — אי אפשר, כי הוא אינו מקבל מות, ואם חלק הבשר — ידוע כי הבשר בעל תכלית, ואיך נאמר שקבל עונש הבלתי בעל תכלית?

This argument is taken from Bibago, *Derekh Emunah,* p. 99a; cf. also *Magen Avraham* 15, fol. 20a.

199. *Commentary on the Iggeret,* pp. 64–66:

השם יתעלה הושיע את המין האנושי אם על צד החסד אם על צד המשפט. אם על צד החסד ומה חסד עשה לקבל חמשת אלפים מלקיות ולבסוף שיהרג בביזוי גדול כזה... ואם על צד הדין ואיפה משפטיו הצדיקים אשר יעשה האלוה אשר רצה שיענש האלוה בעבור עון אדם הראשון וכתוב איש בחטאו יומתו. ואם יאמרו שלא נענש מצד שהוא אלוה אלא מצד שהוא אדם על שביקש אלה סוף סוף שבה השאלה למה יענש שורש משרשי אדם הראשון בעבור עונש אדם כל שכן לדעתם שלא נולד בחטא אוריגינאל כלל, וכתיב ובנים לא יומתו על אבות. ועוד אם לא יענש אלא מצד שהוא אדם מהו הנה בזה להיות אדם הראשון כולל המין שממנו יצאו ובעבור זה נענשו כולם לדעתם לא היה די לו במיתת האיש הזה לכפר העוון כי אתה אמרת כי לא מת אלוה ולא נענש כלל זולתי מצד היותו אדם ולא מצד היותו אלוה וכולל המין כלו. אם כן אין תועלת בקבלת האלוה הבשר ועם כל זה יצדק עליו שהאלוה נתלה ומת כמו שיצדק על הסוחר הגנב שנתלה שהסוחר תלוי אף על פי שלא נתלה מצד שהוא סוחר אלא מצד מה שהוא גנב.

Cf. Profiat Duran, *Kelimat Ha-Goyim* I, *Ha-Ẓofeh,* 3, p. 112.

Chapter Six

1. Though Jews no longer practiced animal sacrifice after 70 C.E., the issue was still debated, since (1) Jews prayed for the restoration of the sacrificial system, and,

moreover, (2) the sacrifices were a target of the general Christian argument that the precepts of the "Old Law" (Torah) were deficient as compared to those of the New Law.

2. Shem Tov ibn Shapruṭ, *Even Boḥan,* I:2, fol. 7a:
גם שהעבודות ההם היו מזוהמות בשריפת הבשרי׳ והחלבי׳ והזאת הדמי׳ אמנם עבודתנו היא נקייה בלחם וביין ומכפרת כל העבירות בשלימות באכלנו את לחם אלוקינו ונהיה קדש ומי שאלהיו בקרבו לא יירא דבר רע.
The idea that, by eating the bread, the worshiper would have his God in him comes from John 6:56: "He who eats my flesh and drinks my blood abides in me, and I in him."

3. This may well refer to the numerous examples of Eucharistic miracles that were proffered as evidence of the real presence of Christ in the Eucharist. Cf. Peter Browe, *Die Eucharistischen Wunder des Mittelalters* (Breslau, 1938). What Albo may have been saying was that even if such miracles actually occurred, they did so irregularly. The sacrifices produced results continuously.

4. Joseph Albo, *Sefer Ha-'Iqqarim,* III:25, ed. and trans. Husik, p. 231. The last statement, *Ha-roẓeh leshaker yarḥiq 'edav,* first used in a polemical context by Naḥmanides, was a popular expression employed by Jewish polemicists in the Middle Ages, though it was not talmudic. Cf. N. Brüll, *Jahrbücher für Jüdische Geschichte und Literatur* 7 (1885): 28, no. 44, and *Vikuaḥ Ha-Ramban,* p. 310; cf. n. 55.

5. *Even Boḥan,* I:2, fol. 9b:
גם מה שאמרת שקרבנותנו מזוהמות ושלכם נקיי׳ אלו נמצאו בקרבנות שלכם הסגולות הנמצאות בקרבנות שלנו בהורדת אש מהשמי׳ והראות כבוד ה׳ וחרב לא תעבור בארצכם היה ראוי להשיבך. אבל בדבר שאין שום סגולה נראית בו אין להעריך אותו עם בעל הסגולות הנפלאות. היתכן שנאמ׳ שהכסף יותר ראוי שיזון כי הוא יותר נקי מהבשר.
Justification of the sacrificial system had an important place in medieval Jewish literature other than strictly polemical works. Cf. Saadia, *al-Amānāt,* III:10, Judah Halevi, *Kuzari,* II:25–26, Maimonides, *Guide,* III:32, 46. Cf. also, Isaac Heinemann, *Ta'ame Ha-Miẓvot Be-Sifrut Yisrael,* I (Jerusalem, 1954), index, p. 207, s.v. *korbanot.*

6. Duran's account is given in *Kelimat Ha-Goyim,* chap. 6, *Ha-Ẓofeh,* 3, pp. 171–72. Lombard was quoted explicitly by Duran, and Posnanski gives appropriate references to *Sententiae,* Liber IV, Dist. 8–13, Migne, *PL* 192, 856–68. A number of Duran's statements are not found in Lombard's work.

7. *Maṭ'im,* as distinguished from *Ṭo'im,* the first Christians, who, though they had mistaken beliefs, did not try to impose these beliefs on others. The former, however, were the real cause of the spread of Christianity and its "erroneous" doctrines.

8. Christian thinkers normally stressed both the virgin birth and crucifixion aspects of the body of Christ. For instance, cf. Lombard's quotation from Ambrose that the bread is that "qui manu sancti Spiritus formatus est in utero Virginis, et igne passionis decoctus in ara crucis," *Sent.,* Dist. 11, col. 862. The following formulation is found in Berengarius' confession of 1079: "Verum Christi corpus, quod natum est de Virgine et quod pro salute mundi oblatum in cruce pependit—It is the true body of Christ, which was born of the Virgin and which, offered for the salvation of the

world, was suspended on the Cross." See *Denz.*, no. 355; trans., Deferrari, p. 144.

9. Cf. Thomas, *ST*, III, 74, 3; *SCG*, IV, 69, p. 531.

10. *ST* III, 75, 6: "Forma substantialis panis non manet."

11. Lombard, Dist. 12, 1, col. 864; "Potius mihi videtur fatendum existere sine subjecto, quam esse in subjecto." This was not Thomas' view, for he held that the accidents remained with dimensive quantity *(quantitas dimensiva)* as subject (*ST* III, 77, 2). Ockham, however, went back to the view that the accidents remained without a subject and denied that *quantitas* remained in the Eucharist. Cf. *De Corpore Christi*, in *The De Sacramento Altaris of William of Occam*, ed. T. Bruce Birch (Burlington, Iowa, 1930), chap. 16, pp. 240–45, and chap. 23, pp. 284–85. Also, G. Buescher, *The Eucharistic Teaching of William Ockham* (Washington, 1950), pp. 119–40.

12. Lombard did not express it this way, but cf., e.g., Alger of Liège, *De Sacramentis Corporis et Sanguinis Dominici*, chap. 14, *PL* 180, 780: "Credendum est, quod eodem tempore et vere est in sacramento suo in terris, et vere in coelo sedet ad dextram Patris—It is to be believed, that at the same time that he is truly in his sacrament on earth, he is truly sitting in heaven at the right side of the Father." A. J. Macdonald states that the question of Christ's location both in heaven and on earth at the same time was a favorite problem in the first half of the twelfth century; *Berengar and the Reform of Sacramental Doctrine* (London, 1930), p. 393.

13. *Sent.*, Dist. 12, 5, col. 865: "Quia forma panis ibi frangitur, et in partes dividitur, Christus vero integer manet, et totus est in singulis—Since the form of the bread is broken there and divided into parts, Christ truly remains entire, and the whole is in each part." Cf. also *ST* III, 76, 3: "Utrum sit totus Christus sub qualibet parte specierum panis vel vini—Is the whole Christ under each and every part of the species?"

14. The history of this image is not quite clear. In *ST* III, 76, 3, Thomas quoted it as "some say" *(quidam dicunt)*. In his *Commentary on the Sentences* IV, 10, 3 (*Opera* [Venice, 1780], 12, p. 198), he cited Augustine as the source, as did Alexander of Hales in his *Summa Theologiae* IV, 10 (Venice, 1575, p. 195c). Augustine, however, did not use such an image. Two theologians who did employ the analogy were Innocent III (ca. 1160–1216), *De Sacra Altaris Mysterio* IV, 8; *PL* 217, 861, and William of Auxerre (ca. 1150–1231), *Summa Aurea* (Paris, 1500), fol. 259d, quoted in Joseph Strake, *Die Sakramentenlehre des Wilhelm von Auxerre* (Paderborn, 1917), pp. 130–31, n. 2. Lombard did not mention this image at all. Thomas rejected the use of the mirror image. His reasoning was: "The multiplication of these images occurs in the broken mirror as the result of many different reflections in the different pieces, but here it is one consecration that is the sole cause of Christ's body being in the sacrament" (*St* III, 76, 3); trans. William Barden, *St. Thomas Aquinas Summa Theologiae* 58, *The Eucharistic Presence* (New York, 1965), p. 103.

15. Ibid., 74, 5; *SCG* IV, 69, p. 531. Note that the wine was of secondary importance, reflecting the custom of offering only the bread to the laity; *ST* III, 80, 12.

16. Cf. John 6:56.

17. The question of the status of the wicked priest's offering of mass was a com-

mon topic. Besides *Sent.* IV, Dist. 13, 1, cols. 867–68, cf. *ST* III, 82, 5, 7.

18. *ST* III, 78, 4.

19. This calculation was based on Jer. *Berakhot* 9:1 (13a); there are 500 years from the earth to the first firmament, each firmament (of seven) is a 500 years' journey, each firmament is 500 years from the next, and then there is an additional 515 years to the heavens. This adds up approximately to 8,000 years. Cf. Posnanski, pp. 172–73, n. 5.

20. אחד מעיקרי דתם אשר יסדוהו המטעים הוא כי ישו באותה הכמות אשר נתלה בה יבוא ויחול תוך איזו כמות שתהיה מן הלחם העשוי מן החטה ושיפשיט הלחם הצורה הלחמית ויקבל גשם ישו כולו ויישארו עם זה מקרי הלחם עומדים בעצמם בזולת נושא האיכות והכמות וזולתו, והוא הוא בעצמו היושבי בשמים ואשר בא אל הבמה עם השארו שם. והוא הוא האחד בעצמו במקומות מתחלפים, והוא הוא המתנועע בעצמו בבמה בכמה מקומות והוא בשמים, ובאיזה חלק שייחלק מן הלחם יימצא כולו על הכמות אשר נתלה בה, כעניין מראה הנשברת אשר בכל חלק ממנה תימצא תמונת המביט בה בכללה, ועל דרך זה יימצא ביין העצור מן הענבים הנקרב בבמה, ועם אכילת הלחם הזה ושתיית היין הזה יתאחד גוף ישו עם גוף האוכלו והשותהו ויעמוד ככה עצור תוך בטנו עד אשר יפסדו מקרי הלחם הנשארים אחרי הפסד צורתו. וזה אמנם יימצא לדעתם בלחם ויין אחר שייאמרו עליהם מאמרים מה על פי הכומר המקריב המיוחד לעבודה זו גדול או קטון חכם או סכל צדיק או רשע כי הממלא מקום ישו בארץ והוא האפיפיור כביר כח לתת לכל כומר הכח הזה כי הסגולה היא דבקה במאמרים ההם להוריד גוף המשיח משמי שמי קדם ולהביאו ממרחק ממקום מהלך שמונת אלפים שנה בשעה אחת אל הבמה ובבמות בלתי תכלית עם היותו יושב שם שקט ושאנן.

21. *'Iqqarim,* trans. Husik, p. 232. Though this exposition is a faithful rendition of the Christian doctrine, it is possible that Albo did not have a full understanding of the Eucharist, because he said that the bread and wine were not a sacrifice. The use of the Eucharist as a sacrifice as well as a sacrament was well attested in Christian sources (e.g., *Sent.* IV, Dist. 12, 7, cols. 866–67; *ST* III, 83, 1; for the Catholic-Protestant debate on the sacrificial nature of the Eucharist, cf. Francis Clark, *Eucharistic Sacrifice and the Reformation* [London, 1960]). It is possible that Albo meant his statement that the Eucharist was not a sacrifice to be an argument against the mass rather than a description of it. If so, it compares with the argument made by Abraham Farissol that the bread and wine should not be considered a sacrifice since nothing is being sacrificed to God; *Magen Avraham,* chap. 37, fol. 37b:
אבל במעשה לחם ויין שהם מגישים על מזבחותם אינו נראה לעין השכל שיקרא קרבן ושיצדק עליו שם קרבן יען כי אינם מקריבים דבר לה׳ וגם ה׳ לא יקחנו.

22. *Biṭṭul 'Iqqare Ha-Noẓrim,* fol. 3a.

23. *Even Boḥan,* XII:4 (other recension, XV), fols. 155a–b.

24. *Magen Avot,* I:3, published in *Keshet U-Magen,* p. 26a.

25. *Hoda'at Ba'al Din,* p. 23.

26. *Vikuaḥ,* p. 451.

27. *Magen Avraham,* 20, fols. 24a–b.

28. *Ḥerev Pifiyot,* pp. 78–83.

29. *Kur Maẓref,* pp. 19a–b; his description was taken from Albo.

30. *Pilpul,* p. 33.

31. *Asham Talui Ḥeleq Sheni,* JTSA ms. 2232, fol. 26b. Segré lived in the eighteenth century.

32. Fols. 45a–47a; this account is an almost verbatim copy of Shem Tov ibn Shapruṭ's *Even Boḥan.*

33. Fol. 4b.

34. *Sent.*, Dist. 11, 3, col. 862: "Mysterium fidei credi salubriter potest, investigari salubriter non potest."

35. *Sermones de Festivitatibus Christi* (Hagenau, 1510), 19C; quoted in Heiko A. Obermann, *The Harvest of Medieval Theology* (Cambridge, Mass., 1963), p. 272, n. 86: "Apud quem [deum] non est impossibile omne verbum, qui de nihilo mundum creavit et in nihilum cum placeret redigere potest." For a modern restatement of this idea, cf. J. Pohle, "Eucharist," *Catholic Encyclopedia,* V (New York, 1909), p. 573: "By the very fact that the Eucharistic mystery does transcend reason, no rationalistic explanation of it, based on a merely natural hypothesis and seeking to comprehend one of the sublimest truths of the Christian religion as the spontaneous conclusion of logical processes, may be attempted by a Catholic theologian."

36. P. 173:
והנה הם ידחו כל ספק כשיאמרו כי העניין האלהי הוא למעלה מהשכל האנושי וכי יד השכל קצרה מהשיג אלה התעלומות והרזים הגדולים והנסתרים והנעלמים כי אחרי שישו אמר זה ויסד השורש הזה עליו אין להרהר אחריו כי הוא האמת הגמור וכי בסיבת סודות הדת האמונה בטוחה והחקירה מסוכנת.
Cf. Posnanski's n. 5 for Lombard source.

37. As Duran stated, his method in his *Iggeret* was much different.

38. *Even Boḥan,* XII:5, fols. 155a–157a.

39. *Magen Avraham,* chap. 20, fols. 24a–25a. Both of these authors also used rational arguments, again drawing from Duran.

40. *SCG* IV, 63, p. 526; trans. O'Neill, IV, p. 257. In fact, the use of philosophy, both realist, by Thomas and his school, and nominalist, by Ockham and his followers, was a common practice in discussions of transubstantiation.

41. *Denz.*, no. 430.

42. Ibid., nos. 873a–893.

43. Cf., e.g., Macdonald, op. cit., pp. 258–62; J. H. Strawley, "Eucharist (to end of Middle Ages)," in Hastings, *Encyclopedia of Religion and Ethics* (New York, 1914), V, p. 554. It should be remembered that both sides of the issue quoted Augustine for support.

44. He was called the first to hold this error by Thomas, *ST* III, 75, 1. Cf. Berengarius' *De Sacra Coena,* ed. W. H. Beekenkamp (The Hague, 1941). For literature on Berengarius, see Macdonald, op. cit., and especially the extensive bibliography, pp. 415–30. For anti-Berengarian literature, cf. *PL* 219, 857–58, index: "Libri de Eucharistia Tractantes."

45. E.g., in *Liber De Mysteriis, PL* 16, 403–26, on the Eucharist, chaps. 8–9, cols. 419–26; and *De Sacramentiis,* ibid., cols. 435–82, especially bks. 4–6, cols. 455–82.

46. The term "transubstantiation" was first used by Hildebert of Tours, *Sermones de Diversis* VI, "Ad Sacerdotes," *PL* 171, 771–76 ("transubstantionis," col. 776). As a verb, it was first used by Stephen of Autun, *Tractatus de Sacramento*

Altaris, PL 172, 1273–1308, cf. col. 1293. Both of these authors were from the early twelfth century. Lombard and Hugh of Saint Victor, one of Lombard's chief sources, did not use the term (in the same century). The description of the two traditions is obviously simplistic. The literature on the subject is extensive. Besides Macdonald, op. cit., cf. Charles E. Sheedy, *The Eucharistic Controversy of the Eleventh Century against the Background of Pre-Scholastic Theology* (Washington, 1947), and Josef R. Geiselmann, *Die Eucharistielehre der Vorscholastik,* Forschungen zur christlischen Literatur und Dogmengeschichte, vol. 15, nos. 1–3 (Paderborn, 1926).

47. *Denz.*, no. 430.

48. Ibid., no. 544.

49. The literature on this topic is enormous. Cf., e.g., Kilian McDonnell, *John Calvin, the Church, and the Eucharist* (Princeton, 1967), bibliography, pp. 383–400.

50. Cf. above. It was the work of Berengarius that caused the Church to formulate its Eucharistic doctrine explicitly.

51. Profiat Duran appears to be the first in his *Iggeret Al Tehi Ke-'Avotekha.* Earlier, nonphilosophical arguments can be found. The anonymous author of *Niẓẓaḥon Yashan* asked how the priest could think that the bread and wine, which he had made, could possibly be God; p. 76. Joseph Ha-Meqanneh quoted scriptural objections to the mass, e.g., Hos. 9:4; *Sefer Yosef Ha-Meqanneh,* p. 85. Cf. also Meir ben Simeon, *Milḥemet Miẓvah,* fols. 98a–b.

52. Cf. Herbert Thurston, "Exposition of the Blessed Sacrament," *Catholic Encyclopedia,* V (New York, 1909), pp. 713–14. One argument against this theory is that the Jewish polemicists of this period did not connect host worship with idolatry. If, indeed, the exposition of the host were the cause of this new interest in transubstantiation, it would seem logical that such a connection be made. Accusations of idolatry against host adoration were made almost contemporaneously in England by John Wyclif (in *De Eucharistia,* ed. Johann Loserth [London, 1892]; cf. McDonnell, op. cit., pp. 55–57). Such an accusation was also made by a later Jewish writer, Isaac of Troki (16th cent.). Cf. *Ḥizzuk Emunah,* I:2, p. 39:

ואפי׳ בבתי עבודתם עדיין לא פסקו עצבי כסף וזהב ופסילי עץ ואבן ובפרט פסילי הלחם שהם עובדים ומשתחוים להם כפי מה שהורגל מקדמת דנא.

Cf. also I:50, p. 280. Solomon ibn Verga described a celebration of a Feast with a procession of cross and host in *Shevet Yehuda,* p. 123.

53. Cf. Baer, *History,* II, pp. 38–39. On host desecrations, see Cecil Roth, "Host, Desecration of," *EJ,* VIII, pp. 1040–44. Roth connected the proliferation of host desecration libels with the statement on transubstantiation of the Fourth Lateran Council, 1215; cf. *Denz.*, no. 430. There were, however, earlier Christian warnings against Jewish access to the host. Cf. Blumenkranz, "Les Auteurs Chrétiens," *REJ* 114 (1955): 45–46, 87–89.

54. *Kelimat Ha-Goyim,* p. 174: כבר הרגישו קצתם בחלשותו.

55. Ratramnus (9th cent.) was the first to distinguish between *figura* and *veritas* in the Eucharist. Cf. *De Corpore et Sanguine Domini, PL* 121, 103–70, and ed. Van den Brink (Amsterdam, 1954).

56. *Commentary on the Iggeret*, p. 88:
וזה אין בו ספק אצלם ואין משימין לזה צורה אבל יאמינוהו כפשוטו והסובר בו סברות ממנו יאמרו כי הוא מין ואפיקורוס.

57. Pp. 84–128.

58. Ibid., p. 78: אל תהי כאבותיך אשר הביאם יסודות השכל להודות בהתחלות העייוניות למודיות טבעיות אלהיות.

Though the context here was not that of transubstantiation, this theme was picked up in the next section, where the Eucharist was the topic. This categorization of the principles that were in conflict with the Eucharistic doctrine might be compared with Wyclif's statement that transubstantiation "subverts Grammar, Logic, all natural science and even (which is still worse) . . . completely destroys the sense of the Gospel," *Trialogus*, p. 261, cited in *De Eucharistia*, p. iii.

59. *'Iqqarim*, III, p. 232.

60. *Vikuaḥ*, p. 451.

61. *Beḥinat Ha-Dat*, pp. 12–13. Del Medigo stated that the doctrines of Trinity and incarnation were in conflict with first principles.

62. P. 175:
שרשים חולקים על טבע המציאות ומכחישים המוחשות וחולקים על המושכלות הראשונים.

63. *Magen Avraham*, fol. 24b:
הנה הוא מבואר הביאור שכלו חולק כנגד השכל וכנגד המושכל והמפורסם וכנגד האמת.

64. E.g., Crescas and Simon Duran, op. cit.

65. *Physics* 4, 1, 208b, 6–8; trans. R. P. Hardie and R. K. Gaye, in *The Basic Works of Aristotle*, ed. R. McKeon, (New York, 1941), pp. 269–70.

66. Ibid., 8, 216a, 26–216b, 12. Cf. H. A. Wolfson, *Crescas' Critique*, pp. 146–49, 342–43.

67. *On Generation and Corruption* 1, 5, 321a, 8–10. This reference and the one from *Physics* 4, 1, were given by Joseph ben Shem Tov, *Commentary on the Iggeret*, op. cit., p. 68; cf. Posnanski's notes.

68. *Iggeret*, p. 84: יכנס העולם כלו בגרגיר חרדל.
On the use of this phrase, cf. Wolfson, *Crescas' Critique*, pp. 342–43.

69. *'Iqqarim*, trans. Husik, p. 233. The reference to quantity most likely was an allusion to the problem of the disparate sizes of the body of Jesus and the host.

70. *Iggeret*, p. 84: כי לפי האמונה גוף המשיח הגדול ישוב לכמות העוגה הקטנה ככף איש ואפשר הוא האמן בו שיכנס העולם כלו בגרגיר חרדל.

71. *ST* III, 76, 1; trans., Barden, p. 93. Cf. also *SCG* IV, 62, p. 525.

72. Ibid., trans., p. 97.

73. *Even Boḥan*, fol. 156b.

74. *Magen Avot* I:3 in *Keshet U-Magen*, p. 26b.

75. *On the Heavens* 1, 2–3.

76. This phrase was borrowed from the well-known prayer *Asher Yaẓar* (*Authorized Daily Prayer Book*, ed. Joseph H. Hertz, rev. ed. [New York, 1952], p. 10). The sarcastic intent is obvious.

77. *Iggeret,* p. 94:
ואל תאמן מהמנע מהגרם השמיימי התנועה הישרה. ולזה תמנע אצלו הקריעה וגם כן השבירה. כי תמיד כל היום לא יחשה גשם המשיח בעלותו ורדתו דרך ישרה יעשהו נקבים נקבים חלולים חלולים בוא יבוא עד שמיום עלותו שמים ועד עתה סביב אלף ושלש מאות וששים שנה. קרוב הוא שנעשה כל גופו ככברה או ימחץ וירפאהו בזולת סמים מדביקים אך ברצונו לבד או באמירה.

78. *Biṭṭul,* fol. 16a. Joseph ben Shem Tov, the translator, also referred to "neqavim, ḥalulim."

79. *'Iqqarim,* p. 232.

80. *Biṭṭul,* fol. 16a: *guf 'ilui glorifiqa'do.* See Crescas' refutation below.

81. *Commentary on the Iggeret,* p. 98.

82. *Tractatus Guilhermi Parisiensis De Sacramentis Cur Deus Homo,* 1496, fol. 26a: "In quo respondeo: non per motum qualis corporis, i.e. transitum continuum . . . Et hic effectus unus est dotis corporis glorificatorum qui nominatur agilitas—To which I respond: this is not through bodily motion, i.e., continuous movement . . . But this is one of the effects of the bodily quality which is called the agility of glorification." Cf. also Salvatore Bonano, *The Concept of Substance and the Development of Eucharistic Theology to the Thirteenth Century* (Washington, 1960), p. 25.

83. *Commentary on Sententiae,* IV, Dist. 11, 1; in 1491 ed., par. 4: "Sed corpus christi cum sit gloriosum simul cum pane potest esse."

84. Cf. Bonano, op. cit., p. 39. Albertus also referred to the "corpus gloriosum" of Christ in his *De Sacramentis,* V, 1, Q.1, A.2, and Q.4, A.1, in *Opera Omnia,* 26 (Aschendorff, 1958), pp. 51, 62.

85. Cf. C. J. Corcoran, "Glorified Body," *New Catholic Encyclopedia,* VI (New York, 1967), pp. 512–13; A. Choller, "Corps Glorieux," *Dictionnaire de Théologie Catholique,* III (Paris, 1908), pp. 1879–1906. The basic New Testament source for this belief is 1 Cor. 15. Cf. also Phil. 3:21. Cf. also *ST* III, supp., Q.81–87.

86. *Commentary on the Iggeret,* p. 98:
וכי אף לאחרי תחייתם יזכו כולם להיות גופם על זה האופן.

87. *Biṭṭul,* fol. 16a:
וזה מהעניינים הנאמרים בדברים מבהילים ואין להם לא מציאות ולא צייור שכלי כלל.

88. *Biṭṭul,* fol. 15a. The relationship between virgin birth and the Eucharist was also assumed by Christians, e.g., Hugh of Saint Victor, *Summa Sententiarum,* VI, 4, *PL* 176, 141. Cf. A. J. Macdonald, "Berengar and the Virgin Birth," *JThS* 30 (1929): 291–94, especially p. 293, where other references are given.

89. For Crescas' belief in the necessity of a body having extension (three-dimensionality), cf. Wolfson, *Crescas' Critique,* pp. 261, 590–91.

90. והוא שהגשם המתעלה אשר יקראו גלוריפיקאדו לא ירצו בו שהו׳ גשם בלתי מרחקי׳ שא״כ היה גשם ולא גשם. ואם יש לו מרחקים לא יעבור בין דברים אין ביניהם מרחקים כמו שהוא צדדי רחם הבתולה וזה מבואר שיביא זה אל סתירה שהיו שם מרחקים שלא יהיו שם מרחקים. אבל אם אפשר שיכנס זה הגשם הגלוריפיקאדו בגשם אחר לא יהיה נעדר המרחקי׳ אחר שהמרחקי׳ נכנסי׳ בגדרו, אבל יאמינו כי (כי) יהיה זה כיכנסו מרחקי הגשם במרחקי הגשם האחר עם שהוא נמנע גמור שישובו שתי אמות אמה ויהיה החלק כמו הכל ויהיה אפשר שיכנס העולם בגרגיר חרדל.

91. *Commentary on the Iggeret*, pp. 98–100. He quoted *On the Heavens* 1, 1, *Physics* 4, and the definitions at the beginning of Euclid's *Elements*.

92. *Magen Avraham*, fol. 25a:
אולם בירידת גוף המשיח שלהם כלו בגוף הלחם וביד כל לחם ולחם מכהני המשיח ובכל הבמות הוא הפך זה כי אמונת ההרכבה הזאת היא הרכבה גופנית ממש מגוף מפואר אלקי אל גוף בלתי מפואר לפאר אותו וישוב הגוף שהוא בלתי מפואר להיות גוף מפואר אלקי או הגוף מפואר האלקי להיות גם הוא בלתי מפואר עם היות נשאר תמיד ג״כ ממשי חמרי מקמח ומים ויאכל הכהן את הגוף ההוא המפואר עם חלקי מקרי הלחם אם שניהם כלו אלוק אחד הוא.

93. *Iggeret*, p. 94: בחר לך אחת מאלה אשר תראה יותר חולקת על המושכל וטבע היצירה.

94. *Metaphysics* 10, 1, 1053a, 31. Cf. Euclid's *Elements*, bk. VII, def. 2.

95. *Iggeret*, pp. 84–86:
ושמספר גשמי המשיח אשר בבמות מתחלפות לאלפים ולרבבות ומאות אינו קבוץ אחדים אבל העשרה והמאה והאלף והאחד כולו אחד.

96. *Even Boḥan*, fol. 156b.

97. *De Sacra Coena*, p. 109; cf. Macdonald, *Berengar and the Reform*, p. 310. It is possible that the origin of this argument was Plato's *Parmenides*, 131. The question there was how the one form can participate in many objects simultaneously.

98. This phraseology, though presumably in incorrect order, was also found in *Iggeret*, p. 84.

99. *Biṭṭul*, fol. 16a:
כי כאשר יאמ׳ שהאלהים הבן נשא׳ שם על השמים עם היותו שם ביד הכומר, שיהיה מקומות מתחלפי׳ רבים בעת אחת וכמו שנראה אותו בבמות לאלפים ולרבבות ולמאו׳ יתרבו האלוקות או יהיה גשם א׳ בעצמו במקומות רבים בעת אחד.

100. *'Iqqarim*, trans., Husik, p. 232.

101. *Magen Avraham*, fol. 24b:
איך יתכן להאמין שישוב ברגע א׳ עצם א׳ נפרד כלו מקובץ בכמה עצמים נפרדים אחרים ובכמה מקומות נפרדות.

102. *Mishneh Torah, Sefer Madda'*, H. Yesode Ha-Torah, I:8.

103. *ST* III, 75, 1, trans., p. 55.

104. *SCG* IV, 62, p. 525; trans., p. 255.

105. In Jewish literature, this exchange is recorded in Farissol's *Magen Avraham*, fols. 24a–25a. Yom-Tov Lipmann Mühlhausen mentioned this Christian objection without relating it to transubstantiation; cf. *Sefer Niẓẓaḥon*, pp. 19–20. In Christian literature, this argument has been preserved in the fifteenth-century Hans Folz, *Die Reimpaarsprüche*, ed. Hanns Fischer, Münchener Texte und Untersuchungen zur deutschen Literatur des Mittelalters, bd. 1 (Munich, 1961), quoted in H. H. Ben-Sasson, "Jewish-Christian Disputation in the Setting of Humanism and Reformation in the German Empire," *HThR* 59 (1966): 375–76; and in the sixteenth-century F. Machado, *Espellio de Christãos Novos*, Ms. National Library of Lisbon F.G. 6747, fol. 44. I owe the latter reference to Prof. Frank Talmage. The Christian polemical use of the Jewish image of Elijah warrants a separate study.

106. *ST* III, 75, 7.

107. *Physics* 4, 11, and 6, 4; cf. *On the Heavens* 1, 6, 273a, 21–274a, 18, and

Wolfson, *Crescas' Critique*, pp. 144–47, 341–42.

108. *Iggeret*, p. 86.

109. *Biṭṭul*, fol. 15b.

110. *'Iqqarim*, III, p. 232.

111. *Biṭṭul*, fol. 15b:

ואינו אפשר שיהיה נברא שם למה שיתחייב שהאלהים יהיה נברא ושיהיה נפסד ובטולים אחרים רבים.

112. *SCG* IV, 63, p. 526.

113. *Iggeret*, p. 86.

114. *Physics* 5, 5–6.

115. *Iggeret*, p. 100.

116. *Metaphysics* 3, 2, 996b, 29: 4, 4, 1005b, 36. Cf. 4, 4, 1007b, 18: contradictories cannot be predicted at the same time. In 4, 2, 1004b, 28, rest is described as the contrary of motion.

117. *Even Boḥan*, fol. 156b.

118. *Magen Avot*, in *Keshet U-Magen*, p. 26a.

119. *ST* III, 76, 6; trans., p. 113. Ockham presented this problem in the opposite manner, namely, the body of Christ was at rest on the altar and moving in the heavens to other altars; cf. Buescher, op. cit., pp. 115–16.

120. *ST*, ibid.

121. This theme runs throughout *De Sacra Coena*, e.g., pp. 41–42, 110–12, 117–18, 126–27; Cf. Macdonald, *Berengar and the Reform*, pp. 316–20.

122. Op. cit., in passim, e.g., pp. 51–52, 62–69, 132–36.

123. *Metaphysics* 5, 8, 1017b, 24.

124. *Posterior Analytics* 1, 4, 73b, 9.

125. *Metaphysics* 7, 2, 1028b, 32; cf. *Physics* 1, 4, 188a, 6–9.

126. *Iggeret*, p. 100. Joseph ben Shem Tov, p. 106, quoted *Physics* 1, 9, concerning the impossibility that the material substratum cease to be.

127. *Biṭṭul*, fol. 16a:

כאשר יעלה אל השמים ישארו המקרים שהם איכיות העוגה גוונה ריחה תמונתה טעמה וזולתם עומדים בעצמם בלא נושא וזה דבר נגד כל טבע ויכולת.

128. *Magen Avot* in *Keshet U-Magen*, p. 26b. For the Mu'tazilite background, see Maimonides, *Guide*, I:73:10.

129. *Even Boḥan*, fol. 157a.

130. *'Iqqarim*, p. 233.

131. *ST* III, 75, 5.

132. Ibid., 77, 1; trans., p. 125.

133. *SCG* IV, 62, p. 525.

134. See above.

135. *Iggeret*, p. 108: חוש הראות לא יטעה במושגיו כל זמן שיהיה הכלי בריא והאמצעי נאות.

136. *Even Boḥan*, fol. 157a.

137. *'Iqqarim*, p. 233.

138. *Beḥinat Ha-Dat*, pp. 12–13:

החושים כלם יחד טועים במוחש מה מיוחד, רצוני לומר חושי האנשים כלם ובכל הזמנים.

139. Ibid.; Reggio has censored the passage concerned from p. 16. Cf. Julius Guttmann, "Elia del Medigos," p. 202. The correct text is:
ואולם שיקבצו הסותרים מבואר ממאמרם המפורסם באחדות האל ואולם שיכחישו המוחש ויניחו יתר הענינים אשר ספרנום מבואר מענין קרבנם.

140. *De Sacramentiis* IV, 4 (20), *PL* 16, 462: "Sed forte dicis: Speciem sanguinis non video."

141. *De Sacra Coena,* p. 95.

142. *Sent.*, IV, Dist. 12, 2, col. 865.

143. Op. cit., p. 20, cf. p. 78.

144. *ST* III, 75, 5; cf. 77, 1.

145. *SCG* IV, 62, quoting *On the Soul* 3, 6, 430b, 29.

146. *Physics* 1, 5, 188a, 31–188b, 2; cf. *On Generation* 1, 6.

147. *Metaphysics* 3, 4.

148. *Iggeret,* p. 100.

149. Ibid.

150. *Biṭṭul,* fol. 16a:
יזונו המקרים ההם וזה דבר יראה בנסיון אכל יאכל הכהן עוגה א׳ גדולה שיהיה נזון וישובו המקרים עצם ר״ל האברים כדין כל זן.

151. *Even Boḥan,* fol. 157a.

152. *Magen Avot* in *Keshet U-Magen,* p. 26b.

153. *'Iqqarim,* p. 233. Cf. Thomas, who admitted that the accidents did nourish, *ST* III, 77, 6.

154. *Beḥinat Ha-Dat,* p. 13. Reggio explained that del Medigo was referring to nominalist philosophy.

155. *Magen Avraham,* fol. 24b: ואיך יתכן שישוב העצם מקרה והמקרה עצם.

156. *ST* III, 75, 4.

157. *Beḥinat Ha-Dat,* p. 13.

158. *ST* III, 75, 6. Thomas stated, quoting Aristotle, *On the Soul* 2, 4, 416b, 12, that food gave nourishment only insofar as it was substance.

159. Ibid., and A.5.

160. *Iggeret,* p. 108. Joseph ben Shem Tov, p. 112, based this argument on Euclid's *Elements,* bk. I, common notion no. 5. It may have its origins in Plato's *Parmenides,* 145.

161. *Magen Avot* in *Keshet U-Magen,* p. 26b.

162. *Even Boḥan,* fol. 156b.

163. *Magen Avraham,* fol. 24b.

164. *Guide,* III:15.

165. Ibid., I:73:10. Notice that one of the impossible items cited there is the existence of accidents without a subject. Cf. above chap. 3.

166. *Iggeret,* pp. 114–16:
ובכלל אחי לא תודה חלילה לך בהקדמה האומרת לנמנע טבע קיים קיום עומד אי איפשר לו השתנותו ולכל הנמנעות בחוק השכל והטבע הנזכרות וכהנה רבות לא אדע ספורות תהיינה מחשבותיך אמונות השלט יכולת המשיח על כל דבר קרוב או רחוק איפשר או נמנע הכזב מה שלא בא על סותרו מופתו האמן במחוייב כי שוא תהיה תמורתו.

167. *Beḥinat Ha-Dat*, pp. 16–17:
ואם יאמר אומר הנכם גם אתם אומרים שהאל יכול על כל דבר ואם כן יתכן מציאות קצת מאלה, נשיב שאנחנו בעלי הדת לא נאמר שיתואר השם ביכולת על הסותרים ולא על החולפים אבל נאמר שלא יחפוץ בם כלל.

168. *Biṭṭul*, fol. 16a: בכל מקום אפשר לברא בן האלהים ובכל מקום אפשר הפסדו.

Chapter Seven

1. Ḥasdai Crescas, *Biṭṭul*, fol. 2b:
האמונה נצרית היא שהבתולים בשום זמן לא נקרעו לא בזמן הלידה ולא לפניו ולא לאחריו.
Cf. Augustine, *Sermo* CXCV, *PL* 39, 2107: "Maria virgo ante partum, virgo in partu, virgo post partum." See also Thomas, *ST* III, Q.28; the first three questions to be considered about Mary are: (1) utrum fuerit virgo in concipiendo Christum, (2) utrum fuerit virgo in partu, and (3) utrum permansuerit virgo post partum. The answer to all three questions is in the affirmative.

2. *Ḥagigah* 14b–15a: בתולה שעיברה.

3. *Magen Avraham*, chap. 11, fols. 14b–15a:
הנה אנחנו לא נוכל לכחש בה האפשרות בו י"ת לברוא בריאה א' בתוך בתולה ואפי' לא ידעה איש אחר אשר ברא כל יש מן האין הגמור אבל נכחש שאין צורך ההגשמה.

4. The name usually associated with this belief is Helvidius (ca. 382), against whom Jerome wrote *De Perpetua Virginitate B. Mariae Adversus Helvidium*, *PL* 23, 193–216. Tertullian, who did not agree that Mary remained a virgin *in partu*, stated that she led a normal married life; cf. *De Monogamia* 8, *PL* 2, 939. Defenders of Mary's virginity *post partum* included Pope Siricius (*Letter to Anysius*, *Denz.*, 91), Ambrose (*De Institutione Virginis*, *PL* 16, 319–48), and Augustine (*Sermo* CXCV, *PL* 39, 2107). For Ambrose's attitude toward Mary, see Charles W. Neumann, *The Virgin Mary in the Works of Saint Ambrose* (Freiburg, 1962). For a general history of Marian theology, see Hilda Graef, *Mary: A History of Doctrine and Devotion*, 2 vols. (New York, 1963–65).

5. A typical and comprehensive treatment of New Testament sources concerning Mary was given by Profiat Duran, *Sefer Kelimat Ha-Goyim* 9, *Ha-Ẓofeh*, 4, pp. 43–45. He quoted Matt. 1:25, 12:47, 13:54–57, and John 2:1–4, 19:26–27, to prove that Joseph had marital relations with Mary and that Jesus had siblings (and that devotion to Mary had no New Testament basis). The Christians were well aware that the implications of these and other verses contradicted their dogma, necessitating an exegesis that was not in conflict with doctrine. Cf., e.g., Thomas, *ST* III, 28, 3.

Of interest in this connection is the Jewish-Christian debate over the meaning in Matt. 1:25 of *donec* (Greek ἕως, Hebrew *'ad*, "until") compared with Gen. 49:10, the Shiloh passage. The Jewish argument was to the effect that if *'ad* in the latter passage (Septuagint ἕως, Vulgate *donec*) meant the end of Judah's dominion after Shiloh comes, the *donec* in Matthew should mean the end of Mary's virginity after the birth of Jesus. Cf. Duran, op. cit., p. 44; Isaac Troki, *Ḥizzuk Emunah*, II:3, p. 288; De

Modena, *Magen Va-Ḥerev,* p. 61; Aaron Ḥayyim Voltera?, *Makkot Li-Khesil Me'ah,* fol. 2b; and others.

6. The literature on the subject is extensive; cf. Graef, op. cit., vol. 1, bibliography, pp. 356–61.

7. *De Carne Christi* 23, ed. Ernest Evans, *Tertullian's Treatise on the Incarnation* (London, 1956), pp. 74–79.

8. *Homilies on Luke* 14, *PG* 13, 1836–37; cf. n. 40. Cf. also Graef, op. cit., pp. 43–46, Neumann, op. cit., p. 111.

9. *Epistola ad Epictetus* 5, *PG* 26, 1057; cf. Graef, op. cit., pp. 51–53.

10. Op. cit., p. 76: "Nam nupsit ipsa patefacti corporis lege, in quo nihil interfuit de vi masculi admissi an emissi; iden illud sexus resignavit."

11. Ibid., pp. 4–7. Tertullian stated explicitly that Marcion's denial of the real nativity and the real flesh were intertwined.

12. Cf. Graef, op. cit., pp. 41–42, and Neumann, op. cit., p. 110.

13. Trans., J. H. Bernard, *Studies and Texts,* 8:3 (Cambridge, 1912), p. 86.

14. M. R. James, *The Apocryphal New Testament* (Oxford, 1924), pp. 46–47.

15. Trans. R. H. Charles (London, 1900), p. 76.

16. *Homiliae VIII in Hexaemeron* 7, *PG* 29, 180, Graef, pp. 62–64.

17. E.g., *Oratio in Diem Natalem Christi, PG* 46, 1136, Graef, pp. 64–68.

18. Op. cit., Graef, pp. 89–94, Neumann, pp. 142–52.

19. See Neumann, op. cit., pp. 105–77 for a full treatment.

20. *Sermo* CXCV, *PL* 39, 2107; Graef, pp. 94–100.

21. Cf. Neumann's long discussion of the problem, op. cit., pp. 105–77.

22. *Denz.,* no. 256: "Incorruptibiliter eam genuisse, indissolubili permanente et post partum eiusdem virginitate." For various Church documents concerning Mary, see Paul F. Parmer, *Mary in the Documents of the Church* (Westminster, Md., 1952).

23. *De Eo Quod Christus ex Virgine Natus Est, PL* 121, 81–102.
There is evidence that this question of the manner of Jesus' birth was known to some Jewish polemicists. The author of *Vikuaḥ Radaq* asked why, if the impregnation was through the ear, parturition was not through the same organ. In fact, the Bogomils believed that both impregnation and parturition were through the ear, while the Cathars held this for impregnation only. Cf. *Vikuaḥ Radaq,* p. 86; trans., Frank Talmage, "An Hebrew Polemical Treatise," p. 341. A much later author, Isaac Lupis (1695), stated that according to Christian sages the Holy Spirit entered through the brain, and hence Jesus should have exited thereby or through Mary's mouth. See *Kur Maẓref,* p. 2b.

24. *Opusculum de Partu Virginis, PL* 120, 1365–86. There is some disagreement about the relation between the works of Ratramnus and Radbertus. The problem is whether the latter wrote in response to the former's work or in reaction to other current beliefs. See E. Dublanchy, "Marie," *Dictionnaire de Théologie Catholique,* IX (Paris, 1927), pp. 2382–83, and Graef, op. cit., pp. 176–80. Ratramnus and Radbertus figured strongly in the Eucharistic controversy of the ninth century. On the connections between the dogmas of transubstantiation and virgin birth, see the

preceding chapter and the discussion below on the interpenetrability of bodies. Cf. also, A. J. Macdonald, "Berengar and the Virgin Birth." Macdonald argues that Berengarius' rejection of the real presence was not accompanied by a denial of virgin birth *in partu.*

25. *Sermo* IV, *PL* 157, 249: "Quod matrem Domini et ante partum et post partum praedicant quidem virginem, sed portam ventris ejus apertam in suo partu, et post partum statim clausam fuisse fotentur . . . Insanum est hoc dicere, et credere profanum."

26. Durandus a Sancto Portianus, *In Sententias Theologicae Petri Lombardi Commentariorum* (Lugduni, 1563), p. 344b: "Sed etiam propter integritatem membri corporalis, nec tamen propter hoc in nativitate Christi fuerunt duo corpora simul scilicet corpus Christi cum corpore matris, quia est alius modus possibilis, scilicet quod virtute divina fuerit facta dilatatio membrorum et meatuum naturalium sine interruptione, vel aliqua fractione."

27. Ibid.: "Quod duo corpora ex hoc quod habent duas quantitates non possunt simul esse in eodem loco."

28. Cf. Francis Suarez, *The Dignity and Virginity of the Mother of God,* trans. Richard J. Obrien (West Baden Springs, Ind., 1954), pp. 44–58; also Dublanchy, op. cit., pp. 2385–86; Joseph Koch, *Durandus de S. Porciano O.P.,* Beiträge zur Geschichte der Philosophie des Mittelalters, 26 (Munster, 1927), pp. 197–394; Joseph C. Fenton, "Our Lady's Virginity *in Partu,*" *American Ecclesiastical Review* 130 (1954): 51–53.

29. כניסת הגשמים בגשמים נמנע; Duran, *Iggeret,* p. 56. Duran presented this statement as מאמר האומר, a favorite expression of his. Cf. *Kelimah, Ha-Ẓofeh* 3, p. 102, n. 2.

30. *Commentary on the Iggeret,* p. 68.

31. *Magen Va-Ḥerev,* p. 55. De Modena's account here was taken word for word from Joseph ben Shem Tov.

32. 4, 1, 208b, 6–8.

33. 1, 5, 321a, 8–10.

34. יכנס העולם כולו בגרגיר חרדל. This phrase was used by Crescas, *Biṭṭul,* fol. 15a, Joseph ben Shem Tov, *Commentary on the Iggeret,* p. 68, and De Modena, *Magen Va-Ḥerev,* p. 55 in virgin birth contexts, and by Duran, *Iggeret,* p. 84, concerning transubstantiation. On the use of this phrase, cf. Wolfson, *Crescas' Critique,* pp. 342–43.

35. Joseph ben Shem Tov, ibid., and De Modena, ibid.

36. Ibid. Simon Duran used the same argument, saying that by accepting the virgin birth, Christians did not reject the possibility of interpenetrability—הכנסת גשם בגשם.

37. 1, 1.

38. *Biṭṭul,* fol. 15a:

א״א שיהיה בזולת מרחקים וזה מצד שהמרחקים נכנסו בגדרו כמו שנא׳ בתחלת ספר השמים והעולם שהגשם הוא אשר לו כל המרחקים ר״ל הג׳ שהם האורך והרוחב והעומק.

39. Ibid.:
הבתולה צדדי רחמה דבוקי׳ ואין ביניהם מרחקים ואם יעבור גוף בין אותם הצדדים יהיה שם מרחקים והם מרחקי הגשם העובר ויתחייב א״כ שיהיה ביניהם מרחקים וכבר הונח שאין ביניהם מרחקים זה חלוף בלתי אפשר.

40. "Phantasticum"; De Modena, op. cit., p. 55: פאנטאסטיקו.

41. *ST* III, 28, 2; trans. Thomas R. Heath, *St. Thomas Aquinas Summa Theologiae,* vol. 51, *Our Lady* (New York, 1969), p. 41.

42. Ibid.

43. Ibid.; cf. De Modena, op. cit., pp. 55–56, where this paragraph is quoted from Thomas.

44. *Biṭṭul,* fol. 15a; cf. Joseph ben Shem Tov, *Commentary on the Iggeret,* pp. 98–100, and the above chapter on transubstantiation.

45. *Magen Va-Ḥerev,* p. 55: מאושר, ר״ל גלוריפיקאדו.

46. Ibid., quoting *ST* III, 28, 2.

47. *ST,* ibid.: "Sed corpus Christi in sua conceptione non fuit gloriosum, sed passibile."

48. Ibid.; Heath's note, op. cit., p. 44, n. 13, attributes this view to Innocent III, *De Sacra Altaris Mysterio* IV, 12 (*PL* 217, 864). In that work, Innocent cited the four properties of glorified bodies: subtlety, clarity, agility, and impassibility. He attributed Jesus' acquisition of each property to a different stage in his life. Thomas rejected this, maintaining that the glorified body came only after Jesus' death.

49. "Facta sunt miraculose per virtutem divinam," *ST,* ibid., trans., p. 45.

50. "Hic si ratio quaeritur, non erit mirabile: si exemplum poscitur, non erit singulare," *Epistola* 137, 2, 8, *PL* 33, 519.

51. Cf. *Denz.,* no. 282, n. 1.

52. *Divinae Institutiones* IV, 12, *PL* 6, 478: "animalia quaedam vento et aura concipere solere omnibus notum est."

53. *Homiliae VIII in Hexaemeron, PG* 29, 180.

54. *Hexaemeron* V, 20, *PL* 14, 247–48.

55. Evodius, *Epistola III* (to Augustine), *PL* 33, 702–4. For a discussion of nonsexual reproduction, see Richard A. Beatty, "Parthenogenesis in Vertebrates," in Charles B. Metz and Alberto Monroy, eds., *Fertilization,* I (New York), 1967, pp. 413–40.

56. Op. cit., pp. 226–27.

57. Mingana, op. cit., p. 154.

58. We see this image, for instance, in Peter Damian (d. 1072), *Sermo* I, *PL* 144, 508; Bernard of Clairveaux, *Super Missus Est Homiliae* II, *PL* 183, 61–71; and Albertus Magnus, *Mariale* 34; cf. Robert J. Buschmiller, *The Maternity of Mary in the Mariology of St. Albert the Great* (Freiburg, 1959), pp. 70–71.

59. Pp. 11–12.

60. *Even Boḥan* II:1, fol. 60b.

61. *Magen Va-Ḥerev,* p. 55.

62. Fol. 14b, taken from *Even Boḥan.*

63. *Kur Maẓref,* p. 2a.

64. Jacob ben Reuben: אבן תרשיש לבנה; Ibn Shapruṭ: אבן ספיר; De Modena: ספיר או זכוכית; Lupis: זכוכית.

65. *Milḥamot Ha-Shem,* pp. 11–12:
אם תקח אבן תרשיש לבנה ותשים אותה לניצוץ השמש, תראה זריחת השמש עוברת מעבר על עבר, והאבן שלמה וקיימת שאין בה נקב.

66. *Magen Va-Ḥerev,* p. 55: כן וכ״ש אדון השמש והעולם יכול לעבור במסך רחם הבתולה בלי שיקרענה.
Cf. *Even Boḥan,* fol. 60b: ואם ככה בשמש כ״ש באדוניו שיכול לפעול ככה.

67. On the relationship between Jacob ben Reuben and Alan of Lille, see D. Berger, op. cit. Alan of Lille wrote after Jacob ben Reuben, cf. p. 38, n. 23.

68. *Contra Haereticos* III, 17, *PL* 210, 415: "Sed sicut fenestra vitrea dicitur aperiri radio solis . . . secundum sui subtilitatem naturae." For a modern source, see William Begley [A Bibliophile], *The Virgin Birth* (Edinburgh, 1905), p. 75, who stated that there was abundant authority that Jesus passed through Mary like sun through crystal.

69. *Milḥamot Ha-Shem,* pp. 13–14:
הרי אם תקח עששית אחת, ותכסה אותה בקלף לבן, ותדליק הנר בתוכה, תראה ניצוצי האור בתוכה עד למרחוק, והקלף עודנו קיים, כי דבר נראה הוא לעינים שאין להב הנר עובר בעד הקלף, שאם יעבר בו ינקבנו נקב גדול, אך חוזק המאור נוגע בצדי לבנת הקלף, שהוא לבן מאד ודק ומאיר סביביו, אך אין דרך העברה בו. ובענין זה אם תקח כוס של זכוכית ותמלאהו יין, תראה על כף היד אור כמראה היין אדמדם, והכוס עודנו שלם וקיים, שאין דרך העברה בו, אך מפני בהירת הזכוכית, שהוא בהיר ולבן, נראה מה שבתוכו מבחוץ, ואין דרך העברה נזכר עליו לעולם. וכמו כן באבן תרשיש, שיש עליה בהירות גדולה ותוקף החמה שהיא מאירה על כל דבר, אינו דין שכאשר תגיע הלת השמש על התרשיש שתזרח מכל צדדיה ותאיר על כל עבר פניה. על כן אין להשוות העברת ילוד אשה דומה להלת השמש על התרשיש, כי אין שם דרך העברה לעולם משום צד ולא משום עניין שידמה לעניין שאתה מדמה. ואם תאמר בעניין אלה המאורות שאמרתי היה ענין האלהות, זה לא יתכן, שזה נמנע מגרם, וזה בהולדו לא נמנע מגרם, ואין להשוות הבורא יתברך לכל אלה, יהי שמו מבורך.

70. Ibn Shapruṭ, fol. 61a, offered only the example of the candle surrounded by paper; De Modena, p. 55, stated that the body of the sun did not pass through the glass, only its lightness, שאין בו ממש. Lupis, p. 3a, also contrasted the incorporeal light and the corporeal body of Jesus.

71. *Kur Maẓref,* p. 22a:
ומה אוסיף עוד בביטול הדעה הזר הזה אחר שאין לו מהסברא ולא מהשכל על מה לסמוך.

Chapter Eight

1. Eastern Jewish polemicists used exact quotations or close paraphrases of their Arabic sources.

2. Profiat Duran, who most likely was baptized and lived ostensibly as a Christian, was apparently an exception. His quotations of Christian authors, e.g., Peter Lombard and Nicholas De Lyra, are too exact to have been learned by hearsay.

3. Cf. above, chap. 4. Peter Lombard and Thomas Aquinas, for instance, mentioned this doctrine but gave it little prominence.

4. E.g., the works of Peter Alfonsi, Peter of Blois, the anonymous French poet, and Nicholas De Lyra.

5. Thus, some Christians employed images of the Trinity in works against heretics. Cf. Anselm's use of the image of the Nile River in his refutation of Roscelin.

6. It is possible that the Jewish polemicists were, indeed, knowledgeable of the subtleties of Christian doctrines but chose to ignore them. Since Christian conversionary attempts and the Jewish counter-arguments were probably directed at the masses, it is to be expected that the level of discourse would not be very high. The Jewish defense was directed at the Christian attack.

7. See Talmage, "An Hebrew Polemical Treatise."

8. *Iggeret,* p. 88.

9. Louis I. Newman's *Jewish Influence on Christian Reform Movements* (New York, 1925) does not deal with these questions.

10. Cf. *Magen Va-Ḥerev,* in passim.

11. Apparently Eastern Jews did read both Christian and Muslim literature in order to understand and criticize Christianity.

12. A study of the Hebrew translations of Christian technical terms is another desideratum.

13. This is the reason why polemics were written in Hebrew, not Latin, and were directed at the anti-Jewish polemical arguments rather than at the more sophisticated philosophical presentation of Christian doctrines.

14. It is true that some Jews considered the Christian misinterpretation of the Bible more understandable, since the Latin was thought by them to be a faulty translation. Since reason, however, was considered universal, the Jews could not imagine that the Christians would disregard its dictates. Nevertheless, it cannot be asserted that the Jewish polemicists put more weight on philosophical than on other arguments.

15. Cf. Wolfson, "The Muslim Attributes," and "Extradeical and Intradeical."

Bibliography

Manuscripts.

Abner of Burgos. *Sefer Teshuvot La-Meḥaref.* Parma ms. 2440 (De Rossi 533).
Abraham Ger of Cordova. *Ẓeriaḥ Bet El.* JTSA ms. 2296.
Alatino, Azriel Petaḥya ben Moses. *Vikuaḥ.* JTSA ms. 2461.
Al-Baṣīr, Yūsuf. *Kitāb al-Muḥtawī.* JTSA ms. 3391.
Crescas, Ḥasdai. *Biṭṭul 'Iqqare Ha-Noẓrim.* JTSA ms. 2209.
———. *Or Ha-Shem.* JTSA ms. 2514.
Farissol, Abraham. *Magen Avraham.* JTSA ms. 2433.
Ha-Levi, Moses. *Ma'amar Elohi.* Bodleian ms. 1324.5.
[Ha-Yiẓhari, Mattityahu ben Moses?] *Aḥiṭov Ve-Ẓalmon.* JTSA ms. 2452.
Ibn Shapruṭ, Shem Tov. *Even Boḥan.* JTSA ms. 2426.
Joseph ben Shem Tov. *Commentary on Aristotle's Ethics.* Paris, Bibliothèque National ms. 996.
[Kevod Elohim?] Bodleian ms. 2175.
Machado, F. *Espellio de Christãos Novos.* Ms. National Library of Lisbon F.G.6747.
Meir ben Simeon. *Milḥemet Miẓvah.* Parma ms. 2749 (De Rossi 155).
[Morpugo, Samson ben Joshua Moses?] *Ḥerev Pifiyot.* JTSA ms. 2227.
Segré, Joshua. *Asham Talui Ḥeleq Sheni.* JTSA ms. 2232.
[Voltera, Aaron Ḥayyim?] *Makkot Li-Khesil Me'ah.* JTSA ms. 2214.
JTSA ms. 2207, untitled, no author.

Printed Works

Aaron ben Elijah of Nicomedia. *Ez Ḥayyim.* Edited by Franz Delitsch. Leipzig, 1841.
———. *The Tree of Life by Aaron Ben Elijah of Nicomedia.* Translated by Moses Charner. New York, 1949.
Abelard, Peter. *Introductio ad Theologiam. PL* 178, 979–1114.
———. *Theologia Christiana. PL* 178, 1113–1330.
Abravanel, Isaac. *Sefer Yeshu'ot Meshiḥo.* Koenigsberg, 1861.
Abū-l-Barakat. "La Lampe des Ténèbres." Edited by L. Villecourt et al. *Patrologia Orientalis* 20 (1929): 575–734.
Abū Qurra, Theodore. *Die Arabischen Schriften des Theodor Abū Qurra.* Edited by G. Graf. Paderborn, 1910.
———. *Les Oeuvres Arabes de Théodore Aboucara.* Edited by Constantine Bacha. Beirut, 1904.
———. *Varia Opuscula. PG* 97, 1461–1602.

Abū Rā'iṭa, Ḥabīb ibn Ḥidma. *Die Schriften des Jakobiten Ḥabīb ibn Ḥidma Abū Rā'iṭa.* Edited by G. Graf. Scriptores Arabici, 14–15. Louvain, 1951.
Alan of Lille. *De Fide Catholica contra Hareticos Liber Tertius c. Judaeos. PL* 210, 399–422.
Albalag, Isaac. *Sefer Tiqqun Ha-De'ot.* Edited by Georges Vajda. Jerusalem, 1973.
Albertus Magnus. *De Sacramentis, Opera Omnia,* 26. Aschendorff, 1958.
Albo, Joseph. *Sefer 'Iqqarim.* Edited by Isaac Husik. Philadelphia, 1929.
Alexander of Hales. *Summa Theologiae.* Venice, 1575.
Alger of Liège. *De Sacramentis Corporis et Sanguinis Dominici. PL* 180, 727–854.
Altercatio Aecclesie contra Synagogam. Edited by Bernhard Blumenkranz. *Revue du Moyen Age Latin.* Strasbourg, 1954.
Altmann, Alexander. "The Divine Attributes." In *Faith and Reason,* edited by Robert Gordis and Ruth Waxman, pp. 9–29. New York, 1973.
———. "Ma'amar be-Yiḥud Ha-Bore'." *Tarbiẓ* 27 (5718 [1957–58]): 301–9.
———. "Moses Ben Joseph Ha-Levi." *EJ,* XII, pp. 421–22.
———. *Moses Mendelssohn.* Philadelphia, 1973.
Ambrose. *De Institutione Virginis. PL* 16, 319–48.
———. *De Sacramentiis. PL* 16, 435–82.
———. *Hexaemeron. PL* 14, 133–288.
———. *Liber De Mysteriis. PL* 16, 403–26.
Anastasius of Sinai. *A Dissertation against the Jews. PG* 89, 1203–82.
Andronicus (Pseudo). *Dialogue of a Christian and a Jew against the Jews. PG* 133, 791–924.
Anselm of Canterbury. *Cur Deus Homo. PL* 158, 359–432.
———. *De Conceptu Virginali et de Peccato Originali. PL* 158, 431–64.
———. *Liber de Fide Trinitatis et de Incarnatione Verbe. PL* 158, 259–84.
———. *Monologium. PL* 158, 141–224.
———. *Proslogion. PL* 158, 223–42.
———. *Trinity, Incarnation, and Redemption.* Edited by Jasper Hopkins and Herbert Richardson. New York, 1970.
———. *Why God Became Man.* Translated by Joseph M. Colleran. Albany, New York, 1969.
Aristotle. *The Basic Works of Aristotle.* Edited by Richard McKeon. New York, 1941.
Armstrong, A. H., ed. *The Cambridge History of Later Greek and Early Medieval Philosophy.* London, 1967.
Ascension of Isaiah. Translated by R. H. Charles. London, 1900.
Athanasius. *De Decretis. PG* 25, 411–76.
———. *Epistola ad Epictetus. PG* 26, 1049–70.
———. *Oratio de Incarnatio Verbi. PG* 25, 95–198.
———. *Orationes contra Arianes. PG* 26, 9–526.
Augustine. *Contra Faustum. PL* 42, 207–518.
———. *De Trinitate. PL* 42, 815–1098.

———. *Enarratio in Psalmos. PL* 36, 67–37, 1968.
———. *Enchiridion ad Laurentium. PL* 40, 231–90.
———. *On the Trinity.* Translated by A. W. Haddan. In Whitney J. Oates, *Basic Writings of Saint Augustine,* II, pp. 667–878. New York, 1948.
———. *Sermo XIII de Tempore. PL* 39, 1997–2001.
———. *Sermo* CXCV. *PL* 39, 2107–10.
Authorized Daily Prayer Book. Edited by Joseph H. Hertz. New York, 1952.
Averroes. *Kitāb al-Kashf 'an Manāhij . . .* Edited by M. J. Müller. *Philosophie und Theologie von Averroës.* Munich, 1859.
———. *Tafsir ma ba'd at-Tabi'at.* Edited by Maurice Bouyges. III, Beirut, 1948.
———. *Tahafot at-Tahafot.* Edited by Maurice Bouyges. Beirut, 1930.
———. *Tahafut al-Tahafut (The Incoherence of the Incoherence).* Translated by Simon van den Bergh. London, 1954.
Bacher, Wilhelm. "Inedited Chapters of Jehuda Hadassi's *Eshkol Hakkofer.*" *JQR,* o.s. 8 (1896): 431–44; reprinted at end of *Eshkol Ha-Kofer,* 1971.
———. "Judeo-Christian Polemics in the Zohar." *JQR,* o.s. 3 (1891): 781–84.
Baer, Yitzhak. *A History of the Jews in Christian Spain.* Philadelphia, 1966.
———. "Le-Vikoret Ha-Vikuḥim Shel R. Yeḥiel Mi-Paris Ve-Shel R. Moshe ben Naḥman." *Tarbiẓ* 2 (5691 [1930–31]): 172–87.
———. "Rashi Ve-Ha-Meẓi'ut Ha-Historit Shel Zemano." *Tarbiẓ* 20 (5709 [1949]): 320–32.
———. "Torat Ha-Qabbalah Be-Mishnato Ha-Qeristologit Shel Avner Mi-Burgos." *Tarbiẓ* 27 (5718 [1957–58]): 278–89.
Baḥya ibn Pakuda. *The Book of Direction to the Duties of the Heart.* Translated by Menahem Mansoor. London, 1973.
———. *Kitāb al-Hidāya ila Farā'iḍ al-Qulūb.* Edited by A. S. Yahuda. Leiden, 1912.
Bandinelli, Roland [Pope Alexander III]. *Die Sentenzen Rolands nachmals Papstes Alexander III.* Edited by Ambrosius M. Gietl. Freiburg, 1891.
Al-Bāqillānī, Abū Bakr. *Kitāb al-Tamhīd.* Edited by Richard J. McCarthy. Beirut, 1957.
Baron, Salo W. *A Social and Religious History of the Jews.* Vol. V, Philadelphia, 1957, IX, Philadelphia, 1965.
Basil. *Epistola* 38. *PG* 32, 325–40.
———. *Epistola* 52. *PG* 32, 391–96.
———. *Homiliae VIII in Hexaemeron. PG* 29, 1–208.
Baumgartner, Ch. *Le Péché Originel.* Paris, 1969.
Bea, Augustin. *The Church and the Jewish People.* New York, 1966.
Beatty, Richard A. "Parthenogenesis in Vertebrates." In *Fertilization,* edited by Charles B. Metz and Alberto Monroy, I, pp. 413–40. New York, 1967.
Begley, William [A Bibliophile]. *The Virgin Birth.* Edinburgh, 1905.
Benjamin ben Moses of Rome. *Teshuvot Ha-Noẓrim.* Edited by Shlomo Ḥanokh Degel-Zahav. *Koveẓ 'al Yad* 15 (1899).
Ben-Sasson, Ḥayyim Hillel. "Disputations and Polemics." *EJ,* VI, pp. 79–103.
———. "Jewish-Christian Disputation in the Setting of Humanism and Reforma-

tion in the German Empire." *HThR* 59 (1966): 369–90.

Ben Yehuda, Eliezer. *A Complete Dictionary of Ancient and Modern Hebrew.* New York, 1960.

Berengarius of Tours. *De Sacra Coena.* Edited by W. H. Beekenkamp. The Hague, 1941.

Berger, David. "Gilbert Crispin, Alan of Lille, and Jacob ben Reuben: A Study in the Transmission of Medieval Polemic." *Speculum* 49 (1974): 34–47.

Bergmann, J. "Deux Polémistes Juifs Italiens." *REJ* 40 (1900): 188–205.

Bernard of Clairveaux. *Super Missus Est Homiliae. PL* 183, 55–88.

Bibago, Abraham. *Derekh Emunah.* Constantinople, 1522. Reprinted, Gregg Publishers, England, 1969, and Jerusalem, 5730 (1969–70).

Blau, Joseph. *The Christian Interpretation of the Cabala.* New York, 1944.

Blumenkranz, Bernhard. *Les Auteurs Chrétiens Latins du Moyen Age sur les Juifs et le Judaïsme.* Paris, 1963; and *REJ* 109 (1948–49): 3–67; 111 (1951–52): 5–61; 113 (1954): 5–36; 114 (1955): 37–90; 117 (1958): 5–58.

———. *Die Judenpredigt Augustins.* Basel, 1946.

———. "Die jüdischen Beweisgründe in Religionsgespräch mit den Christen in den christlich-lateinischen Sonderschriften des 5. bis 11. Jahrhunderts." *Theologische Zeitschrift* 4 (1948): 119–47.

———. *Juifs et Chrétiens dans le Monde Occidental, 430*–1096. Paris, 1960.

———. "Un Pamphlet Juif Médio-Latin de Polémique Antichrétienne." *Revue d'Histoire et de Philosophie Religieuses* 34 (1954): 401–13.

Bonano, Salvatore. *The Concept of Substance and the Development of Eucharistic Theology to the Thirteenth Century.* Washington, 1960.

Bonaventure. *Commentary on Sententiae.* 1491.

Braude, Morris. *Conscience on Trial.* New York, 1952.

Briel, Judah. "Hashmaṭot Bi-Defuse S. Beḥinat Ha-Dat." *Oẓar Tov (Magazin für die Wissenschaft des Judenthums)* 4 (1878): 082–084.

Browe, Peter. *Die Eucharistischen Wunder des Mittelalters.* Breslau, 1938.

———. *Die Judenmission im Mittelalter und die Päpste.* Rome, 1942.

Brown, Francis, et al. *A Hebrew and English Lexicon of the Old Testament.* Oxford, 1962.

Browne, Laurence E. *The Eclipse of Christianity in Asia.* New York, 1967.

Brüll, N. "Sprüchwörter in der nachtalmudischen Literatur des Judentums." *Jahrbücher für Jüdische Geschichte und Literatur* 7 (1885): 18–30.

Buescher, G. *The Eucharistic Teaching of William Ockham.* Washington, 1950.

Buschmiller, Robert J. *The Maternity of Mary in the Mariology of St. Albert the Great.* Freiburg, 1959.

Cappuyns, Maïeul. *John Scot Érigène.* Brussels, 1964.

Castro, Michael G. de. *Die Trinitätslehre des hl. Gregor von Nyssa.* Freiburg, 1938.

Cheikho, Louis. *Vingt Traités Théologiques.* Beirut, 1920.

Choller, A. "Corps Glorieux." *Dictionnaire de Théologie Catholique,* III, pp. 1879–1906. Paris, 1908.

Clark, Francis. *Eucharistic Sacrifice and the Reformation.* London, 1960.
Clement of Alexandria. *Deux Dialogues Christologiques.* Edited by G. M. de Durand. Sources Chrétiennes, no. 97. Paris, 1964.
Cohen, Martin. "Reflections on the Text and Context of the Disputation of Barcelona." *HUCA* 35 (1964): 157–92.
Corcoran, C. J. "Glorified Body." *New Catholic Encyclopedia,* VI, pp. 512–13. New York, 1967.
Crescas, Ḥasdai. *Biṭṭul 'Iqqare Ha-Noẓrim.* Edited by Ephraim Deinard. Kearny, N.J., 1904; 1st ed., Salonika[?], 1860[?].
———. *Or Ha-Shem.* Vienna, 1861, reprinted.
Crispin, Gilbert. *Disputatio Christiani cum gentili.* Edited by Clement C. J. Webb. "Gilbert Crispin, Abbot of Westminster: Dispute of a Christian with a Heathen touching the Faith of Christ." *Mediaeval and Renaissance Studies* 3 (1954): 55–77.
———. *Disputatio Judei cum Christiano de Fide Christiana,* ed. Bernhard Blumenkranz, *Gisleberti Crispini Disputatio Iudei et Christiani et Anonymi Auctoris Disputationis Continuatio.* Utrecht, 1956.
Crispin, Pseudo-Gilbert. *Disputatio Ecclesiae et Synagogae.* Edited by E. Martène and U. Durand. *Thesauras Novus Anecdotum,* 5, pp. 1497–1506. Paris, 1717.
Cusanus, Nicolas (Nicholas of Cusa). *Of Learned Ignorance.* Translated by Germain Heron. London, 1954.
Damian, Peter. *Sermo* I. *PL* 144, 505–14.
Davidson, Israel. "The Author of the Poem *Zikheron Sefer Niẓẓaḥon.*" *JQR* 18 (1927–28): 257–65.
———. "Note on *Zikheron Sefer Niẓẓaḥon.*" *JQR* 19 (1928–29): 75–76.
Del Medigo, Elijah. *Beḥinat Ha-Dat.* Edited by Isaac Reggio. Vienna, 1833, reprinted.
Denifle, H. "Quellen in Disputation Pablos Christiani . . . " *Historisches Jahrbuch der Görres-Gesellschaft* 8 (1887): 225–44.
Denziger, Henry. *Enchiridion Symbolorum.* Freiburg, 1957.
———. *The Sources of Catholic Dogma.* Translated by Roy J. Deferrari. London, 1957.
Dieterici, F. *Alfarabi's philosophische Abhandlungen.* Leiden, 1890 (Arabic), 1892 (German).
Dublanchy, E. "Marie." *Dictionnaire de Théologie Catholique,* IX, pp. 2339–2474. Paris, 1927.
Dunash Ibn Tamim [attributed]. *Perush Sefer Yeẓirah.* Edited by Leopold Dukes. *Shire Shelomo,* pp. ii–viii. Hannover, 5618 (1857–58); reprinted, Jerusalem, 5729 (1968–69).
Duran, Profiat. *Iggeret Al Tehi Ke-'Avotekha.* National and University Library, Jerusalem, ms. Heb. 8° 757 (Posnanski critical edition), printed Jerusalem 5730 (1969–70).
———. *Sefer Kelimat Ha-Goyim.* Edited by Adolf Posnanski. *Ha-Ẓofeh Me-'Ereẓ*

Hagar 3 (5674 [1913–14]): 99–113, 143–80; 4 (5675 [1914–15]): 37–48, 81–96, 115–32.

Duran, Simon. *Keshet U-Magen.* Livorno, 5523 (1762–63); reprinted, Jerusalem, 5730.

———. *Magen Avot.* Livorno, 1785; reprinted, Jerusalem, n. d.

Duran, Solomon ben Simon. *Milḥemet Miẓvah.* Livorno, 5523 (1762–63); reprinted, Jerusalem, 5730 (1969–70).

Durandus of Saint-Pourçain. *In Sententias Theologicae Petri Lombardi Commentariorum.* Lugduni, 1563.

Eisenstein, J. D. *Oẓar Vikuḥim.* New York, 1928.

Elijah Ḥayyim ben Benjamin of Genazzano. *Vikuaḥ.* Edited by Judah Rosenthal. *Meḥkarim U-Meqorot,* I, pp. 431–55. Jerusalem, 1967.

Emery, R. W. "New Light on Profayt Duran *The Efodi.*" *JQR* 58 (1967–68): 328–37.

Epiphanius. *Adversus Haereses Panarium, PG* 41, 173–1200.

Erigena, John Scotus. *De Divisione Naturae. PL* 122, 439–1022.

Ess, Josef van. "The Logical Structure of Islamic Theology." In G. E. von Grunebaum, *Logic in Classical Islamic Culture,* pp. 21–50. Wiesbaden, 1970.

Euclid. *Elements.*

Evodius. *Epistola* III (to Augustine). *PL* 33, 702–4.

Fenton, Joseph C. "Our Lady's Virginity in Partu." *American Ecclesiastical Review* 130 (1954): 46–53.

Frankl, P. F. *Ein Mu'tazilitischer Kalam aus dem 10 Jahrhundert.* Vienna, 1872.

Fritsch, Erdmann. *Islam und Christentum im Mittelalter.* Breslau, 1930.

Fulbert of Chartres. *Sermo* I. *PL* 141, 317.

Funkenstein, Amos. "Ha-Temurot Be-Vikuaḥ Ha-Dat Ben Yehudim le-Noẓrim Be-Me'ah Ha-Yod-Bet." *Ẓion* 33 (1968): 125–49.

Geiselmann, Josef R. *Die Eucharistielehre der Vorscholastik.* (Forschungen zur christlischen Literatur und Dogmengeschichte, 15, nos. 1–3), Paderborn, 1926.

Gelber, N. M. "Die Taufbewegung unter den polnischen Juden in XVIII Jahrhundert." *MGWJ* 68 (1924): 225–41.

Geronimo de Santa Fé, *Hebraeomastix* in *Bibliotheca Magna Patrum,* XXVI, pp. 528–54. Lyons, 1677.

Gershom ben Judah Meor Ha-Golah. *Seliḥot U-Fizmonim.* Edited by A. M. Habermann. Jerusalem, 1944.

Al-Ghazālī, Abū Ḥamid. *Tahāfut al-Falasifah.* Edited by Maurice Bouyges. Beirut, 1927.

———. *Al-Ghazali's Tahafut al-Falasifah.* Translated by Sabih A. Kamali. Lahore, 1958.

——— [attributed]. *Réfutation Excellente de la Divinité de Jesus-Christ d'après les Évangiles.* Edited and translated by Robert Chidiac. Paris, 1939.

Gilson, Etienne. *History of Christian Philosophy in the Middle Ages.* New York, 1955.

Ginzburg, I. O. "Arabskiy i Yevreyskiy Varianti Filosofskovo Sochinyeniya Ali-Mokammisa (IX–X vv.)." *Zapiski Kollegii Vostokovêdov* 5 (1930): 481–506.

Golb, N. "The Hebrew Translation of Averroes' *Faṣl al-Maqāl*." *PAAJR* 25 (1956): 99–113; 26 (1957): 41–64.

Goldstein, Daniel. *Seder Ha-Seliḥot*. Jerusalem, 5725 (1964–65).

Goldziher, I. "Uber muhammedanische Polemik gegen Ahl-al-Kitab." *Zeitschrift der Deutschen Morgenländischen Gesellschaft* 32 (1878): 341–87.

Gottheil, Richard. "Some Geniza Gleanings." *Mélanges Hartwig Derenbourg*, pp. 84–106. Paris, 1909.

Graef, Hilda. *Mary: A History of Doctrine and Devotion*. 2 vols. New York, 1963–65.

Graetz, Heinrich. *History of the Jews*. Philadelphia, 1894.

Graf, G. *Die Philosophie und Gotteslehre des Jaḥjâ ibn 'Adî und Spateren Autoren*. Munster, 1910.

Gregory of Nazianzus. *Oratio* 31. *PG* 36, 133–72.

———. *Epistola 101 ad Cledonium*. *PG* 37, 175–94.

Gregory of Nyssa. *De Communibus Notionibus*. *PG* 45, 175–86.

———. *Oratio in Diem Natalem Christi*. *PG* 46, 1127–50.

———. *Quod Non Sit Tres Dii, ad Ablabium*. *PG* 45, 115–36.

Gregory of Tours. *Historiae Francorum Libri Decem*. *PL* 71, 161–572.

Grillmeyer, Aloys, and Bacht, Heinrich. *Das Konzil von Chalcedon*. 3 vols. Würzburg, 1951–54.

Guttmann, Jacob. *Die Religionsphilosophie des Saadia*. Göttingen, 1882.

Guttmann, Julius. "Elia del Medigos Verhältnis zu Averroës in seinem *Bechinat Ha-Dat*." *Jewish Studies in Memory of Israel Abrahams*, pp. 192–208. New York, 1927.

———. *Philosophies of Judaism*. Translated by David W. Silverman. New York, 1964.

Hadassi, Judah. *Eshkol Ha-Kofer*. Eupatoria ed., 1836; reprinted. Westmead, England, 1971.

Hailperin, Herman. *Rashi and the Christian Scholars*. Pittsburgh, 1963.

Halevi, Judah. *Kitāb al-Khazarī*. Edited by Hartwig Hirschfeld. Leipzig, 1887, reprinted.

———. *The Kuzari*. Translated by Hartwig Hirschfeld. New York, 1964.

Ḥayyim ibn Musa. *Magen Va-Romaḥ*. National and University Library, Jerusalem, ms. Heb. 8° 787 (Posnanski ms.), published, Jerusalem, 5730 (1969–70).

Heinemann, Isaac. *Ta'ame Ha-Miẓvot Be-Sifrut Yisrael*. Jerusalem, 1954.

Herford, R. Travers. *Christianity in Talmud and Midrash*. London, 1903.

Hergenröther, Joseph. *Die Lehre von der göttlichen Dreieinigkeit nach dem heiligen Gregor von Nazianz*. Regensburg, 1850.

Hermann. *Sententie Hermanni (Petri Abelardi, Epitome Theologiae Christianae)*. *PL* 178, 1685– 1758.

Ḥesronot Ha-Shas. Tel Aviv, 1966.

Hildebert of Tours. *Sermones de Diversis. PL* 171, 751–950.
Hirschfeld, Hartwig. "The Arabic Portion of the Cairo Geniza." *JQR* o.s. 15 (1903): 677–97.
Hippolytus. *Contra Haeresin Noeti. PG* 10, 803–30.
Honorius Augustodunensis. *Elucidarium. PL* 172, 1109–76.
Horst, L. *Des Metropolitan Elias von Nisibis Buch von Beweis des Glaubens.* Colmar, 1886.
Hugh of Saint Victor. *De Sacramentis. PL* 176, 173–618.
———. *On the Sacraments of the Christian Faith.* Translated by Roy J. Deferrari. Cambridge, Mass., 1951.
———. *Summa Sententiarum. PL* 176, 41–174.
——— [attributed]. *Apologia de Verbe Incarnata, PL* 177, 295–316.
Husik, Isaac. *A History of Medieval Jewish Philosophy.* Philadelphia, 1940.
Ibn Daud, Abraham. *The Book of Tradition (Sefer Ha-Qabbalah).* Edited by Gerson D. Cohen. Philadelphia, 1967.
Ibn Ezra, Abraham. *Commentary on Genesis.*
Ibn Verga, Solomon. *Shevet Yehuda.* Edited by Y. Baer and E. Shohat. Jerusalem, 1947.
Innocent III. *De Sacra Altaris Mysterio. PL* 217, 763–916.
Isidore of Seville. *Contra Judaeos. PL* 83, 449–538.
Jacob ben Reuben. *Milḥamot Ha-Shem.* Edited by Judah Rosenthal. Jerusalem, 1963.
Jaeger, Werner. *The Theology of the Early Greek Philosophers.* Oxford, 1967.
James, M. R. *The Apocryphal New Testament.* Oxford, 1924.
Jastrow, Marcus. *A Dictionary of the Targumim, the Talmud Babli and Yerushalmi, and the Midrashic Literature.* New York, 1950.
Jellinek, A. "Christlicher Einfluss auf die Kabbalah." *Beiträge zur Geschichte der Kabbala,* II, pp. 51–56. Leipzig, 1857.
Jerome. *De Perpetua Virginitate B. Mariae Adversus Helvidium. PL* 23, 193–216.
Jerome of Jerusalem. *Dialogus de Sancta Trinitate, PG* 40, 847–60.
John of Damascus. *De Fide Orthodoxa. PG* 94, 781–1228.
Joseph Ha-Meqanneh Official. *Sefer Yosef Ha-Meqanneh.* Edited by Judah Rosenthal. Jerusalem, 1970.
Joseph Ibn Ẓaddiq. *Sefer Ha-'Olam Ha-Qaṭan.* Edited by S. Horovitz. Breslau, 1903, reprinted (with discrepancy in page numbers).
Judah ben Barzilay of Barcelona. *Perush Sefer Yeẓirah.* Edited by S. J. Halberstam. Berlin, 1885.
Juster, Jean. *Les Juifs dans l'Empire Romain,* I. Paris, 1914.
Justin Martyr. *Dialogue with Trypho. PG* 6, 471–800.
———. *Writings of Saint Justin Martyr.* Translated by Thomas B. Falls. New York, 1948.
Kahn, Z. "Étude sur le Livre de Joseph Le Zélateur." *REJ* 1 (1880): 222–46; 3 (1881): 1–38.

Kaminka, A. "Note on Meshullam ben Uri," *JQR* 18 (1927–28): 437.
Kaspi, Joseph. *Maskiyot Kesef.* Edited by S. Z. Werbluner. *Sheloshah Qadmone Mefarshe Ha-Moreh.* Jerusalem, 1961.
Katz, Jacob. *Exclusiveness and Tolerance.* Oxford, 1961.
Kaufman (Even Shmuel), Yehuda. *R. Yom-Tov Lipmann Mühlhausen.* New York, 1927.
Kaufmann, David. *Geschichte der Attributenlehre.* Gotha, 1877.
Kimḥi, David. *Commentary on Ezekiel.*
———. *Commentary on Psalms: Selections.* Edited by Frank Talmage. In Joseph Kimḥi, *Sefer Ha-Berit,* pp. 71–79. Jerusalem, 1974. Also known as *Teshuvot Radaq La-Noẓrim.* Edited by Theodor Hackspan. In Yom–Tov Lipmann Mühlhausen, *Sefer Niẓẓaḥon,* pp. 196–200. Altdorf, 1644. *Ḥesronot Ha-Shas,* pp. 87–92.
Kimḥi, Pseudo-David. *Vikuaḥ Radaq.* Edited by Frank Talmage. In Joseph Kimḥi, *Sefer Ha-Berit,* pp. 83–96.
Kimḥi, Joseph. *The Book of the Covenant.* Translated by Frank Talmage. Toronto, 1972.
———. *Sefer Ha-Berit.* Edited by Frank Talmage. Jerusalem, 1974. Also *Milḥemet Ḥovah,* pp. 18b–38a. Constantinople, 1710.
Klatzkin, Jacob. *Oẓar Ha-Munaḥim Ha-Filosofiim.* 4 vols. Berlin, 1928–33.
Koch, Joseph. *Durandus de S. Porciano O.P.* Beiträge zur Geschichte der Philosophie des Mittelalters, 26. Munster, 1927.
Krauss, Samuel. *Das Leben Jesu nach juedischen Quellen.* Berlin, 1902.
———. "Fragment Polémique de la Gueniza." *REJ* 63 (1912): 63–74.
Lactantius. *Divinae Institutiones. PL* 6, 111–822.
Lauterbach, Jacob Z. "Jesus in the Talmud." *Rabbinic Essays,* pp. 473–570. New York, 1973.
———. "Substitutes for the Tetragrammaton." *PAAJR* 2 (1930–31): 39–67.
Levi ben Abraham of Villefranche. "Pereq Mi-Sefer *Livyat Ḥen.*" Edited by Moritz Steinschneider. *Jeshurun* (Kobak), 8 (1875): 1–13.
Levi ben Gerson. *Milḥamot Ha-Shem.* Riva di Trento, 1560, reprinted.
Lewin, A. "Die Religionsdisputation des R. Jechiel von Paris 1240 am Hofe Ludwigs des Heiligens ihre Veranlassung und ihre Folgen." *MGWJ* 18 (1869): 97–110, 145–56, 193–210.
Lieberman, Saul. *Shkiin.* 2nd ed. Jerusalem, 1970.
Loeb, Isidore. "La Controverse de 1240 sur le Talmud." *REJ* 1 (1880): 247–61; 2 (1881): 248–70; 3 (1882): 39–57.
———. "La Controverse de 1263 à Barcelone." *REJ* 16 (1887): 1–18.
———. *La Controverse Religieuse entre les Chrétiens et les Juifs au Moyen Age en France et en Espagne.* Paris, 1888.
———. "Polémistes Chrétiens et Juifs en France et en Espagne." *REJ* 18 (1889): 43–70, 219–42.
Löwinger, S. "Liquṭim Mi-*S. Magen Avraham.*" *Ha-Ẓofeh Le-Ḥokhmat Yisrael* 12

(1928): 277–97.
———. "Recherches sur l'oeuvre apologétique d'Abraham Farissol." *REJ* 105 (1939): 23–52.
Lombard, Peter. *Sententiae. PL* 192, 519–964.
Lorki, Joshua. *Nusaḥ Ha-Ketav.* Edited by Eliezer Ashkenazi. *Divre Ḥakhamim,* pp. 41–46. Metz, 1849. Also L. Landau, *Das Apologetische Schreiben des Josua Lorki.* Antwerp, 1906.
Lull, Raymund. *El "Liber Predicationis Contra Judaeos."* Edited by José Mª Millás-Vallicrosa. Madrid-Barcelona, 1957.
———. *Disputatio Fidelis et Infidelis, Raymundus Lullus Opera,* IV. Mainz, 1737; reprinted, Frankfurt/Main, 1965, pp. 377–429.
Lupis, Isaac. *Kur Maẓref Ha-'Emunot U-Mar'eh Ha-'Emet.* Edited by Isaac Altaris. Metz, 1847.
Luscombe, D. E. *The School of Peter Abelard.* Cambridge, 1969.
Macdonald, A. J. *Berengar and the Reform of Sacramental Doctrine.* London, 1930.
———. "Berengar and the Virgin Birth." *JThS* 30 (1929): 291–94.
Mandonnet, Pierre F. *Siger de Brabant et l'Averroïsme Latin au XIIIme Siècle.* Louvain, 1908–11.
Marmorstein, Arthur. *Studies in Jewish Theology.* London, 1950.
Martini, Raymund. *Pugio Fidei.* Edited by Carpzov. Leipzig, 1687.
Marx, Alexander. "The Polemical Manuscripts in the Library of the Jewish Theological Seminary." *Studies in Jewish Bibliography and Related Subjects,* pp. 247–78.
Maximinus the Arian. *Tractatus V Contra Judaeos. PL* 57, 793–806.
McCarthy, R. J. *The Theology of al-Ash'ari.* Beirut, 1952.
McDonnell, Kilian. *John Calvin, the Church, and the Eucharist.* Princeton, 1967.
McGiffert, Arthur C. *Dialogues between a Christian and a Jew . . .* New York, 1889.
Mendelssohn, Moses. *Moses Mendelssohn: Gesammelte Schriften.* Jubiläumsausgabe. Berlin, 1930.
———. *Jerusalem and Other Writings.* Translated by Alfred Jospe. New York, 1969.
Menges, Matthew C. *The Concept of Univocity Regarding the Predication of God and Creature According to William Ockham.* St. Bonaventure, N.Y., 1952.
Merchavia, Ch. *Ha-Talmud Be-Re'i Ha-Noẓrut.* Jerusalem, 1970.
Merlin, Nicholas. *Saint Augustin et les Dogmas du Péché Originel et de la Grâce.* Paris, 1931.
Millás-Vallicrosa, José Mª "Aspectos Filosoficos de la Polemica Judaica en Tiempos de Ḥasday Crescas." *Harry A. Wolfson Jubilee Volume,* pp. 561–76. New York, 1965.
Mingana, A. "The Apology of Timothy the Patriarch before Caliph Mahdi." *Woodbrooke Studies,* fasc. 3. *Bulletin of the John Rylands Library,* 12, 1 (1928): 137–298.
Modena, Judah Aryeh de. *Magen Va-Ḥerev.* Edited by S. Simonsohn. Jerusalem, 1960.

Moses ben Maimon. *Dalālat al-Ḥa'īrīn.* Edited by Solomon Munk. Jerusalem, 1929.
———. *Epistle to Yemen.* Edited by Abraham S. Halkin. Translated by Boaz Cohen. New York, 1952.
———. *Le Guide des Égarés.* Translated by Solomon Munk. Paris, 1856.
———. *The Guide of the Perplexed.* Translated by Shlomo Pines. Chicago, 1963.
———. *Maqāla fi Teḥiyyat Ha-Metim (Treatise on Resurrection).* Edited by Joshua Finkel. New York, 1939.
———. *Mishneh Torah.*
———. *Maimonides' Treatise on Logic (Maḳālah Fi-Ṣinā'at Al-Manṭik).* Edited by Israel Efros. New York, 1938.
Moses ben Naḥman. *Vikuaḥ Ramban.* Edited by H. D. Chavel. *Kitve Ramban,* I, pp. 299–320. 4th ed. Jerusalem, 1971.
Moses ben Solomon of Salerno. *Ta'anot.* Edited by Stanislaus Simon, *Mose ben Salomo von Salerno und seine philosophischen Auseinandersetzungen mit Lehren des Christentums.* Breslau, 1931.
Moses Ha-Kohen of Tordesillas. *'Ezer Ha-Dat.* Edited by Yehuda Shamir. *Rabbi Moses Ha-Kohen of Tordesillas and His Book 'Ezer Ha-Emunah,* II, pp. 163–81. Coconut Grove, Fla., 1972.
———. *'Ezer Ha-'Emunah.* Edited by Yehudah Shamir. *Rabbi Moses Ha-Kohen of Tordesillas and His Book 'Ezer Ha-Emunah,* II, pp. 5–160. Coconut Grove, Fla., 1972.
Mühlhausen, Yom-Tov Lipmann. *Sefer Niẓẓaḥon.* Edited by Theodor Hackspan. Altdorf, 1644.
Nager, Franz. *Die Trinitätslehre des hl. Basilius des Grossen.* Paderborn, 1912.
Nasi, Don David. *Hoda'at Ba'al Din.* Frankfurt, 1866.
Nemoy, Leon. "Al-Qirqisani's Account of the Jewish Sects and Christianity." *HUCA* 7 (1930): 317–97.
———. "The Attitude of the Early Karaites towards Christianity." in *Salo W. Baron Jubilee Volume II,* pp. 697–716. New York and London, 1975.
Nestor Ha-Komer. Edited by Abraham Berliner. Altona, 1906.
Neubauer, A. D., and Driver, S. R. *The Fifty-Third Chapter of Isaiah According to the Jewish Interpreters.* Oxford, 1876–77.
Neumann, Charles W. *The Virgin Mary in the Works of Saint Ambrose.* Freiburg, 1962.
Neusner, Jacob. *Aphrahat and Judaism.* Leiden, 1971.
Newberry, Thomas. *Solar Light as Illustrating Trinity in Unity.* Glasgow, 18??.
Newman, Louis I. *Jewish Influence on Christian Reform Movements.* New York, 1925.
———. "Joseph ben Isaac Kimchi as a Religious Controversialist." *Jewish Studies in Memory of Israel Abrahams,* pp. 365–72. New York, 1927.
Nicholas de Lyra. *Contra Judaeos probatio temporis incarnationis Christi.* In *Biblia Latina cum Postilla Nic. de Lyra.* Venice, 1481.
Niẓẓaḥon Yashan. Edited by Johannes Wagenseil. *Tela Ignea Satanae.* Altdorf, 1681;

reprinted, Jerusalem, 5730 (1969--70).
Nonnus of Nisibis. *Traité Apologétique.* Edited by A. van Roey. Louvain, 1948.
Obermann, Heiko A. *The Harvest of Medieval Theology.* Cambridge, Mass., 1963.
Ockham. *De Corpore Christi.* In *The De Sacramento Altaris of William of Occam,* edited by T. Bruce Birch. Burlington, Iowa, 1930.
Odes of Solomon. Translated by J. H. Bernard. Studies and Texts, 8:3. Cambridge, 1912.
Odo, Bishop of Cambrai. *Disputatio Contra Judaeum Leonem Nomin de Adventu Christi Filii Dei. PL* 160, 1103–12.
On the Triune Nature of God. Edited by Margaret D. Gibson. *Studia Sinaitica* 7 (1899): 2–36 (English), 74–107 (Arabic).
Origen. *Contra Celsum. PG* 11, 637–1632.
———. *In Lucam Homiliae. PG* 13, 1801–1902.
Pacios Lopez, A. *La Disputa de Tortosa.* Madrid, 1957.
Parkes, James. *The Conflict of the Church and the Synagogue.* London, 1934.
Parmer, Paul F. *Mary in the Documents of the Church.* Westminster, Md., 1952.
Pelikan, Jaroslav. *The Emergence of the Catholic Tradition (100–600).* Chicago, 1971.
———. *The Light of the World.* New York, 1962.
———. *The Spirit of Eastern Christendom (600–1700).* Chicago, 1974.
Peter Alfonsi. *Dialogus. PL* 157, 535–672.
Peter of Blois. *Contra Perfidium Judaeorum. PL* 207, 825–70.
Peter of Cluny. *Tractatus Adversus Judaeorum Inveteratam Duritiem. PL* 189, 507–650.
Pflaum, H. "Poems of Religious Disputations in the Middle Ages." *Tarbiẓ* 2 (5691 [1930–31]): 443–76.
Philo. *De Aeternitate Mundi.* Translated by F. H. Colson. *Philo,* IX, Loeb Classical Library. Cambridge, Mass., 1961.
Photius. *Bibliotheca* 230. *PG* 103, 1023–88.
Pines, Shlomo. *Beiträge zur Islamischen Atomenlehre.* Berlin, 1936.
Plato. *Parmenides.*
Pohle, J. "Eucharist." *Catholic Encyclopedia,* V, pp. 572–90. New York, 1909.
Posnanski, Adolf. "La Colloque de Tortoṣe et de San Mateo (7 février 1413–13 novembre 1414)." *REJ* 74 (1922): 17–39, 160–68; 75 (1922): 74–88, 187–204.
———. *Schiloh. Ein Beitrag zur Geschichte der Messiaslehre.* Leipzig, 1904.
Prestige, G. L. *God in Patristic Thought.* London, 1959.
Al-Qirqisānī, Ya'qūb. *Kitāb al-Anwār wal-Marāqib.* Edited by Leon Nemoy. New York, 1939–43.
Radbertus, Paschasius. *Opusculum de Partu Virginis. PL* 120, 1365–86.
Rankin, Oliver S. *Jewish Religious Polemic.* Edinburgh, 1966.
Rappa, Jonah Ha-Kohen. *Pilpul 'al Zeman Zemanim Zemanehem.* Edited by George Belasco. London, 1908.
Ratramnus. *De Corpore et Sanguine Domini.* Edited by Van den Brink. Amsterdam,

1954; and *PL* 121, 103–70.
———. *De Eo Quod Christus ex Virgine Natus Est. PL* 121, 81–102.
Rawidowicz, Simon. "Saadya's Purification of the Idea of God." In *Saadya Studies,* edited by E. I. J. Rosenthal, pp. 139–65. Manchester, 1943. Reprinted in *Studies in Jewish Thought,* edited by N. Glatzer, pp. 246–68. Philadelphia, 1974.
Renan, Ernest. *Averroes et l'Averroïsme.* Paris, 1852.
———. *Les Écrivains Juifs Français du XIVe Siècle.* (Histoire Littéraire de la France, 31.) Paris, 1893.
Roman, Abraham. *Sela' Ha-Maḥloket.* In *Milḥemet Ḥovah.* Constantinople, 1710.
Rondet, Henri. *Original Sin.* Shannon, 1972.
Rosenthal, E. I. J. "Anti-Christian Polemic in Medieval Bible Commentaries." *JJS* 11 (1960): 115–35.
Rosenthal, Judah. "Hagganah Ve-Hatqafah Be-Sifrut Ha-Vikuaḥ Shel Yeme Ha-Benayim." *The Fifth World Congress of Jewish Studies, Proceedings,* Hebrew sec., pp. 345–58. Jerusalem, 1971.
———. "Ha-Pulmus Ha-'Anṭi Noẓri Be-Rashi 'al Ha-Tanakh." In *Rashi, Torato Ve-'Ishiyuto,* edited by Simon Federbusch, pp. 45–59. New York, 1958. Reprinted in *Meḥkarim U-Mekorot,* I, pp. 101–13. Jerusalem, 1967.
———. "Ribbit Min Ha-Nokhri." *Meḥkarim U-Mekorot,* I, pp. 253–323. Jerusalem, 1967.
———. "Sifrut Ha-Vikuaḥ Ha-'Anṭi-Noẓrit 'Ad Sof Ha-Me'ah Ha-Shemoneh-'Esreh." *Areshet* 2 (1960): 130–79; "Milu'im," 3 (1961): 433–39.
———. "The Talmud on Trial." *JQR* 47 (1956): 58–76, 145–69.
Rossi, G. B. de. *Bibliotheca Judaica Anti-Christiana.* Parma, 1800.
———. *Mss. Codices Hebraici.* Parma, 1803.
Roth, Cecil. "The Disputation of Barcelona (1263)." *HThR* 43 (1950): 114–44.
———. "Host, Desecration of." *EJ,* VIII, pp. 1040–46.
Saadia Gaon. *The Book of Beliefs and Opinions.* Translated by Samuel Rosenblatt. New Haven, 1948.
———. *Saadya Gaon: Book of Doctrines and Beliefs.* Translated by Alexander Altmann. *Three Jewish Philosophers.* New York, 1972.
———. *Kitāb al-Amānāt wa'l-I'tiqādāt.* Edited by S. Landauer. Leiden, 1880.
Saenger, M. "Ueber den Verfasser des polemischen Werkes: *S. Ha-Kelimah* oder *Kelimat Ha-Goyim," MGWJ* 3 (1854): 320–27.
Sanz Artibucilla, José Mª "Los Judios en Aragon y Navarra. Neuvos Datos Biograficos Relativos a Šem Ṭoḇ Ben Iṣḥaq Šaprut." *Sefarad* 5 (1945): 337–66.
Sbath, Paul. *Vingt Traités Philosophiques et Apologétiques d'Auteurs Arabes Chrétiens du IXe au XIVe Siècle.* Cairo, 1929.
Schlosberg, Léon. *Controverse d'un Évêque.* Vienna, 1880 (Arabic); Versailles, 1888 (French).
Schoeps, Hans. J. *The Jewish-Christian Argument.* New York, 1963.
Scholem, Gershom. *Kabbalah.* New York, 1974.
Schreiner, Martin. *Der Kalam in der Jüdischen Literatur.* Berlin, 1895.

Schweid, Eliezer. "Omanut Ha-Di'alog Be-Sefer *Ha-Kuzari* U-Mashma'utah Ha-'Iyunit." *Ṭa'am Va-Haqashah*, pp. 37–79. Ramat Gan, 1970.
———. "'To'ar 'Azmi' be-Mishnat Ha-Rav Ḥasdai Crescas," *Ṭa'am Va-Haqashah*, pp. 149–71.
Seiferth, Wolfgang. *Synagogue and Church in the Middle Ages*. New York, 1970.
Sellers, Robert V. *The Council of Chalcedon*. London, 1953.
Sermonetta, Giuseppe. *Un Glossario Filosofico Ebraico-Italiano del XIII Secolo*. Rome, 1969.
Servetus, Michael. *De Trinitate Erroribus Libri Septem*. 18th cent. forgery of 1531 ed.
———. *The Two Treatises of Servetus on the Trinity*. Translated by Earl M. Wilbur. Cambridge, Mass., 1932.
Shahrastānī. *Kitāb al-Milal wal-Niḥal (Book of Religious and Philosophical Sects)*. Edited by William Cureton. London, 1842.
Sheedy, Charles E. *The Eucharistic Controversy of the Eleventh Century against the Background of the Pre-Scholastic Theology*. Washington, 1947.
Shehaby, Nabel. *The Propositional Logic of Avicenna*. Dordrecht, Holland, 1973.
Shereshevsky, E. "Rashi's and Christian Interpretations." *JQR* 61 (1970): 76–86.
Simon, Marcel. *Verus Israel*. Paris, 1948.
Solomon ben Adret. *Teshuvot Ha-Rashba*. Salonika, 5575 (1814–15).
Solomon ben Moses ben Yekutiel. *'Edut Ha-Shem Ne'emanah*. Edited by Judah Rosenthal. *Meḥkarim U-Mekorot*, I, pp. 373–422. Jerusalem, 1967.
Southern, R. W. "St. Anselm and Gilbert Crispin, Abbot of Westminster." *Mediaeval and Renaissance Studies* 3 (1954): 79–115.
Stein, S. "A Disputation on Moneylending between Jews and Gentiles in Me'ir b. Simeon's *Milḥemeth Miṣwah* (Narbonne, 13th Cent.). *JJS* 10 (1959): 45–61.
Steinschneider, Moritz. *Al-Farabi*. St. Petersburg, 1869.
———. *Die Hebräischen Übersetzungen des Mittelalters und die Juden als Dolmetscher*. Berlin, 1893.
———. *Jewish Literature*. London, 1857.
———. *Polemische und apologetische Literatur in arabischer Sprache*. Leipzig, 1877.
Stephen of Autun. *Tractatus de Sacramento Altaris*. *PL* 172, 1273–1308.
Stern, S. M. "'Abd al-Jabbār's Account of How Christ's Religion Was Falsified by the Adoption of Roman Customs." *JThS*, n.s. 19 (1968): 128–86.
Strake, Joseph. *Die Sakramentenlehre des Wilhelm von Auxerre*. Paderborn, 1917.
Strawley, J. H. "Eucharist (to end of Middle Ages)." In *Encyclopedia of Religion and Ethics*, edited by James Hastings, V, pp. 540–63. New York, 1914.
Suarez, Francis. *The Dignity and Virginity of the Mother of God*. Translated by Richard J. Obrien. West Baden Springs, Ind., 1954.
Sweetman, J. Windrow. *Islam and Christian Theology*, II:1. London, 1955.
Talmage, Frank. "An Hebrew Polemical Treatise, Anti-Cathar and Anti-Orthodox." *HThR* 60 (1967): 323–48.
———. "Judaism on Christianity: Christianity on Judaism." *The Study of Judaism*, pp. 81–112. New York, 1972.

———. "R. David Kimḥi as Polemicist." *HUCA* 38 (1967): 213–35.
Tatian. *Oratio adversus Graecos. PG* 6, 803–88.
Tennant, F. R. *The Sources of the Doctrine of the Fall and Original Sin.* New York, 1968.
Tertullian. *Adversus Praxeam. PL* 2, 153–96.
———. *De Carne Christi.* Edited by Ernest Evans. *Tertullian's Treatise on the Incarnation.* London, 1956.
———. *De Monogamia. PL* 2, 929–54.
Theodoret. "Dialogue II 'Inconfusus.'" In *Later Treatises of S. Athanasius . . . and an Appendix on S. Cyril of Alexandria and Theodoret,* translated by William Bright, Oxford, 1881.
Thomas Aquinas. *Commentary on the Sentences, Opera,* 12. Venice, 1780.
———. *On the Truth of the Catholic Faith.* Translated by Anton C. Pegis et al. New York, 1955–57.
———. *Summa Contra Gentiles.* Rome, 1934.
———. *Summa Theologiae.*
———. *St. Thomas Aquinas Summa Theologiae,* 58. *The Eucharistic Presence.* Translated by William Barden. New York, 1965.
———. *St. Thomas Aquinas Summa Theologiae,* 51. *Our Lady.* Translated by Thomas R. Heath. New York, 1969.
———. *St. Thomas Aquinas Summa Theologiae,* 6. *The Trinity.* Translated by Ceslaus Velecky. London, 1965.
Thurston, Herbert. "Exposition of the Blessed Sacrament." *Catholic Encyclopedia,* V, pp. 713–14. New York, 1909.
Trachtenberg, Joshua. *The Devil and the Jews.* London, 1943.
Tractatus Adversus Judaeum. PL 213, 747–808.
Troki, Isaac. *Faith Strengthened.* Translated by Moses Mocatto. London, 1850.
———. *Ḥizzuk Emunah.* Edited by David Deutsch. Breslau, 1873.
The Trophies of Damascus (Les Trophées de Damas). Edited by Gustave Bardy. *Patrologia Orientalis* 15 (1927): 171–292.
Urbach, Ephraim E. "Étude sur la Littérature Polémique au Moyen-Age." *REJ* 100 (1935): 49–77.
Vajda, Georges. "A propos de la Perpétuité de la Rétribution d'Outre Tombe en Théologie Musulmane." *Studia Islamica* 11 (1959): 29–38.
———. "La Démonstration de l'Unité Divine d'après Yūsuf al-Baṣīr." In *Studies in Mysticism and Religion Presented to Gershom G. Scholem,* edited by E. E. Urbach et al., pp. 285–315. Jerusalem, 1967.
———. "La Finalité de la Création de l'Homme selon un Théologian Juif du IXe Siècle." *Oriens* 15 (1962): 61–85.
———. *Isaac Albalag.* Paris, 1960.
———. "Le Problème de l'Unité de Dieu d'après Dāwūd ibn Marwān al-Muqammiṣ." In *Jewish Medieval and Renaissance Studies,* edited by Alexander Altmann, pp. 49–73. Cambridge, Mass., 1967.

Vernet, F. "Juifs (Controverse avec les)." *Dictionnaire de Théologie Catholique*, VIII, pp. 1870–1914. Paris, 1924.

Vikuaḥ Tortosa. Edited by Kobak. *Jeshurun* 6 (1868): 45–55.

Wagenseil, Johannes. *Tela Ignea Satanae*. Altdorf, 1681.

Watt, W. Montgomery. *The Formative Period of Islamic Thought*. Edinburgh, 1973.

Waysbaum, M. "Isaac of Troki and Christian Controversy in the XVI Century." *JJS* 3 (1952): 62–77.

Wensinck, A. J. *The Muslim Creed*. Cambridge, 1932.

Werblowsky, R. J. Zwi, and Bleeker, C. Jouco. *Types of Redemption*. Leiden, 1970.

Wheelwright, Philip. *The Presocratics*. New York, 1966.

William of Auvergne. *Tractatus Guilhermi Parisiensis De Sacramentis Cur Deus Homo*. 1496.

William of Auxerre. *Summa Aurea*. Paris, 1500.

William of Champeaux [attributed]. *Dialogus inter Christianum et Judaeum*. *PL* 163, 1045–72.

William of St. Thiéry. *De Erroribus Guillelimi de Conchis*. *PL* 180, 333–40.

Williams, A. Lukyn. *Adversus Judaeos*. Cambridge, 1935.

———. *A Manual of Christian Evidences for the Jewish People*. 2 vols. London, 1911–19.

Williams, Norman P. *The Ideas of the Fall and of Original Sin*. London, 1927.

Wilms, Franz-Elmar. *Al-Ghazālī's Schrift Wider die Gottheit Jesu*. Leiden, 1966.

Wolfson, Harry A. "The Amphibolous Terms in Aristotle, Arabic Philosophy and Maimonides." *HThR* 31 (1938): 151–73. Reprinted, *Studies in the History of Philosophy and Religion*, I, pp. 455–77. Cambridge, Mass., 1973.

———. "Avicenna, Algazali, and Averroes on Divine Attributes." *Homenaje a Millás-Vallicrosa*, II, pp. 545–71. Barcelona, 1956. Reprinted, *Studies*, pp. 143–69.

———. "Crescas on the Problem of Divine Attributes." *JQR*, n.s. 7 (1916–17): 1–44, 175–221.

———. *Crescas' Critique of Aristotle*. Cambridge, Mass., 1929.

———. "Extradeical and Intradeical Interpretations of Platonic Ideas." *Religious Philosophy*, pp. 27–68. Cambridge, Mass.,

———. "The Muslim Attributes and the Christian Trinity." *HThR* 49 (1956): 1–18.

———. "Philosophical Implications of Arianism and Apollinarianism." *Religious Philosophy*, pp. 126–57. Cambridge, Mass., 1961.

———. "Philosophical Implications of the Problem of Divine Attributes in the Kalam." *JAOS* 71 (1959): 73–80.

———. *The Philosophy of Spinoza*. Cambridge, Mass., 1961.

———. *The Philosophy of the Church Fathers*. I, Cambridge, Mass., 1964.

———. *The Philosophy of the Kalam*. Cambridge, Mass., 1976.

———. "The Plurality of Immovable Movers in Aristotle, Averroes, and St.

Thomas." *Harvard Studies in Classical Philology* 63 (1958): 233–53. Reprinted, *Studies*, pp. 1–21.

———. "Saadia on the Semantic Aspect of the Problem of Attributes." In *Salo W. Baron Jubilee Volume*, II, pp. 1009–1021, New York and London, 1975.

———. "Saadia on the Trinity and Incarnation." In *Studies and Essays in Honor of Abraham A. Neumann*, edited by M. Ben-Horin et al., pp. 547–68. Leiden, 1962.

Wyclif, John. *De Eucharistia*. Edited by Johann Loserth. London, 1892.

Yaḥya ben 'Adī. *Petits Traités Apologétiques de Yaḥyâ ben 'Adî*. Edited by Augustin Périer. Paris, 1920.

———. "Un Traité de Yaḥyâ ben 'Adî, Défense de la Trinité contre les Objections d'al-Kindī." Edited by Augustin Périer. *Revue de l'Orient Chrétien* 22 (1920): 4–21.

Yair ben Shabbetai. *Ḥerev Pifiyot*. Edited by Judah Rosenthal. Jerusalem, 1958.

Yeḥiel of Paris. *Vikuaḥ Rabbi Yeḥiel Mi-Paris*. Edited by Reuben Margoliot. Lwow, n.d.

Index of Citations

General Index

Aaron ben Elijah of Nicomedia; 62, 203.
'Abd al-Jabbār; 197, 202.
Abelard, Peter; 63, 68, 100, 203, 204, 225.
Abner of Burgos (Alfonso of Valladolid); 6, 7, 15, 64, 78, 102, 122, 129, 176.
Abraham bar Ḥiyya, 14.
Abravanel, Don Isaac; 17, 89, 110, 176, 218.
Abrogation of the Law; 5, 18, 19.
Abū al-Hudhayl al-'Allaf, Muhammed ibn; 61.
Abū Hāshim 'Abd al-Salām; 61.
Abū-l-Barakāt ibn Kabar; 77.
Abū Qurra, Theodore; 94–95, 225.
Abū Rā'iṭa, Ḥabīb ibn Ḥidma; 94–95, 193, 221.
Adam; 107, 118, 133, 157.
Admissibility, Kalam Theory of; 29–32.
Agent Intellect; 129.
Alan of Lille; 6, 100, 102, 103, 158, 178, 224, 255.
Alatino, Azriel Petaḥia ben Moshe; 18, 99, 102, 185.
Albalag, Isaac; 78–79, 185, 213.
Albertus Magnus (the Great); 142, 247, 254.
Albigensians; 138.
Albo, Joseph; 18, 34–36, 37, 47, 79, 81, 136, 140, 141, 142, 144, 146, 147, 148, 149, 177, 184, 210, 241, 243.
Alexander of Hales; 242.
Alfarābī; 212, 213.
Alfonsi, Peter; 64, 122, 174, 176, 204, 256.
Alger of Liège; 138, 242.
Al-Muqammiẓ, Dāwūd ibn Marwān; 22, 52–55, 56, 57, 61, 93–96, 109, 181, 191–95, 199, 221, 231.
Altercatio Aecclesie Contra Synagogam; 177.
Alvare, Paul; 180.
Ambrose; 138, 148, 154, 157, 241, 251.
Anastasius of Sinai; 200.
Andronicus, Pseudo-; 200.
Angels; 68, 145, 189, 191.
Anselm of Canterbury; 107, 125, 133, 163, 185, 189, 204, 210, 220, 225, 226, 227, 230, 233, 236, 256.
Anti-Attributists; 55, 62, 104, 194.
Aphrahat; 177.
Appolinarius; 226, 239.
Arianism; 187, 218.
Arians; 105.
Aristotelianism; 19, 20, 31, 48, 51, 62–63, 76, 77, 78, 79, 80, 82–83, 92, 99, 151, 163, 189, 213, 217.
Aristotelians; 10, 28, 49, 64, 77, 78, 104, 189, 218.
Aristotle (see also Index of Citations); 31, 41, 42, 49, 50, 52, 87, 92, 102, 110, 117, 128, 140, 142, 144, 146, 147, 155, 156, 190, 195, 205, 212, 219, 228, 232, 237, 238, 250.
Arius; 84.
Armenians; 138.